PROBLEM SOLVING AND PROGRAMMING IN C

THEORY, PROBLEMS AND APPLICATIONS

REVISED & ENLARGED EDITION

"We want that education by which character is formed, strength of mind is increased, the intellect is expanded, and by which one can stand on one's own feet..."

. . . Swami Vivekananda

"The meaning of education is to encourage in people a sense of self-introspection, the ability to grasp and to develop the capacity for constructive works..."

. . . Dr. S. Radhakrishnan

"Always surround yourself with the kind of people who can make you believe that you can do it..."

. . . R. S. Salaria

"Treat others the way you wish to be treated..."

. . . R. S. Salaria

"May the blessings of the almighty go with this book to one and all..."

. . . R. S. Salaria

PROBLEM SOLVING AND PROGRAMMING IN C

THEORY, PROBLEMS AND APPLICATIONS

REVISED & ENLARGED EDITION

Prof. R. S. Salaria

Alumnus of IIT, Delhi.

Certified Software Quality Professional, Govt. of India.

SUN Certified Programmer, SUN Microsystems, USA.

SUN Certified Trainer, SUN Microsystems, USA.

Head

Deptt. of Computer Science & Engineering

Rayat-Bahra University, Mohali,

PUNJAB.

Former Head

Deptt. of Computer Science & Engineering

Thapar University,

PATIALA-147004.

Assisted by

Anita Salaria

KHANNA BOOK PUBLISHING CO. (P) LTD.

Publisher of Engineering and Computer Books

4C/4344, Ansari Road, Darya Ganj, New Delhi-110002

Phone : 011-23244447-48 **Mobile:** +91-9910909320

E-mail : contact@khannabooks.com

Website : www.khannabooks.com

Dear Readers,

To prevent the piracy, this book is secured with HIGH SECURITY HOLOGRAM on the front title cover. In case you don't find the hologram on the front cover title, please write us to at contact@khannabooks.com or whatsapp us at +91-99109 09320 and avail special gift voucher for yourself.

Specimen of Hologram on front Cover title:

Moreover, there is a SPECIAL DISCOUNT COUPON for you with EVERY HOLOGRAM.

How to avail this SPECIAL DISCOUNT:

Step 1: Scratch the hologram
Step 2: Under the scratch area, your "coupon code" is available
Step 3: Logon to www.khannabooks.com
Step 4: Use your "coupon code" in the shopping cart and get your copy at a special discount
Step 5: Enjoy your reading!

Price: ₹ 425.00

ISBN: 978-93-82609-49-0

Problem Solving and Programming in C
by R.S. Salaria

First Edition: 2017
Reprint: 2023

To view complete list of books, Please scan the QR Code:

Published by:
Khanna Book Publishing Co. (P) Ltd.
CIN: U22110DL1998PTC095547

Visit us at: **www.khannabooks.com**
Write us at: **contact@khannabooks.com**

Printed in India by: Vaibhav Products, Delhi.

Dedication

Our Dearest Parents,
Daughters Surbhi & Mehak,
Beloved Readers,

AND

Our Country Men/Women at Large.

My Slogan for My Fellow Citizens

India . . .
. . . is a Great Country

AND

Indians . . .
. . . are Outstanding.

Preface to Revised & Enlarged Edition

Continuing with the tradition of providing the rich content on the subject of *"Problem Solving & Programming in C"*, which can make Computer Science and Information Technology students' competent professionals, the present edition lays more emphasis on the overall layout of the subject matter so as to make it more appealing and attractive. I am certain that the present edition will help the students in inculcating the habit of reading and self-learning.

Most of the topics are thoroughly revised, presented in a kind of manner with visuals where ever possible so that the students can grasp them with quite each.

Chapter 1 is completely re-written with the aim of providing enough problems so that reader can master the art of problem solving, program planning and design.

Chapter 8 is partially re-organized and re-written with the aim that the readers can master the various aspects associated with functions, organizing multi-function and multi-file programs.

Appendix A containing Frequently Asked Questions (FAQs) is added to help the students to prepare for short questions that are mostly asked in viva voce examinations and placement interviews.

I am hopeful that this edition will be going beyond your expectations. Do keep on writing, as your valuable feedback and suggestions will help me in tuning the book to your expectations.

. . . R. S. Salaria
Email : *rssalaria@yahoo.com*

Preface to First Edition

This book is designed to serve as textbook for the students of BCA, BSc (Computer Science), BSc (IT), PGDCA, MSc (Computer Science), MSc (IT), BTech and MCA of different Indian universities and deemed universities.

While writing the book, special emphasis is given to keep the language very simple and lucid; level of presentation is kept simple and illustrative so that even an average reader can grasp the subject matter with quite ease. Practically this book will provide you every thing you need on the subject of "*Problem Solving and Programming in C*".

The areas of strength of this book are in terms of that

- It provides a comprehensive coverage of the subject in a very lucid manner.
- It demonstrates the development of programs in a good programming style, as inline with the industry standards.
- It provides large number of ready to run example programs, for reference.
- It provides large number of multiple choice questions.
- It provides challenging exercises to test your knowledge about the subject learned.
- It also provides large number of challenging programming exercises to test your programming skills acquired.

I am certain that you will enjoy reading this book. I do need a little favour from your side in the form of your response about the book. Your free and frank comments, suggestions, and positive criticism will help me to improve the book further to meet your expectations.

. . . R. S. Salaria

Acknowledgments

It is my pleasure to take this opportunity to sincerely thank all the teachers who have adopted my book and introducing it to their students. I am also thankful for their appreciations that I have been receiving from them in the form of emails and letters.

I would be failing in my duty if go without appreciating the response and interest shown by the students in my books. They are always a source of inspiration for me and I feel honoured because of their faith in me.

Finally, I must thank my publisher, Mrs. Anita Salaria, Managing Director, Salaria Publishing House, for their aggressive marketing and thus establishing the book as one of the best text books on the subject of *"Problem Solving and Programming in C"*.

. . . R. S. Salaria

Sharing of Word of Wisdom with Teachers

Dear friends, let us remind ourselves that teachers can be categorized as follows:

Mediocre Teacher Tells
Good Teacher Explains
Superior Teacher Demonstrates
Great Teacher Inspires

Now you are to find out where you fit-in and where you want to be.

We believe that in addition to academic qualifications, a teacher must possess the following essential qualifications:

- Capability of providing inspirational leadership,
- Desire to teach,
- Knowledge of the subject and its relationship to other subjects, and
- Ability to transfer the knowledge to the students so that it is alive and meaningful.

If you possess all of the above essential qualifications, hats-off to you. Even if you lack in one or more of the above essential qualifications, but make a commitment to yourself to acquire those, we are certain that sooner you can become a great teacher.

For those who neither possess the above essential qualifications and nor prepared to acquire them, we pray the almighty to find a suitable place for them in some other profession.

We also want to share with you our views about the (holistic) education. Holistic education has two aspects:

- First aspect of it teaches us how to make living, and
- Second aspect of it teaches us how to live life.

We, as teachers, have to shoulder the responsibility of imparting both aspects of education so that we can contribute our share in the development of the country by producing individuals who are globally competent in their respective disciplines and are well equipped with morals and values of joyful life (*honesty, sincerity, integrity, loyalty, commitment*, . . .).

We sincerely advise you to treat your every student as your own child, the best in you will automatically come out - you know every parent want to give *the best* to their child.

As rightly said,

"A Teacher is a Nation builder"
and
"Teaching is a noble profession"

Enjoy your profession . . .

Wish you a nice time ahead.

. . . R. S. Salaria

Sharing of Word of Wisdom with Students

My beloved students, we would like to remind you that we can categorize people as:

People who watch the things happening,
People who look into how things are happening, and
People who make the things happen.

Now you are to find out where you fit-in and where you want to be.

We firmly believe that youth of our country is second to none, and this fact is recognized world wide.

Our honorable former president Late Dr. APJ Kalam (first and may be the last president known as *people's president*) has been saying at all the platform that in India there is no dearth of resources and talent, only thing we need to change is *the mindset* (we have to shed *chalta hai* attitude). He has set a vision for us to see India a developed country by 2020, and the basis for his vision is the talent of our youth.

Take some time to discover yourself and try to assess how much talent you possess. Utilize your period of study to harness that talent. I can assure you that you will have a great future.

We want to share a popular game with you which all of us used to play in our childhood. The game is of burning a peace of paper using a lens under the sun. When the lens and the paper are held stationery, it starts burning in a few seconds. However, if you keep moving either the paper or the lens, the paper will never burn. *Why it happens so?* The answer is simple – the light energy emitted by the sun is not focused. The same is with us. We have enough energy in ourselves, but we don't focus it, rather we waste it in meaningless acts. The next question arises is – *where to focus our energy?* The natural answer of this question should be – what you want to become in your life (that basically defines your goal). So you need to focus your entire energy on your goal, and surely you will achieve your goal.

We would also like to share with you a scene from the popular epic – *Mahabharta*. When Dronacharya, Guru of Pandvas, asked his disciples to aim at the eye of the sparrow placed on a tree. All his disciples, except Arjuna, replied in a same manner – *Guru ji, we see a sparrow*. However, when the turn of Arjuna came, his reply was – *Guru ji, I see only the eye*. That is the kind of the focus you also need to develop in your life.

The next point is that when you have identified your goal, you need to identify the steps that you need to follow in order to accomplish your goal. Once the goal and the steps to accomplish your goal are identified, write them nicely on a piece of a paper and paste that paper at a place which you visit regularly. Whenever you will visit that place, the writing on the paper will remind you about your goal and what you have to do to achieve your goal.

The final word, you may set any goal for yourself and that may be of becoming a successful doctor, an engineer, an administrator or a businessman, but you must also try to be a *nice human being*. You know a nice human being is like a fruit of all seasons, and is welcome every where, anytime. We believe, the basic mantra to become a nice human being is too simple and can be stated as

"Treat the others the way you want to be treated, in other words, don't do anything with others which you wish others shouldn't do with you."

Enjoy your student life and make best use of it . . .

Wish you good luck and a nice time ahead.

. . . R. S. Salaria

Contents at a Glance

Table of Contents

CHAPTER 3: DATA TYPES, VARIABLES AND CONSTANTS 69-92

CHAPTER 4: OPERATORS AND EXPRESSIONS 93-128

Problem Solving and Program Planning

Learning Objectives

After reading this chapter, students will have the ability to:

- explain the importance of problem solving
- explain the importance of program planning and design
- explain the various program design tools
- design solutions of typical problems

1.1 INTRODUCTION

Suppose you are asked by your mathematics teacher to solve an arithmetic problem and you are not familiar with the steps involved in solving that problem. In such a situation, you will not be able to solve the problem. The same principle applies to writing the program. A programmer cannot write instructions for a computer unless the programmer knows how to solve the problem manually.

Let us imagine that you know the steps to be followed for solving the given problem but while solving the problem, you forget to apply some of the steps or you apply some of the steps in wrong sequence. Obviously, you will get a wrong answer. Similarly, while writing a program, if the programmer leaves out some of the instructions or writes the instructions in wrong sequence, the computer will give a wrong answer.

Thus, to write an effective and efficient program, it is necessary that the programmer must write each and every instruction in the proper sequence. However, the sequence of instructions, *referred to as logic*, of a program can be very complex. Therefore, in order to ensure that the program instructions are appropriate for the given problem and are in the correct sequence, program must be planned before they are written.

In this chapter, we will learn about the various tools that can be used to plan the program. Further, the use of each of these tools will be demonstrated by considering number of problems with whom you are already familiar.

1.2 PROBLEM SOLVING

As mentioned earlier, you will not be able to solve a problem if you don't know the steps involved in solving that problem. The same principle applies to writing a program. A programmer cannot write instructions to be given to the computer unless the programmer knows how to solve the problem manually.

Therefore, it is very important that before attempting to write a program, the programmers must solve the problem manually. While solving a problem, the programmer will be able to learn about the various steps to be performed and the sequence in which these steps are to be performed.

To demonstrate how the programmer should proceed, let us consider a familiar example of finding the roots of a quadratic equation of type

$ax^2 + bx + c = 0$ provided $a \neq 0$.

The roots of such an equation are given by the formula:

$$root_{1,2} = \frac{-b \pm \sqrt{b^2 - 4ac}}{2a}$$ where $b^2 - 4ac$ is known as the discriminant.

Depending on the sign of the discriminant, there are three are mutually exclusive possibilities for the roots:

Case 1: If $b^2 - 4ac < 0$, then the root are imaginary, and we can compute real part and imaginary part separately as

$$\text{real part} = -\frac{b}{2a} \quad \text{and} \quad \text{imaginary part} = \frac{\sqrt{-(b^2 - 4ac)}}{2a}$$

Once we know the real and imaginary part of the root, we can determine the actual roots as (real part $\pm$ *i* imaginary part).

Case 2: If $b^2 - 4ac = 0$, then the roots are real and equal, and are computed as

$$\text{each root} = -\frac{b}{2a}$$

Case 3: If $b^2 - 4ac > 0$, then the roots are real and distinct and are computed as

$$\text{root1} = \frac{-b - \sqrt{b^2 - 4ac}}{2a} \quad \text{and} \quad \text{root2} = \frac{-b + \sqrt{b^2 - 4ac}}{2a}$$

Therefore, we will proceed as

For a given set of values of *a*, *b* and *c*, compute expression $b^2 - 4ac$. Now compare the computed value of $b^2 - 4ac$ with zero. If it is less than zero, compute the roots as shown in case 1; if it is equal to zero, compute the roots as shown in case 2; and if it is greater than zero, compute the roots as shown in case 3.

In this book, for each problem considered, we will first see how to solve it.

1.3 PROGRAM PLANNING AND DESIGN

Planning is very important in every walk of life. Even for our routine kind of things, we have to plan. Such a plan of doing things is also as *process*. For example, we have to plan our monthly budget otherwise things can go astray and we may not enough money left in our pocket towards the end of the month.

Planning should not be in the mind only (*adhoc process*), you must write it down, *i.e.*, you must document it (*defined process*). The results of *adhoc process* are not guaranteed where as the results of *defined process* are guaranteed and predictable.

Likewise, if you know the steps to be followed for solving a given problem but you have not documented them, you may forget to apply some of the steps or you may apply some of the steps in wrong sequence. Obviously, you will get a wrong answer. Similarly, while writing a program, if the programmer leaves out some of the instructions or writes the instructions in wrong sequence, the computer will give a wrong answer.

The various tools collectively referred to as *program design tools*, that helps in planning the program are *algorithm*, *flowchart* and *pseudocode*.

In the subsequent section, we will discuss about these tools, and demonstrate their use through illustrative examples.

1.4 ALGORITHMS

An *algorithm* is defined as a finite sequence of instructions defining the solution of a particular problem, where each instruction is numbered.

However, in order to qualify as an algorithm, every sequence of instructions must satisfy the following criteria:

- ***Input***: There are zero or more values which are externally supplied.
- ***Output***: At least one value is produced.
- ***Definiteness***: Each step must be clear and unambiguous, *i.e.*, having one and only one meaning).
- ***Finiteness***: If we trace the steps of an algorithm, then for all cases, the algorithm must terminate after a finite number of steps.
- ***Effectiveness***: Each step must be sufficiently basic that it can in principle be carried out by a person using only paper and pencil. In addition, not only each step is definite, it must also be feasible.

Example 1.1:

Formulate an algorithm to display the nature of roots of a quadratic equation of type

$ax^2 + bx + c = 0$ provided $a \neq 0$.

Solution: Roots of the quadratic equation are given by the formula:

$$x_{1,2} = \frac{-b \pm \sqrt{b^2 - 4ac}}{2a}$$

where the expression $b^2 - 4ac$ is known as the discriminant.

Depending on the sign of discriminant, there are three possibilities for roots:

1. If $b^2 - 4ac < 0$, then the root are imaginary.
2. If $b^2 - 4ac = 0$, then the roots are real and equal.
3. If $b^2 - 4ac > 0$, then the roots are real and distinct.

The complete algorithm will look like

Algorithm 1.1

Step 1: Input values of *a, b* and *c*

Step 2: Compute $b^2 - 4ac$ and denote its value by variable *disc*

Step 3: Is *disc* < 0? If yes then goto step 7 else goto step 4

Step 4: Is *disc* > 0? If yes then goto step 9 else goto step 5

Step 5: Output "roots are real and equal"

Step 6: Goto step 10

Step 7: Output "roots are imaginary"

Step 8: Goto step 10

Step 9: Output "roots are real and distinct"

Step 10: Stop

1.5 FLOWCHARTS

A flowchart is a pictorial representation of an algorithm. A flowchart uses different shapes to denote different types of instructions. The actual instructions are written within the shapes using clear and concise statements. These shapes are connected by directed lines to indicate the sequence in which instructions are to be executed.

Normally, an algorithm is first represented in the form of a flowchart and then the flowchart is expressed in some programming language to prepare a program. The main advantage of this approach in program writing is that while drawing a flowchart, one is not concerned with the details of the syntax of the programming language. Moreover, since a flowchart shows the sequence of instructions in a pictorial form, any error in logic can be detected more easily that in the case of a program. Once the flowchart is ready, the programmer can forget about the logic and can concentrate only on coding the instructions in each shape in terms of the syntax of the programming language. This will ensure an error-free program.

A flowchart, therefore, is a picture of the logic to be implemented by the program. It is simply a tool assisting the programmer to lay out, in a visual, two-dimensional format, ideas on how to organize a sequence of steps necessary to solve a problem by computer. It is basically the plan to be followed when the program is written. It acts like a road map for a programmer and guides him/her how to go from the starting point to the final point while writing a program.

Experienced programmers most often skip the flowchart while writing the program. However, for a beginner, it is recommended that flowchart must be drawn first in order to reduce the number of errors and omissions in the programs. Moreover, it is a good practice to have a flowchart because flowchart is very helpful during the testing of a program as well as while incorporating further modifications in the program.

Flowchart Symbols

As mentioned, flowchart uses boxes of different shapes to denote different types of instructions. The communication of the program logic through flowcharts is made easier through the use of symbols that have standardized meanings. For example, a diamond always means a decision. Only few symbols are needed to represent the necessary instructions in a flowchart. These symbols are standardized by American National Standards Institute (ANSI). Table 1.1 shows various symbols used in flowcharts along with their name and brief description.

Oval Symbol – This symbol is used to indicate the beginning (START) and ending (STOP) in the program logic flow. It is the first and the last symbol in the program logic.

Parallelogram Symbol – This symbol is used to denote the input to the program or output from the program. If there is a program instruction to input data from any input device, that may include keyboard, disk, tape, etc., that step will be indicated in the flowchart with this symbol. Similarly, if there is an instruction to output data to any output device, that may include terminal screen, printer, disk, tape, etc., that step will be indicated in the flowchart with this symbol.

Table 1.1: Various flowchart symbols and their brief description

Symbol	Name	Purpose
	Oval	*Terminal* - to mark the beginning and end of the program logic flow.
	Parallelogram	*Input/Output* - to denote the input to the program or output from the program.
	Rectangle	*Processing* - to denote the arithmetic operations and movement of data.
	Diamond	*Decision* - to denote a point where decision has to be made to branch to one of the alternatives.
	Small circle	*Connector* - To provide a logical link between segments of a flowchart.
	Directed lines	*Flow Lines* - To indicate the sequence in which instructions are to be executed.

Rectangle Symbol – This symbol is used to denote the arithmetic and data movement instructions. Thus, all arithmetic instructions such as addition, subtraction, multiplication and division are shown by this symbol. The other instructions such as moving data from one location in memory to other locations are also shown using this symbol. When more that one arithmetic and data movement instructions are to be executed consecutively, they can be placed in the same symbol and they are assumed to be executed in the order of their appearance.

Diamond Symbol – This symbol is used to denote a point where decision has to be made to branch to one of the alternatives.

It is important to note that the criteria for making the decision should be indicated clearly within the decision box. Moreover, the expression upon which each of the possible exit paths will be executed should be identified and all the possible paths should be accounted for. During execution, the appropriate path is followed depending upon the result of the decision.

Small Circle Symbol – This symbol is used to provide a logical link between segments of a flowchart. If a flowchart is very long, the flow lines start criss-crossing at many places that cause confusion and thus reduce understandability of the flowchart. Moreover, there are instances when a flowchart becomes too long to fit in a single page and the use of flow lines becomes impossible.

Thus, whenever a flowchart becomes complex enough that the number and direction of flow lines is confusing or it spreads over more than one page, it is useful to utilize the connector symbol as a substitute for flow lines. This symbol represents an entry from, or an exit to another part of the flowchart. A connector symbol is represented by a small circle and a letter or a digit is placed within the small circle to indicate the link. A pair of identically labeled connector symbols is commonly used to indicate a continued flow when the use of flow line is confusing. Therefore, two connectors with identical label serve the same function as a long flow line. That is, they show an exit to another section of the flowchart, or they indicate an entry from another section of the flowchart.

Now the question arises – *How is it possible to determine if a connector is used as an entry or an exit point*?

It is very simple – if an arrow enters into a connector, it is an exit point and the program control is transferred to an identically labeled connector that does have an outlet; if an arrow leaves a connector, it is an entry point and the control is received from an identically labeled connector. It may be noted that connectors do not represent any operation and their use in a flowchart is only for the sake of convenience and clarity.

Directed Lines – These lines are used to indicate the sequence in which instructions are to be executed. The normal sequence is from top to bottom and left to right. The crossing of these lines should be avoided whenever possible.

1.6 PSEUDOCODE

Pseudocode is another design tool that can be used for planning the program. The word "pseudo" means imitation or false and the word "code" refers to the instruction written in a programming language. Pseudocode, therefore, is an imitation of actual computer instruction. Pseudo instructions are phrases written in English like statements. Instead of using symbols to describe the logic of the program, as in flowcharts, pseudocode uses a structure that resembles computer instructions. Because, it emphasizes the design of the program, pseudocode is also called *Program Design Language* (PDL).

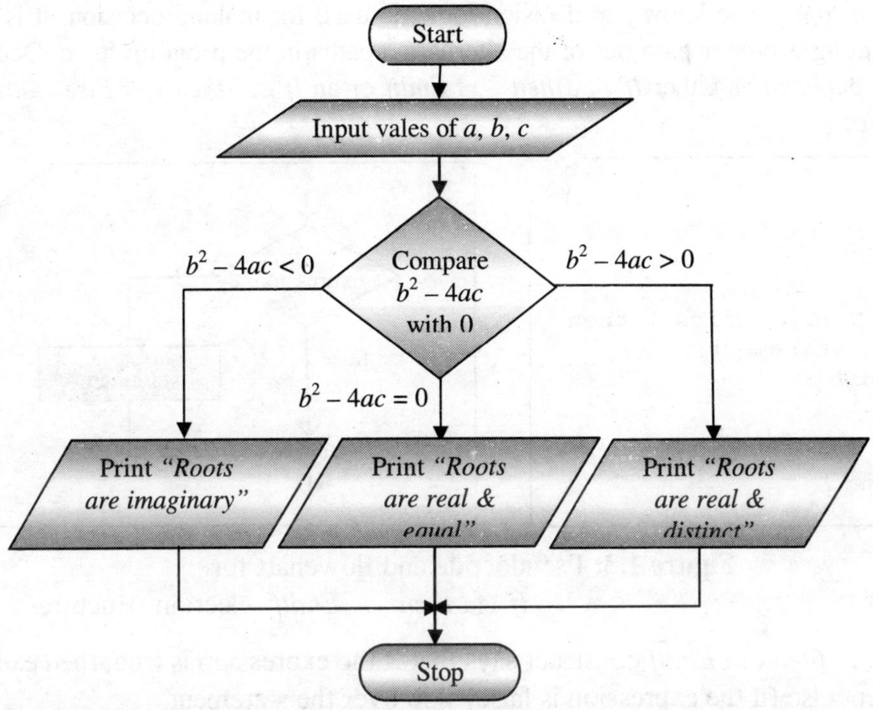

Figure 1.1: Flowchart to find the nature of roots of a quadratic equation

Pseudocode is made up of the following basic logic structures that have proved to be sufficient for writing any computer program:

1. Sequence
2. Selection (*If . . . then . . . Endif, If . . . then . . . Else . . .Endif*)
3. Iteration (*For . . . Endfor, While . . . Endwhile, Do . . . While*)

Sequence logic is used for performing instructions one after another in sequence. Thus, for sequence logic, pseudocode instructions are written in the sequence in which they are to be executed. The flow of logic is from top to bottom.

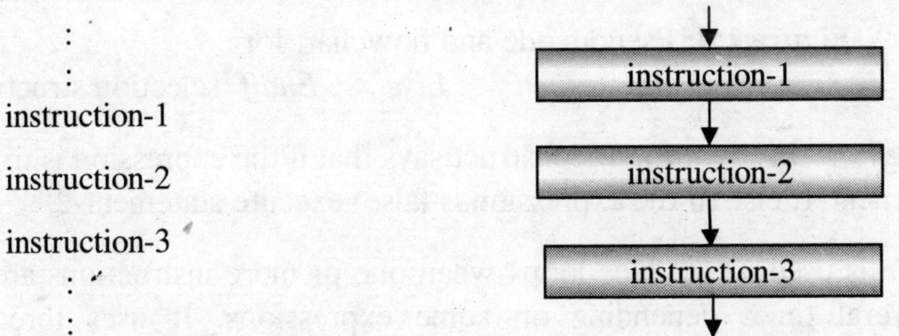

Figure 1.2: Pseudocode and flowchart for sequence structure

Selection logic, also known as decision logic, is used for making decision. It is used for selecting a proper path out of the alternative paths in the program logic. Decision logic is depicted as either *If . . . then . . . Endif* or an *If . . . then . . . Else . . . Endif* structure.

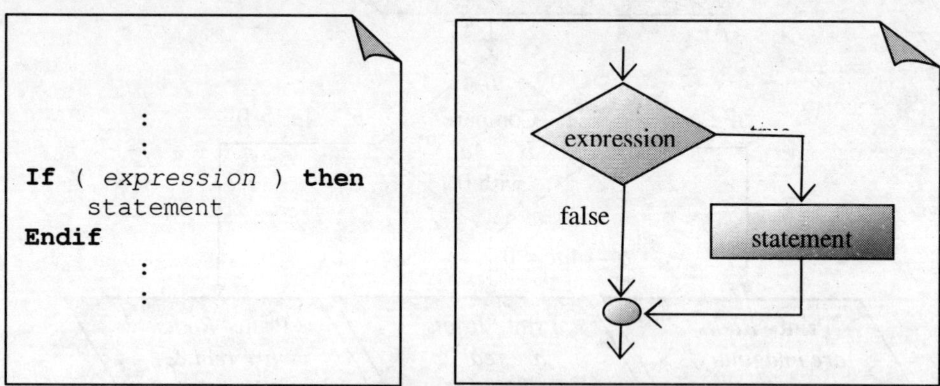

Figure 1.3: Pseudocode and flowchart for *If . . . then . . . Endif* selection structure

The *If . . . then . . . Endif* construct says that if the expression is true, then execute statement else (if the expression is false) skip over the statement.

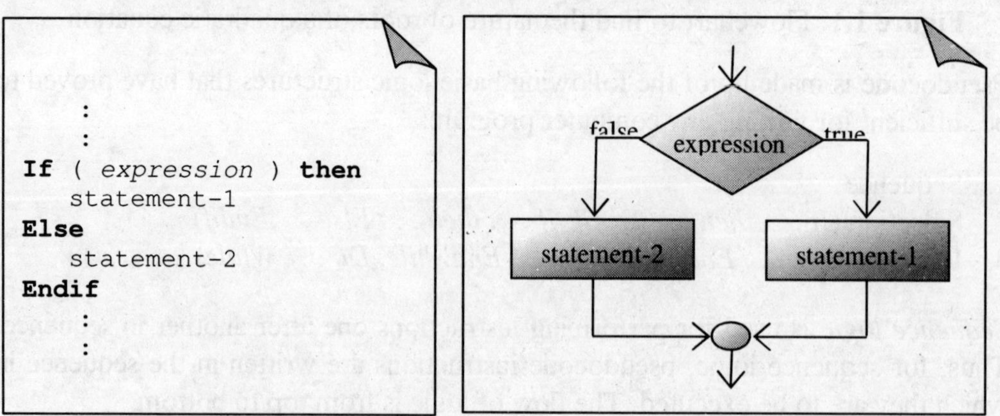

Figure 1.4: Pseudocode and flowchart for *If . . . then . . . Else . . . Endif* selection structure

The *If . . . then . . . Else . . . Endif* construct says that if the expression is true then execute statement-1, else (if the expression is false) execute statement-2.

Iterative logic is used to produce loops when one or more instructions are to be executed several times depending on some expressions. It uses three loop structures called *For . . . Endfor*, *While . . . Endwhile* and *Do . . . While*.

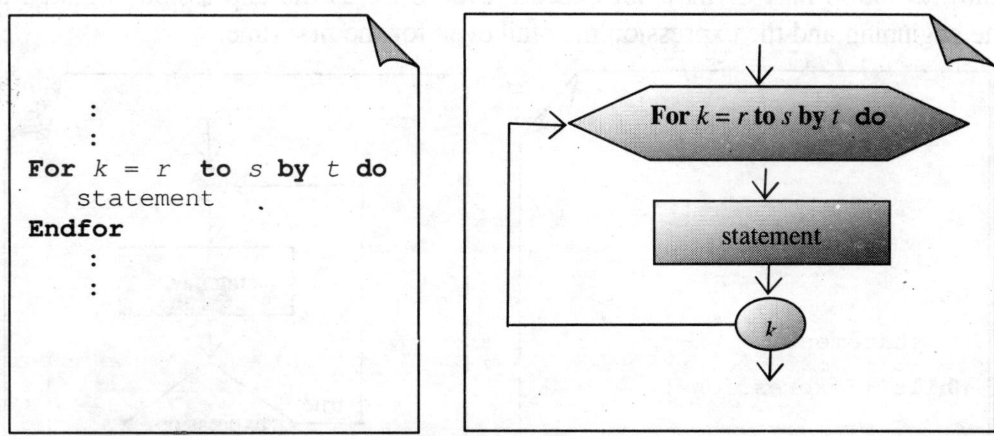

Figure 1.5: Pseudocode and flowchart *For . . . Endfor* iterative structure

It uses an index variable *k* to control the loop. Here *r* is called the initial value, *s* is called the final value and *t* is called the step size, which may be positive (increment) or negative (decrement).

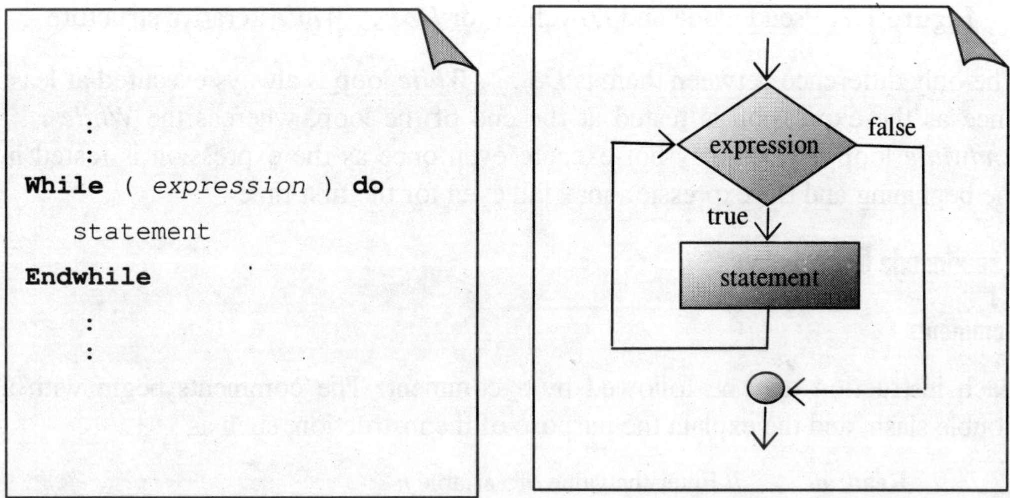

Figure 1.6: Pseudocode and flowchart for *While . . . Endwhile* iterative structure

The *For . . . Endfor* loop is used when the number of iterations is known. On the other side, *While . . . Endwhile* and *Do . . . While* loops are used when the number of iterations is not known. Both *While . . . Endwhile* and *Do . . . While* continues to execute as long as the expression is true.

The only difference between them is *Do . . . While* loop is always executed at least once as the expression is tested at the end of the loop, whereas the *While . . .*

Endwhile loop may or may not execute even once as the expression is tested in the beginning and the expression may fail even for the first time.

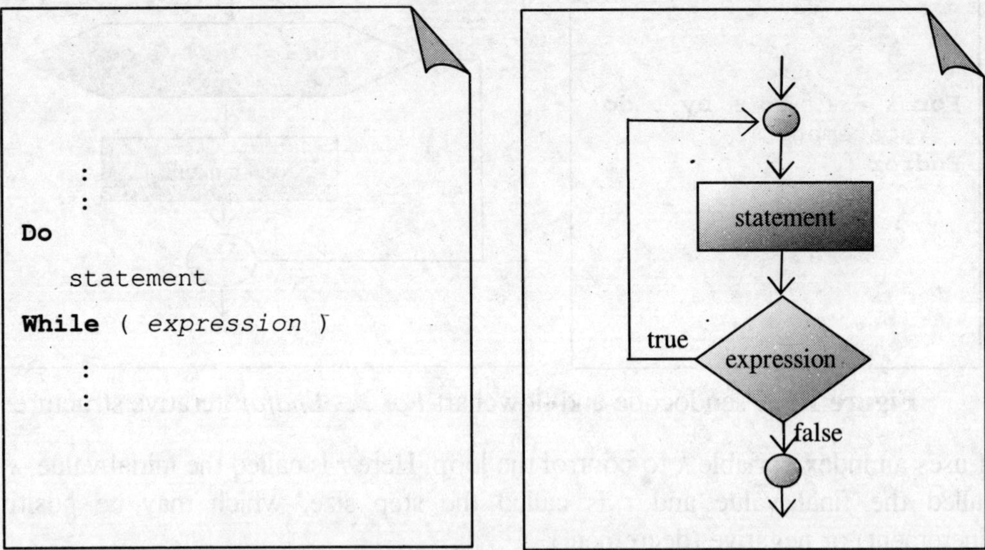

Figure 1.7: Pseudocode and flowchart for *Do . . . While* iterative structure

The only difference between them is *Do . . . While* loop is always executed at least once as the expression is tested at the end of the loop, whereas the *While . . . Endwhile* loop may or may not execute even once as the expression is tested in the beginning and the expression may fail even for the first time.

Pseudocode Description

Comments

Each instruction may be followed by a comment. The comments begin with a double slash, and the explain the purpose of the instruction, such as

Read: *n* // Enter the value of variable *n*

Appropriate use of comments enhances the readability of the pseudocode, which in turn helps in maintaining the pseudocode.

Variable Names

For variable names, we will use italicized lowercase letters such as *max*, *loc*, etc., whereas for defined constants, if any, we will use uppercase letters.

Assignment Statement

The assignment statement will use the notation as

Set $max = a_i$

to assign the value of a_i to *max*. The right hand side of the assignment statement can have a *value, a variable* or *an expression*.

However, if several assignment statements appear in the same line, such as

Set $k = 1$, $loc = 1$, $max = a_i$

then they are executed from left to right.

Input/Output

Data may be input and assigned to variables by means of a *read* statement with the following format

Read: *Variable list*

where the *Variable list* consists one or more variables separated by comma.

Similarly, the data held by the variables and the messages, if any, enclosed in double quotes can be output by means of a *write* statement with the following format

Print: *message* and/or *Variable list*

where the *message* and the variables in the *Variable list* are separated by comma.

Execution of Instructions

The instructions in the pseudocode are usually executed one after the other as they appear in the pseudocode. However, there may be instances when some instructions are skipped or some instructions may be repeated as a result of certain expressions.

Completion of the Algorithm

The pseudocode is completed with the execution of the last instruction. However, the pseudocode can be terminated at any intermediate state using the *exit* instruction.

Pseudocode to display the nature of roots of a quadratic equation of the type

$ax^2 + bx + c = 0$ provided $a \neq 0$.

Pseudocode 1.1

```
Begin
   Read: a, b, c
   Set disc = b^2 – 4ac
   If ( disc < 0 ) then
      Print: "roots are imaginary"
   Else
      If ( disc > 0 ) then
         Print: "roots are real and distinct"
      Else
         Print: "roots are real and equal"
      Endif
   Endif
End.
```

If you look at the algorithm, flowchart and pseudocode for program design to find the nature of the roots of the quadratic equation, you will find that the logic in flowchart is easy to understand whereas the pseudocode is much closer to the actual program.

In this chapter, we will consider flowchart and pseudocode to express the design of the program.

1.7 ILLUSTRATIVE EXAMPLES

Example 1.2:

Draw flowchart and write pseudocode to find the largest of three numbers, say *a*, *b*, *c*.

Solution: We first compare *a* with *b*. If *a* is greater than *b* then we compare *a* with *c*. If *a* is greater than *c*, then *a* is taken as the largest number otherwise we take c as the largest number.

However, if *a* is not greater than *b*, we compare *b* with *c*. If *b* is greater than *c* then *b* is taken as the largest number otherwise we take *c* as the largest number.

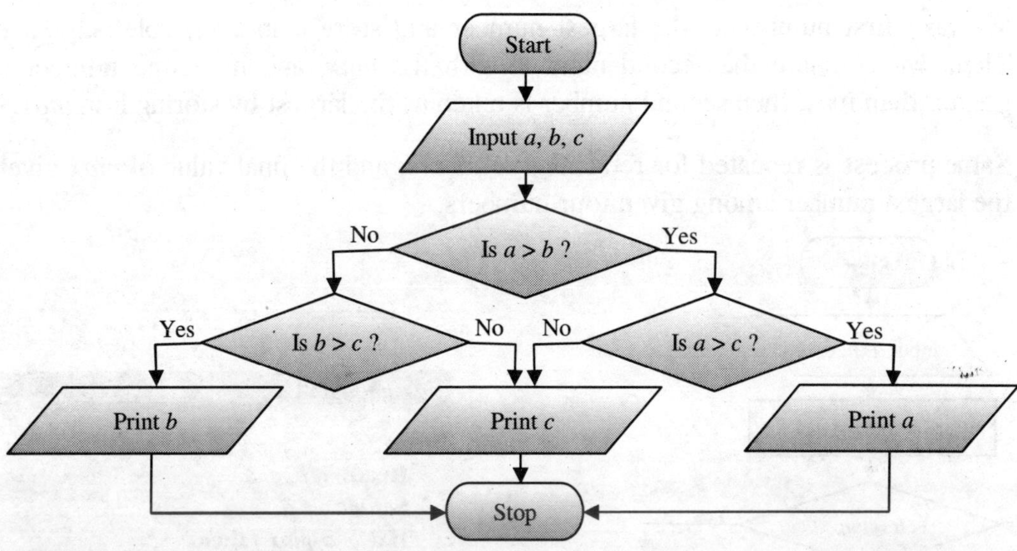

Pseudocode 1.2

```
Begin
    Read: a, b, c
    If ( a > b ) then
        If ( a > c ) then
            Print: a
        Else
            Print: c
        Endif
    Else
        If ( b > c ) then
            Print: b
        Else
            Print: c
        Endif
    Endif
End.
```

Figure 1.8: Flowchart & pseudocode to find largest of three numbers

Example 1.3:

Draw flowchart and write pseudocode to find the largest of four numbers, say *a*, *b*, *c*, *d*.

Solution: For four or more numbers, the solution of Example 1.2 will become very cumbersome. Therefore, we will follow an alternate approach.

We take first number as the largest number and store it in a variable, say *max*. Then, we compare the second number with the *max*, and if second number is greater than max, then second number is taken as the largest by storing it in *max*.

Same process is repeated for remaining numbers, and the final value of *max* given the largest number among given four numbers.

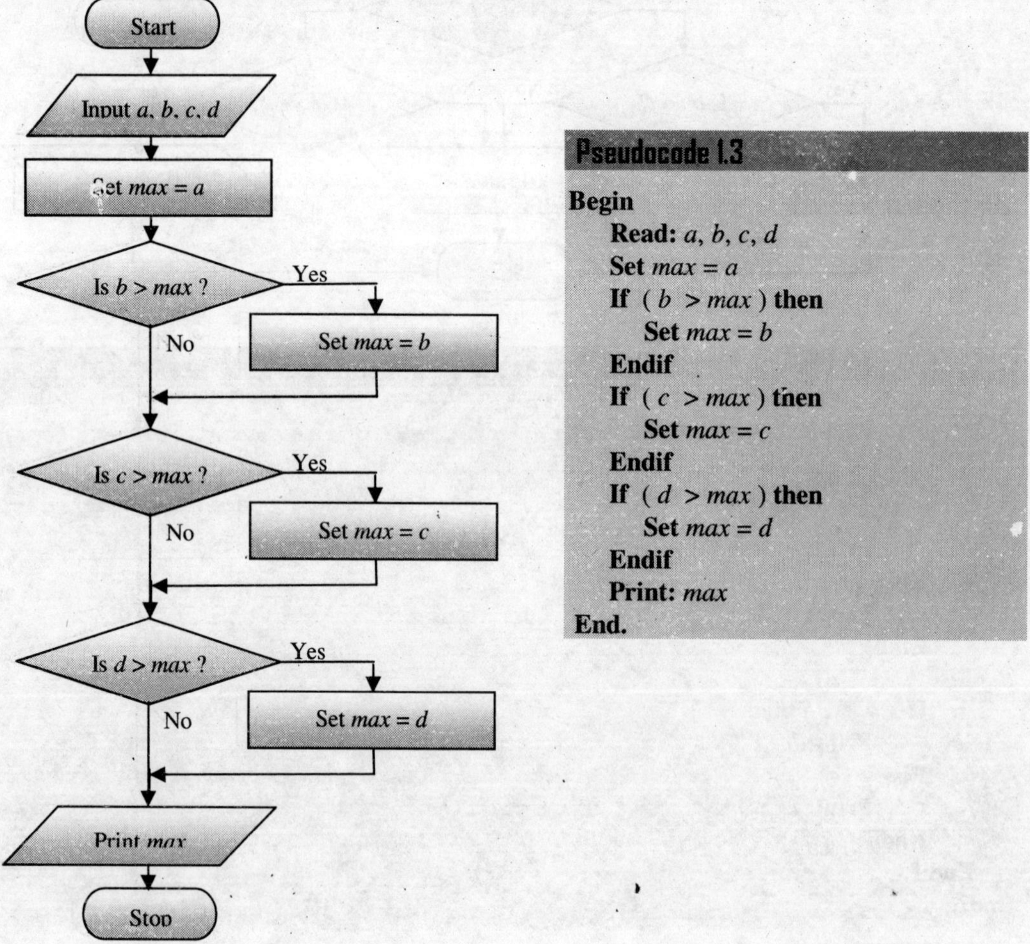

Pseudocode 1.3

```
Begin
    Read: a, b, c, d
    Set max = a
    If ( b > max ) then
        Set max = b
    Endif
    If ( c > max ) then
        Set max = c
    Endif
    If ( d > max ) then
        Set max = d
    Endif
    Print: max
End.
```

Figure 1.9: Flowchart & pseudocode to find largest of four numbers

Example 1.4:

Fibonacci sequence is given below:

0 1 1 2 3 5 8 13 21 . . .

Draw a flowchart and write pseudocode to generate the above sequence up to the term less than or equal to 100.

Solution: Observe that, leaving first two terms, each term is obtained as the sum of the immediately preceding two terms.

If we use variable *previous* for previous term, *current* for current term, *next* for next term, and setting *previous* and *current* to values 0 and 1 respectively, i.e., first two terms of the sequence, then the entire sequence can be generated by using the recurrence relation

next = *previous* + *current*
replace *previous* by *current*
replace *current* by *next*

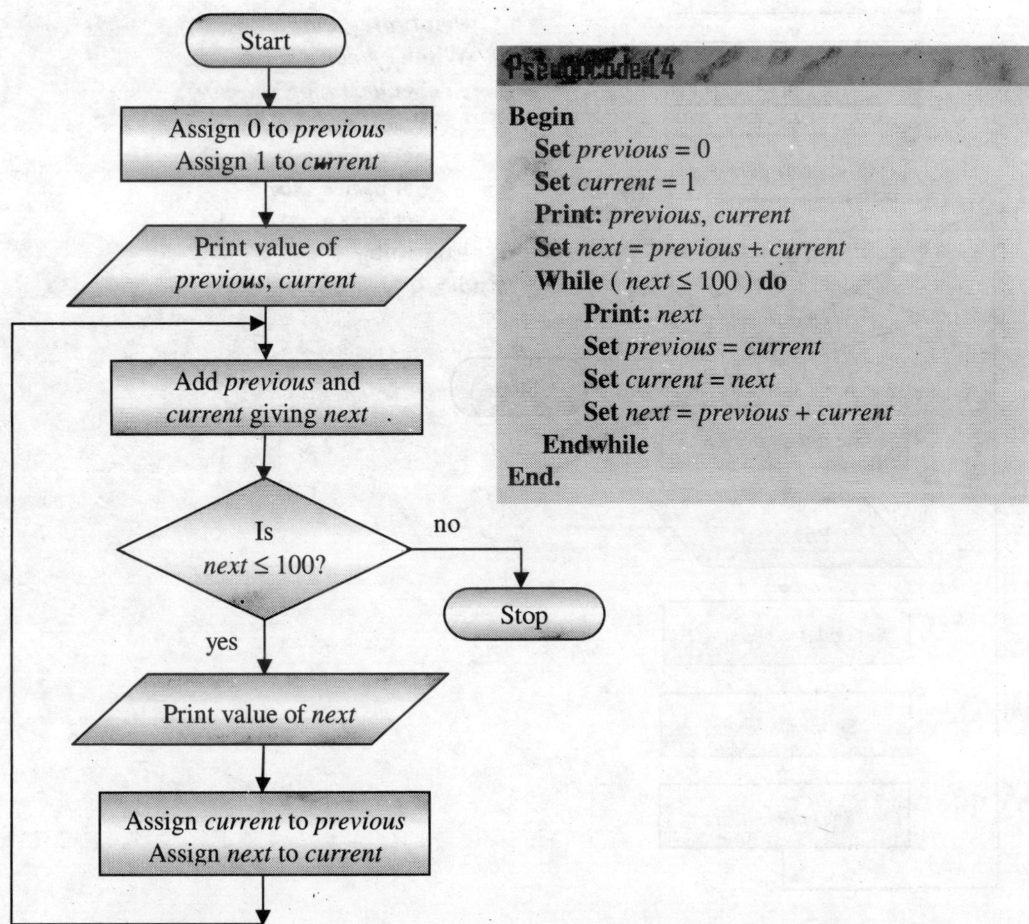

Pseudocode1.4

```
Begin
   Set previous = 0
   Set current = 1
   Print: previous, current
   Set next = previous + current
   While ( next ≤ 100 ) do
       Print: next
       Set previous = current
       Set current = next
       Set next = previous + current
   Endwhile
End.
```

Figure 1.10: Flowchart & pseudocode to generate the Fibonacci sequence with last term less than or equal to 100

Example 1.5:

Draw a flowchart and write pseudocode to print first *n* terms of the Fibonacci sequence. For example, if input value for *n* is 8, the output should be

0 1 1 2 3 5 8 13

Solution:

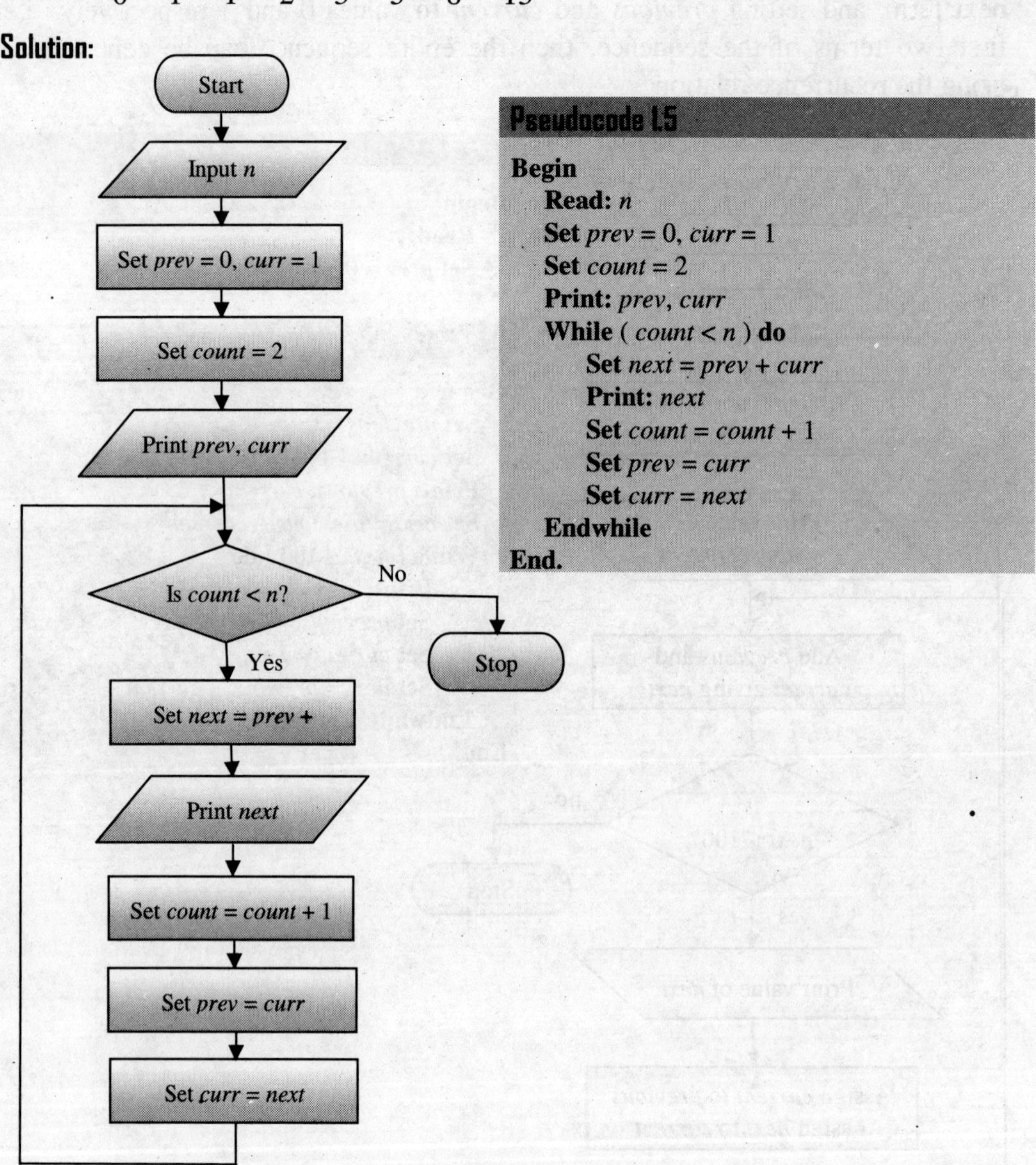

Pseudocode 1.5

```
Begin
    Read: n
    Set prev = 0, curr = 1
    Set count = 2
    Print: prev, curr
    While ( count < n ) do
        Set next = prev + curr
        Print: next
        Set count = count + 1
        Set prev = curr
        Set curr = next
    Endwhile
End.
```

Figure 1.11: Flowchart & pseudocode to print first *n* terms of the Fibonacci sequence

Example 1.6:

Draw a flowchart and write pseudocode to print *n*th term of the Fibonacci sequence. For example, if input value for *n* is 8, the output should be

13

Solution:

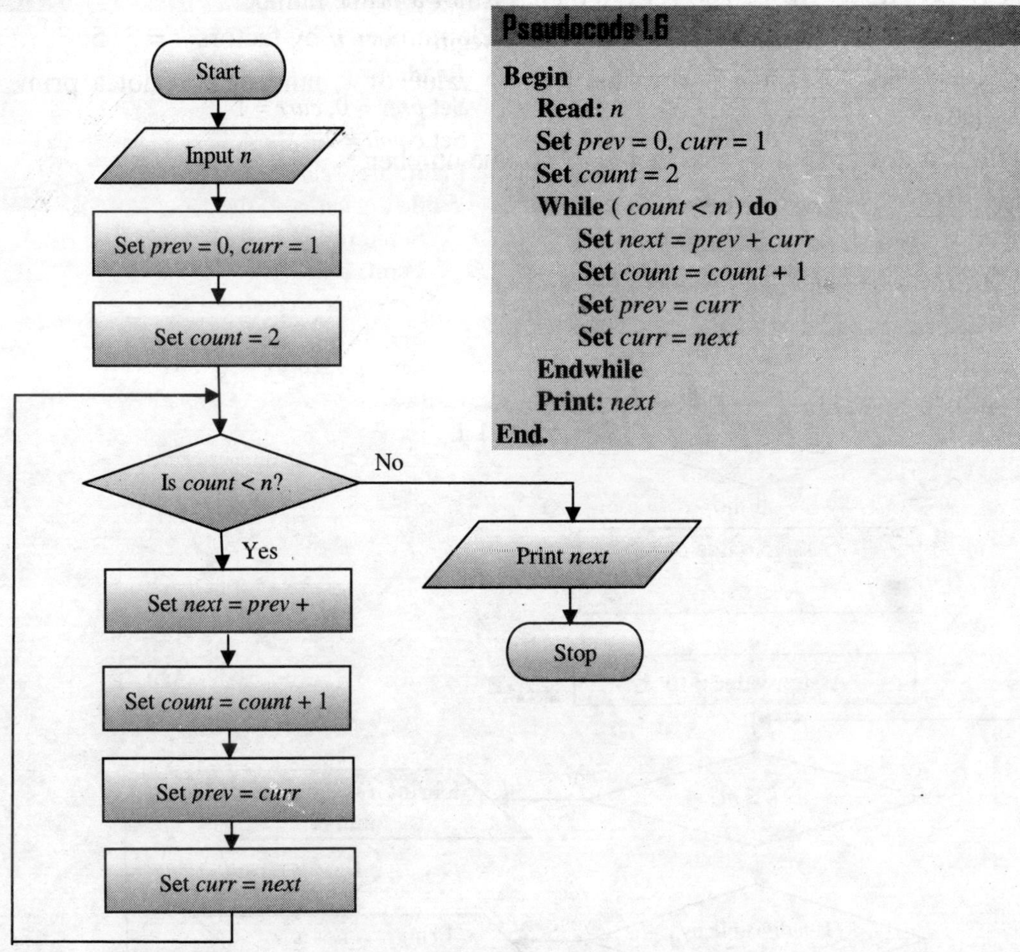

Pseudocode 1.6

```
Begin
    Read: n
    Set prev = 0, curr = 1
    Set count = 2
    While ( count < n ) do
        Set next = prev + curr
        Set count = count + 1
        Set prev = curr
        Set curr = next
    Endwhile
    Print: next
End.
```


Figure 1.12: Flowchart & pseudocode to print *n*th term of the Fibonacci sequence

Example 1.7:

Program to find whether the given natural number n is a prime number or not.

Solution: A natural number is said to be prime if it divisible by 1 and itself only, *i.e.*, it cannot be factorized. In addition, to this definition, an even number except 2 is not a prime number. Therefore, our test criteria becomes

1. If n is greater than 2 and is even then n is not a prime number.
2. If test at step 1 fails, then we try to divide number n by factors $k = 3, 5, 7, \ldots \sqrt{n}$. Therefore, if n is divisible by any value of k, number n is not a prime number.
3. If test at step 2 also fails, then n is a prime number.

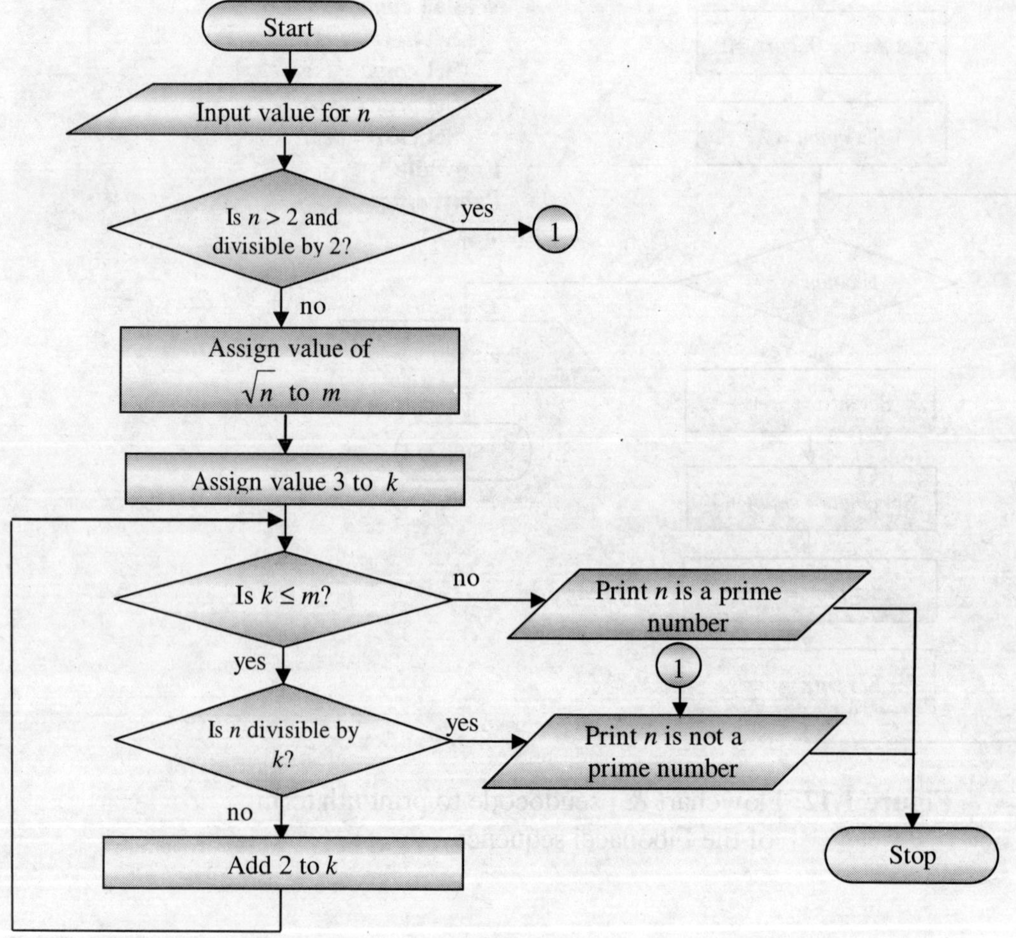

Figure 1.13: Flowchart to check whether number n is prime or not

Following is the pseudocode to find whether the given positive number *n* is a prime number or not.

Pseudocode 1.7

```
Begin
   Read: n
   If ( n > 2 and n mod 2 == 0 ) then
        Print: n, " is not a prime number"
        Exit
   Else
       Set m = √n
       For k = 3 to m by 2 do
           If ( n mod k == 0 ) then
                Print: n, " is not a prime number"
                Exit
           Endif
       Endfor
       Print: n, " is a prime number"
   Endif
End.
```

Example 1.8:

To find highest common factor (HCF)/, also known as greatest common divisor (GCD), of two natural numbers *m* and *n*.

Solution:

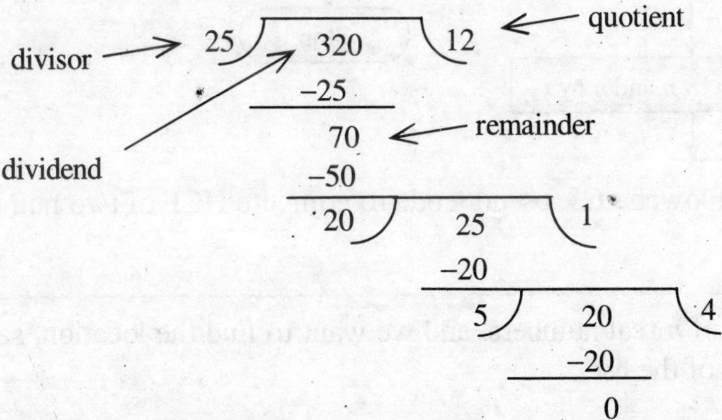

Figure 1.14: Illustration of computational procedure for HCF/GCD

Figure 1.14 demonstrates the long/continued division method to find the HCF/GCD of two natural numbers. You must have observed that in successive divisions, the divisor of the previous division becomes dividend, remainder of becomes divisor, and division is again carried out. This process is carried out till the reminder becomes zero, and the current divisor is taken as HCF/GCD of the given natural numbers.

This process can be implemented by using the following steps

1. Perform division.
2. If remainder is zero, then stop and take the divisor as HCF/GCD.
3. Replace dividend by divisor.
4. Replace divisor by remainder.
5. Repeat from step 1.

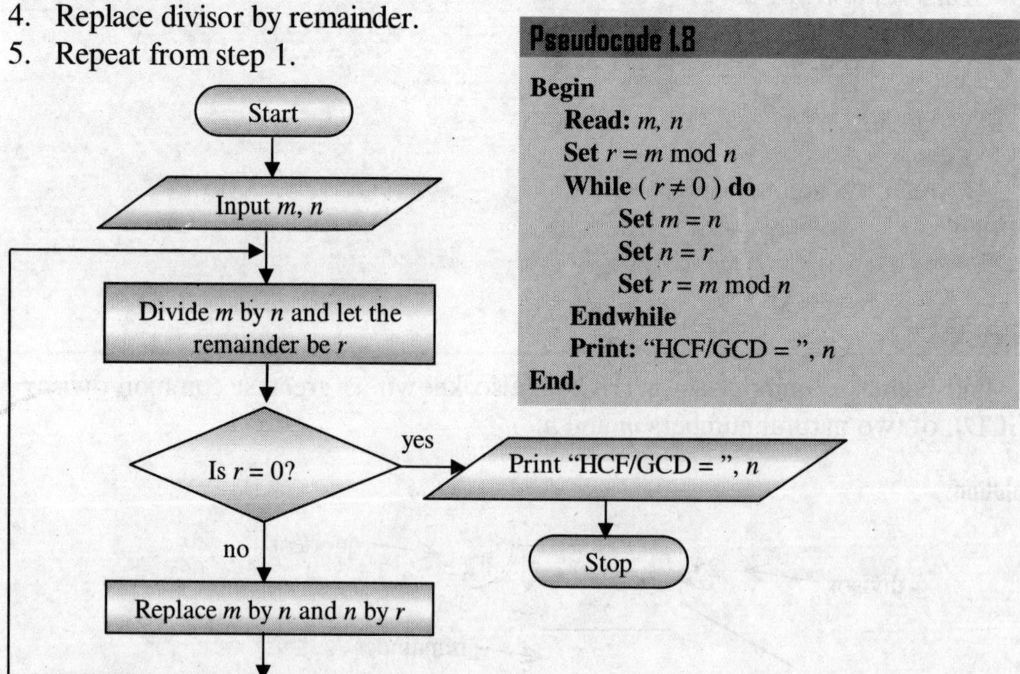

Pseudocode 1.8

Begin
    Read: *m*, *n*
    Set $r = m \bmod n$
    While ($r \neq 0$) **do**
        Set $m = n$
        Set $n = r$
        Set $r = m \bmod n$
    Endwhile
    Print: "HCF/GCD = ", *n*
End.

Figure 1.15: Flowchart & pseudocode to compute HCF of two numbers

Example 1.9:

Suppose *a* is a list of *n* real numbers, and we want to find the location, say *loc*, of the largest element of the list.

Solution: *This problem can be solved as follows*: We begin with *loc* = 1, and *max* = *a*[1]. We then compare *max* with each successive element *a*[*k*] of the list. If *a*[*k*] is greater than *max*, we then update *loc* and *max* as *loc* = *k* and *max* = *a*[*k*], respectively. The final value of *loc* gives the location of the largest element of the list.

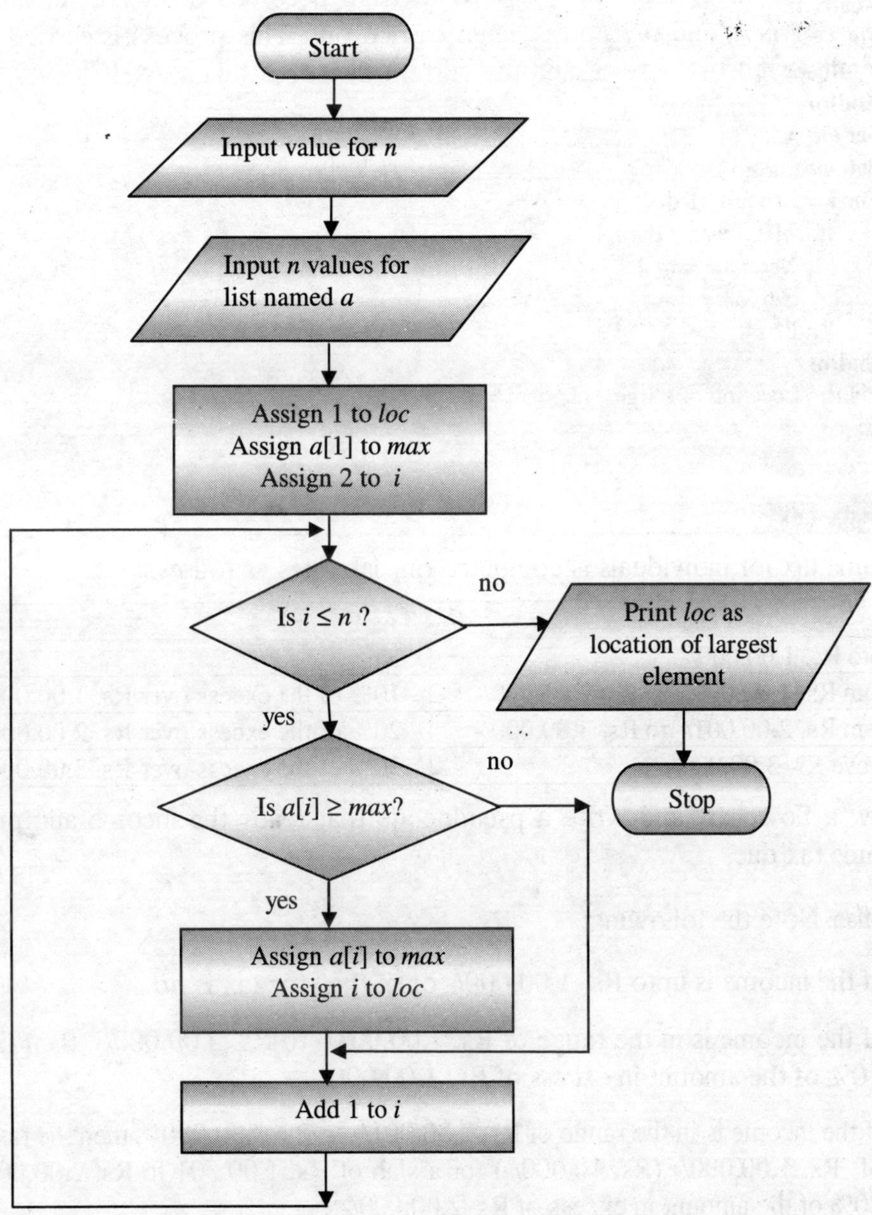

Figure 1.16: Flowchart to find the location of the largest element from a list of numbers

Pseudocode 1.9

```
Begin
   Read: n
   For i = 1 to n by 1 do
      Read: a[i]
   Endfor
   Set loc = 1
   Set max = a[1]
   For i = 2 to n by 1 do
        If ( a[i] > max ) then
           Set max = a[i]
           Set loc = i
        Endif
   Endfor
   Print: "Location of Largest element = ", loc
End.
```

Example 1.10:

Income tax for individuals is computed on slab rates as follows:

Income	Tax Payable
Upto Rs. 1,00,000/-	Nil
From Rs. 1,00,001/- to Rs. 2,00,000/-	10% of the excess over Rs. 1,00,000/-
From Rs. 2,00,001/- to Rs. 3,00,000/-	20% of the excess over Rs. 2,00,000/-
Above Rs. 3,00,000/-	30% of the excess over Rs. 3,00,000/-

Draw a flowchart and write a pseudocode that reads the income and prints the income tax due.

Solution: Note the following:

- If the income is upto Rs. 1,00,000/- only, then the tax is *nil*.
- If the income is in the range of Rs. 1,00,001/- to Rs. 2,00,000/-, then the tax is 10% of the amount in excess of Rs. 1,00,000/-.
- If the income is in the range of Rs. 2,00,001/- to Rs. 3,00,000/-, then the tax is 10% of Rs. 1,00,000/- (Rs. 10,000/-) for a slab of Rs. 1,00,001 to Rs. 2,00,000/- plus 20% of the amount in excess of Rs. 2,00,000/-.
- If the income is more than Rs. 3,00,000/-, then the tax is 10% of Rs. 1,00,000/- (Rs. 10,000/-) for a slab of Rs. 1,00,001 to Rs. 2,00,000/- plus 20% of Rs. 1,00,000/- (Rs. 20,000/-) for a slab of Rs. 2,00,001 to Rs. 3,00,000/- plus 30% of the amount in excess of Rs. 3,00,000/-.

Let us have hands on by computing the tax if the given income is

(*a*) Rs. 2,50,000/-
(*b*) Rs. 1,75,000/-
(*c*) Rs. 3,20,000/-

(*a*) *Tax Computations for income of Rs. 2,50,000/-*

For first Rs. 1,00,000/-	Tax is Nil
For next Rs. 1,00,000/-	Tax is 10,000/- (@ 10%)
For next Rs. 50,000/-	Tax is 10,000/- (@ 20%)
Total Tax due	Rs. 20,000/-

(*b*) *Tax Computations for income of Rs. 1,75,000/-*

For first Rs.1,00,000/-	Tax is Nil
For next Rs. 75,000/-	Tax is 7,500/- (@ 10%)
Total Tax due	Rs. 7,500/-

(*c*) *Tax Computations for income of Rs. 3,20,000/-*

For first Rs. 1,00,000/-	Tax is Nil
For next Rs. 1,00,000/-	Tax is 10,000/- (@ 10%)
For next Rs. 1,00,000/-	Tax is 20,000/- (@ 20%)
For next Rs. 20,000/-	Tax is 6,000/- (@ 30%)
Total Tax due	Rs. 36,000/-

Pseudocode 1.10

```
Begin
   Read: income
   If (income < 100000) then
      Set tax = 0
   Else if (income < 200000) then
      Set tax = 0.01 × (income – 100000)
   Else if (income < 300000) then
      Set tax = 10000 + 0.02 × (income – 200000)
   Else
      Set tax = 30000 + 0.03 × (income – 300000)
   Endif
   Print: tax
End.
```

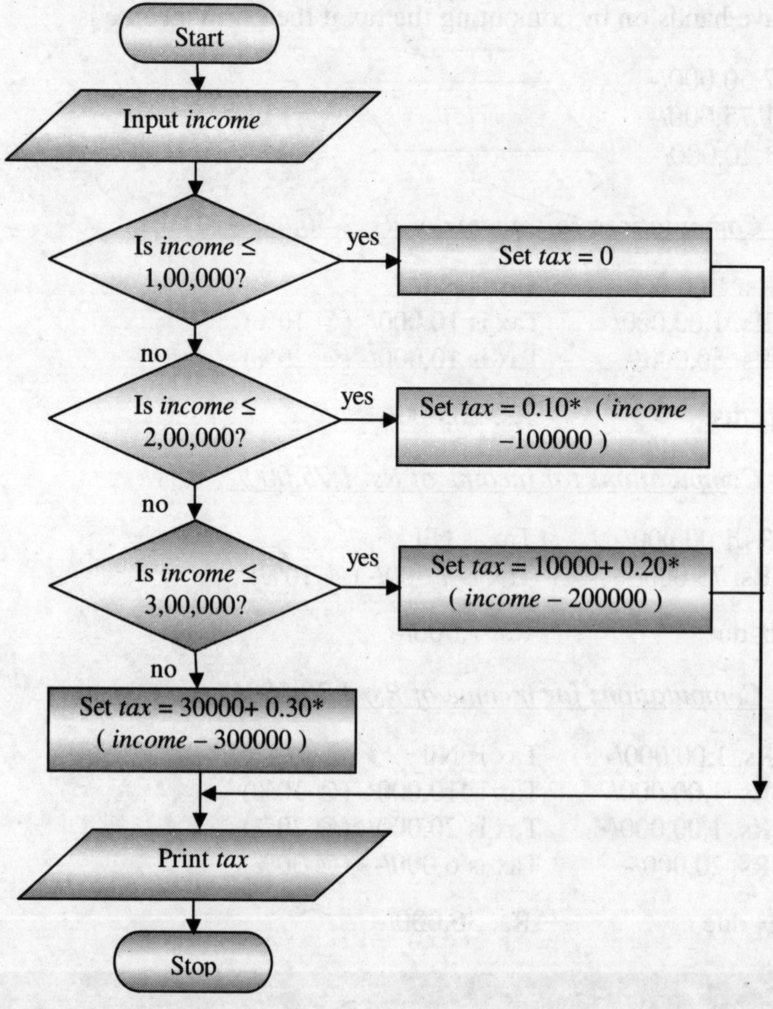

Figure 1.17: Flowchart to compute tax

Example 1.11:

Given measure of three line segments as *a*, *b*, and *c*. Draw a flowchart and also write pseudocode to check whether the line segments can be used to make a triangle.

Solution: By the Triangle Inequality, in order for three line segments to make a triangle, the sum of the lengths of any two line segments must exceed the length of the third line segment.

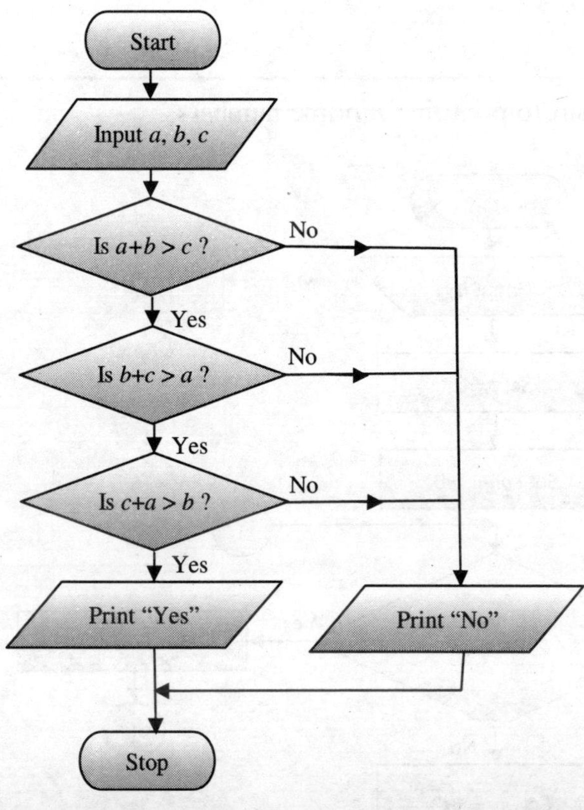

Pseudocode 1.11

```
Begin
   Read: a, b, c
   If ( a + b > c ) then
       If ( b + c > a ) then
           If ( c + a > b ) then
               Print: "Yes"
           Else
               Print: "No"
           Endif
       Else
           Print: "No"
       Endif
   Else
       Print: "No"
   Endif
End.
```

Figure 1.18: Flowchart & pseudocode to check whether a triangle can be formed from given three line segments

Example 1.12:

Draw a flowchart to print first n prime numbers.

Solution:

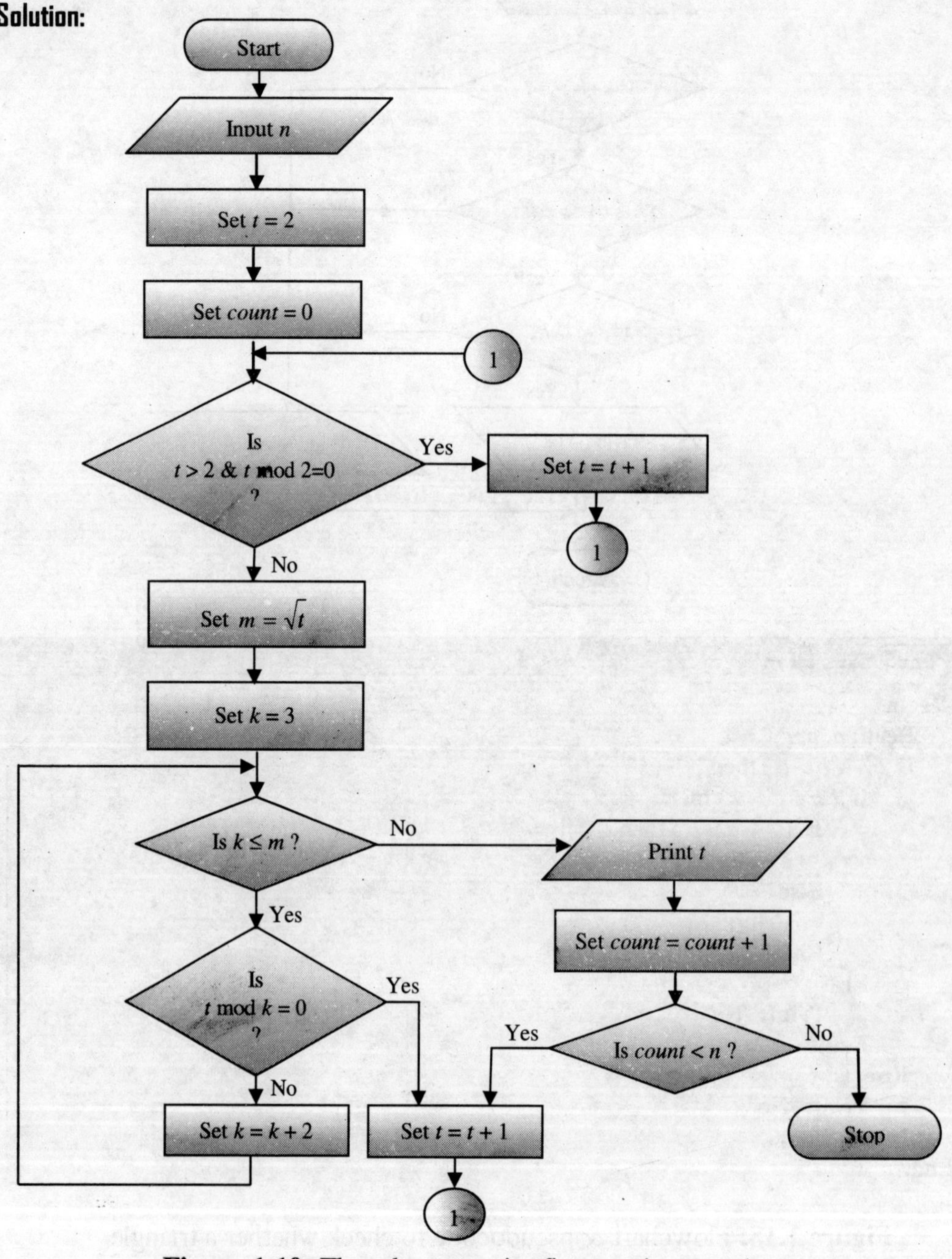

Figure 1.19: Flowchart to print first n prime numbers

Example 1.13:

Draw a flowchart to print *n*th prime number.

Solution:

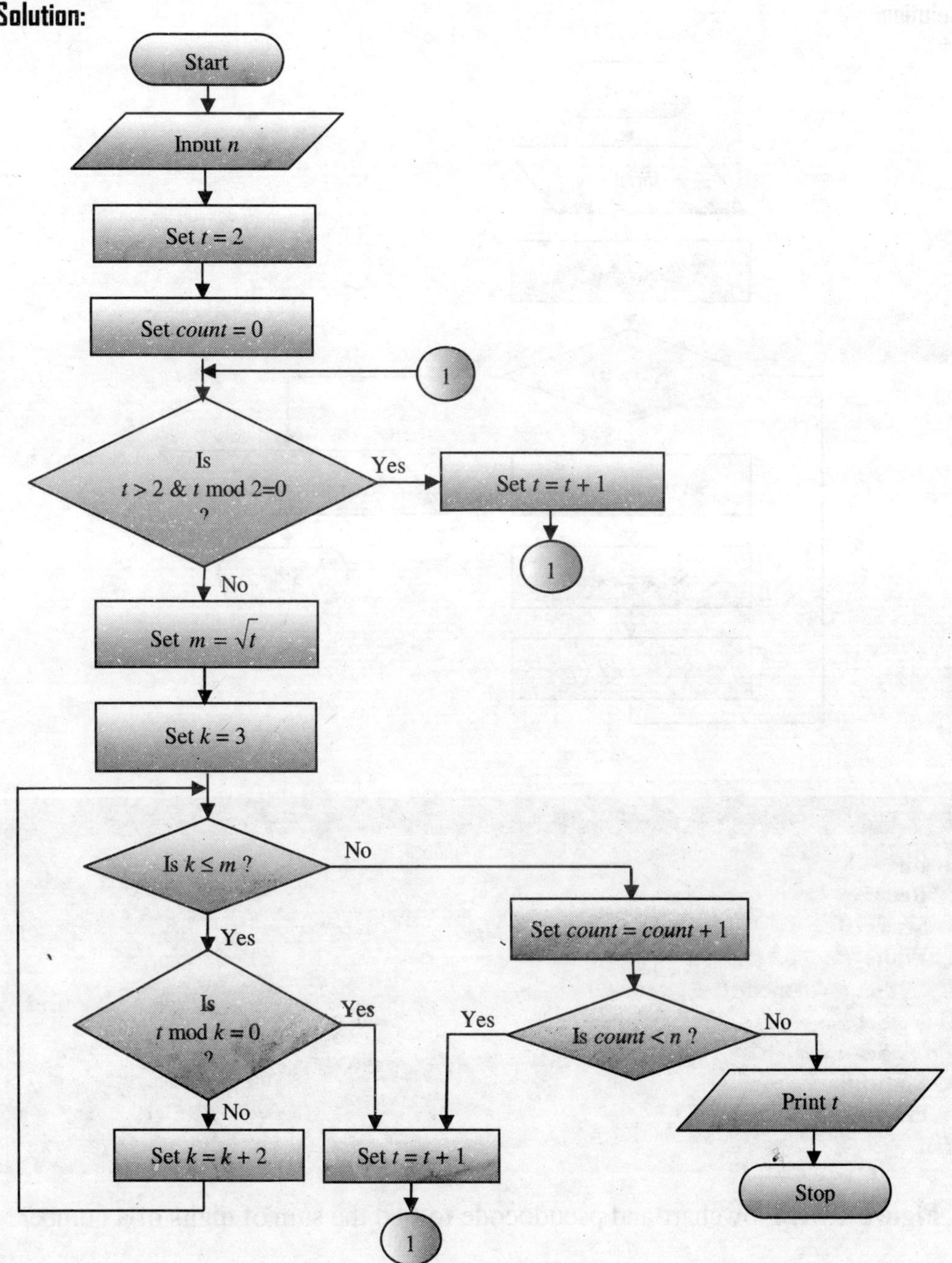

Figure 1.20: Flowchart to print *n*th prime number

Example 1.14:

Draw a flowchart and write pseudocode to find the sum of digits of a number *n*.

Solution:

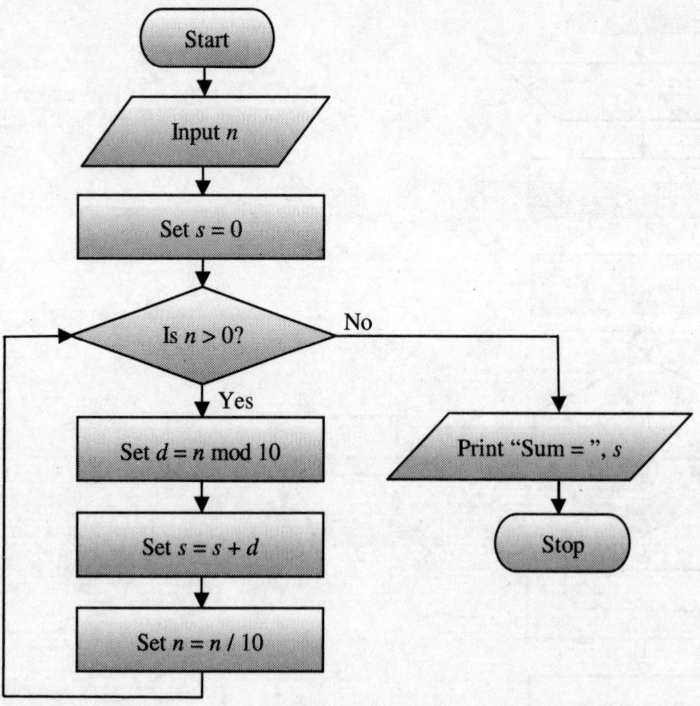

Pseudocode 1.12

Begin
  Read: n
  Set $s = 0$
  While $(n > 0)$ **do**
    Set $d = n$ mod 10
    Set $s = s + d$
    Set $n = n / 10$
  Endwhile
  Print: "Sum = ", s
End.

Figure 1.21: Flowchart and pseudocode to find the sum of digits of a number

Example 1.15:

Draw a flowchart and write pseudocode to find the largest digit of a number *n*.

Solution:

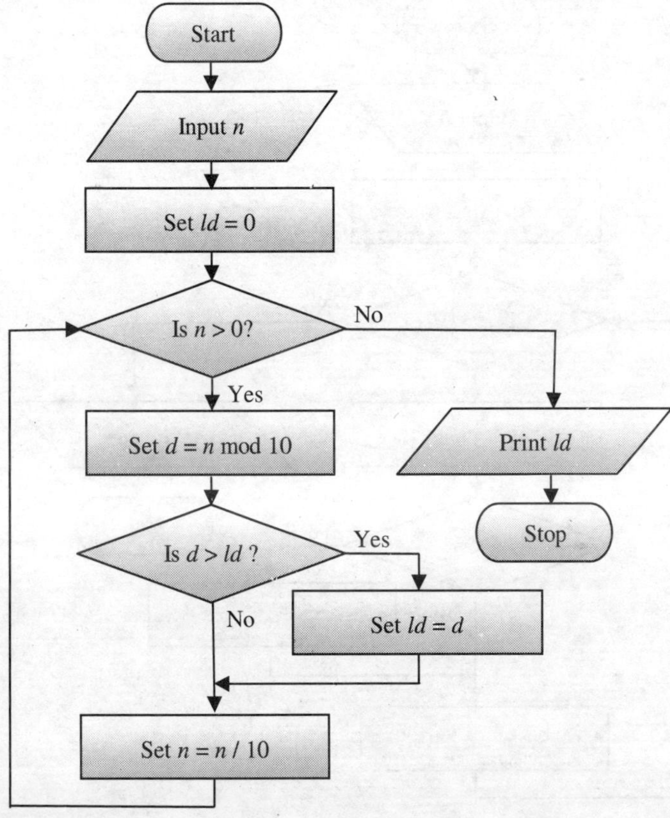

Pseudocode 1.13

```
Begin
   Read: n
   Set ld = 0
   While ( n > 0 ) do
      Set d = n mod 10
      If ( d > ld ) then
         Set ld = d
      Endif
   Endwhile
   Print: "Largest digit = ", ld
End.
```

Figure 1.22: Flowchart and pseudocode to find the largest digit of a number

Example 1.16:

Draw a flowchart and write pseudocode to find the largest digit of a number *n*.

Solution:

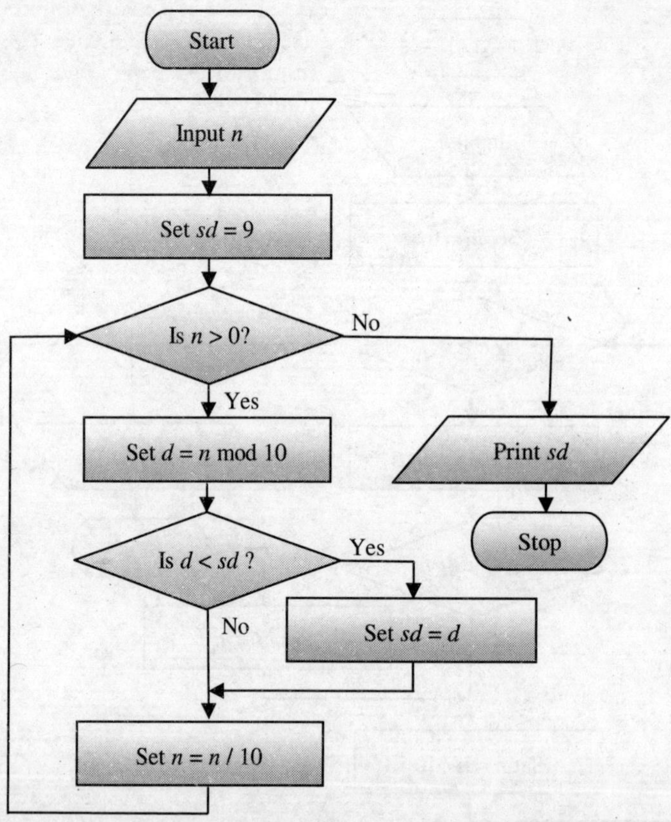

Pseudocode 1.14

Begin
  Read: *n*
  Set *sd* = 9
  While (*n* > 0) **do**
    Set *d* = *n* mod 10
    If (*d* < *sd*) **then**
      Set *sd* = *d*
    Endif
  Endwhile
  Print: "Smallest digit = ", *sd*
End.

Figure 1.23: Flowchart and pseudocode to find the smallest digit of a number

Example 1.17:

Draw a flowchart and write pseudocode to check whether the given number *n* is palindrome or not.

Solution:

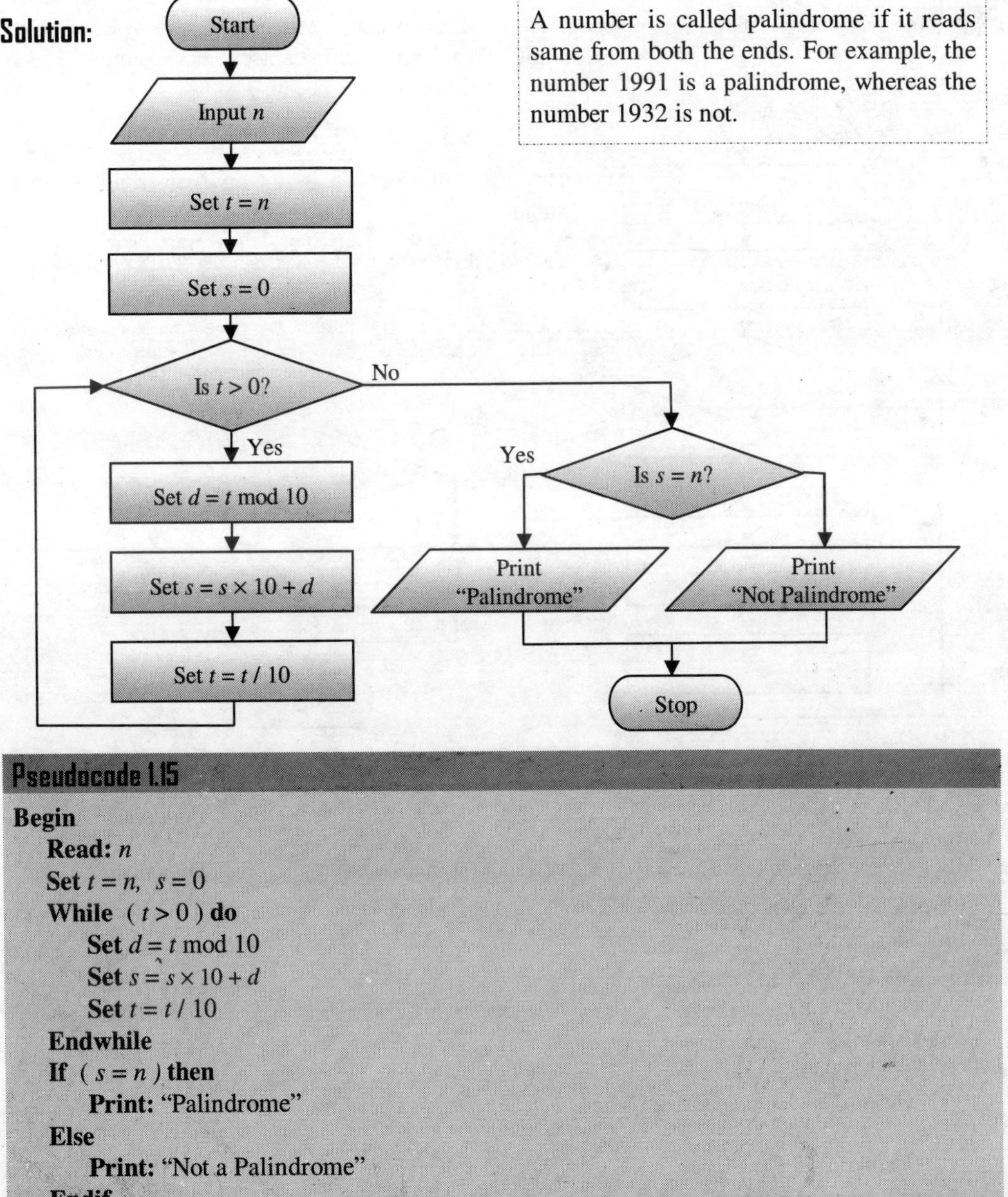

A number is called palindrome if it reads same from both the ends. For example, the number 1991 is a palindrome, whereas the number 1932 is not.

Pseudocode 1.15

```
Begin
    Read: n
    Set t = n,  s = 0
    While ( t > 0 ) do
        Set d = t mod 10
        Set s = s × 10 + d
        Set t = t / 10
    Endwhile
    If ( s = n ) then
        Print: "Palindrome"
    Else
        Print: "Not a Palindrome"
    Endif
End.
```

Figure 1.24: Flowchart & pseudocode to check whether the given number *n* is palindrome or not

Example 1.18:

Draw a flowchart and write pseudocode to check whether the given number n is Armstrong number or not.

Solution:

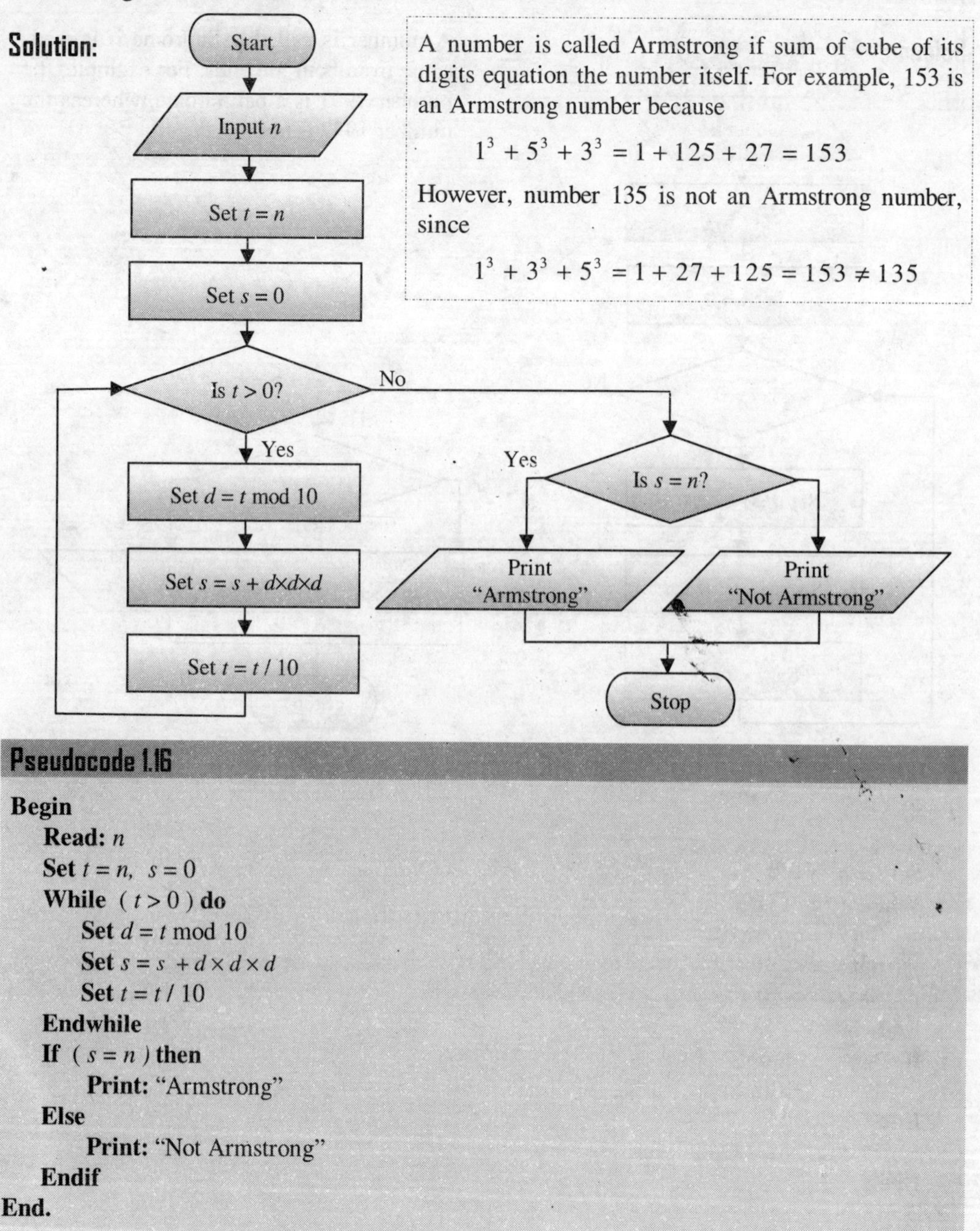

Pseudocode 1.16

```
Begin
   Read: n
   Set t = n,  s = 0
   While  ( t > 0 ) do
       Set d = t mod 10
       Set s = s + d × d × d
       Set t = t / 10
   Endwhile
   If  ( s = n ) then
       Print: "Armstrong"
   Else
       Print: "Not Armstrong"
   Endif
End.
```

Figure 1.25: Flowchart and pseudocode to check whether the given number n is Armstrong number or not

Example 1.19:

A notion of *well-ordered* number is introduced here. Any number whose digits from left to right are in increasing order (with no digit repeated) is called a *well-ordered* number. For example, number 138 is called *well-ordered* because the digits in the number (1, 3, 8) increase from left to right, *i.e.*, 1 < 3 < 8. On the other hand, the number 365 is not *well-ordered* because 6 is larger than 5.

Draw a flowchart and also write pseudocode to check whether the given number *n* is *well-ordered* not.

Solution:

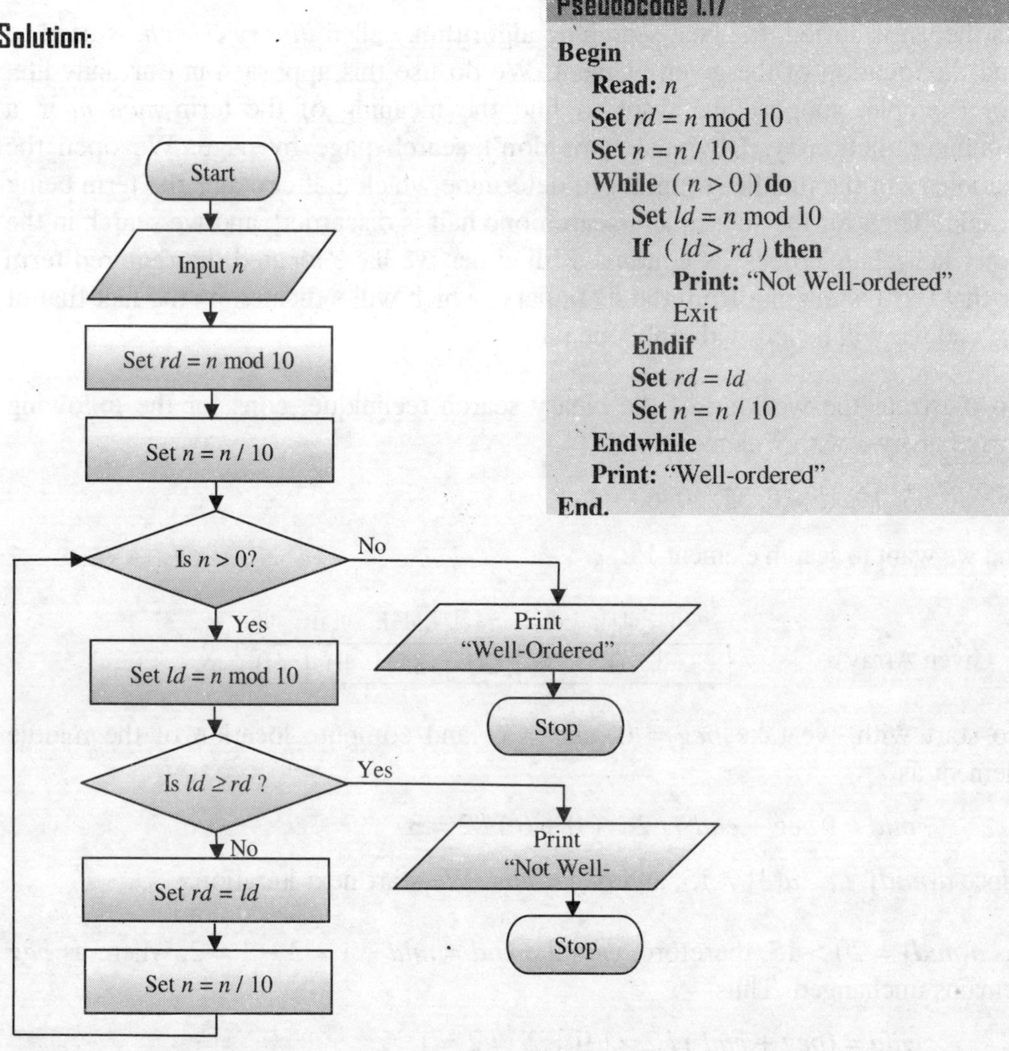

Pseudocode 1.17

```
Begin
    Read: n
    Set rd = n mod 10
    Set n = n / 10
    While ( n > 0 ) do
        Set ld = n mod 10
        If ( ld > rd ) then
            Print: "Not Well-ordered"
            Exit
        Endif
        Set rd = ld
        Set n = n / 10
    Endwhile
    Print: "Well-ordered"
End.
```

Figure 1.26: Flowchart and pseudocode to check whether the given number *n* is well-ordered or not

Example 1.20:

Write a pseudocode to search a given element in a list, named *a* having *n* elements, which is maintained in ascending order.

Solution:

Searching is a process of finding the location of given element in the list. The search is said to be successful if the given element is found, *i.e.*, the element does exist in the list; otherwise unsuccessful.

As the list is sorted, the best searching algorithm, called *binary search,* is used to find the location of the given element. We do use this approach in our daily life. For example, suppose we want to find the meaning of the term *modem* in a computer dictionary. Obviously, we don't search page by page. We open the dictionary in the middle (roughly) to determine which half contains the term being sought. Then for the subsequent search one half is discarded, and we search in the other half. This process is continued till either we have located the required term or that term is missing from the dictionary, which will indicated by the fact that at the end we will be left with only one page.

To illustrate the working of the binary search technique, consider the following sorted array *a* with 7 elements

3, 10, 15, 20, 35, 40, 60

and we want to search element 15.

	a[0]	*a*[1]	*a*[2]	*a*[3]	*a*[4]	*a*[5]	*a*[6]
Given Array *a*	3	10	15	20	35	40	60

To start with, we take *beg* = 0, *end* = 6, and compute location of the middle element as

$$mid = (beg + end) / 2 = (0 + 6) / 2 = 3$$

Since *a*[*mid*], *i.e.*, *a*[3] ≠ 15, and *beg* < *end*. We start next iteration.

As *a*[*mid*] = 20 > 15, therefore, we take *end* = *mid* – 1 = 3 – 1 = 2, where as *beg* remains unchanged. Thus

$$mid = (beg + end) / 2 = (0 + 2) / 2 = 1$$

Since *a*[*mid*], *i.e.*, *a*[1] ≠ 15, and *beg* < *end*. We start next iteration.

As $a[mid] = 10 < 15$, therefore, we take $beg = mid + 1 = 1 + 1 = 2$, where as *end* remains unchanged.

Since $beg = end$, again compute location of the middle element as

$$mid = (beg + end) / 2 = (2 + 2) / 2 = 2$$

Since $a[mid]$, *i.e.*, $a[2] = 15$, the search terminates on success.

In case, the value of variable *beg* becomes greater than variable *end*, it indicates that search is unsuccessful.

Pseudocode 1.18

```
Begin
    Read: n
    For i = 0 to (n–1) by 1 do          // input elements of sorted list
        Read: a[i]
    Endfor
    Read: item
    Set beg = 0
    Set end = n–1
    Set mid = ( beg + end ) / 2
    While ( ( beg ≤ end ) and ( a[mid] ≠ item ) ) do
        If ( item < a[mid] ) then
            Set end = mid-1
        Else
            Set beg = mid+1
        Endif
        Set mid = ( beg + end ) / 2
    Endwhile
    If ( beg > end ) then
        Print: "Search unsuccessful"
    Else
        Print: item, " found at location ", mid
    Endif
End.
```

Example 1.21:

Write a pseudocode to sort a list, named *a* having *n* elements, in ascending order.

Solution: Sorting is the process of arranging the elements in some logical order. This logical order may be ascending or descending in case of numeric values or dictionary order in case of alphanumeric values. We do, almost, use this process daily in our routine activities. For example, we do arrange our class notes in order of date so we can refer them quickly later on. Like this there are many situations, which you can enumerate.

Bubble sort is one of most popular technique for this purpose. It requires $(n-1)$ pass to sort an array. In each pass, every element $a[i]$ is compared with $a[i+1]$, for $i = 0$ to $(n-k)$, where k is the pass number and if they are out of order, *i.e.*, if $a[i] > a[i+1]$, they are swapped (interchanged).

This will cause the largest element to move or bubble up. Thus, after the end of first pass the largest element in the array will be placed in nth position, and on each successive pass, the next largest element is placed at position $(n-1)$, $(n-2)$, ..., 2, respectively. For more clarity, carefully examine the following steps.

Pass 1.

Step 1. If $a[0] > a[1]$ then swap $a[0]$ and $a[1]$.
Step 2. If $a[1] > a[2]$ then swap $a[1]$ and $a[2]$.
:
Step $n-1$. If $a[n-2] > a[n-1]$ then swap $a[n-2]$ and $a[n-1]$.

Pass 2.

Step 1. If $a[0] > a[1]$ then swap $a[0]$ and $a[1]$.
Step 2. If $a[1] > a[2]$ then swap $a[1]$ and $a[2]$.
:
Step $n-2$. If a$[n-3] > a[n-2]$ then swap $a[n-3]$ and $a[n-2]$.

:

Pass *k*.

Step 1. If $a[0] > a[1]$ then swap $a[0]$ and $a[1]$.
Step 2. If $a[1] > a[2]$ then swap $a[1]$ and $a[2]$.
:
Step $n-k$. If $a[n-k+1] > a[n-k]$ then swap $a[n-k+1]$ and $a[n-k]$.

:

Pass *n*–1.

Step 1. If $a[0] > a[1]$ then swap $a[0]$ and $a[1]$.

Note that, the output of a given pass becomes the input for the next pass.

To illustrate the working of bubble sort method, consider the sorting of the following array in ascending order.

12 40 3 2 15

Note that, the output of a given pass becomes the input for the next pass.

Given array can be shown as

a[0]	a[1]	a[2]	a[3]	a[4]
12	40	3	2	15

Pass-1:

a[0]	a[1]	a[2]	a[3]	a[4]
(12)	(40)	3	2	15

(*a*) Compare a[0] and a[1]. Since $a[0] < a[1]$ (12 < 40), no action is taken.

a[0]	a[1]	a[2]	a[3]	a[4]
12	(40)	(3)	2	15

(*b*) Compare a[1] and a[2]. Since $a[1] > a[2]$ (40 > 3), swap these elements.

a[0]	a[1]	a[2]	a[3]	a[4]
12	3	(40)	(2)	15

(*c*) Compare a[2] and a[3]. Since $a[2] > a[3]$ (40 > 2), swap these elements.

a[0]	a[1]	a[2]	a[3]	a[4]
12	3	2	(40)	(15)

(*d*) Compare a[3] and a[4]. Since $a[3] > a[4]$ (40 > 15), swap these elements.

a[0]	a[1]	a[2]	a[3]	a[4]
12	3	2	15	40

Thus, after first pass, the largest element, 40, has moved to its final position. However, the rest of the numbers, which may have changed their positions, are yet to be sorted. The shaded part shows the elements that have been sorted.

For the remaining passes, only comparisons and swaps, if required, are shown.

Pass-2:

a[0]	*a*[1]	*a*[2]	*a*[3]	*a*[4]	Action
(12)	(3)	2	15	40	Swap
3	(12)	(2)	15	40	Swap
3	2	(12)	(15)	40	No swap
3	2	12	15	40	

After second pass, the second largest element, 15, has moved to its final position.

Pass-3:

a[0]	*a*[1]	*a*[2]	*a*[3]	*a*[4]	Action
(3)	(2)	12	15	40	Swap
2	(3)	(12)	15	40	No swap
2	3	12	15	40	

After third pass, the third largest element, 12, has moved to its final position.

Pass-4:

a[0]	*a*[1]	*a*[2]	*a*[3]	*a*[4]	Action
(2)	(3)	12	15	40	No swap
2	3	12	15	40	

After fourth pass, the fourth largest element, 3, has moved to its final position. Thus, the array is completely sorted in 4 passes.

The above sorting process can also be visualized as shown below:

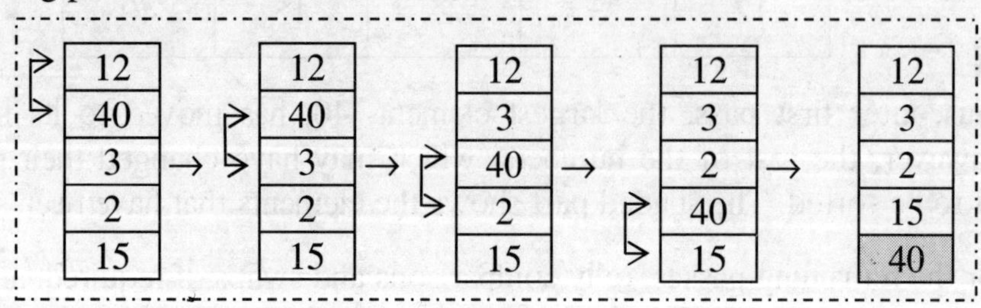

Given Array

Pass 1

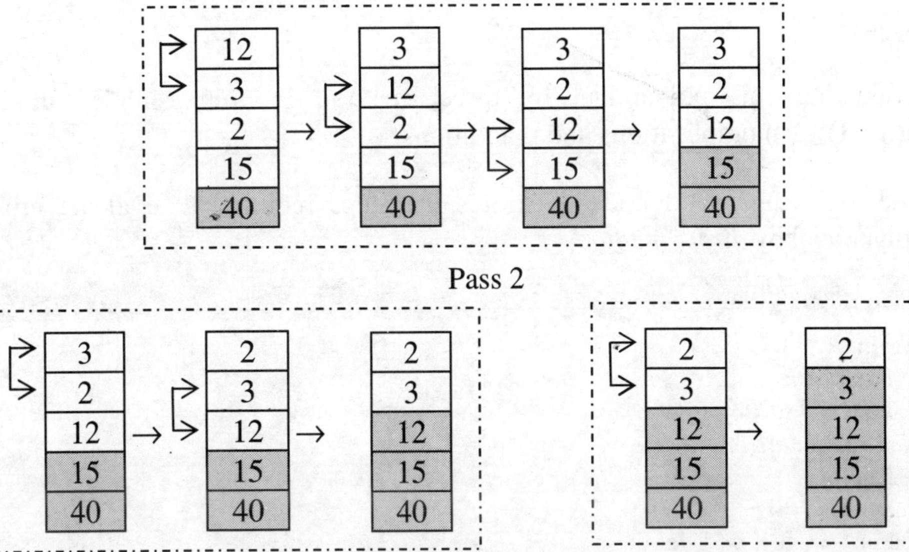

Figure 1.27: Illustration of Bubble sort method

Pseudocode 1.19

```
Begin
    Read: n
    For i = 0 to (n–1) by 1 do
        Read: a[i]
    Endfor
    For k = 1 to (n–1) by 1 do
        For j = 0 to (n–k–1) by 1 do
            If a[j] > a[j+1] then
                Set temp = a[j]          // variable temp is used to facilitate
                Set a[j] = a[j+1]        // interchange of values
                Set a[j+1] = temp
            Endif
        Endfor
    Endfor
    For i = 0 to (n–1) by 1 do
        Print: a[i]
    Endfor
End.
```

Example 1.22:

Write a pseudocode to evaluate n^{th} degree polynomial of type

$$a_n x^n + a_{n-1} x^{n-1} + a_{n-2} x^{n-2} + ... + a_2 x^2 + a_1 x + a_0 \qquad \text{where } a_n \neq 0.$$

Solution:

Evaluating this polynomial by direct method is quite simple but involves $n(n-1)/2$ multiplications and n additions.

The following pseudocode illustrates the steps required to evaluate nth degree polynomial by *direct method.*

Pseudocode 1.20a

```
Begin
  Read: x, n
  For i = 0 to n by 1 do
     Read: a[i]
  Endfor
  Set sum = 0
  For i = 0 to n by 1 do
     Set sum = sum + a[i] × x^i
  Endfor
  Print: sum
End.
```

The polynomial of above type can be efficiently evaluated by using *Horner's method.* In Horner's method, the number of multiplications is reduced to n. This method is based on the following alternate method of writing the polynomial as

$$a_0 + x(a_1 + x(a_2 + x(a_3 + ... + x(a_{n-2} + x(a_{n-1} + a_n x)))))$$

The following pseudocode illustrates the steps required to evaluate nth degree polynomial by *Horner's method.*

Algorithm 1.20b

```
Begin
  Read: x, n
  For i = 0 to n by 1 do
     Read: [i]
  Endfor
  Set sum = a[n]
  For i = n to 1 by −1 do
     Set sum = a[i−1] + sum × x
  Endfor
  Print: sum
End.
```

1.9 QUICK RECAP

In this chapter, we have learnt that

- We cannot solve a problem unless you do not know the steps (rules) to solve it.
- Before planning a program for a given problem, we should solve the problem manually in order get more insight into the steps required for finding the solution of the problem.
- Once we know how to solve the problem, we should plan the program using an algorithm, a flowchart or a pseudocode.
- In an algorithm the steps are numbered and these steps are executed in their increasing order.
- In a flowchart, the flow lines show the order of execution of the various steps.
- In a pseudocode, the steps (instructions) are executed in sequence as they appear except in case of a decision or a loop.

1.10 REVIEW EXERCISES

1. Why is it advisable to plan the program before writing it?
2. What is an algorithm? What are the essential characteristics for a sequence of instructions to qualify as an algorithm?
3. What is a flowchart? What are the various symbols used in flowcharts?
4. What is a pseudocode? Why is it so called?
5. Among algorithm, flowchart and pseudocode, which makes the logic of the underlying program clearer and easily understandable?
6. Given a chance to plan a program, will you prefer to choose algorithm, flowchart or a pseudocode? Give reasons for your choice.

10. Draw a flowchart to find the largest of the five numbers represented by variables *a*, *b*, *c*, *d*, and *e*.
11. Write a pseudocode to display first 20 prime numbers.
12. Write a pseudocode to find the sum of first 100 odd numbers.
13. Suppose an amount *p* is deposited in a commercial bank, which pays compound interest at the rate of *r*% annually, for *n* years. Write a pseudocode that prints the amount in account after each year.

14. Write a pseudocode to find LCM and HCF of two natural number *m* and *n*.
15. Write a pseudocode to find factorial of a natural number *n*.
16. Write a program to print first *n* pairs of twin prime numbers. Note that two consecutive prime numbers are said to twin prime numbers if they differ by 2.
17. A department store places an order with a company for *n* pieces of miners, *m* pieces of toasters, and *p* number of fans. The cost of items are as follows:

Item Description	Price per Unit (in Rupees)
Miners	1,500
Toaster	200
Fan	450

The discount allowed for various items are 5% for miners, 15% for fan, and 10% for toaster. The company charge 10% as sales tax on all items on net value after deducting the discount.

Write a pseudocode that reads *m*, *n*, and *p* and computes the amount to be paid by the store.

18. The monthly telephone bill is to be computed as follows:

Minimum Rs. 200 for upto 100 calls
plus Rs. 0.60 per call for next 50 calls
plus Rs. 0.50 per call for next 50 calls
plus Rs. 0.40 per call for any call beyond 200 calls.

The input contains name of the customer and number of calls made and the desired output is the name and telephone bill to be paid by the customer. Draw a flowchart for logical steps needed to accomplish the above task.

19. State pollution control board has the following classification policy:

Pollution Index	Classification
< 30	Pleasant
30 – 60	Unpleasant
> 60	Hazardous

Draw a flowchart that accepts the pollution index and prints the appropriate classification.

❑ ❑ ❑

2 Overview off C Language

Learning Objectives

After reading this chapter, students will have the ability to:

- history and evolution of C language
- why C language is called middle level language
- key characteristics of C language
- potential areas where C language is predominantly used
- general structure of C program
- steps required in building a C program
- usage of various C Compilers

2.1 INTRODUCTION

One of the difficult aspects of learning a programming language is that almost each and everything is interrelated. Therefore, it seems almost impossible to understand anything before you know little about everything. So, before we start learning C language, it would be a nice experience to have an idea about the historical development and evolution of one of the much talked computer programming language, where it stands, and how many different versions of C are available.

We will also discuss about various other aspects associated with the C language.

2.2 HISTROY AND EVOLUTION OF C LANGUAGE

The development of C language shook the entire computer world. It fundamentally changed the way the programming was approached and thought about. The creation of C language was a direct result of the need for a structured, efficient, high-level language that could replace the assembly language code when creating system programs such as operating systems, compiler, linkers, editors, etc.

As you probably may be aware that when a new computer language is designed, the trade-offs in the areas such as following are made:

- Ease of use versus power
- Safety versus efficiency
- Rigidity versus extensibility

Prior to C language, the programmers have to make a choice between languages that optimized one set of attributes or the other. For example, although FORTRAN could be used to write fairly efficient programs for scientific applications, it lacks features for writing system programs. BASIC was easy to learn but it was not very powerful. It also lack in structure which made its usefulness for large systems questionable. Assembly language can be used to produce highly efficient programs, but it is not easy to learn and use effectively. Further, debugging assembly code is difficult and can be nightmare on occasions.

Another significant problem with the earlier languages was that they were not designed around structured principles. These languages depend heavily on GOTO as primary means of program control. As a result of the heavy use of GOTO statements, the large programs become a mass of tangled jumps and conditional branches which make them virtually impossible to comprehend. While Pascal language was structured, it was not designed for efficiency and also lacked features necessary to make it applicable to wide range of programs. Therefore, there was no such language that can reconcile the conflicting attributes that had dogged earlier efforts, and hence the need for such a language was pressing.

By the early 1970s, the computer revolution was beginning to take hold, and the demand for software was rapidly outpacing the programmer's ability to produce it. A great deal of effort was expanded in the academic circles in an attempt to create a better computer language. At the same time, the computer hardware was becoming common enough and was reaching the masses. No longer were the computers kept behind the locked doors. For the first time, the programmers were able to get unlimited access to the computers. This unlimited access to computer allowed programmers the freedom to experiment. It also allowed programmers to create their own customized tools. On the eve of the creation of the C language, the stage was set for a quantum leap forward in computer languages.

Invented and first implemented by Dennis Ritchie, a system programmer at Bell Laboratories, on a DEC PDP-11 computer system running the UNIX operating system. Later on, the UNIX operating system was rewritten almost entirely in C language. The development of C language was the result of the development process that started with an older language known as Basic Combined Programming Language (BCPL), developed by Martin Richards. The BCPL language influenced a language called B language, developed by Ken Thompson., which lead to the development of C language in the 1970s. It was a mere coincidence that the letters B and C are in alphabetic order.

For many years the de facto standard for C language was the one supplied with the UNIX operating system and described in book entitled "*The C Programming Language*" by Brain Kernighan and Dennis Ritchie (Prentice-Hall, 1978). The C language was formally standardized in December 1989, when the American National Standards Institute (ANSI) standard for C was adopted.

The creation of C language was considered many to have marked the beginning of the modern age of programming languages. It successfully synthesized the conflicting attributes that had troubled earlier languages. The result was a powerful, efficient, structured language that was relatively easy to learn. It also included one other, nearly intangible aspect – it was a programmer's language. Prior to its creation, other computer languages were generally designed either as academic exercises or by the bureaucratic committees. The C language stands different. It was designed, developed, and implemented by the working programmers, reflecting the way they approached the job of programming. Its features were honed, tested, thought about, and rethought by the people who actually used the language. The result was a language that programmers liked to use. Indeed, the C language quickly attracted many followers who had a near-religious zeal for it. As such it found wide and rapid acceptance in the programmer community. In short, the C language is a language designed by and for programmers.

2.3 ANATOMY OF COMPUTER LANGUAGES

To see how C language compares with other programming languages, let us have a look on the programming languages in general. The programming language can be divided into two broad categories, depending on their level of interaction with the underlying hardware of the computer:

- Low-level Languages
- High-level Languages

2.3.1 Low-level Languages

In this category, we have machine language and assembly language. These languages permit the efficient use of the computer. But the problems with these languages are:

- These languages are hardware dependent, *i.e.*, programs written using these languages is not portable, i.e., cannot be used on other computers.
- Programming using these languages is not an easy job. One must have thorough knowledge of the architecture of the computer.

2.3.2 High-level Languages

In this category, we have FORTRAN, BASIC, PASCAL, COBOL, PL/1, etc. These languages are designed for better programming efficiency, *i.e.*, faster program development. These languages have following advantages:

- The syntax for writing program instructions is very much like English statements. This enables the readers to learn high-level languages (HLLs) quickly. In addition, the programs written in HLLs can be easily understood, which facilitates its maintenance.

- The programs written in HLLs are not hardware dependent. This means that program written for one machine can be transferred to another machine with minimal changes or none at all.

The C language stands between these two categories. That is why it is often called *middle-level* language, since it was designed to have best of both the worlds, *i.e.*, a good programming efficiency as well as good machine efficiency.

- To achieve programming efficiency, the C language has all the elements as of any other modern high-level language.
- To achieve machine efficiency, the C language has requisite features to access any hardware component of the system, to operate at register level, and to interface with high-speed assembly language routines.

2.4 CHARACTERISTICS OF C LANGUAGE

The C language was and will remain as one of the popular programming languages. Some of the key characteristics that add to its popularity are:

- It is a general purpose programming language, and therefore, can be used to solve vide variety of problems.
- It is supports structuring programming, and therefore, programs developed in it can easily be understood.
- It is free form, *i.e.*, no rigid format for writing programs. Any instruction can start from anywhere and end anywhere. In addition, a single instruction can span (can be written in) many lines.
- It is case sensitive. It distinguishes between lowercase (small) and uppercase (capital) alphabets.
- It was the first language to provide rich set of operators.
- It allows you, through pointers, to access any storage location and the devices connected to your computer through your program.
- It allows you to manipulate internal processor registers, and thus it is very useful for low-level programming.
- It is portable, that means any program written in it can be used on any computer without or with little modification(s).
- It allows you to develop your own library of functions that can be linked to your any program like standard library functions.

2.5 APPLICATION AREAS OF C LANGUAGE

The strength of C language makes it a natural choice for

- Systems programming that include writing software for language translators, device drivers, editors, linkers, loaders, etc.
- Network software to implement different communication protocols.
- Graphics programming that include writing software for graphical user interfaces (GUIs), scientific visualisation, and presentation graphics, etc.
- Embedded systems where C routines are interfaced high speed assembly language routines and the resulting code is stored in ROM chip which is a part of the embedded system.

2.6 GENERAL STRUCTURE OF A C PROGRAM

The usual order of statements written in a C program is as follows:

```
Section 1: Comments

Section 2: Preprocessor Directives

Section 3: Global Declarations

Section 4:

void main(void)
{
    Local Declarations

    Statements
}

Section 5: Other Functions as
           required
```

Figure 2.1: General Structure of a C Program

Section 1 is optional. If present it contains the description about the program. This description usually contains the information about the task being accomplished by the program. In addition, it can also contain the name of the author (programmer), the date on which it was written, the date on which it was last modified, etc.

Section 2 contains the preprocessor directives. The frequently used preprocessor directives are *include* and *define*. These directives tell the preprocessor how to prepare the program for compilation. The *include* directive tells which header files are to be included in the program and the *define* directive is usually used to associate an identifier with a literal (constant) that is to be used at many places in the program.

Section 3 is optional. If present, it contains the global declarations. These declarations usually include the declaration of the data items (variables) which are to be shared between many functions in the program. In addition, these declarations can also include the decorations of functions (prototypes), except the *main()* function, to be used in the program.

Section 4 contains the *main()* function. The execution of the program always begins with the execution of the *main()* function. The *main()* function can call any number of other functions, and those called function can further call other functions. The first section in the *main()* function, as well as other functions, contains local declarations. These declarations are local in the sense that they pertain to the requirements of that function only. The second section in the *main()* function, as well as in other functions, contains the statements that defines the actions to be performed by the function.

Section 5 is also optional. If present, it contains the other functions.

If the problem to be solved is simple and small in size, then on!/ the *main()* function is sufficient to accomplish the task. However, if the problem is complex and the size of the problem is large, it is divided into small and independent subproblems, and then we write separate functions for each subproblem. The *main()* function coordinates the execution of these functions by appropriate calls to these functions, and synthesizes the solutions of the subproblems obtained from these functions.

2.7 SAMPLE C PROGRAM

In order to have a feel of the organization of a C program, let us consider the simple example C program, given overleaf.

Problem considered is very straightforward and familiar to you. We want to write a program that converts temperature in Celsius scale to its equivalent temperature in Fahrenheit scale.

We know the relation between temperature in Celsius and Fahrenheit is:

$$\frac{C}{100} = \frac{F-32}{180} \qquad \text{Simplifying, we get} \quad F = 1.8 \times C + 32$$

Listing 2.1

```
 1: /*
 2: * Program to convert temperature from Centigrade scale
 3: * to Fahrenheit scale
 4: */
 5: #include <stdio.h>
 6: int main(void)
 7: {
 8:   float fahrenheit, centigrade;
 9:   printf( "\nEnter temperature in Celsius scale: ");
10:   scanf( "%f", &centigrade );
11:   fahrenheit = 1.8 * centigrade + 32;
12:   printf( "\nEquivalent temperature in Fahrenheit scale");
13:   printf( " = %.2f\n",fahrenheit);
14:   return 0;
15: }
```

Here the line numbers are added for ready reference.

Test Run

```
Enter temperature in Celsius scale: 30
Equivalent temperature in Fahrenheit scale = 86.00
```

Dissection of the Program

If you are familiar with other programming languages, this program may look strange to you. One reason for this strangeness is that the entire program is written in lowercase letters. In most other languages, usually uppercase letters are used, though they permit the use of lowercase letters. So you have to become accustomed to lowercase as quickly as possible. Also, it is important to remember that C language is case sensitive, *i.e.*, it differentiates between lowercase and uppercase letters. Lowercase letters are characteristic of the C language.

A C program is written in a free format. By free format, we mean that an instruction can start anywhere in a line and can end anywhere. Even an instruction can span many lines. Spacing is of no consequence in C language, it is used to enhance the readability of the program.

Lines 1-4 demonstrate the style used in C language to add comments in a program. This is done by starting the comments with two characters '/*' and ending with the characters '*/'. Between these pair of characters, called *delimiters*, any characters may be included in either uppercase or lowercase.

In other words, a comment appears as follows:

```
/*  You type here what you want   */
```

In addition to this style, comments can also be added after the instruction on the same line as shown below:

```
#include<stdio.h>     /* include stdio.h file */
```

Comments may not be essential in a simple program, but in complex programs they are lifesaver. For any program, no matter how well it is written, the day will come when we have to make amendments to incorporate the changing conditions. The chances are quite high that the original author of the program may have left the organization. Even the original author may not remember the logic of a program that he wrote several months or years ago.

In order to reduce the burden on the person, who will make amendments to the program, ample comments should be included at the time when the program is being written. Too often we postpone the task of adding comments until the program is finally Okayed, but this practice is not very useful.

Some programmers feel that C language is such a concise and cryptic language that every line of code should be accompanied by a comment. But too many comments actually reduce the readability of the program. Still, it is better to have too many comments than few.

Line 5 demonstrates the way pre-processor directives are used. These directives instruct the compiler process the source code in a specific way. In this case, *include* directive, also called *file inclusion* directive, and instructs the compiler to include the specified file at this point. In this case, the specified file is a header file (a file with extension *.h*) that is part of the C compiler.

The other often-used pre-processor directive is *#define* whose syntax is

```
#define MAX 100
```

This directive, called *macro expansion* directive, tells the compiler to replace every occurrence of MAX with value 100 during pre-processing. There are many other directives that we will discuss later.

Line 6 specifies a function named *main*. This is a special name that is recognized by the system. It points to the precise place in the program where execution begins. Every C program must have a *main* function. We cannot have more than one main function in a program.

Every C function has a return type associated with it. Where return type is one of the data types that determine the type of the value returned by the function. If a function is not supposed to return any value, its return type is specified as *void*. Since main function is the function from where execution begins, it will usually be declared with type *int*. A pair of parentheses follows the word main. The matter, if any, contained in these parentheses specifies the formal arguments of the function. If there are no arguments, we write *void*.

The *main()* Function

The *main()* function is a part of every C program. The C language permits following forms of *main()* function:

- `main()`
- `main(void)`
- `void main()`
- `int main()`
- `void main(void)`
- `int main(void)`

The empty pair of parenthesis indicates that the *main()* function takes no arguments. This may be explicitly indicated by using the keyword *void* inside the parenthesis. We may also specify the keyword *void* or *int* before the word main. When the keyword *void* is used, it indicates that the function *main()* does not return any value to the operating system. When the keyword *int* is used, it indicates that the function *main()* will return an integer value to the operating system. Value 0 is returned to the operating system to indicate that the program terminated on completion of its intended task whereas the value 1 is used to indicate that the program terminated prematurely (could not complete its intended task).

Line 7 contains character '{', called left brace or left curly bracket. There is also matching right brace '}' in line 14, which appears at the end of the main function. These pair of matching braces encloses the body of the function.

Line 8 declares two variables, *fahrenheit* and *centigrade* of type *float*, which can represent and store two real numbers (float) in computer memory. Variable *centigrade* is used to hold the value, representing temperature in Celsius scale, entered by the user during program execution. Variable *fahrenheit* is to used to hold the computed value, representing temperature in Fahrenheit scale, equivalent to given temperature in Celsius scale. Note that the names of the variables used are self-explanatory. It is always recommended to use meaningful names. This will help to increase the readability of the program.

Line 9 uses library function *printf()* that displays "*Enter temperature in Celsius scale:* " on the computer screen. We call these kinds of messages as *user prompts* as they guide the user to enter the desired input. In this case, the value to be entered is temperature in Celsius scale.

You must have observed that the entire sequence of characters enclosed in double quotes is not printed. Then, *what is the role of characters '\n' in the beginning*? These two characters together represent the *new line* character. Although *new line* character is a combination of two characters, *i.e.*, '\' and 'n', they are translated by the C compiler into a single character. The *new line* character instructs the compiler to advance to the next line before printing subsequent information.

Line 10 uses another library function *scanf()* that accepts the user input and stores in variable *centigrade* (in fact, in a memory location that is reserved for the *centigrade*). The first argument is a *format string* that is enclosed in double quotes and tells the system how the entered values are to be interpreted. Following the format string, there will be a list of one or more variables; each variable prefixed with character '&', called *address of operator.*

Line 11 is an assignment statement that computes the temperature in Fahrenheit scale equivalent to given temperature in Celsius scale, and assigns to variable *fahrenheit, i.e.*, stores in variable *fahrenheit.*

Lines 12-13 uses library function *printf()* that outputs the stored value in variable *fahrenheit* along with the message "*Equivalent Temperature in fahrenheit* = ". The use of these kinds of messages is not mandatory, but is very useful as they make the output easy to interpret.

Line 14 uses *return* statement, which on execution terminates the execution of the program and return the control back to the operating system. In addition, it also returns value 0 to the operating system indicating that the program terminated on success. In case of failure, value 1 is returned. This retuned value can be used by the operating system for deciding further line of action.

Line 15 marks the end of the *main* function as well as end of the program as this is the only function in the program.

- If there is more than one function in a file, each will have its own body enclosed in pair of braces.
- Variables can only be declared in the beginning of a block before any executable statement.

2.8 PROGRAM DEVELOPMENT LIFE CYCLE

Program development life cycle (PDLC) is a systematic way of developing quality programs (and hence software). It provides an organized plan for breaking down the task of program development into manageable chunks, each of which must be successfully completed before moving on to the next phase. The program development process is divided into following phases:

- Defining the problem
- Designing the program
- Building the program
- Testing the program
- Documenting the program
- Deploying and maintaining the program

2.8.1 Defining the Problem

The first step in developing a program is to define the problem. In major software projects, this is a job for system analyst, who provides the results of their work to programmers in the form of a *program specification*. The program specification precisely defines the input data, the processing that should take place, the format of the output reports and the user interface. Depending on the size of the job, the program development might be handled by an individual or a team.

2.8.2 Designing the Program

An architect doesn't design a home just by going to the site with a bunch of boards and bricks. After determining the needs of the house's owner, the next step in designing a house is an architectural drawing – a plan drawn up on the paper that can be discussed and reviewed until everything is right. Likewise, programmers create program designs. Like an architect's drawing, the program design specifies the components that make the program work.

Program design begins by focusing on the main goal that the program is trying to achieve and then breaking the program into manageable components, each of which contributes to this goal. This approach of program design is called *top-down program design* or *modular programming*. The first step involves identifying the *main routine* (*main()* function), which is the program's major activity. From there, programmers try to break down the various components of the main routine into smaller units called *modules*, until each module is highly focused. Experience shows that this is the best way to ensure program quality. If an error appears in a program designed this way, it is relatively easy to identify the module that must be causing the error.

For each module, the programmer draws a conceptual plan using an appropriate program design tool to visualize how the module will do its assigned job.

The various familiar program design tools are:

- **Structure charts** – A *structure chart*, also called *hierarchy chart*, show the top-down design of a program. Each box in the chart indicates a task that the program must accomplish. The top module, called the *main module* or *control module*, oversees the transfer of control to other modules.

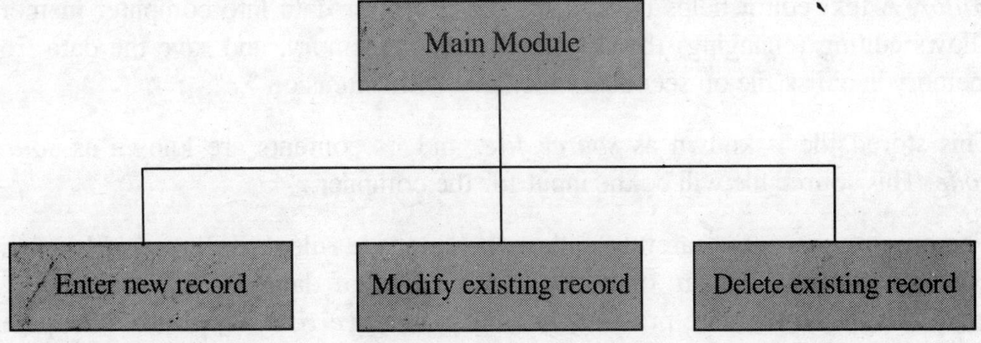

Figure 2.2: Structure Chart for a Data Entry Program

- **Algorithms** – An *algorithm* is a step-by-step description of how to arrive at a solution. Algorithms are not restricted to computers. In fact, we use them every day.
- **Flowcharts** – A *flowchart* is a diagram that shows the logic of the program. Programmers create flowcharts either by hand using a flowchart template or on the computer. Each flowcharting symbol has a meaning. For example, parallelogram indicates an input or output, rectangle indicates a process, and diamond indicates a condition.
- **Pseudocodes** – A *pseudocode* is another tool to describe the way to arrive at a solution. In some sense, it is considered as a form of an algorithm. The only difference is that instead of expressing the action to be carried in form of steps, they are expressed in program language like constructs.

We have already discussed in detail about various program design tools such as *algorithms*, *flowcharts* and *pseudocodes*, in *Chapter 1*. The use of these tools was also demonstrated by taking familiar illustrative examples.

2.8.3 Building the Program

Once the design of the program is ready, the next step is to convert the program design into a computer program. During this conversion each of the steps of the program design is coded as one or more C language instructions. Here also it is recommended that one should write the program first on a piece of paper before keying in the computer.

Creating and Editing Programs

Once the program is ready on paper, we key in computer memory using a *text editor*. A text editor helps us to enter the character data into computer memory, allows editing (changing) the data in computer memory, and save the data from memory in a disk file on secondary memory with extension ".*c*".

This stored file is known as *source file*, and its contents are known as *source code*. This source file will be the input for the compiler.

The programmer must carefully follow the language rules, which precisely specify how to express certain operations. Violation of language rules results in grammatical errors, more precisely known as *syntax errors*. Program development tool - *Compiler*, will check these syntax errors. These syntax errors must be eliminated before moving further.

Compiling Programs

The source code in the source file, stored on the disk, must to be translated into machine language. This job is done by the *compiler*. The C compiler actually is a combination of two separate programs – the *preprocessor* and the *translator*.

The *preprocessor* reads the source code and prepares it for translation. While reading the source code, it scans the code for preprocessor directives and processes them accordingly. For example, when it encounters the *include* directive, it substitutes that directive with the contents of the specified header file (such as *stdio.h*), and when it encounters the *define* directive, it substitutes the identifier with the specified literal (constant). The output from the preprocessor is an intermediate file, known as *translation unit*.

The translator reads the translation unit instruction-by-instruction and checks them for their grammatical accuracy. If there is a syntax error in it, it flags an error message – called *diagnostic message* on the screen. These diagnostics messages help the programmer to identify the cause of the syntax error and the place where it is present.

Therefore, if there is even a single syntax error, the translation process, known as *compilation*, is terminated. In that case, open the source file using the text editor, and make the necessary corrections and repeat the compilation.

However, if there are no syntax errors in the translation unit, the translator rereads the instruction from the beginning, translates them into machine language, and writes them onto a disk file. The translated version of the source code is known as *object code*, and is stored in the disk file with extension "**.obj*".

Linking Programs

Once the source code is translated into object code, though it is in machine language, still it is not in executable form. The reason being is that it may be referring to other functions which are not included in the object code. These referred functions can be library functions (pre-written functions supplied with the compiler in the form of libraries) or user-defined functions stored in other source files and which are compiled separately. All these functions also need to be included in the object code to get a final machine code which is in the executable form, known as *executable code*. This task is performed by the *linker*.

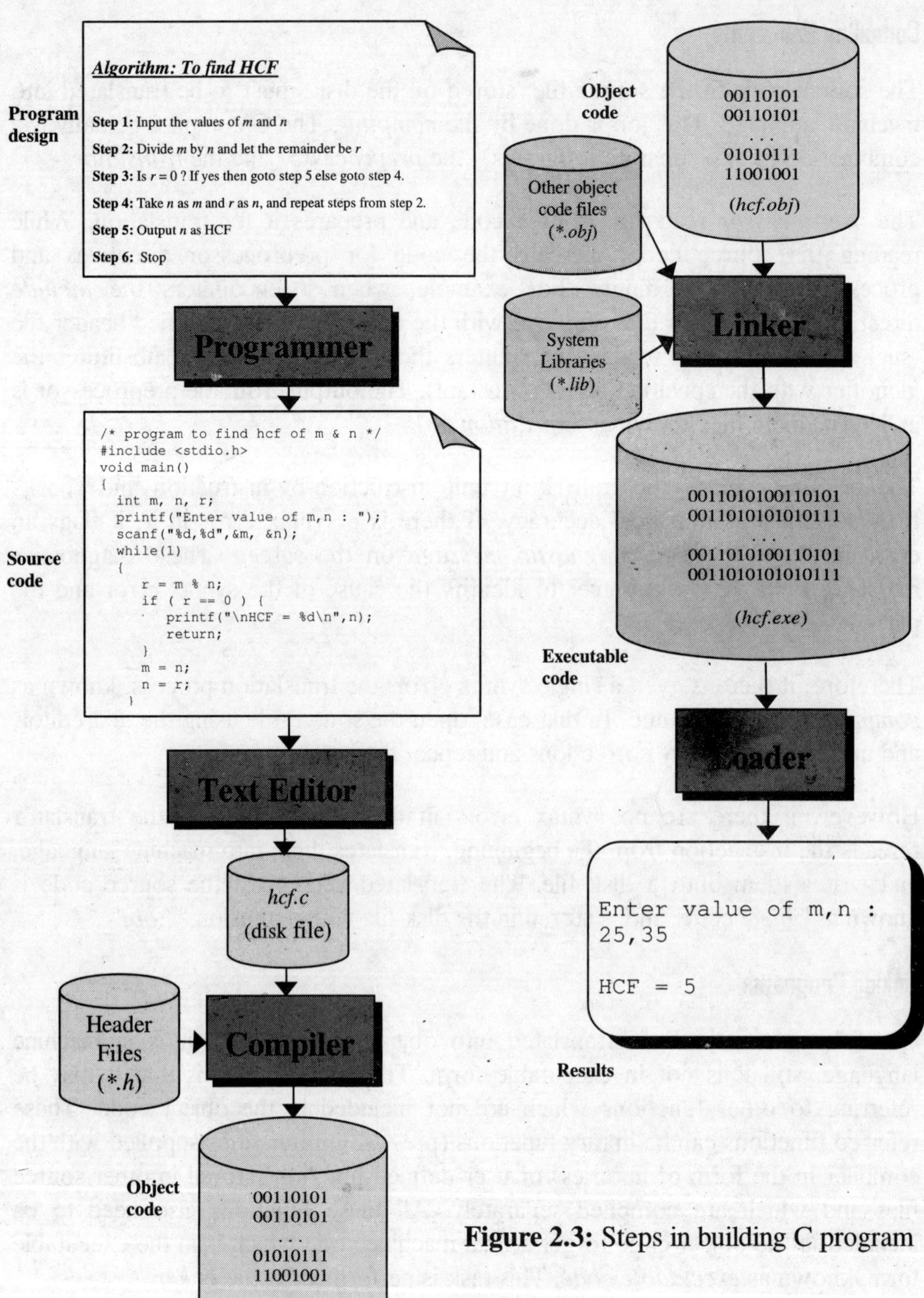

Figure 2.3: Steps in building C program

A *linker* is a development tool that extracts the referred library functions from the system libraries, reads the object codes of the user-defined functions from the object files and integrates them with the current object code to produce the final executable code, which is stored in disk file with extension "*.*exe*". This executable code is the final form of the program that is ready for execution.

Executing Programs

Once the program is linked, it is ready for execution. To execute a program we give an operating system command, such as *run*, to load the program into computer memory and execute it. Getting the program into memory is the function of an operating system program known as *loader*. The loader locates the executable program in the secondary storage, reads it and brings into the computer memory. Once the program is loaded, the operating system transfers the control to the program and the program begins its execution.

All the programs either developed by you or purchased off-the self are executed under the supervision of the operating system. Remember that operating system is resource manager of the computer system, and the resources required by the executing programs allocated by the operating system and are reclaimed when the program finishes its execution or program explicitly hands over the resources.

The complete process of *designing*, *creating*, *compiling*, *linking* and *executing* the program, referred to as building the program, is depicted in Figure 2.3.

2.8.4 Testing the Program

Even when the program is executing, the output of the program may not be correct. This will be because of logical errors in the program. A *logical error* is a mistake that the programmer made while designing the solution to the problem. For example, a programmer tells the computer to calculate the net pay by adding deductions to the gross salary instead of subtracting. A program development tool, such as compiler, cannot detect these errors. Therefore, the programmer must find and correct logical errors by carefully examining the program output for a set of data for which results are already known. Such type of data is known as *test data*.

Syntax errors and logical errors collectively are known as *bugs*. The process of identifying and eliminating these errors is known as *debugging*.

2.8.5 Documenting the Program

After testing, the program development is almost complete. The *structure charts*, *algorithms*, *pseudocodes*, and *flowcharts* developed during the design phase become documentation for others who are associated with the program. In addition, more documentation needs to be done as the programs are being coded such as list of variable names and definitions, description of files that the program need to work with, and format of output that the program produces. All of this documentation needs to be saved and placed together for future reference.

This phase ends by writing a manual that provides an overview of the program's functionality, tutorials for the beginner, in-depth explanations of major program features, reference documentation of all program commands and a thorough description of the error messages generated by the program. This manual is given to the user when the program is installed.

2.8.6 Deploying and Maintaining the Program

In the final phase, the program is deployed (installed) at the user's site. Here also, the program is kept under watch till the user gives green signal to it. Users may discover errors that were not caught in the testing phase, no matter how exhaustively the program was tested.

Even after the development project is complete, it needs to be maintained and evaluated regularly. In program maintenance, the programming team fixes program errors that users discover during its day-to-day use. In periodic evaluations, the team asks whether the program is fulfilling its objectives. This evaluation may lead to modifications to update the program or to add more features for the user. It may even lead to a decision to abandon the current system and develop a new one, and so the program development life cycle begins afresh.

2.9 USING VARIOUS C COMPILERS

2.9.1 Using C Compiler on Windows Platform

If you are using Window based platform, then Turbo C/C++ Compiler is the user's preferred choice. Turbo C/C++ Compiler can be used in two different ways:

- The first and frequently used method for creating programs is Turbo C/C++'s Integrated Development Environment (IDE). In this environment, all the necessary operations for program development are available in a unified screen display with menus and windows. It provides an ideal environment for learning C language. You can start IDE in one of the following ways:

- o Type TC at the command prompt.
- o Execute TC file using the Run command from Startup button.
- o Select and double click on the TC using Window Explorer.
- o Double click on the icon representing the short cut for TC.

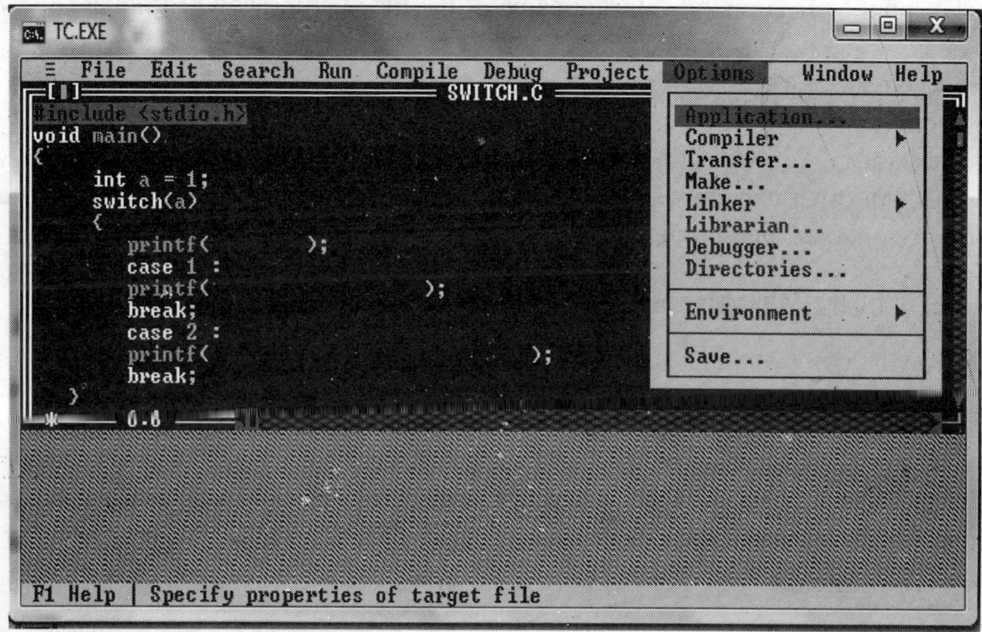

Figure 2.2: IDE of Turbo C++, which can be used create C programs as well as C++ programs

- ❑ The second method is a traditional C command-line system in which the functions of editing, compiling, linking, and executing a program are invoked from the command prompt as separate programs. This system is relatively inefficient. Though, it must be used in certain complex situations, such as linking your C code with a code written in assembly language. It is used as

```
>TCC myprog.c
```

The program will be compiled and if there is no syntax error, it subsequently will be linked with system libraries and the executable code is stored in file *myprog.exe*. To run the program, by entering name of file at command prompt as

```
>myprog
```

2.9.2 Using C Compiler on Unix Platform

Type the command at

```
>cc myprog.c
```

The program will be compiled and if there is no syntax error, it subsequently will be linked with system libraries and the executable code is stored in file *a.out*.

To run the program, by entering name of the file at command prompt as

```
>a.out
```

Note that for every file compiled, the executable code is always stored in file *a.out*.

Therefore if you want to compile and run more programs and the same time want to retain other executable codes for future use, first rename the file *a.out* to a file of your choice, and proceed with the compilation of another file.

2.9.3 Using C Compiler on Linux Platform

Type the command at

```
>gcc myprog.c
```

The program will be compiled and if there is no syntax error, it subsequently will be linked with system libraries and the executable code is stored in file *a.out*.
To run the program, by entering name of the file at command prompt as

```
>a.out
```

Like Unix platform, on Linux platform for every file compiled, the executable code is always stored in file *a.out*. Therefore if you want to compile and run more programs and the same time want to retain other executable codes for future use, first rename the file *a.out* to a file of your choice, and proceed with the compilation of another file.

2.10 SOME KEY POINTS TO REMEMBER

List of some key points about which every C programmer must be aware:

- The C language is a free form language, *i.e.*, any instructions can start from anywhere and end anywhere. Even a single instruction can span many lines.
- Pre-processor directive can be used anywhere in the C program but the recommended place is in the beginning of the source file.
- Each instructions end with character semicolon ';'.
- The C language is a case sensitive, *i.e.*, it will treat identifiers abc, Abc, aBc, ABC, abC, etc. as different identifiers.

- The C program is usually written in lower case. Uppercase letters are usually used for symbolic names and predefined names.
- Comments can be placed anywhere.
- Execution of program always begins with first executable statement in *main* function.
- Variable can only be declared in the beginning of the function, *i.e.*, prior to any executable statement.
- Entire calculations involving real numbers are done in double precision mode, *i.e.*, with 12 decimal digits precision.
- A C program can contain any number of functions. It basically depends on the size and complexity of the problem under consideration.

2.11 QUICK RECAP

In this chapter, we have learnt that

- Dennis Ritchie developed C language at Bell Laboratories.
- The C language is successor of B language that in turn is successor of Basic Combined Programming Language (BCPL).
- The C language is middle level language and is portable.
- Key application areas of C language include systems programming, network programming, GUI, scientific visualization, embedded systems, etc.
- General structure of a C program consists of five sections are – comments, preprocessor directives, global declarations, *main()* function, and other functions as required.
- Program development life cycle (PDLC) is a systematic way of developing quality programs.
- Program development life cycle is divided into six phases are – namely defining the problem, designing the program, building the program, testing the program, documenting the program, and deploying & maintaining the program.
- Different steps in building a program are – creation, compilation, linking, and executing.
- Text editor is a program that helps us in entering and changing the program in computer memory, and finally saving on a disk file.
- Source code is program written in a high-level language such as C and is stored in a disk file known as source file.
- A compiler is a program that translates the C program to the machine language. It has two components – *preprocessor* and *translator*. The preprocessor processes the program and prepares it for translation. The translator does the final translation.

- Process of translating the source program into object program is known as *compilation.*
- Object code is program in machine language that produced by the compiler and is stored in a file known as object file.
- Linker is a program that adds the machine language of library functions from system libraries and user-defined function, and produces final executable program.
- Executable code is a program in machine language that produced by the linker and is stored in a file known as run file, which is ready for execution.
- Loader is a program that transfers the executable program from a disk file on a secondary into computer memory and prepares it for execution.
- Testing is the process to ensure that program works correctly for all possible inputs to the program.
- Debugging is the process of identifying, locating and fixing the bugs. It is not an independent activity in the program development process, it is always associated with testing.

2.12 MULTIPLE CHOICE QUESTIONS

1. If a program written in any language on a given platform can be transported to another platform without any change or with minimal number of changes, then the language is said to ____________.

   (*a*) Understandable (*b*) Readable (*c*) Portable (*d*) Maintainable
2. Who developed C language?

   (*a*) Von Neuman (*b*) Dennis Ritchie (*c*) Peter Norton (*d*) Ken Thompson
3. Which of the following character is used to terminate an instruction in a C program?

   (*a*) , (comma) (*b*) : (colon) (*c*) ; (semicolon) (*d*) . (period)
4. How many *main* functions can be used in a C program?

   (*a*) 0 (*b*) 1 (*c*) 2 (*d*) Any number
5. Which of the following cannot be a first letter of an identifier?

   (*a*) digit (*b*) underscore (*c*) alphabet (*d*) All
6. Which of the following are used to enclose the body of a function?

   (*a*) [ ] (*b*) { } (*c*) ( ) (*d*) None
7. The C language can be used on which of the following platforms?

   (*a*) Unix (*b*) Windows (*c*) Linux (*d*) All
8. The C language is a ____________ language.

   (*a*) High (*b*) Low (*c*) Middle (*d*) Symbolic

9. The total number of phases in the development of a program is ___.

   (*a*) 6 (*b*) 7 (*c*) 5 (*d*) 9

10. Which of the following errors does the compiler catch?

    (*a*) Logical errors (*b*) Runtime errors (*c*) Syntax errors (*d*) Al

11. The acronym ANSI stands for ________________.

    (*a*) American National Standards International
    (*b*) American National Software Incorporation
    (*c*) American National Standards Institute
    (*d*) American National Standards Instructions

12. Find the odd term

    (*a*) Source code (*b*) Object code (*c*) Executable code (*d*) ASCII code

13. The term *bug* refers to ________.

    (*a*) Syntax error (*b*) Logical error (*c*) Runtime error (*d*) All

14. Testing of a program is done to ensure that

    (*a*) it should not contain any syntax error (*b*) it performs its intended task
    (*c*) it compiles successfully (*d*) it should not run infinitely

15. The acronym ASCII stands for ________________.

    (*a*) American Standard Code for International Information
    (*b*) American System for Compiler Information International
    (*c*) American System for Code Information International
    (*d*) American Standard Code for Information Interchange

16. Which of the following statements is not true about C language?

    (*a*) Every instruction is terminated by semicolon
    (*b*) It is case insensitive
    (*c*) Comments can be placed any where in the program code
    (*d*) It has features of both high-level and low-level languages

17. The term *debugging* refers to the process of ________.

    (*a*) translating the source code to object code
    (*b*) linking the object code with the system libraries
    (*c*) identifying the bugs and fixing them
    (*d*) None of above

18. The term *portability* means that ________________.

    (*a*) Program code is understandable
    (*b*) Program code is maintainable
    (*c*) Program code is bug free
    (*d*) Program code can be transported without/with minimal changes to another computer

19. The C programs are converted into machine language using ________.

    (*a*) Assembler (*b*) Interpreter (*c*) Compiler (*d*) Operating system

20. Extension of file containing machine code produced by the compiler is ______.

    (*a*) *.com (*b*) *.exe (*c*) *.c (*d*) *.obj

2.13 REVIEW EXERCISES

1. Name the predecessor of the C language.
2. Name the person who developed C language.
3. When and where the C language was developed?
4. Why C language is called middle-level language?
5. List the application areas of C language.
6. Describe the general structure of a C program.
7. What is PDLC? Describe various phases of PDLC.
8. Describe the following - *text editor*, *compiler*, *linker*, *loader*.
9. What symbol or character is used to terminate every C statement?

❑ ❑ ❑

3 Data Types, Variables and Constants

Learning Objectives

After reading this chapter, students will have the ability to:

- explain the concept of character set
- explain what does tokens mean
- explain the rules for naming an identifier
- explain the concept of data types and various data types supported by C language
- explain the fundamental data types
- explain about literals, constants, symbolic constants and variables
- describe the declaration and initialization of variables
- explain the various type modifiers
- explain the concept of storage class and its types

3.1 INTRODUCTION

A program must be able to store its input somewhere so that it can work with the data and process it into a form that is meaningful to the user. All the data processed by a program is stored either as a *variable* or as a *constant*. Each variable in C language has some characteristics associated with it, called its *storage class*.

The ability to divide the data into different types is one of the most important features of the modern programming languages. It enables us to work with relatively complex data objects instead of elementary data objects that a computer can understand and manipulate.

This chapter attempts to describe these semantic units of the C language.

3.2 CHARACTER SET

In a most basic sense, a C program is a sequence of characters. When these characters are submitted to the compiler, they are interpreted in various contexts as characters, identifiers, constants, and statements. The characters used in a C source program belong to the American Standard Code for Information Interchange (ASCII pronounced as *ass-kee*) set.

The characters in C language are grouped into the following categories:

- Letters
- Digits/Numerals
- Special characters
- White space characters

Table 3.1: Character set of C Language

Letters	**Digits/Numerals**
Uppercase : A–Z Lowercase : a–z	All decimal digit : 0–9

Special Characters

, comma	. period	: colon
; semicolon	~ tilde	! exclamation mark
# hash/number sign	% percentage sign	^ caret
& ampersand	* asterisk	– hyphen/minus sign

<table>
<tr><td>+ plus sign</td><td>= equal sign</td><td>| vertical bar</td></tr>
<tr><td>′ single quote</td><td>″ double quote</td><td>/ slash</td></tr>
<tr><td>\ backslash</td><td>_ underscore</td><td>$ dollar sign</td></tr>
<tr><td>[left bracket</td><td>] right bracket</td><td>(left parenthesis</td></tr>
<tr><td>) right parenthesis</td><td>{ left brace</td><td>} right brace</td></tr>
<tr><td>< left angle bracket or less than sign</td><td>> right angle bracket or greater than sign</td><td>? question mark</td></tr>
<tr><td></td><td></td><td>@ at the rate of sign</td></tr>
<tr><th colspan="3">White Space Characters</th></tr>
<tr><td>Blank space</td><td>Horizontal Tab</td><td>Carriage return</td></tr>
<tr><td>Formfeed</td><td>Newline</td><td></td></tr>
</table>

All C compilers ignore white space characters. These characters are basically used to enhance the readability and understandability of a C program.

3.3 TOKENS

A *token* is a smallest entity that have a meaning in itself. A C program is a sequence of tokens.

Tokens in C language can be classified into following categories:

- Keywords
- Identifiers
- Literals
- Punctuators
- Operators

3.3.1 Keywords

Every word in C++ is either classified as a *keyword* or an *identifier*.

Keywords are basically those words that have predefined and fixed meaning and these meanings cannot be changed. These keywords serve as basic building blocks for forming program instructions (statements). All keywords are written in lowercase. There incorrect usage results in a syntax error.

The list of keywords of C language, as per American National Standard Institute (ANSI) standard, is given in Table 3.2.

Table 3.2: Keywords in C

asm	default	for	short	union
auto	do	goto	signed	unsigned
break	double	if	sizeof	void
case	else	int	static	volatile
char	enum	long	struct	while
Const	extern	register	switch	
continue	float	return	typedef	

3.3.2 Identifiers

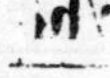

An identifier is basically a name in a program. Identifiers can be used to denote variables, arrays and functions. These user-defined names consist of sequence of characters, where each character can be a letter, a digit or an underscore '_', and cannot start with a digit. Both uppercase and lowercase letters are permitted, however, lowercase are commonly used. The underscore is usually used to link the two or more words to create meaning full names.

Since C language is case sensitive (it distinguishes between lowercase and uppercase), therefore, the identifiers *price* and *Price* will be treated as two different identifiers.

RULES FOR IDENTIFIERS

1. The first character must be an alphabet or an underscore.
2. Must consist of letters, digits or underscore only.
3. Cannot use a keyword.
4. Cannot contain a white space.

Examples of valid identifiers:

```
myFile      roll_no     date_of_birth     _chk
file10      N1TO10      area              AbCdE
```

Examples of invalid identifiers:

`my-File`	contains character other than letter, digit and underscore
`pin.code`	contains character other than letter, digit and underscore
`12file`	starts with a digit

3.3.3 Literals

A *literal*, often referred to as constants, refer to fixed value that do not change during the execution of a program. The C++ language supports following types of literals:

- Integer Literals
- Real Literals
- Single Character Literals
- String (multi-character) Literals

We will learn about these literals in section 3.4.

3.3.4 Punctuators

Punctuators are also called separators. Various punctuators used in C are described below.

Table 3.3: List of punctuators and their description

Punctuators	Description
Brackets [ ]	Used to enclose array subscripts.
Parentheses ( )	Used to enclose arguments in function declaration as well as function definition, parameters in function calls and expressions.
Braces { }	Used to enclose the block of statements. Also used to enclose list of elements while initializing arrays.
Comma ,	Used to separate arguments in function definition, and parameters in function call.
Semicolon ;	Used to terminate a statement.
Equal to sign =	Used to initialize a variable and as an assignment operator.
Pound sing #	Used for preprocessor directives.

3.3.5 Operators

Operators are the verbs of C language that let the user perform computations on values. You can think of operators as verbs and of operands as the subjects and object of those verbs. The C language's rich set of operators is one of its distinguished features.

These operators can be enumerated in following categories:

- Arithmetic Operators (+, -, *, /, %)
- Relational Operators (<, <=, >, >=, ==, !=)
- Logical Operators (!, &&, ||)

- Bit-wise Operators (~, >>, <<, &, |)
- Special Operators
  - Increment & Decrement Operators (++ - -)
  - The *sizeof* Operator
  - The *addressof* Operator (&)
  - Indirection Operator (*)
  - Ternary/Conditional Operator (? :)
  - Scope Resolution Operator (::)
  - Comma Operator (,)

We will learn about those categories of operators as prescribed in *Chapter 4*.

3.4 DATA TYPES

As mentioned earlier, the ability to divide the data into different types is one of the most important features of the modern programming languages. It enables us to work with relatively complex data objects instead of elementary data objects that a computer can understand and manipulate. We can deal with integer number, real numbers, and characters; all of which are familiar entities. At the bit level, the computer may not understand these concepts. Therefore, it is up to the compiler to make sure that the computer handles bits and bytes in a way consistent with their data type.

A *data type* is just an interpretation applied to a string of bits. Formally, *data type* is defined as a finite set of values along with well-defined set of rules for operations that can be performed on these values.

Data in C language belongs to one of following types:

1. Fundamental Data Types
   - Integer (*short int, int, long int*)
   - Real/Floating-point (*float, double, long double*)
   - Character (*char*)
2. Derived Data Types
   - Array
   - String
   - Structure
   - Union
   - Enumeration
   - Pointer
3. The *void* Data Type

In this chapter, we will discuss about fundamental data types and *void* data type. The other data types will be introduced briefly and will we discuss at length the relevant sections.

3.4.1 Fundamental Data Types

Under fundamental data types, also referred to as standard/primitive data types, we have integer numbers, real numbers, and characters. The various kinds of data types supported by C under this category are summarized in Table 3.4 along with description and their memory requirements.

In Turbo C implementations, *short integers* and *normal integers* are synonymous, but in on computer built on other processors such as Motorola, a short integer value occupies half word, a normal integer value occupies full word, and a long integer values occupies double word.

Table 3.4: Fundamental data types and their memory requirements

Name	Description	Bytes
Integer		
short int	Small whole numbers	2
int	Medium whole numbers	2
long int	Large whole numbers	4
Real/Floating-point		
float	Small real numbers	4
double	Large real numbers	8
long double	Very large real numbers	10
Character		
char	A Single Character	1

By default, integer and character data types are signed and can take negative as well as positive values. However, they can be prefixed with word *unsigned* to include positive range only.

In C language, it is mandatory to declare the data types of the variables to be used in a program unit. This not only helps to organize the program in a better way, but also helps the compiler in allocating the appropriate memory.

3.4.1.1 Integer Data Type

The integer data type consists of a subset of integers. An integer value is an exact representation of the corresponding integer. Table 3.5 shows the different types of integer numbers, their memory requirements, and the range of values for each type.

Table 3.5: Type of Integer Numbers

Type	Bytes	Range
short int or int	2	–32768 to +32767
long int	4	–2147483648 to +2147483647
unsigned short int or unsigned int	2	0 to 65535
unsigned long int	4	0 to 4294967295

An integer value consists of a sequence of digits preceded by an optional sign, plus (+) or minus (–). A decimal point and comma is not allowed in an integer value.

An integer value can be expressed in the following notations:

- Decimal (base 10) – a sequence of digits starting with a digit other than zero.
- Octal (base 8) – a sequence of digits (0 to 7) starting with 0.
- Hexadecimal (base 16) – a sequence of digits (0 to 7) and letters (*a* to *f* or *A* to *F*) starting with 0*x* or 0*X*.

Table 3.6 lists the integers from 0 to 16, showing their equivalents in the octal and hexadecimal number systems.

Table 3.6: Number Systems

Decimal number	Octal number	Hexadecimal number	Decimal number	Octal number	Hexadecima l number
0	0	0	8	10	8
1	1	1	9	11	9
2	2	2	10	12	a/A
3	3	3	11	13	b/B
4	4	4	12	14	c/C
5	5	5	13	15	d/D
6	6	6	14	16	e/E
7	7	7	15	17	f/F
			16	20	10

The range of values for *int* type can be viewed as shown in Figure 3.1.

A similar view holds for other integer types. Important point to learn from this view is that when we exceed the boundary values, the C system will not give an error rather automatically takes corresponding value from this view.

For example, if current value of a variable, say *i*, is 32767 and you try to increment the value of *i* by 1. The C system rather than giving an error-indicating overflow takes value –32768.

The following are valid integer values of type *int*:

```
  123          +123          0        32765
 3445         0x23a       7523        -2000
 0300         -3578       0032        -0120
```

The following are invalid integer values of type *int* because of the reasons as given:

```
  .123      (Decimal point not allowed)
 3,452      (Comma not allowed)
 45234      (Value larger than permissible range)
```

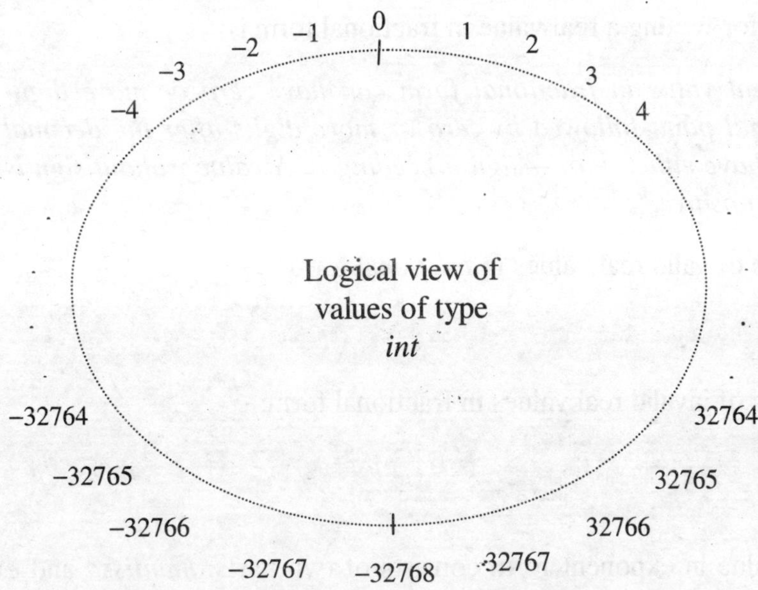

Figure 3.1: Logical view of values of type *int*

3.4.1.2 Real/Floating-point Data Type

The real/floating-point data type consists of a subset of the real numbers. A real value is an approximation of the desired real number correct to certain decimal positions. A real value of type *float* is accurate to six decimal positions, a real value of type of *double* is accurate to twelve decimal positions, and a real value of type of *long double* is even accurate to more than twelve decimal positions.

Table 3.7 shows the different types of real numbers, their memory requirements, and the range of values for each type.

Table 3.7: Type of Real Numbers

Type	Bytes	Range
float	4	3.4×10^{-38} to $3.4\times10^{+38}$
double	8	1.7×10^{-308} to $1.7\times10^{+308}$
long double	10	3.4×10^{-4932} to $1.1\times10^{+4932}$

Real values are numbers having fractional parts. The real values can be specified in two forms – *fractional form* (*fixed-point form*) and *exponent form* (*scientific notation*). A real value in fractional form consists of signed or unsigned digits including a decimal point.

The rule for writing a real value in fractional form is:

> *"A real value in fractional form can have zero or more digit before a decimal point followed by zero or more digits after the decimal point. It may have either + or – sign preceding it. A value without sign is assumed to be positive."*

Examples of valid real values in fractional form:

```
-123.345     +125.50     .456     1234.
```

Examples of invalid real values in fractional form:

```
      15          (Decimal point missing)
  12,34.23        (Comma not allowed)
```

A real value in exponent form consists of two parts: *mantissa* and *exponent*. For example, in value 2.5E–1 (which is equivalent to 2.5×10^{-1}), mantissa part is 2.5 and exponent part is –1. Here E–1 represents 10^{-1}, and letter *E* (or *e*) stands for *exponent*.

The rule for writing a real value in exponent form is given below:

> *"A real value in exponent form has two parts – mantissa and en exponent. The mantissa can either be an integer value or a real value in fractional form. The mantissa is followed by a letter E (or e) and the exponent. The exponent must be an integer value."*

Examples of valid real values in exponent form:

```
+1.25E12    .0001E+2    1.E-2    100.00E0     5E+10
```

Examples of invalid real values in exponent form:

```
+145.80E      (No digit specified for exponent)
6.35E5.5 (Exponent cannot be a fraction)
12,235E-5     (No comma allowed)
```

3.4.1.3 Character Data Type

The character data type (*char*) consists of ASCII characters. A character value occupies 1-byte of memory. A character variable can be signed (default) or unsigned, which means they have a range of –128 to +127 and 0 to 255, respectively. A character constant is an ASCII character enclosed by a pair of single quotation marks. Within the range specified above, character variable behaves like an integer variable and vice versa.

Table 3.8 gives a list of common escape sequences.

Table 3.8: Common Escape Sequences

Escape Sequence	Represents	Effect
\n	Newline	has the effect of both a carriage return and linefeed, *i.e.*, the subsequent output starts from new line.
\t	Tab	moves over to the next eight-space-wide field.
\b	Backspace	moves the cursor one space left.
\r	carriage return	carriage return.
\f	formfeed	advances to the top of the next page on printer.
\a	beep	produces one audio tone of the speaker
\'	single quote	insert character ' in the output
\"	double quote	insert character " in the output
\\	backslash	insert character \ in the output
\0	null	terminates a string

The C language allows certain characters that cannot be entered/typed directly from the keyboard such as *backspace*, *tab*, *carriage return*, *newline,* etc. These characters are represented by a sequence that begin with character \ (back slash), and are known as *escape sequences*.

An escape sequence actually represents a single character.

3.4.2 The *void* Data Types

The *void* data type, also known as *empty* data type, is useful in many situations.

These are enumerated below:

1. When used as a function return type, *void* means that the function does not return a value. For example, we may write as

```
void functionName(int x, int y )
{
    . . . .
}
```

   to indicate that the *functionName()* does not return a value.

2. When used in the function heading, *void* means that the function does not take any argument. For example, we may write as

```
int functionName(void )
{
    . . . .
}
```

   to indicate that the *functionName()* does not take any argument.

3. Used to declare generic pointers as shown below:

```
void *ptr;
```

We will discuss about functions in *Chapter 8* and about pointers in *Chapter 12*.

3.5 LITERALS/CONSTANTS

A constant (also known as simply literal or literal constant) refers to fixed values that do not change during the execution of a program. The C language supports several types of constants as illustrated in Figure 3.2.

Integer Literal

An *integer literal* refers to a sequence of digits. Such a sequence without a leading sign is assumed as positive integer literal.

Following are valid integer literals of type *int*:

```
     123          +123          0       32765
    3445          7523      -2000       0300
```

Following are invalid integer literals of type *int* because of the reasons as given:

```
    .123      (Decimal point not allowed)
   3,452      (Comma not allowed)
   45234      (Value larger than permissible range)
```

An integer literal by default is treated as an integer value of type *int*, and the compiler reserves 2-bytes of memory for its storage.

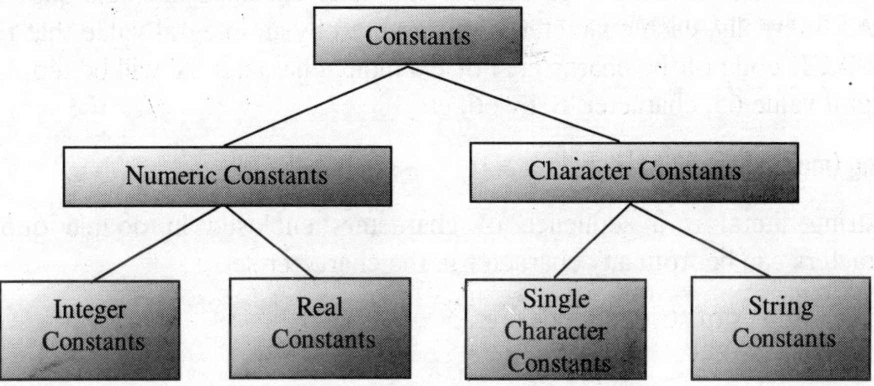

Figure 3.2: Types of Constants

Real Literals

A *real literal* are numbers having fractional parts. The real literals can be specified in two forms – *fractional form* (*fixed-point form*) and *exponent form* (*scientific notation*). A real literal in fractional form consists of signed or unsigned digits including a decimal point.

Examples of valid real literals in fractional form:

```
   -125.50      +100.5      1.      .454
```

Examples of valid real literals in fractional form:

```
        155     (Decimal point missing)
  12,500.25     (Comma not allowed)
```

A real literal in exponent form consists of two parts: *mantissa* and *exponent*. For example, in literal 5.25E+2 (which is equivalent to 5.25×10^2), mantissa part is 5.25 and exponent part is +2. Here E+2 represent 10^2, and letter *E* (or *e*) stands for *exponent*.

Examples of valid real literals in exponent form:

```
   1.25E12      .0001E+2      5.E-3      100.00E0      5.5E+10
```

Examples of invalid real literals in exponent form:

```
+145.80E      (No digit specified for exponent)
12.35E5.5     (Exponent cannot be a fraction)
12,75E-5      (Comma allowed)
```

Single Character Literals

A character literal consists of a single character enclosed in single quotes (') such as 'A'. Internally, each character is represented by an integral value that represents the ASCII code of the character. For example, character 'A' will be represented by integral value 65, character 'B' by 66, etc.

String (multi-character) Literals

A string literal is a sequence of characters enclosed in double quotes. The characters can be from any character in the character set.

Valid examples of string literals are:

```
"hello"    "Well done . . ."    "123.24"    "X"    "10+5"
```

Note that single character literal such as 'A' is not equivalent to single character string literal as "A".

Escape sequences can also appear in a string literal. For example printing string

```
"\"String literals are double-quoted.\""
```

will give the following result

```
"String literals are double-quoted."
```

3.6 SYMBOLIC CONSTANTS

A symbolic constant is a name that substitutes a literal constant. As an example, assume that we are computing the area of circle with given radius using the following statement:

```
area = 3.14159 * radius * radius;
```

In the above statement, numeric constant 3.14159 represents the value of the mathematical constant π, and can be replaced by symbolic constant named *PI*. The task is accomplished as follows:

```
#define PI 3.14159
area = PI * radius * radius;
```

In the above statements, *#define* pre-processor directive associates the name PI with the numeric constant 3.14159. Note that no semicolon is used after the *#define* preprocessor directive, and also to other directives as well.

During the compiling, the preprocessor will replace each occurrence of name PI with numeric constant 3.14159.

The use of symbolic constant has following advantages:

- The use of symbolic constants enhances the readability of the program, as the appropriately chosen names pronounce much as their counter parts in the real world (actual use).
- Suppose the same numeric constant is used at many places in the program, and you want to change its value, you can do it in following ways:
    - At every place, change the value manually in the program, which is cumbersome and time consuming. Also there may be chances that at some place values may be left unchanged.
    - Use symbolic constant, *i.e.*, associate a name with the constant, and then at each place of the value use symbolic constant. Now, if you want to change the value of the constant, you have to do only at one place. During compilation, every occurrence of the symbolic constant will be replaced with the new value.

3.7 VARIABLES

A variable provides us with named storage that we can write to, retrieve, and manipulate throughout the course of the program. In other words, variables are memory locations in the computer's memory that holds data. Contents of a variable may vary — hence the name *variable*.

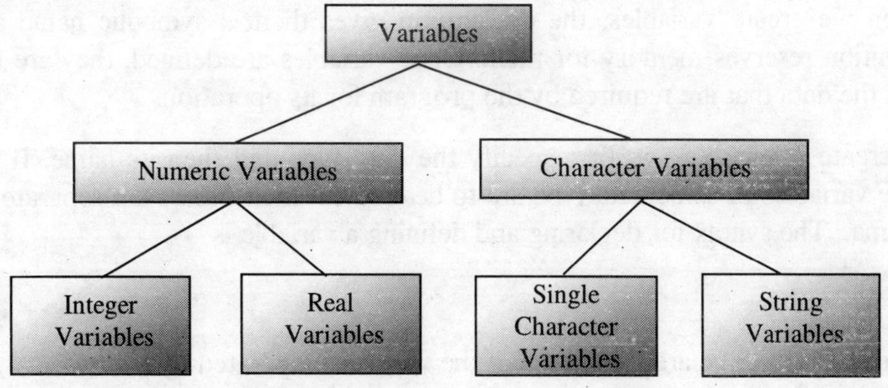

Figure 3.3: Type of variables in C

Unlike a constant, a variable is *addressable* and its address can be accessed using *addressof* (&) operator.

There are two values associated with a variable:

1. Its data value that is stored at some memory address. This sometimes referred to as variable's *rvalue* (pronounced as "are-value"). We may think *rvalue* as meaning *read value*. Both a literal constant and a variable can serve as *rvalue*.
2. Its address value that is its address in memory within which its data value is stored. This sometimes referred to as variable's *lvalue* (pronounced as "ell-value"). We may think *lvalue* as meaning *location value*. Only a variable can serve as *lvalue*.

Consider the following statement

```
y = y + 3.5;
```

Here variable *y* appears on both sides of an assignment operator. The right-hand instance is read. Its associated data value is fetched from its address in memory. The left-hand instance is written. The result of the addition operation is stored at its location value and its previous value is overwritten. Therefore, variable *y* on the left-hand side serves as *lvalue* and on the right-hand side it serves as *rvalue*.

3.7.1 Declaring Variables

In C language, each variable in a program must be declared and defined. Declaration is used to name a variable while definition is used to create (allocate memory) a variable. The definition of variable assumes that the declaration of the variable has been done or is being done at the same time.

When we create variables, the declaration gives them a symbolic name and the definition reserves memory for them. Once variables are defined, they are used to hold the data that are required by the program for its operation.

To create a variable, we first specify the data type and then its name. If two or more variables of same data type are to be created, their names are separated using comma. The syntax for declaring and defining a variable is

```
type v1, v2, . . ., vn;
```

where *v1*, *v2*, ..., *vn* are the names of the variables separated by comma.

A variable's type can be any of the fundamental data types or user-defined data types. The one exception is the *void* type, *i.e.*, a variable cannot be of type *void*.

Following are some examples of variable declarations and definition:

```
int count, m, n;
float
value, sum;
char ch;
double deviation;
long amt;
unsigned k;
short srno;
unsigned char chr;
```

First statement declares variables *count*, *m* and *n* of type *int*. Compiler reserves 2-bytes for each of these variables.

Second statement declares variable *value* and *sum* of type *float*. Compiler reserves 4-bytes for each of these variables.

Third statement declares variable *ch* of type *char*. Compiler reserves 1-bytes for it.

Fourth statement declares variable *deviation* of type *double*. Compiler reserves 8-bytes for it.

Fifth statement declares variable *amt* of type *long* (*long int*). Compiler reserves 4-bytes for it.

Sixth statement declares variable *k* of type *unsigned* (*unsigned int*). Compiler reserves 2-bytes for it.

Seventh statement declares variable *srno* of type *short* (*short int*). Compiler reserves 2-bytes for it.

Eighth statement declares variable *chr* of type *unsigned char*. Compiler reserves 1-bytes for it.

3.7.2 Initializing Variables

It is important to note that during the declaration and definition, a variable is normally not initialized. However, in C language, it is possible to give an initial value to a variable during its declaration and definition. To do that, a variable is followed by character '=' and then the value to be given to the variable. Consider the following statement

```
int sum = 0;
```

It declares variable *sum* of type *int*, reserves 2-bytes of memory for it, and places integer value 0 in those 2-bytes, *i.e.*, initializes variable *sum* to a value 0.

As declarations and definitions of variables of same type can be combined in one statement, likewise initialization of variables of same type can also be done. The following statement illustrates this:

```
int sum = 0, count = 0;
```

3.7.3 The *const* Access Modifier

When the *const* access modifier is used along with the variable, it allows the value to be assigned once and that too using initialization. Afterwards, the value of this variable cannot be modified, *i.e.*, variable behaves as a constant. Consider the following declaration statement

```
const float pie = 3.1428;
```

It stores real constant in a variable *pie* (π – a useful constant in mathematics).
Any further assignment to this variable *pie* is not permitted, *i.e.*, any assignment statement of type

```
pie = value/variable/expression/function-call;
```

will result in a syntax error as the compiler will not allow to do that.

However, it is possible to modify the value of a constant stored in a variable indirectly using a pointer. As in above declaration, the statement

```
*(float *)&pie = 3.5;
```

will modify the value of pie.

3.7.4 The Type Modifiers

The *type* modifiers changes the meaning of the fundamental data type with which they are used. The type modifiers supported by the C language are *unsigned*, *signed*, *short*, and *long*.

3.7.4.1 The *signed* Type Modifier

The *signed* type modifier can only be used with *int* and *char* fundamental data types. Even if the signed modifier is omitted, it is assumed by default. When a variable is of signed type, implicitly or explicitly, it can hold negative as well as positive values.

In the following cases, variable *x* can hold any value in the range –32768 to +32767, and variable *y* can take any value in the range –128 to +127.

```
signed int x;               signed char y;
int x;                      char y;
```

3.7.4.2 The *unsigned* Type Modifiers

The *unsigned* type modifier can also be used only with *int* and *char* fundamental data types. When it is used, a variable can hold only positive values.

In following cases, variable *x* can hold any value in the range 0 to 65535, and variable *y* can take any value in the range 0 to 255.

```
unsigned int x;                unsigned char y;
```

3.7.4.3 The *short* Type Modifier

The *short* type modifier can be used only with *int* fundamental data type. With *short* type modifier, the base type can be omitted, and it is assumed to be *int*. When it is used, a variable use memory as half of the memory as that of base type *int*, and can hold only smaller values. However, in the implementations of C language such as Turbo C, *int* and *short int* are synonymous, *i.e.*, both use 16-bits (2 bytes).

Both of the following statements serve the same purpose, and variable *x* can hold values in the range –32768 to 32767.

```
short int x;        OR        short x;
```

3.7.4.4 The *long* Type Modifier

The *long* type modifier can be used with *int*, *float*, and *double* fundamental data types. With *long* type modifier, the base type can be omitted, and it is assumed to be *int*. When it is used, a variable use memory as double of the memory as that of base type, and can hold large values.

Both of the following statements serve the same purpose.

```
long int x;      OR      long x;
```

Following statements also serve the same purpose.

```
long float x;    OR      double x;
```

Table 3.8 sums up the fundamental data types, their possible combinations with type modifiers, memory requirements for each and the range of values on Turbo C/C++ compiler.

3.7.5 The *volatile* Modifier

The *volatile* modifier indicates to the computer that the variable can be changed by external programs, *i.e.*, other than this program. Normally, variables used in a program belong to only C compiler. When the compiler owns a variable, it can store and handle it in any way necessary to optimize the program. For example, a C compiler may think that it is more efficient to remove a variable from RAM and put in a register. However, sometimes variables are shared between your program and some other facilities outside your C program, such as input/output routines. To tell the compiler that the variable is shared, we declare it with modifier *volatile*. This way we are telling the compiler this variable may be referenced or changed by other entities.

The following example declares an integer variable as volatile

```
volatile int x;
```

Table 3.8: Possible combinations of type modifiers and fundamental data types

Type	Memory Requirement	Range
unsigned char	1 byte	0 to 255
char	1 byte	–128 to 127
unsigned int	2 bytes	0 to 65,535
int	2 bytes	–32,768 to 32,767
short int	2 bytes	–32,768 to 32,767
long int	4 bytes	–2,147,483,648 to 2,147,483,647
long	4 bytes	–2,147,483,648 to 2,147,483,647
unsigned long	4 bytes	0 to 4,294,967,295
float	4 bytes	3.4×10^{-38} to $3.4\times10^{+38}$
long float	8 bytes	1.7×10^{-308} to $1.7\times10^{+308}$
double	8 bytes	1.7×10^{-308} to $1.7\times10^{+308}$
long double	10 bytes	3.4×10^{-4932} to $1.1\times10^{+4932}$

3.8 STORAGE CLASSES

Every variable in C language possesses a characteristic called its *storage class*. The storage class defines two main characteristics of the variable, apart from the place of storage and the initial value. These are

- Lifetime
- Visibility or scope

Lifetime — *Lifetime* of a variable is the length of time it retains a particular value.

Visibility — *Visibility* or *scope* of a variable refers to those parts of a program that will be able to recognize it.

At first instance, a question arises: *why are storage classes necessary*? The answer is that by using variables with the appropriate lifetime and visibility, we can write programs that use memory more efficiently, run faster, and are less prone to programming errors. The correct use of storage class is especially important in large programs.

The storage class precedes the variable's declaration and tells the compiler regarding *where the variable should be stored*, *what should be its initial value*, *what will be its scope*, and for *how much time it will be available for use*.

The C language supports following four storage classes:

- auto
- static
- extern
- register

If storage class in variable declaration is omitted, it is assumed of type *auto*, *i.e.*, storage class is *auto* by default. Let us examine these storage classes one by one.

For example, consider the following declaration statement

```
static unsigned int x;
```

It tells the compiler that the storage class for variable *x* is static, which signifies the following things:

- Variable *x* will be stored in computer main memory.
- Since variable *x* is not initialized, it will automatically be initialized with value is 0.
- Variable *x* will be visible to the block in which it is declared.
- The variable *x*, if declared in a function other than *main()* function, will retain its value during different function calls.

We will learn more about storage classes in *Chapter 8*.

3.9 QUICK RECAP

In this chapter, we have learnt that

- A value coded directly or represented through a variable that does not change during the course of program execution is called a constant, where as those values that may change is called a variable.
- Data type is a set of values along with set of permissible operations.
- Various data types supported by C language are named as simple data types, structured data types, pointer data type, enumerated data type and void data type.
- Simple data types consist of integers (*short*, *int*, *long*), real numbers (*float*, *double, long double*) and characters (*char*).
- Derived data types consist of arrays, strings, structures, unions, enumerations, and pointers.
- Every data item to be processed by the program needs to be declared.

3.10 MULTIPLE CHOICE QUESTIONS

1. Which of the following is not a valid identifier in C language?

   (*a*) EMP_CODE (*b*) rollno123
   (*c*) a1b2c3d4 (*d*) 3a2b1c

2. Which of the following is not a valid data type in C language?

   (*a*) Char (*b*) float
   (*c*) long (*d*) double

3. Which of the following declarations is not correct?

   (*a*) float a; (*b*) int b = 4;
   (*c*) unsigned char c; (*d*) unsigned float d;

4. Which of the following is not a valid integer constant of type *int*?

   (*a*) 3750 (*b*) 32800
   (*c*) –32767 (*d*) 0

5. A variable of type *int* in C can take a value in the range

   (*a*) 0 to 32767 (*b*) 0 to 65535
   (*c*) –32768 to 32767 (*d*) –32767 to 32768

6. Which of the following is not a reserved word in C language?

   (*a*) for (*b*) goto
   (*c*) doo (*d*) switch

7. Which of the following is not a valid storage class?

   (*a*) automatic (*b*) static
   (*c*) register (*d*) extern

8. How much memory is required to store a value of type *double*?

   (*a*) 4 bytes (*b*) 6 bytes
   (*c*) 8 bytes (*d*) 10 bytes

9. Which of the following modifier is used to declare a variable as constant?

   (*a*) unsigned (*b*) short
   (*c*) signed (*d*) const

10. Which of the following doesn't denote a primitive data value in C?

    (*a*) "a" (*b*) 'k'
    (*c*) 35.25 (*d*) 014

11. The storage class controls

    (*a*) life time of a variable (*b*) scope of a variable
    (*c*) Both (*a*) & (*b*) (*d*) None of above

12. A character variable can store - - - - - character(s).

    (*a*) 1 (*b*) 256
    (*c*) 8 (*d*) 255

13. Storage class of a variable determines

    (*a*) Which section of the program can access a variable?
    (*b*) For how long variable exists.
    (*c*) Its initial value if it is not explicitly initialized.
    (*d*) All of above

14. Which of the following storage classes is a default storage class?

    (*a*) register (*b*) extern
    (*c*) static (*d*) None

15. Which of the following is not a storage class?

    (*a*) register (*b*) external
    (*c*) auto (*d*) static

16. Scope of the variable refers to
    (*a*) Part of a program in which the variable can be recognized.
    (*b*) Duration for which the variable retains a given value during execution.
    (*c*) Value of the variable.
    (*d*) Data type of the variable.
17. Lifetime of the variable refers to
    (*a*) Part of a program in which the variable can be recognized.
    (*b*) Value of the variable.
    (*c*) Duration for which the variable retains a given value during execution.
    (*d*) Data type of the variable.

3.11 REVIEW EXERCISES

1. What are various data types supported by C language? Give memory requirement of each. Also give at least two examples of each data type.
2. List various types of operators available in C language and also give their precedence, if any.
3. Suppose *x*, *y*, and *z* have been declared variables of type *float*, write a C segment which changes the values of *x*, *y*, and *z* so that *x* has *y*'s value, *y* has *z*'s value, and *z* has *x*'s value.
4. What is an integer? Which of the following are invalid 2-byte integers, and why?

```
123      -435     +4567    32767
-32768   +32768   -40000   4.50
```

5. What is a variable? What are the rules for naming a variable? Which of the following are invalid variable names and why?

```
roll-no   12_items  temperature
height    float     Interest_Paid    SUM
```

6. What is another name for floating point numbers?
7. What is a character constant? What is the maximum number of character that a variable of type *char* can hold?

❑ ❑ ❑

4 Operators and Expressions

Learning Objectives

After reading this chapter, students will have the ability to:

- various operators and their usage
- concept of precedence and associativity among operators
- various type of expressions and their evaluation
- type conversion in assignment and expressions
- assignment statement and its forms
- library functions

4.1 INTRODUCTION

Operators are the verbs of a language that let the user perform computations on values. You can think of operators as verbs and of operands as the subjects and object of those verbs. C language's rich set of operators is one of its distinguished features.

An *expression* is a formula consisting of one or more operands and zero or more operators linked together to compute a value. The computed values are to be stored in a variable for future use. This is done using an assignment statement.

In a computer program, variety of computations is to be performed as per requirements of the problem in hand. Yet there are some routine type computations that may be part of almost every program. Therefore as a convenience, every modern programming language provides a support for these routine type computations in the form of library functions.

This chapter attempts to describe these semantic units of the C language.

4.2 OPERATORS

As mentioned earlier, operators are the verbs of a language that let the user perform computations on values. You can think of operators as verbs and of operands as the subjects and object of those verbs.

The C language's rich set of operators is one of its distinguished features. These operators can be enumerated in following categories:

- Arithmetic Operators
- Relational Operators
- Logical Operators
- Bitwise Operators
- Special Operators
    - Increment & Decrement Operators
    - The *sizeof* Operator
    - The *addressof* Operator
    - Indirection Operator
    - Conditional Operator
    - Comma Operator

4.2.1 Precedence and Associativity of Operators

Precedence is used to determine the order in which different operators are evaluated in an expression.

Associativity is used to determine the order in which different operators with same precedence are evaluated in an expression.

Precedence is applied before associativity to determine the order in which expressions are evaluated. Associativity is applied later, if necessary.

Precedence

The concept of precedence is well defined in the subject of mathematics. You must be aware of rule BODMAS – Brackets, Of, Division, Multiplication, Addition, and Subtraction. In algebra, division and multiplication is performed before addition and subtraction.

The following is a simple example of precedence:

```
5 + 3 * 4
```

This expression consists of one addition and one multiplication operator. As you know from the knowledge of algebra, multiplication has higher precedence than addition, and this multiplication is performed before addition.

Therefore, the expression will be evaluated as

```
( 5 + ( 3 * 4 ) ) → ( 5 + 12 ) → 17
```

giving value 17 as the value of the entire expression.

Associativity

Associativity is applied when more then one operator of same precedence is used in an expression. Associativity can be *left-to-right* or *right-to-left*. Left-to-right associativity evaluates the expression by starting on the left and moving to the right whereas the right-to-left associativity evaluates the expression by starting on the right and moving to the left.

The following is a simple example of associativity:

```
2 + 5 + 7
```

This expression consists of two addition operators. Here the associativity determines how the sub expressions are grouped together. Since the addition operator has left-to-right associativity, the expression will be grouped as

```
( ( 2 + 5 ) + 7 ) → ( 7 + 7 ) → 14
```

giving value 14 as the value of the entire expression.

We will learn more about precedence and associativity as we proceed with the discussion on various operators.

The precedence of operators is also some time known as hierarchy amongst operators. The precedence of operators will be given a level (rank) with lower number denoting the higher precedence. There are total of 15 levels of precedence, level 1 denoting the highest precedence and level 15 denoting the lowest precedence.

Appendix B summarizes the precedence and associativity of all the operators supported by C language.

4.2.2 Arithmetic Operators

Different arithmetic operators supported by C language are listed in Table 4.1. All of the operators may be used as binary operators, which appear between their operands. The plus (+) and minus (–) may also be used as unary, and precede their operand.

Table 4.1: Arithmetic Operators

Symbol Used	Operation Performed	Precedence Level	Associativity
+	Addition	4	Left-to-right
–	Subtraction	4	Left-to-right
*	Multiplication	3	Left-to-right
/	Division	3	Left-to-right
%	Modulus	3	Left-to-right

1. Modulus (%) operators, that give remainder, work only on operands of type *int*, *long int*.
2. There is no operator for exponentiation operation in C language.

Integer Arithmetic

When both the operands are integers, the operations will be called *integer arithmetic* and will always yield an integer value. Consider the following statements

```
int x = 13, b = 5;
```

then we have the following results:

```
x - y = 8
```

```
x + y = 18
x * y = 65
x / y = 2 (decimal part truncated)
x % y = 3 (remainder of division)
```

In the integer division, if both the operands are of same sign, the result of the division is truncated towards 0. If one of them is negative, direction of truncation is implementation dependent. On Turbo C/C++ compilers, it is towards 0.

Therefore,

`3/4, -3/-4, -3/4` and `3/-4`

all yields value 0 on Turbo C/C++ compiler.

Similarly in modulus operation, the sign of the result is always the sign of the first operand. Therefore,

```
-13/5 = -3        -13/-5 = -3        13/-5 = 3
```

Real Arithmetic

When both the operands are real numbers, the operations will be called *real arithmetic* and will always yield a real value. The real operand may be in *fractional form* or *exponent form*. Since real numbers (floating-point values) are rounded to permissible number of significant digits, the result of arithmetic operations is an approximate value of the correct result.

That is

```
 6.0 /  7.0  =  0.857143
-1.0 /  3.0  = -0.333333
 3.0 / -2.0  = -1.500000
```

The modulus operation cannot be used with real operands.

Mixed-mode Arithmetic

When one of the operands is real and the other is integer, the operations will be called *mixed-mode arithmetic* and will always yield a real value. The integer operand is converted into real operand and then the real arithmetic is performed, resulting in a real value.

That is

```
 6 / 7.0  →   6.0 / 7.0  =  0.857143
-1.0 / 3  →  -1.0 / 3.0  =  -0.333333
```

Note that

```
15 / 10.0 = 1.5
15.0 / 10 = 1.5
```

where as

```
15 / 10 = 1
```

4.2.3 Relational Operators

These operators are used to compare the values of the operands that must be compatible, in order to facilitate decision-making. If the comparison succeeds, they return a value 1 (equivalent to Boolean value *true*) and if comparison fails then returns value 0 (equivalent to Boolean value *false*).

The C language supports all six relational operators. These relational operators are listed in Table 4.2, along with their descriptions.

Table 4.2: Relational Operators

Symbol Used	Operation Performed	Precedence Level	Associativity
<	Less than	6	Left-to-right
<=	Less than or equal to	6	Left-to-right
>	Greater than	6	Left-to-right
>=	Greater than or equal to	6	Left-to-right
==	Equal to	7	Left-to-right
!=	Not equal to	7	Left-to-right

Note that in C language, the non-zero value is treated as equivalent to Boolean true and zero value as equivalent to Boolean false. Further note that, there is no support for Boolean data as such in C language in old versions of C language. The new version of C language, known as C99 standard, supports the Boolean type.

Table 4.3 lists some example relational expressions and the result of their evaluation.

Table 4.3: Relational Expressions

Relation Expressions	Result of operation
`20 >  10`	1
`15 != 12`	1
`15 == 13`	0
`20 >= 35`	0
`10 <= 19`	1
`13 >  20`	0

Expressions such as

```
100 >= 59        15 < 25
```

are known as relational expressions.

However, if the relational expression is of following type

```
a + b == x + y
```

then firstly arithmetic expressions on both the sides of the relational operators are evaluated then the comparison is performed, *i.e.*, arithmetic operators have a higher precedence that relational operators.

Relational Operators Complement

Among six relational operators, they form three pairs in which each one complements the other and vice versa, as shown below:

>	is complement of	<=
<	is complement of	>=
==	is complement of	!=

We can simplify an expression involving the NOT and the relational operators using the complements as shown below:

Actual one	Simplified one
`!(x < y)`	`x >= y`
`!(x > y)`	`x <= y`
`!(x != y)`	`x == y`
`!(x <= y)`	`x > y`
`!(x >= y)`	`x < y`
`!(x == y)`	`x != y`

4.2.4 Logical Operators

These operators are used to form compound conditions by joining two or more simple conditions formed using relational operators. Different logical operators supported by C language are listed in Table 4.4.

Table 4.4: Logical Operators

Symbol Used	Operation Performed	Precedence Level	Associativity
!	Logical NOT	10	Left-to-right
&&	Logical AND	11	Left-to-right
||	Logical OR	12	Left-to-right

NOT Operator

The NOT operator (!) is a unary operator. It inverts the value, *i.e.*, it changes a *true* value to *false* and false value to *true*.

Table 4.5: Rules for Logical Operators

NOT Operation

x	*!x*
false	true
true	false

AND Operation

x	*y*	*x&&y*
false	false	false
false	true	false
true	false	false
true	true	true

OR Operation

x	*y*	*x || y*
false	false	false
false	true	true
true	false	true
true	true	true

AND Operator

The AND operator (&&) is a binary operator. Four distinct combinations of values of its operands are possible. The result is *true* only when both the operands are *true*, in all other cases, the result is *false*.

OR Operator

The OR operator (||) is also a binary operator. Four distinct combinations of values of its operands are possible. The result is *false* only when both the operands are *false*, in all other cases, the result is *true*.

Evaluating Logical Expressions

There are two methods to evaluate a logical expression. In the first method, the expression must be completely evaluated before the result is determined. This means that AND expression must be completely evaluated even when the first operand is *false* and it is therefore known that result will be *false*. Likewise, an OR expression must be completely evaluated even when the first operand is *true* and it is therefore known that result will be *true*.

In the second method, also known as *short-circuit evaluation*, the expression need not be evaluated completely. As soon as it is known that what the final result will be, the rest of the expression is not evaluated. Therefore, in evaluating the AND expression, if the first operand is *false*, the second operand is not evaluated since it is apparent that the result will be *false*. Likewise, in evaluating the OR expression, if the first operand is *true*, the second operand is not evaluated since it is apparent that the result will be *true*.

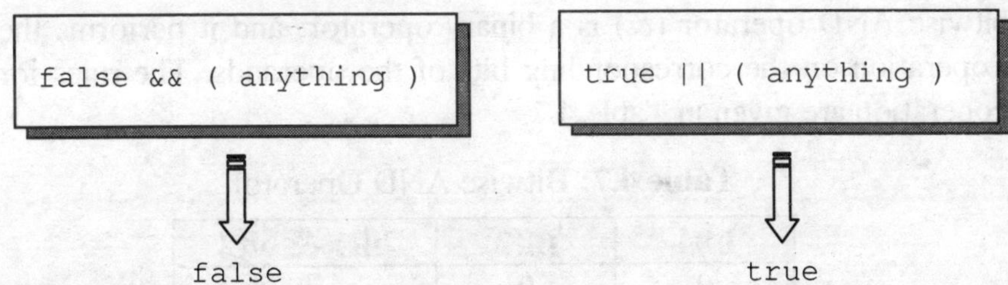

Figure 4.1: Short-circuit evaluation of AND/OR Operation

4.2.5 Bitwise Operators

These operators operate at bit-level, and allow us to manipulate the individual bits. Specifically, these operators find their use in low-level programming.

Different bit-wise operators supported by C language are listed in Table 4.6.

Table 4.6: Bitwise Operators

Symbol Used	Operation Performed	Precedence Level	Associativity
>>	Shift-right	5	Left-to-right
<<	Shift-left	5	Left-to-right
~	1's Complement	2	Left-to-right
&	Bitwise AND	8	Left-to-right
^	Bitwise Exclusive OR	9	Left-to-right
|	Bitwise Inclusive OR	10	Left-to-right

To illustrate the working of bitwise operators, consider the following declarations statement

```
int a = 20, b = 94, c, d;
```

The value of *a* will be internally stored as 0000000000010100, and of *b* as 0000000001011110, *i.e.*, as two byte binary numbers.

4.2.5.1 Logical Bitwise Operators

The logical operators look at data to be manipulated as individual bits. Following four operators are used to manipulate the bits: bitwise AND (&), bitwise inclusive OR (|), bitwise exclusive OR (^), and one's complement (~). The first three are binary operators while the fourth one is unary operator.

4.2.5.1.1 Bitwise AND Operator

The bitwise AND operator (&) is a binary operator, and it performs the bitwise AND operation on the corresponding bits of the operands. The rules for bitwise AND operation are given in Table 4.7.

Table 4.7: Bitwise AND Operator

bit1	bit2	bit1 & bit2
0	0	0
0	1	0
1	0	0
1	1	1

```
Operand 1        ----    0000000000010100
Operand 2        ----    0001000010001110
Bitwise AND      ----    0000000000000100
```

This can be accomplished using the statement of type

```
c = a & b;
```

Using the value of *a* and *b*, as per type declaration statement, find out the value of *c*.

4.2.5.1.2 Bitwise Exclusive OR Operator

The bitwise exclusive OR operator (^) is a binary operator, and it performs the bitwise exclusive OR operation on the corresponding bits of the operands. The rules for bitwise exclusive OR operation are given in Table 4.8.

Table 4.8: Bitwise Exclusive OR Operator

bit1	bit2	bit1 ^ bit2
0	0	0
0	1	1
1	0	1
1	1	0

```
Operand 1                 ----   0000000000010100
Operand 2                 ----   0001000010001110
Bitwise Exclusive OR      ----   0001000010011010
```

This can be accomplished using the statement of type

```
c = a ^ b;
```

Using the value of *a* and *b*, as per type declaration statement, find out the value of *c*.

4.2.5.1.3 Bitwise Inclusive OR Operator

The bitwise inclusive OR operator (|) is a binary operator, and it performs the bitwise inclusive OR operation on the corresponding bits of the operands. The rules for bitwise inclusive OR operation are given in Table 4.9.

Table 4.9: Bitwise Inclusive OR Operator

bit1	bit2	bit1 | bit2
0	0	0
0	1	1
1	0	1
1	1	1

```
Operand 1                 ----   0000000000010100
Operand 2                 ----   0001000010001110
Bitwise Inclusive OR      ----   0001000010011110
```

This can be accomplished using the statement of type

```
c = a | b;
```

Using the value of *a* and *b*, as per type declaration statement, find out the value of *c*.

4.2.5.1.4 One's Complement Operator

One's complement operator is a unary operator. The One's complement is obtained by just inverting the individual bits.

That is, if the value of *a* is 0000000000010100, then its one's complement will be 1111111111101011

This can be achieved by using ~ operator as shown in the following statement

```
c = ~a;
```

4.2.5.2 Shift Operators

The shift operators move bits of the operand to the left or right. When applied to unsigned numbers, these operators are independent of the underlying implementation (hardware and software). When applied on signed numbers, however, the implementation is left to the software engineer who designs the system.

It is often known for which hardware and software platform the compiler is written. Therefore, the C standard leaves the implementation details up to the compiler writer (there is no standard), the code that shifts signed negative numbers may not be portable to other platforms.

4.2.5.2.1 Bitwise Shift-Right Operator

The shift-right operator is a binary operator where the value of the second operand specifies the by how many bit positions the value of the first operand is to be right shifted. The rightmost bit is discarded, whereas the 0 or 1 (depending on whether the operand is positive number or negative number) is inserted in the leftmost bit position.

Consider the following statement

```
c = a >> 1;
```

This statement causes the value of *a* (0000000000010100) shifted to right by one bit and 0 bit is added to the left, and finally the resultant value is assigned to variable *c*.

So the value of *c* will be 0000000000001010, *i.e.*, decimal 10. The right shift by 1 bit is equivalent to division by a factor of 2.

However, if the original left most bit is 1 (*i.e.*, the value is negative), then bit 1 is added to the left for every shift.

The signed numbers are stored in two's complement form. In two's complement form, the leftmost bit is used for sign. The sign bit is 0 for positive and 1 for negative numbers. For 2-byte integers, remaining 15 bits hold the magnitude of the number, whereas for 4-byte integers (*i.e.*, long integers) remaining 31-bits contain the magnitude of the number. But for unsigned integers, all the bits are used to hold the magnitude as all the numbers are positive and therefore no bit is used for sign to distinguish positive integers from negative integers.

4.2.5.2.2 Bitwise Shift-Left Operator

Like shift-right operator, shift-left operator is also a binary operator where the value of the second operand specifies the by how many bit positions the value of the first operand is to be left shifted. The leftmost bit is discarded, whereas 0 bit is inserted in the rightmost bit position.

Consider the following statement

```
c = a << 1;
```

This statement causes the value of *a* (0000000000010100) shifted to left by one bit and 0 bit is added to the right, and finally the resultant value is assigned to variable *c*.

So the value of *c* will be 0000000000101000, *i.e.*, decimal 40. The left shift by 1 bit is equivalent to multiplication by a factor of 2.

4.2.6 Special Operators

These operators were not supported by earlier high-level languages, and were incorporated for the first time in C. Most of the later high-level languages are influenced by C and almost all such languages, for example C, JAVA, etc., support these kind of operators. Let us discuss each of them briefly, and their utility you will be able to appreciate in the subsequent sections and chapters.

4.2.6.1 Increment & Decrement Operators

The C language supports two very useful operators – increment operator (++) and decrement operator (−−). These operators can be used with all basic data types. The increment operator adds 1 to the operand, while decrement operator subtracts 1 from the operand.

Both operators are unary operators and can be used in the prefix as well as postfix notation as shown below:

```
++k;    or    k++;
--k;    or    k--;
```

Here, `++k` (as well as `k++`) is equivalent to `k = k + 1` or `k += 1`, and `--k` (as well as `k--`) is equivalent to `k = k - 1` or `k -= 1`.

These operators are most frequently used in *while* and *for* loops as control variables.

While `++k` or `k++` means the same thing when they form statements independently, they behave differently when they are used as part of other expressions.

Consider the following statements

```
int y, k = 5;
y = ++k;
```

In this case, first the value of *k* is incremented and then assigned to *y*, and hence y and k will have same value as 6. Thus, the above statements are equivalent to following statements

```
int y, k = 5;
++k;
y = k;
```

However, if we write the above statements as

```
int y, k = 5;
y = k++;
```

then first the current value of *k* (value 5) is assigned to y and then the value of k is incremented, and hence *y* will have value 5 while and *k* will have value as 6.

Thus, the above statements are equivalent to following statements

```
int y, k = 5;                 int y, k = 5;
y = k;             or         y = k;
++k;                          k++;
```

Similar is the case, when these operators are used in accessing elements of an array.

Therefore, the statement

```
a[i++] = 5;
```

is equivalent to

```
a[i] = 5;
i = i + 1;
```

These operators can also be used in complex expressions, such as

```
k = m++ - j / 10;
```

where exiting value of *m* is used in evaluating the expression, and afterwards *m* is incremented.

Rules for Increment & Decrement Operators

1. These operators are unary operators and require variable as operand.
2. These operators mean the same thing, irrespective whether they are used in prefix or postfix notation, when they form statements independently.
3. When these operators are used in prefix notation in an expression, then first the value of the variable is changed accordingly and the new value is used in evaluating the expression.
4. When these operators are used in postfix notation in an expression, then first the existing value of the variable is used in evaluating the expression and then the value is changed accordingly.
5. The precedence and associativity of these operators is same as that of unary plus and unary minus.

4.2.6.2 The *sizeof* Operator

The *sizeof* operator returns the size, in bytes, of the given operand. The syntax of *sizeof* operator is

```
sizeof( exp )
```

where *exp* represents a data type (built-in or user-defined), a literal/constant or a variable. For example

```
sizeof( float )
```

returns value 4.

Table 4.10: Use of *sizeof* Operator

sizeof Operator used as	Returns	Justification
`sizeof(12)`	2	Integer constant by default belong to data type *int*, and the size for *int* is 2.
`sizeof('a')`	1	Size of Character constant is 1.
`sizeof(int)`	2	Size of data type *int* is 2.
`sizeof(125.25)`	8	Real constant by default belong to data type *double*.
`sizeof(125UL)`	4	Size of data type *unsigned long int* is 4.
`sizeof(125.25F)`	4	Real constant is of data type *float*, and the size for *float* is 4.
`double x;` `sizeof(x);`	8	Variable *x* is of type *double*, and the size for *double* is 8.

The *sizeof* operator finds its use in dynamic memory management, when the programmers need to allocate a memory block of varying size.

4.2.6.3 The *addressof* Operator

Character '&' when prefixed with a variable returns the address of the memory locations, hence its name *addressof* operator. It is used in the *scanf()* function and to initialize the pointers.

Table 4.11: Use of *addressof* (&) Operators

addressof (&) Operator used as	Task Performed

`int y = 10;`
`int *py;`
`Py = &y;`
	First statement declares and defines variable *y* of type *int*. It also initializes it with value 10.
	
	Second statement declares and defines a pointer variable *py* that can hold an address of a memory location reserved for storing value of type *int*.
	
	Third statement assigns the address of variable y to pointer variable *py*.

`int x, y;` `scanf("%d %d", &x, &y);`	First statement declares and defines two variable *x* and *y* of type *int*. Second statement takes two integer values as input from the keyboard and stores those values at addresses of variable *x* and *y*, respectively.

4.2.6.4 Indirection Operator

Character '*' when prefixed with a pointer variable returns the value stored in a memory location whose address is held in pointer variable. That is, value is accessed through the pointer variable indirectly, hence its name indirection operator.

Consider the following statements

```
int y = 10, x;
int *py;
py = &y;
x = *py;
```

The expression *"*py"* returns the values at address which held in pointer variable *py*, *i.e.*, value of variable y which is 10, and that get assigned to variable *x*.

We will learn more about the use of *addressof* (&) and indirection operators (*) in *Chapter 12*.

4.2.6.5 Conditional Operator

Consider the following segment, written in pseudocode

```
if ( a > b ) then
    set big = a
else
    set big = b
endif
```

This segments assigns the maximum of the values of *a* and *b* to *big*. As it is clear that the value assigned to variable *big* will depend on the outcome of the test condition "*a* > *b*". Such expressions are known as *conditional expressions*, and can be written using conditional operator. The syntax of using ternary operator is

```
exp1 ? exp2 : exp3;
```

where *exp1*, *exp2*, *exp3* are expressions.

The expression *exp1* is evaluated first. If it is non-zero (true), then the expression *exp2* is evaluated, and that is the value of the conditional expression; otherwise expression *exp3* is evaluated, and that is the value of the conditional expression. Note that only one of the expression *exp2* and *exp3* is evaluated.

Thus, the above pseudocode segment using conditional operator can be written as

```
big = ( a > b ) ? a : b;
```

Parentheses are not necessary around the first expression of the conditional expression since the precedence of '?:' is very low, just above assignment operator. However, the use of parentheses is recommended as they make the condition part easier to see.

4.2.6.6 Comma Operator

A comma operator is used to combine several related expressions. The group of expressions separated by comma ',' are evaluated left-to-right and the result of the right-most expression becomes the value of the total comma separated expression.

For example, the statement

```
a = ( b = 10, b+1 );
```

first assigns the value 10 to *b*, and then adds 1 to *b* and finally the resultant value, *i.e.*, 11 is assigned to *a*. In the above expression, the use of parenthesis is mandatory because the comma operator has a lower precedence than the assignment operator. In fact comma operator has the lowest precedence among all the operators.

Comma operator can be used in *for loop* to separate expressions, as shown below:

```
for ( i = 0, j = n; i < j; i++, j-- )
{
    // some code
}
```

In the above *for loop*, first variable *i* is initialized to 0 and then variable *j* is initialized to *n*, and this happens only once. Then for every subsequent iteration, first variable *i* is incremented and then variable *j* is decremented before testing the terminating condition which states that the loop will execute till the value of *i* is less than *j*.

Comma operator can also be used in *while loop* to separate expressions such as

```
while ( ch = cin.get(), ch != '\r' )
{
    // some code
}
```

In the above *while loop*, the first expression accepts a character input from the user and assigns the same character to *char* variable *ch*, then variable *ch* is tested against carriage return. If the character input is not the carriage return, the loop continues to execute for next iteration.

Following is another example of use of the comma operator to swap the values of two integer variables *x* and *y*:

```
temp = x, x = y, y = temp;
```

Variable *temp* is used as a temporary variable just to facilitate swapping of values.

4.3 EXPRESSIONS

An *expression* is a formula consisting of one or more operands and zero or more operators linked together to compute a value. An operand may be a function reference, a variable, an array element or a constant. In the expression

```
a + b
```

plus character '+' is an operator and *a* and *b* are operands.

There are four types of expressions in C. These are

1. Arithmetic expressions
2. Relational expressions
3. Logical expressions
4. Conditional expressions

Each type of expression takes certain types of operands and uses a specific set of operators. Evaluation of every expression produces a value of specific type. Expressions are not statements, but may be components of statements.

For example, consider the line

```
x = 2.0/3.0 + a * b;
```

The entire line is a statement, but the portion after the equal sign is an expression.

4.3.1 Arithmetic Expressions

An arithmetic expression is made up of operands and arithmetic operators. It produces a value that is of type *int*, *float* or *double*. When an expression involve only integral operands, it is known as *pure integer expression*, when it involves only real operands it is known as a *pure real expression*, and when it involves both integral and real operands it is known as a *mixed mode expression*.

Following are some mathematical expressions and their corresponding C expressions. For simplicity, we have considered only those expressions that don't involve the use of any mathematical or trigonometric functions.

Table 4.12: Some Sample Arithmetic Expressions

Mathematical/Algebraic Expressions	The C Arithmetic Expressions
$\frac{a+b}{2}$	`(a+b)/2`
$a+\frac{b}{c}+d$	`a+b/c+d`
$\frac{ab}{c-d^2}+d$	`(a*b)/(c-d*d)+d`
$1+\frac{a}{b+\frac{1}{c}}$	`1+a/(b+1/c)`
$\frac{\frac{a}{c+b}-e}{d}$	`a/((c+b)/d)-e`
ax^2+bx+c	`a*x*x+b*x+c`
$ut+\frac{1}{2}at^2$	`u*t+0.5*a*t*t`
$m\left(a\times h+\frac{v^2}{2}\right)$	`m*(a*h+(v*v)/2)`

While converting mathematical/algebraic expressions into C arithmetic expressions, parentheses can be used to control associativity and the order in which operators are evaluated. If parentheses are present in an expression, then the expression within the parentheses is evaluated first and within the parentheses the implicit precedence is observed. If there is nesting of parentheses (parentheses inside parentheses), then the inner most parentheses are evaluated first.

4.3.1.1 Evaluation of Arithmetic Expressions

As you know expressions are evaluated by performing one operation at a time, and same is the case when expressions are evaluated by a computer. The order of evaluation of individual operations is governed by the precedence and associativity of operators. However, when individual operations are performed, the following cases can happen:

- When both of the operands are of type integer (*short*, *int*, *long*), the integer arithmetic will be performed and the results of the operation will an integer value. For example, 5/2 will yield 2 not 2.5 as the fractional part is ignored.
- When both of the operands are of type real (*float*, *double*), the real arithmetic will be performed and the results of the operation will a real value. For example, 5.0/2.0 will yield 2.5.
- However, when one operand is of type integer and the second one is of type real, the mixed mode arithmetic will be performed. In this case, first integer operand will be converted into real operand, and then real arithmetic will be performed and the results of the operation will a real value. For example, 5/2.0 or 5.0/2 will yield 2.5, because in the first case first value 5 will be converted to 5.0 and then division will be performed while in the second case value 2 will be converted to 2.0 and then the division will be performed.

To illustrate the way arithmetic expression are evaluated, consider the following expression

```
5 * 4 / ( 1 + 5 * 2 / 3 + 6 ) + 8 * ( 7 / 4 )
```

This expression is evaluated as depicted below:

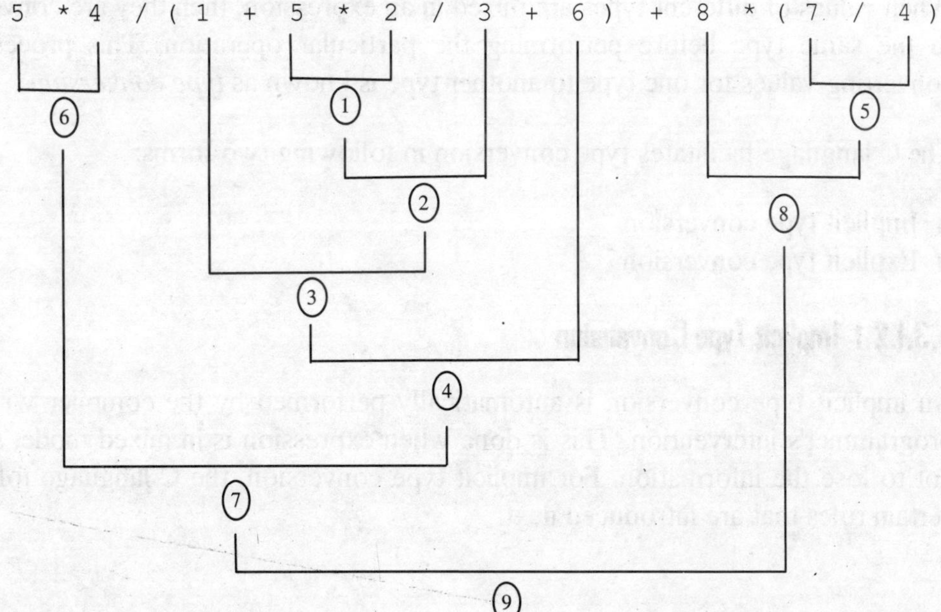

Table 4.13: Illustration of Evaluation of arithmetic expression in tabular form

Operation by Operation Evaluation of Expression	Description of Each operation
`5 * 4 / (1 + 5 * 2 / 3 + 6) + 8 * (7 / 4)`	Given expression
`5 * 4 / (1 + 10 / 3 + 6) + 8 * (7 / 4)`	5 is multiplied by 2 , giving value 10
`5 * 4 / (1 + 3 + 6) + 8 * (7 / 4)`	10 is divided by 3, giving value 3 (as a result of integer division)
`5 * 4 / (4 + 6) + 8 * (7 / 4)`	3 is added to 1, giving value 4
`5 * 4 / 10 + 8 * (7 / 4)`	6 is added to 4, giving value 10
`5 * 4 / 10 + 8 * 1`	7 is divided by 4, giving value 1 (as a result of integer division)
`20 / 10 + 8 * 1`	5 is multiplied by 4, giving 20
`2 + 8 * 1`	20 is divided by 10, giving 2
`2 + 8`	8 is multiplied by 1, giving value 8
`10`	8 is added to 2, giving value 10, which is the final value of the expression.

4.3.1.2 Type Conversion

When values of different types are mixed in an expression, then they are converted to the same type before performing the particular operation. This process of converting values for one type to another type is known as *type conversion.*

The C language facilitates type conversion in following two forms:

- Implicit type conversion
- Explicit type conversion

4.3.1.2.1 Implicit Type Conversion

An implicit type conversion is automatically performed by the compiler without programmer's intervention. This is done when expression is in mixed mode, so as not to lose the information. For implicit type conversion, the C language follows certain rules that are introduced next.

Conversion Rank

Before we discuss how conversions are handled, we will discuss the concept of conversion rank. We can assign a rank to integral and real types. The operand of larger size is given a higher rank than that of a smaller size.

Figure 4.5 shows the ranks that will be used for conversions. The *long double* has a higher rank than a *long int* while the *short* has a higher rank than a *char*.

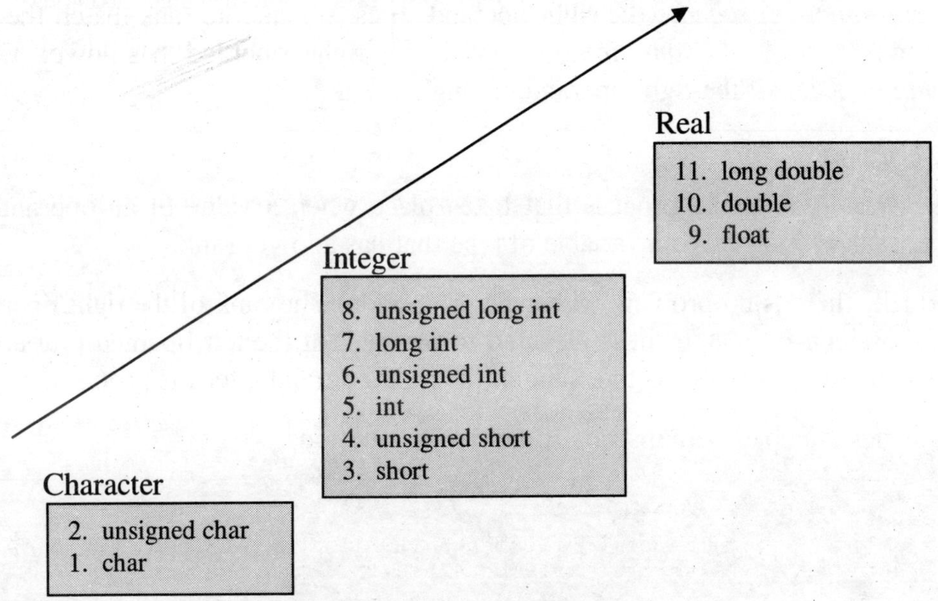

Figure 4.5: Conversion Rank

Conversion in Evaluation of Expressions

When an operation is to be performed on operands of different ranks, then operand of lower rank is converted to type so as to match the operand of higher rank. Once this conversion of the ranks is done, the operation is performed and the result of the operation will of type having higher rank.

For example, suppose variables *x* and *y* are of type *float* and variables `i` and `j` are of type *integer*, in expression:

```
x / i + y * j
```

While evaluating expression "*x/i*", integer operand *i* will be converted to *float* type and then operand *x* will be divided by *i*, and the result of the expression will be a value of type *float*.

Conversions in Assignment Statements

A simple assignment statement involves an assignment operator (=) and two operands. The operand on the left hand side of assignment operator is a variable while the operand on the right side can be a literal/constant, variable or a value after evaluation of an expression.

Depending on the difference of the rank of the operands, the C system tries to either *promote* or *demote* the right operand so as to make its rank match the left operand (variable). *Promotion* occurs if the right operand has lower rank; *demotion* occurs if the right operand has higher rank.

Type Promotion

Type promotion is the process that takes place when a value of an operand of lower rank is assigned to a variable of type that has a lower rank.

Normally there is no problem with type promotion. The rank of the right operand in the assignment statement is elevated to the rank of the left operand (variable). The value of the variable is the value of the right operand after the promotion.

Following examples demonstrate some type promotions:

```
int i;
float f;
i = 'A';      /* value of i will be 65 (ASCII code of character A */
f = 425;      /* value of f will be 425.0  */
```

Type Demotion

Type demotion is the process that takes place when a value of an operand of higher rank is assigned to a variable of type that has a lower rank. If the size of the variable on the left hand side of an assignment operator in an assignment statement can accommodate the value of the operand of higher rank, type demotion will not create any problem. The rank of the right operand in the assignment statement is de-elevated to the rank of the left operand (variable). The value of the variable is the value of the right operand after the demotion.

Following examples demonstrate some type demotions:

```
char ch;
int i;
float f;
ch = 65;      /* value of ch will be 65 which will represent the */
              /* ASCII code of character A */
i = 426.0F;/* value of i will be 426 */
f = 425.75;     /* value of f will be 425.75 */
```

4.3.1.2.2 Explicit Type Conversion

An explicit type conversion is user-defined that forces an operand or expression to be of specific type. The process of explicit type conversion is also known as *type casting*. The syntax for explicit type conversion or type casting is

```
type(operand)      OR      type(expression)
```

Here *type* in the parentheses is referred to as *cast operator*, which has a precedence of 2. As shown in the syntax, to cast data from one type to another type, we specify the new type in parentheses before the value that we want to convert.

For example, to convert variable *x* of type *int* to *float* type, we write the expression as

```
float(x)
```

It is important to note here that in this operation like any other unary operation, the value stored in *x* is still of type *int*, but the value of the expression is promoted to type *float*.

One use of the cast operator is to ensure that the result of a divide operation on integer operands results in a real number.

For example, if we want to calculate the average, which may contain fraction as well, without a cast operator, the result will be an integer number because of integer division. To force the real result, we can write the statement to compute average as

```
average = float(total) / n;
```

In this statement, there is explicit conversion of *total* to *float*, and then implicit conversion of *n* to *float*. Now real division will take place and the result will be a real number, as desired, which will be assigned to *average*.

Can you guess what will be the result of following expression when value of integer variable *x* is 4?

```
(float)(x/10)
```

You may be surprised to find the answer as 0.0. Since no conversion will take place as both the operands are integer, and therefore integer division will take place resulting into value 0 which then will be explicitly converted into 0.0.

To get a real result, the expression should be written as

```
(float) x / 10      or      x / (float) 10
```

Casting can also be useful in many other situations; one of such situation is to round-off a given real value, where the expression can be written as

```
x = int( ( y + 0.5 ) );
```

Suppose *y* is 20.6, (*y*+0.5) will be 21.5, which on casting become 21, the value that will be assigned to *x*.

Casting is also very frequently used with the library functions, which we will discuss in the next section. Majority of the library function takes arguments of type *double* and also return value of type *double*. Therefore, if argument(s) for the library functions is/are of type other than double, they must be casted so that they are converted to type *double* before use. Likewise, the value returned may need to casted to appropriate type before being further used.

For example, to convert variable *x* of type *int* to *float* type, we write expression as

```
y = cos( double(x) );
```

where *cos* is a library function to compute cosine of an argument.

4.3.2 Relational Expressions

Relational expressions compare the values of two operands. A relational expression is used to test a condition in order to decide whether an action should be taken or not. In relational expression, an arithmetic value should not be compared with a string value. Result of a relational expression is either zero or non-zero. Here, non-zero value is equivalent to a boolean *true* and zero to a boolean *false*.

Table 4.14: Sample Relational Expressions

Relation Expression	Description
`x % 2 == 0`	Used to test whether the operand *x* is an even number or not. The relational expression results in value 1 if *x* is even otherwise results in value 0.
`a != b`	Used to test whether the operands *a* is not the same as *b*. The relational expression results in value 1 if *a* is different from *b* otherwise results in value 0.
`a + b == x + y`	Used to test whether value of expression "*a*+*b*" is equal to the value of expression "*x*+*y*" or not.
`x >= 35`	Used to test whether the operand *x* is greater than or equal to 35. The relational expression results in value 1 if *x* is greater than or equal to 35 otherwise results in value 0.

Relational expressions with arithmetic operands may have one operand of *int* type and one of *float* type. In this case, the *int* operand is converted to *float* type before the relational expression is evaluated.

4.3.3 Logical Expressions

A logical expression also produces a zero or non-zero value. A logical expression is used to form a complex test condition in order to take a decision. For example, an assurance company has framed an assurance policy that states like

> *"Assure a person if he is married or his/her age is more than 30 years"*

Suppose marital status of a person is denoted by value '0' if unmarried and '1' if married. Let us further suppose that we use character variable *status* to store this value, and integer variable *age* is used to store age of the person. Then, these two conditions separately can be written as

> **Condition 1** : status = '1'
>
> **Condition 2** : age ≥ 30

So according to the company's policy, the person is eligible for assurance, if at least one of the two conditions is satisfied.

In pseudo-language, the above decision criteria can written as

```
if ( ( status = '1' ) or ( age ≥ 30 ) ) then
   Insure the person
else
   Person not eligible for insurance
endif
```

The above test condition for Assurance Company can be written as

```
status == '1'  ||  age >= 30
```

Table 4.15: Sample Logical Expressions

Logical Expression	Description
`( x > 2 ) && ( x % 2 == 0 )`	Used to form a test condition to check whether the operand *x* is greater than 2 and x is even (divisible by 2). The result of this test condition will be 1 only if both the conditions hold true simultaneously.

Table 4.15: Sample Logical Expressions *contd.*

Logical Expression	Description
`age >= 40 || sex == 'F'`	Used to form a test condition to check whether the operand *age* is greater than or equal to 40 or sex is 'F' (for female). The result of this test condition will be 1 only if either or both the conditions hold true.
`! ( x > 5 ) && ( y == 0 )`	Used to form a test condition to check whether the operand *x* is not greater than 5 and *y* is equal to 0. The result of this test condition will be 1 only if both the conditions hold true simultaneously.

4.3.4 Conditional Expressions

Note that the conditional expression is indeed an expression, and can be used wherever any other expression can be. A conditional expression looks like

```
exp1 ? exp2 : exp3
```

where *exp1* is a simple or compound condition; *exp2* and *exp3* are any other kind of expressions. The final value of this conditional expression depends on the outcome of condition represented by *exp1*. If condition *exp1* evaluates zero (true), then value of the condition expressional will be as represented by *exp2* otherwise as represented by *exp3*. Since, the final value of condition expression depends on the outcome of condition, hence its name.

For example, in the following condition expression

```
big  = a > b ? a : b;
```

it will assume value of *a* if *a* > *b* else as of *b*, and this value of conditional expression is then assigned to variable *big*.

Note that the use of parentheses are not necessary around the first expression of the conditional expression since the precedence of '?:' is very low, just above assignment operator. However, the use of parentheses is recommended as they make the condition part of the expression easier to see.

The above statement using parentheses can be written as

```
big  = ( a > b ) ? a : b;
```

Table 4.16: Sample Conditional Expressions

Logical Expression	Description
`(a%2==0)?1:0`	The conditional expression takes value 1 if *a* is divisible by 2 otherwise it takes value 0.
`(a>b)?((a>c)?a:c):((b>c)?b:c)`	The conditional expression takes largest of the three number (*a*, *b* and *c*) as its value.
`(x>y)? x--: y++`	Decrement *x* if *x* is greater than *y* else increment *y*.

4.4 ASSIGNMENT STATEMENTS

As we know that an expression is a formula consisting of one or more operands and zero or more operators linked together to compute a value. These computed values are to be stored in a variable for future use. This is done by using an *assignment statement*. The C language supports variety of assignment statements.

These are

- Simple assignment statement
- Multiple assignment statement
- Shorthand assignment statement

4.4.1 Simple Assignment Statement

The syntax of simple assignment statement is

```
var = exp;
```

where *var* is a variable or array element reference; *exp* is any expression; and '=' is an *assignment operator.*

The unique feature about C is that it treats assignment operator in a way it treats other operators. For example, the following statement

```
printf( "\nValue of c = %d\n", c = a + b );
```

will be valid. This statement first assigns the sum of variables *a* and *b* of type *int* to variable *c*, also of type *int*, and then the value of variable *c* is printed. The type of the variable or array element and the type of the expression must be compatible.

The following are valid assignment statements:

(Given *a, b, c, y, x, disc* are *float* variables)

(*a*) `a = 5.0;`
(*b*) `y = 4.0 * x + 7.5;`
(*c*) `disc = b * b - 4.0 * a * c;`
(*d*) `x = y;`

The following are invalid assignment statements with the reasons indicated:

(Given *a, b, c, y* are real variables)

(*a*) `b + c = a;` (*b* + *c* is not a valid variable)
(*b*) `abs(a) = x;` (abs(*a*) is not a valid variable)
(*c*) `y = 'R';` (*y* is not a character variable)

4.4.2 Multiple Assignment Statement

If the same value is to be assigned to different variable of same type, the usual way is to use different assignment statement for each variable. However, C language permits us to assign the same value to more than one variable using multiple assignment statement. The syntax of a multiple assignment statement is

```
v1 = v2 = v3 = exp;
```

where *v1*, *v2*, and *v3* are variables of same type; and exp is a literal, variable or expression.

The order of assigning the value is from right-to-left. For example, the following statement assigns value 0 to variables *a*, *b*, *c*, and *d*.

```
a = b = c = d = 0;
```

4.4.3 Shorthand Assignment Statement

Consider the following assignment statements

```
a = a + 5;
a = a / j;
```

Its purpose is to increase the value of *a* by factor of 5, *i.e.*, add value 5 to the current value of variable *a* and assign the new value to *a* itself.

Similarly, in the second assignment statement, the value of *a* is divided by *j*, and the result is again stored in *a*.

Such types of assignment statements are known as *self replacement* statements as the value of one of the variables of the assignment statement is being replaced with a new value.

The same task can also be accomplished using following statements

```
a += 5;
a /= j;
```

The '+=' and '/=' (in general "op=" operator) are called *shorthand assignment operators*, and the entire statements is known as arithmetic assignment statements.

Table 4.17: Use of shorthand assignment operators

Assignment statement with simple assignment operator	Assignment statement with shorthand assignment operator
`k = k + m;`	`k += m;`
`k = k - m;`	`k -= m;`
`k = k * m;`	`k *= m;`
`k = k / ( n + 1 );`	`k /= ( n + 1 );`
`k = k % b;`	`k %= b;`

Only arithmetic and bitwise operators can be combined with the assignment operator.

4.5 LIBRARY FUNCTIONS

Quite often it is necessary to evaluate several mathematical functions that are used quite frequently, such as square root, logarithms, exponentials, etc. They are written and incorporated into the C language. Rather than each user writes these subprograms, C compiler provides these built-in library functions as a convenience.

The programmer has to include *math.h* header file in his program unit. In addition to these functions, there are many other library functions that perform specialized functions, and are defined in different header files. For example, library functions that manipulate strings are defined in *string.h*.

Arguments to certain library functions are limited by the definition of the function. For example, the logarithm of a negative number is mathematically undefined. Similarly, the square root of a negative number is mathematically undefined, and therefore not permitted.

4.5.1 Description of Some Mathematical Functions

The following table describes some popular and frequently used mathematical functions. The user must include header file *math.h* in the program in order to use these functions.

Table 4.18: Some Commonly Used Mathematical Functions

Function	Description
pow(x,y)	Returns *x* raised to power *y, i.e.*, x^y .
pow10(p)	Returns the value 10^p .
exp(x)	Returns *e* to the *xth* power, *i.e.*, e^x .
log(x)	Returns the value of $ln(x)$.
log10(x)	Returns the value of $log10(x)$.
sqrt(x)	Returns the value of $\sqrt{x}$.
sin(x)	Returns the value sine of *x*, where the angle *x* is in radians.
ceil(x)	Returns the smallest integer greater than or equal to *x*.
floor(x)	Returns largest integer less than or equal to *x*.
ploy(x,n, coeffs[])	Returns the value of the polynomial in *x*, of degree *n*, with coefficients *coeffs*[0], *coeffs*[1], . . ., *coeffs*[*n*].

4.5.2 Description of Some Console Handling Functions

Console (screen) related functions are defined in *conio.h*. By default, the screen is set in text mode consisting of 25 rows, and 80 character positions on each row. The user must include header file *conio.h* in the program in order to use these functions.

Table 4.19: Some Commonly Used Console Handling Functions
(*applicable only for Turbo C/C++ Compiler*)

Function	Descriptiom
window(left. top, right, bottom)	Defines active text mode window. The left top corner of text screen is (1,1). By default, active text window is entire screen.
clrscr()	Clears the active text window
gotoxy(x,y)	Positions the cursor in text position at (*x*, *y*), *i.e.*, x^{th} row, and y^{th} column.
textcolor(color)	Sets new character color in text mode.
textbackground(color)	Sets new text background color in text mode.

Turbo C/C++'s IDE provides very good features, and I personally feel every C/C++ programmer must be familiar with it. These features are in the form of on-line help. To know about any library function in detail, just type the name of the function, position the cursor on the name and press *Ctrl+F1*, you will the entire details. Even the Turbo C++ compiler goes one step further by providing examples that illustrate the use of the functions.

4.6 QUICK RECAP

In this chapter, we have learnt that

- The C language supports large number of operators that include increment & decrement operators, bit-wise operators, address operator, indirection operator, and conditional operator.
- The C language supports variety of assignment statements.
- There is a precedence of operators that determines the evaluation of expressions.
- Library functions are the most frequently used functions and are provided as a part of the language so that programmer can directly use them instead of writing their own.
- Type casting or simply called casting is the way we force the conversion of value of a variable or expression to be of particular by prefixing appropriate data type in parenthesis.

4.7 MULTIPLE CHOICE QUESTIONS

1. Which of the following is not an arithmetic operator?

   (*a*) + (*b*) &
   (*c*) % (*d*) *

2. Precedence of operators determines which operator

   (*a*) is used first (*b*) is important
   (*c*) operates on largest numbers (*d*) executes fast

3. The operator % can be applied to

   (*a*) Float values (*b*) Double values
   (*c*) Integral values (*d*) All

4. Expression *x* % *y* is equivalent to

   (*a*) (*x*–(*x*/*y*)) (*b*) (*x*–(*x*/*y*)**y*)
   (*c*) (*y*–(*y*/*x*)) (*d*) (*y*–(*x*/*y*)**x*)

5. Which of the following is not a bit-wise operator?

   (*a*) > (*b*) >>
   (*c*) ^ (*d*) &

6. What will be the value of expression 5 / 6 / 3 + 8 / 3?

   (*a*) 4 (*b*) 2
   (*c*) 2.333 (approx.) (*d*) None

7. In expression *x* / *y*, the value of *y* should be

   (*a*) integer (*b*) non-zero
   (*c*) non-negative (*d*) positive

8. If *x* is a variable of type *int*, which of the following is odd?

   (*a*) *x* << 1 (*b*) *x* = *x* * 2
   (*c*) *x* *= 2 (*d*) *x* <<= 1

9. Consider the following statement in C language

```
x = (a > b) ? ((a > c) ? a : c) : (b > c) ? b : c;
```

   What will be the value of *x* if $a = 3$, $b = -5$, $c = 2$?

   (*a*) 2 (*b*) 3
   (*c*) –5 (*d*) None

10. When a relational expression is false, it has the value _____.

   (*a*) 1 (*b*) 0
   (*c*) –ve (*d*) +ve

11. What will be result if we attempt to compile and execute the following program?

```
#include<stdio.h>
void main()
{
    int y;
    y = 0x10 + 10 + 010;
    printf( "%d", y);
}
```

   (*a*) Code will not compile & compiler will complain about expression "0x10+10+010"
   (*b*) Program will execute and output value 30
   (*c*) Program will execute and output value 34
   (*d*) Program will execute and output value 1010010

12. If *a* = 15 then the statement *b* = *a* << 2; will result in

   (*a*) 30 (*b*) 60
   (*c*) 7 (*d*) None

13. The result of expression ~~7 is

(*a*) 7 (*b*) 1
(*c*) 0 (*d*) None

14. Which of the following is used for exclusive OR operation?

(*a*) << (*b*) |
(*c*) ^ (*d*) &

15. What is the value of *x* after executing the statement?

```
X = 011 | 0x10;
```

(*a*) 25 (*b*) 50
(*c*) 10 (*d*) 15

16. Consider the following code segment

```
int i, j = 10;
i = ++j;
```

The value of *i* and *j* at the end of this segment will be

(*a*) 10, 10 (*b*) 10, 11
(*e*) 11, 10 (*d*) 11, 11

17. Consider the following code segment

```
int x = 6, y = 5, z = -3;
z = ( x == 6 || ++y );
```

The value of *x*, *y* and *z* at the end of this segment will be

(*a*) 6, 6, 1 (*b*) 6, 6, 0
(*c*) 6, 5, 1 (*d*) 6, 5, 0

18. Consider the following code segment

```
int x, y, z;
z = ( x = 5, y = 6, x * y );
```

The value of *z* at the end of this segment will be

(*a*) 5 (*b*) 6
(*c*) 30 (*d*) None

19. Consider the following code segment

```
int x = 5.234, y;
y = sizeof(x);
```

The value of *y* will be

(*a*) 4 (*b*) 2
(*c*) 8 (*d*) Syntax error

4.8 REVIEW EXERCISES

1. List various types of operators available in C language and also give their precedence, if any.
2. Suppose *x*, *y*, and *z* have been declared variables of type *float*, write a C segment which changes the values of *x*, *y*, and *z* so that *x* has *y*'s value, *y* has *z*'s value, and *z* has *x*'s value.
3. In order to store the result of the computation, which statement must be used?
4. What are various forms of assignment statement in C?
5. Which of the following statements are not valid and why?

   (*a*) `float = area * pie * 0.05;` (*b*) `c = 5 / 9 ( f - 32 );`
   (*c*) `pie * r * r = area;` (*d*) `si = p * r * t / 100;`
   (*e*) `area = 3.141 * r ** 2;`
6. Find the value of each of the following expressions.

   (*a*) `3 - 5 * 2.5` (*b*) `10 / ( 2 * 3 )`
   (*c*) `22 % 3 * 12 / 3` (*d*) `( 3 / 7 ) / ( 6 / 5 )`
7. What is the role played by parentheses in expressions?
8. What is the effect of dividing an integer value by a real value? What is this effect called?
9. How would you use the *cast operator* to convert expression `(7*12/10)` to double type?
10. Write C expressions equivalent to the following algebraic expressions:

    (*a*) $a - \frac{a}{a^{-x}} + b$ (*b*) $1 + \frac{1}{a + \frac{1}{a}} + b$ (*c*) $x + \frac{y^{-z}}{k} - \sqrt{x}$

    (*d*) $x^3 - \frac{y^7}{-z} + e^x$ (*e*) $\left(\frac{1-x}{1+x}\right) / \left(\frac{1+y}{1-y}\right)$ (*f*) $\frac{1}{r} = \frac{1}{r_1} + \frac{1}{r_2}$

    (*g*) $\sqrt{\left(x^2 + y^2 + z^2\right)^3}$ (*h*) $\frac{-b - \sqrt{b^2 - 4ac}}{2a}$

❑ ❑ ❑

5 Standard Input/Output

Learning Objectives

After reading this chapter, students will have the ability to:

- standard Input/Output facility provided by C I/O subsystem
- working of character I/O functions
- working of string I/O functions
- working of formatted I/O functions
- various features to format the output

5.1 INTRODUCTION

In almost every computer program, the users have to input some data that will be stored in computer's memory, and then subsequently processed. This input data may be from a keyboard, a disk file, or from another computer via a communication channel. The intermediate and final results of the computations are also stored in computer's memory. And finally, there is need to output the results of the computations so that user can use them in their day-to-day work. The output can be displayed on the computer screen, stored on a disk, or transmitted via a communication channel to other computer.

In microcomputers (PCs), the common input device is the keyboard and the output device is a computer screen, sometimes called the *monitor*. This subsystem comprising keyboard and monitor is referred to as a *console*.

The various forms of input and output, abbreviated as I/O, obviously are very different. It would have been easier if all these forms of I/O can be handled in a unified manner as they are handled in other high level languages, such as in Pascal and FORTRAN. But one of the objectives of Dennis Ritchie, developer of C, was to have C language as compact as possible. Therefore, he deliberately omitted I/O statements that generate extra overhead. Instead, every C compiler provides several I/O functions that can be linked with any C program. Though, these I/O functions are not part of C's formal definition, they have become a standard feature of C language.

This chapter describes the various I/O functions that perform the input from a standard input device and output to a standard output device. To use entire range of I/O functions, we need to include header file named *stdio.h* in all our programs.

5.2 STANDARD INPUT/OUTPUT

When a C program begins execution, it has access to the following pre-defined files:

- The first one, known as the *standard input* (*stdin*), is the file from which input is received. This file is usually a keyboard, but it can also be redirected to obtain input from a disk file or other device.
- The second one, known as *standard output* (*stdout*), is the file to which output is directed. The file is usually a computer screen, but it can be redirected to a disk file or to another device.

- The third one, known as *standard error* (*stderr*), is the file used to keep error messages separate from program's output. For example, if output is going to a disk file, the standard error file can be a computer screen, so that the user sees error messages immediately.

5.3 STANDARD I/O FUNCTIONS

There are many library functions available for standard I/O. These functions are divided into two categories:

- unformatted
- formatted

The only difference between these functions is that the formatted functions permit the input from a standard input device or output sent to a standard output device to be formatted as per requirements. For example, if different values are to be displayed, how much field width i.e. how many columns on screen, is to be used, and how much space between two values is to be given. If a value to be displayed is of real type, then how many decimal places to output.

5.3.1 Unformatted I/O Functions

In the unformatted I/O category, we have functions for performing input/output of one character at a time, known as *character I/O functions* and functions that perform input/output of one string at a time, known as *string I/O functions*. These functions are described in the next sections.

5.3.1.1 Character I/O Functions

For character input, the functions is *getchar()* that is available in all versions of C language. In addition, Turbo C provides two more versions of character input functions in the form of *getche()*, and *getch()*. For character output, the function available is *putchar()*.

***getchar() function*:** This function returns a character that has been recently typed. The typed character is echoed to the computer screen. After typing the appropriate character, the user is required to press *Enter* key.

***putchar() function*:** This function output a character constant or a character variable to the standard output device.

Following character input functions are only supported by Turbo C/C++ Compilers

getche() function: Like *getchar()* function, this function also returns a character that has been recently typed. The typed character is also echoed to the computer screen. But the user is not required to press *Enter* key after typing a character. The advantage of this function over *getchar()* function is that as soon as the user types a character, the character is immediately accepted. In reduces the user's action to single key.

getch() function: This function too returns a character that has been recently typed. But, neither the user is required to press *Enter* key after entering the character nor the typed character is echoed to the computer screen. This function has advantages over the other functions in the applications where the user wants to hide the input.

This input is usually the password used for system security. A *password* is a secret word or a code set by the programmer in case of software or assigned by a system administrator of a multi-user system or a computer network to the individual users. Whenever they want to use that particular software or want to work on that particular system, they have to enter their password. If their password is valid, they will be permitted to use the software or system.

The next program illustrates the working of all these functions. In this program, to display user prompt, the *printf()* function, which will be described in the later sections, is used.

Listing 5.1

```
/* Program to illustrate working of character I/O functions  */
#include <stdio.h>

int main(void)
{
   char ch;

   printf( "\nEnter any character: " );
   ch = getchar();
   printf( "\nCharacter you typed is " );
   putchar(ch);

   printf( "\nEnter any other character: " );
   ch = getche();
   printf( "\nCharacter you typed is " );
```

```
    putchar(ch);
    printf( "\nEnter any other character: " );
    ch = getch();
    printf( "\nCharacter you typed is " );
    putchar(ch);
    return 0;
}
```

Test Run

```
Enter any character: A
Character you typed is A
Enter any other character: x
Character you typed is x
Enter any other character:
Character you typed is H
```

5.3.1.2 String I/O Functions

For string input, the function is *gets()* is used, and for string output, the function is *puts()* is used.

gets() function: This function accepts a string from the standard input device. The length of the string is limited by the declaration of the string variable. The input string may consist of multiple words. Typing Enter key completes the input.

puts() function: This function outputs a string constant or a string variable to the standard output device. The following program illustrates the working of these string I/O functions.

Listing 5.2

```
/* Program to illustrate working of string I/O functions  */
#include <stdio.h>
void main()
{
    char str[31];
    printf( "\nEnter string of length <= 30: " );
    gets( str );
    printf( "\nString you typed is " );
    puts( str );
}
```

Test Run

```
Enter string of length <= 30: string input
String you typed is string input
```

5.3.2 Formatted I/O Functions

In the formatted I/O category, we have *scanf()* function for input and *printf()* function for output. The working of these functions is described in this section.

5.3.2.1 The *scanf()* Function

This function allows us to input data in a fixed format. Its syntax is

```
scanf( "format string", list of addresses of variables );
```

where the *format string* contains the format specifiers that begin with character '%' and are, usually, separated by space or comma.

It returns the number of items read from the keyboard.

Table 5.1 lists various format specifiers used with *scanf()* function. The list of addresses of variables are used so that *scanf()* function can place the data received from a standard input device. The address of a variable is obtained by using address operator, character '&' and pronounced as *addressof* operator.

Table 5.1: List of Format Specifiers

Format Specifier	Used For
%d	signed decimal integer
%ld	signed long decimal integer
%u	unsigned decimal integer
%f	single precision floating real number
%lf	double precision floating real number
%e	floating point (exponential notation)
%x	unsigned hexadecimal integer
%o	unsigned octal integer
%c	single character
%s	single-word string
%[^\n]s	multi-word string

On execution, the input data must be supplied strictly according to the specified format string otherwise results can be very strange. This strange behavior is illustrated next.

Consider the following segment:

```
int a;
float b;
char c;
 :
scanf( "%d,%f,%c", &a, &b, &c );
 :
```

Suppose that the input data is 20 for *a*, 50.25 for *b*, and character 'A' for *c*.

The data must be entered or typed in the following format

```
20,50.25,A
```

In case, if your enter the data as

```
20 50.25 A
```

results can be very surprising.

5.3.2.1.1 Limitation of *scanf()* Function

Consider the following statement

```
scanf( "%d", &intVariable );
```

If we input the value as

```
75.50
```

the *scanf()* function will accept 75 only.

Similarly, in the following statement

```
scanf( "%f", &floatVariable );
```

If we input the value as

```
25
```

the *scanf()* function will store this value as 25.0 i.e. integer value is converted to a real value.

However, in the following statement

```
scanf( "%d,%f", &intVariable, &floatVariable );
```

If we input the above values as

```
75.50,25
```

the *scanf()* function will store a value 75 in *intVariable* but the value of the *floatVariable* will be unpredictable.

5.3.2.2 The *printf()* Function

The *printf()* function allows to output the data in a fixed format. Its general form looks like

```
printf( "format string", list of variables );
```

where the *format string* contains the format specifiers, the sequences that begin with character '\' (back slash), known as *escape sequences*, and the text to be output along with the output data.

It returns the number of characters displayed in the output.

All the format specifiers used with *scanf()* function are valid for *printf()* function. Another format specifier "%p" is used to print the value of a pointer variable in hexadecimal notation. Table 5.2 lists common *escape sequences.*

Table 5.2: Common Escape Sequences

Escape Sequence	Represents	Effect
\n	newline	has the effect of both a carriage return and linefeed, *i.e.*, the subsequent output starts from new line.
\t	tab	moves over to the next eight-space-wide field.
\b	backspace	moves the cursor one space left.
\r	carriage return	carriage return.
\f	formfeed	advances to the top of the next page on printer.
\a	beep	produces one audio tone of the speaker
\'	single quote	insert character ' in the output
\"	double quote	insert character " in the output
\\	Backslash	insert character \ in the output

Consider the following segment:

```
int a = 15;
float b = 23.75;
char c = 'V';
     :
printf( "%d,%f,%c", a, b, c );
     :
```

The output of the above segment will look like

```
15,23.75,V
```

But if the segment is written like

```
int a = 15;
float b = 23.75;
char c = 'V';
     :
printf( "%d%f%c", a, b, c );
     :
```

The output of the above segment will look like

```
1523.75V
```

Needless to say, the output in this form is very difficult to understand.

The above segment can also be written as

```
int a = 15;
float b = 23.75;
char c = 'V';
   :
printf("\nValue of a=%d\nValue of b=%f\nValue of c=%c",
       a, b, c );
   :
```

The output of the above segment will look like

```
Value of a=15
Value of a=23.75
Value of a=V
```

You must have noticed that, in the later case the output is self-explanatory and is the preferred way for the output.

Let us see how the *printf()* function interprets the format string.

We will consider the following example of *printf()* function

```
printf( "\nValue of a = %d\nValue of b = %f\n", a, b );
```

Let us further assume that $a = 15$, and $b = 23.46$.

The *printf()* function examines the format string from left to right. It keeps on sending the characters to the standard output device until it encounters either character '%' or character '\'. The moment it encounters character %, it picks up the corresponding variable and outputs its value in the specified format. Similarly, the moment the character '\' is encountered, it indicates the presence of escape sequence, the action taken will depend on the next character.

In our example, the first character is '\', and the next character is *n*, so the action of '\n' is to insert *newline* character so that subsequent output can continue from the next line. So the string

```
Value of a =
```

is send to the standard output device, and then character % is encountered following by character *d*, so it picks up the variable *a* and print its value. The output up to this stage appears as

```
Value of a = 15
```

As the scanning of the format string continues, it finds another *newline* character, and the subsequent output is sent to the next line up to % character. Up to this the output appears as

```
Value of a = 15
Value of b =
```

Now it picks up the second variable and outputs its value, and after outputting the value of variable *b*, it finds another *newline* character that causes the subsequent output to be sent to the next line. The final output appears as

```
Value of a = 15
Value of b = 23.46
```

5.3.2.2.1 More About *printf()* Function

As you must have observed in the output of the above program that the *printf()* function outputs six decimal digits for a real value, because in the format specifier we have not specified any additional information. In general, to have a control over the output, we can pass additional information to the *printf()* function.

With this additional information, the format specifier for a real value takes the form

```
%w.df
```

where *w* is the total width or space used for outputting a real value including decimal point and the number of decimal digits; and *d* is the number of decimal digits to be outputted.

This field width is the minimum width to be used. If the real value is small, the output value is right justified in the field and if the value can not be accommodated in the specified field width, then the field width is assumed to be large enough to accommodate the output value.

Similarly for a integer value, it takes the form

```
%wd
```

For a string value, it takes the form

```
%ws
```

By default, the output value is always right justified in the field.

The output value can be left justified in the field by writing hyphen '–' after character % as shown below

```
%-5d
```

In this case, the corresponding value will appear left justified i.e. if the value is small, it will be padded with blanks on the right. To fix these ideas, let us consider an example.

Consider the following segment

```
    :
    :
int a = 123;
float b = 123.564;
char name[20] = "Language";
    :
    :

printf( ":%d:   :%f:   :%s:\n", a, b, name);
printf( ":%6d:   :%8.2f:   :%20s:\n", a, b, name);
printf( ":%-6d:   :%-8.2f:   :%-20s:\n", a, b, name);
    :
    :
```

The output of this segment will appear as

```
:123:   :123.564:   :Language:
:    123:   :    123.56:   :                Language:
:123    :   :123.56    :   :Language                :
```

5.4 SUPPLEMANTARY PROBLEMS

Let us write a few example programs to use the features that we have learned so far.

Problem 5.1:

Program to find the sum of digits of a given 4-digit positive integer number.

Listing 5.3

```
/*
*  Program to find sum of digits of a 4-digit positive
*  integer number
*/
#include<stdio.h>
int main(void)
{
   int number, sum, digit1, digit2, digit3;
   int digit4, temporary;
   printf( "\nEnter 4-digit positive number: ");
   scanf( "%d", &number );
   temporary = number;
   digit1 = temporary % 10;
   temporary /= 10;
   digit2 = temporary % 10;
   temporary /= 10;
   digit3 = temporary % 10;
   temporary /= 10;
   digit4 = temporary % 10;
   sum = digit1 + digit2 + digit3 + digit4;
   printf( "\n\nSum of digits of %d = %d\n", number, sum );
   return 0;
}
```

Test Run

```
Enter 4-digit positive number: 2375
Sum of digits of 2375 = 17
```

Problem 5.2:

Program to reverses the digits of a given 4-digit positive integer number.

Listing 5.4

```
/*
*  Program to print 4-digit positive integer number in
*  reverse order
*/
#include<stdio.h>
int main(void)
{
  int number, sum, digit1, digit2, digit3;
  int digit4, temporary;
  printf( "\nEnter 4-digit positive number: ");
  scanf( "%d", &number );
  temporary = number;
  digit1 = temporary % 10;
  temporary /= 10;
  digit2 = temporary % 10;
  temporary /= 10;
  digit3 = temporary % 10;
  temporary /= 10;
  digit4 = temporary % 10;
  sum = digit1*1000+digit2*100+digit3*10+digit4;
  printf( "\nNumber after reversing digits of %d is %d\n",
          number, sum );
  return 0;
}
```

Test Run

```
Enter 4-digit positive number : 2375
Number after reversing the digits of 2375 is 5732
```

Problem 5.3:

Program to convert time in seconds to time in hours, minutes and seconds.

Listing 5.5

```
/*
*   Program to convert time in seconds to time in hours,
*   Minutes and seconds
*/
#include<stdio.h>
void main()
{
  int seconds,minutes, hours, total_seconds, temp;
```

```
  printf( "\nEnter time in seconds: " );
  scanf( "%d", &total_seconds );

  temp = total_seconds;
  hours = temp / 3600;
  temp %= 3600;
  minutes = temp / 60;
  seconds = temp % 60;

  printf( "\nTime in %d seconds = ", total_seconds);
  printf( "%d hour(s),%d minute(s) & %d secs.\n", hours,
          minutes,seconds );
}
```

Test Run

```
Enter time in seconds: 3678
Time in 3678 seconds=1 hour(s),1 minute(s) & 18 secs.
```

Problem 5.4:

Program to compute the area of a triangle whose sides are given.

Suppose that length of the sides is *a*, *b* and *c*, then area of triangle is given by formula

$$\text{Area of triangle} = \sqrt{s(s\text{-}a)(s\text{-}b)(s-c)}, \text{ where } s = \frac{a+b+c}{2}$$

Listing 5.6

```
/*  Program to find area of triangle whose sides are given  */
#include<stdio.h>
#include<math.h>

void main()
{
  float sideA, sideB, sideC, s, area;
  printf( "Enter side A: " );
  scanf( "%f", &sideA );
  printf( "Enter side B: " );
  scanf( "%f", &sideB );
  printf( "Enter side C: " );
  scanf( "%f", &sideC );
  s = ( sideA + sideB + sideC ) / 2;
  area = sqrt((double)(s*(s-sideA)*(s-sideB)*(s-sideC)));
  printf( "\nArea of triangle: %.3f\n", area );
}
```

Test Run

```
Enter side A: 3
Enter side B: 3
Enter side C: 3

Area of triangle: 3.897
```

The program is run for an equilateral triangle with each side equal to 3 units.

Problem 5.5:

On an amount of rupees, say *P*, program to compute simple interest and compound interest if the interest rate is *R%* annually and the time is *N* years.

We know that formulae to compute simple interest and compound interest are

$$\text{Simple interest } (si) = \frac{P \times R \times N}{100}$$

$$\text{Compound interest } (ci) = P\left(1 + \frac{R}{100}\right)^N - P$$

Listing 5.7

```
/*
*    Program to compute simple interest & compound interest
*/
#include<stdio.h>
#include<math.h>
void main()
{
  float p, r, n, si, ci;
  printf( "Enter amount: " );
  scanf( "%f", &p );
  printf( "Enter rate of interest: " );
  scanf( "%f", &r );
  printf( "Enter time: " );
  scanf( "%f", &n );
  si = ( p * r * n ) / 100;
  ci = p * pow((double)1.0+r/100, (double)n ) - p;
  printf( "\nSimple Interest    : %.2f\n", si );
  printf( "\nCompound Interest: %.2f\n", ci );
}
```

Test Run

```
Enter amount: 100
Enter rate of interest: 5
Enter time: 5

Simple Interest  : 25.00
Compound Interest: 27.63
```

Problem 5.6:

Program that reads a lowercase alphabet and prints it in uppercase.

Note that characters are internally represented using ASCII code. The ASCII for lowercase alphabet letters (*a-z*) is 97 decimal to122 and for uppercase alphabet letters (*A-Z*) it is 65 to 90. It means that the ASCII code of lowercase alphabet letters is more by a factor of 32 than corresponding uppercase alphabet letters. Therefore, given a lowercase alphabet letter, by subtracting a value of 32, we get corresponding uppercase alphabet letter.

The following program does this.

Listing 5.8

```
/*
*   Program to reads a lowercase character and outputs it as
*   uppercase character
*/
#include<stdio.h>
void main()
{
  char ch;
  printf( "Enter lowercase alphabet letter: " );
  ch = getchar();
  ch = ch - 32;
  printf( "\nUppercase alphabet letter:  %c\n", ch );
}
```

Test Run

```
Enter lowercase alphabet letter: a

Uppercase alphabet letter: A
```

Problem 5.7:

Program that reads a decimal integer number and prints it equivalent octal number without doing any explicit conversion.

Note that integer numbers (in general all kind of data) are internally represented as binary numbers whether you input as decimal number, octal number or hexadecimal number. The stored binary integer number can be printed either as decimal number, octal number or hexadecimal number using *d*, *o* and *x* specifier in the *printf()* function. The following program does this.

Listing 5.9

```
/*
*  Program that reads decimal integer number and
*  prints it as octal integer number
*/
#include<stdio.h>
void main()
{
  int number;
  printf( "Enter decimal integer number: " );
  scanf("%d", &number );
  printf( "\nEquivalent octal number:  %o\n", number );
}
```

Test Run

```
Enter decimal integer number: 250

Equivalent octal number: 372
```

5.5 QUICK RECAP

In this chapter, we have learnt that

- Input/output is a vital part of every program.
- By default, every C program has access to *stdin*, *stdout* and *stderr* files.
- Input/output in a C program can be formatted or unformatted.
- There are no input/output statements in C. Instead, C language provides specialized function to perform input/output of character and string data.
- In general, it is not possible to read multi-word string with *scanf()* function.
- Using escape sequences, we can format the output as per our requirements.

5.6 MULTIPLE CHOICE QUESTIONS

1. What will be the output of the following code?

```
printf( "%d", 'B' );
```

(*a*) 66 (*b*) B
(*c*) b (*d*) Error

2. What will be the output of the following code?

```
float x = 1 / 2.0 - 1 / 2;
printf( "%.2f", x );
```

(*a*) 0.00 (*b*) 0.50
(*c*) 0.25 (*d*) 1.00

3. What is the function of character hyphen '–' when used after the character % in the field specifier?

(*a*) To print the output left justified (*b*) To print '–' character before output
(*c*) To print the output right justified (*d*) None

4. Which of the following function will prefer to use in case you want to provide the password facility in your program for security purposes?

(*a*) getchar() (*b*) getch()
(*c*) scanf() (*d*) gets()

5. Every escape sequence begins with character

(*a*) % (*b*) /
(*c*) \ (*d*) –

6. If *x* = 12.4568, what value will be printed if the *printf()* function is used as?

```
printf( "%.3f", x );
```

(*a*) 12.457 (*b*) 12.000
(*c*) 12.456 (*d*) 12.4568

7. What will be the output of the following segment of code?

```
int i = -3, j = 2, k = 0, m;
m = ++i && j++ && ++k;
printf("\n%d, %d, %d, %d\n", i, j, k, m);
```

(*a*) -2, 3, 1, 1 (*b*) -3, 2, 0, 1
(*c*) -2, 3, 0, 1 (*d*) -2, 3, 1, 0

8. What will be the output of the following segment of code?

```
int i = -3, j = 2, k = 0, m;
m = ++i || j++ || ++k;
printf("\n%d, %d, %d, %d\n", i, j, k, m);
```

(*a*) -2, 3, 0, 0 (*b*) -2, 2, 0, 1
(*c*) -2, 2, 1, 1 (*d*) -2, 3, 1, 0

9. What will be the output of the following segment of code?

```
printf("%c", 7);
```

(*a*) Syntax error (*b*) Run time error
(*c*) prints value 7 (*d*) None

10. Which would be the output of the following segment of code?

```
int a = 4;
printf("\n%d, %d\n", a++, ++a );
```

(*a*) 4, 5 (*b*) 5, 4
(*c*) 4, 4 (*d*) 5, 5

11. What is the value returned by *printf()* function?
    (*a*) It returns the number of items printed.
    (*b*) It returns the number of character positions printed.
    (*c*) It returns the number of bytes printed.
    (*d*) None of above.
12. What is the value returned by *scanf()* function?
    (*a*) It returns the number of items read.
    (*b*) It returns the number of character in the items read.
    (*c*) It returns the number of bytes read.
    (*d*) None of above.

5.7 REVIEW EXERCISES

1. How many decimal places are displayed when a number has a corresponding format specifier "%f"?
2. How does the %u format specifier compare with %d format specifier?
3. What is the difference between 'x' and "x"?
4. How does the %15s format specifier compare with %–15s format specifier?
5. How the % sign can be printed with a *printf()* function as a part of the output?
6. How the output will appear as a result of the following statement?

```
printf("\n:%20s:\n:% -20s:\n", "Test String", "Test String" );
```

7. Find the errors, if any, in the following segment of code.

```
float a, b;
printf("\nEnter value of a: ");
scanf( "%f", a );
b = a * 3;
printf("\nValue of b = %f\n", b);
```

9. Find errors, if any, in the following program. What will be the output of the C program if it is error free?

```
int i = 3, j = 2, k;
k = 2 * i + j;
i += 3;
```

```
j = i + 2 * j - k;
k += 2 * i;
printf("\ni=%d\tj=%d\tk=%d\n",i,j,k);
```

9. What will the output of the following code?

```
printf(" %d\n", printf("\nGood Bye\n"));
```

10. What will be the output of the following segment of code?

```
int m, j = 1, k = 3;
m = 2 * j + k;
j = 2 * m + j / 3;
k /= 2;
m = j + k+ m;
printf ( "\nj = %d\tk = %d\tm = %d\n", j, k, m );
```

11. What will the output of the following code?

```
int intVar = 20;
printf("\n%d,%d,%d\n", intVar == 20,intVar = 35,intVar < 50);
```

5.8 PROGRAMMING EXERCISES

1. Write a program that accepts a decimal integer and prints it in the octal form.
2. Write a program that accepts a character in uppercase and prints it as lowercase.
3. Write a program that accepts a temperature in Fahrenheit scale and prints its equivalent temperature in Centigrade scale.
4. An amount of rupees, say *P*, is deposited in a commercial bank for *N* years, which pays simple interest at the rate of *R*% annually. Write a C program that prints the amount after *N* years.
5. Write C program to find real roots of a quadratic equation of type $ax^2+bx+c = 0$.
6. Basic salary (BS) of an employee is input through the keyboard. The dearness allowance (DA) is 25% of the basic salary while the house rent allowance (HRA) is 15% of the basic salary. Provident fund (PF) is deducted at the rate of 10% of the gross salary (BS+DA+HRA). Write a program to calculate the net salary (NS).
7. A department store places an order with a company for *n* pieces of miners, *m* pieces of toasters, and *p* number of fans. The cost of items are as follows:

Item Description	Price per Unit (in Rupees)
Miners	1,500
Toaster	200
Fan	450

The discount allowed for various items are 5% for miners, 15% for fan, and 10% for toaster. The company charge 10% as sales tax on all items on net value after deducting the discount. Formulate an algorithm that reads *m*, *n*, and *p* and computes the amount to be paid by the store.

❑ ❑ ❑

6 Decision Making Statements

Learning Objectives

After reading this chapter, students will have the ability to:

- explain the need for control transfer
- explain the kind of control statement available in C language
- explain the working of *if* and *if-else* statements for decision making
- explain the working of nested *if* statements
- explain the usefulness of *else if* ladder in multiple alternatives in decision making
- explain the working of *switch* statement
- use these decision making statements to write programs to solve problems requiring
- decision making

6.1 INTRODUCTION

A computer program is a set of instructions for a computer. These instructions, also known as *statements*, are executed sequentially, *i.e.*, one after the other as they appear in a program. This order of executing the statement works well for simple problems where neither any decision making process is involved nor any repetition of statements is involved. However, in practice, it is often required to change the order of execution of statements or repeat a group of statements for known number of times or until certain specified expressions are met. In such cases, the order in which these statements will be executed is to be controlled.

Changing the order of execution of the statements *i.e.* changing the flow of control, might involve one of the following situations.

- *Jumping* — transferring control from one point to another point in the same program unit.
- *Branching* — executing one group of instructions depending on the outcome of a decision.
- *Looping* — executing a group of instructions repetitively either for a given number of times or until the required expressions are met.

The C Language provides facilities for controlling the order of execution of the statements, which are referred to as *flow control statements* or simply as *control statements*.

The various flow control statements are clubbed in the following categories:

1. *Decision Making Statements* — In this category, C language provides the following statements
   - *if* statement
   - *if – else* statement
   - *else if* ladder
   - *switch* statement
2. *Looping Statements* — In this category, C language provides the following statements
   - *for* statement
   - *while* statement
   - *do – while* statement

3. *Jumping Statements* — In this category, C language provides the following statements
   - *break* statement
   - *continue* statement
   - *goto* statement

This chapter describes various decision making statements, and the *break* statement. The remaining statements will be discussed in *Chapter 11*.

6.2 DECISION MAKING STATEMENTS

These statements allow the execution of selective statements based on certain decision criteria. We will see their working supported by well-designed illustrative examples.

6.2.1 The *if* Statement

The syntax of *if* statement is

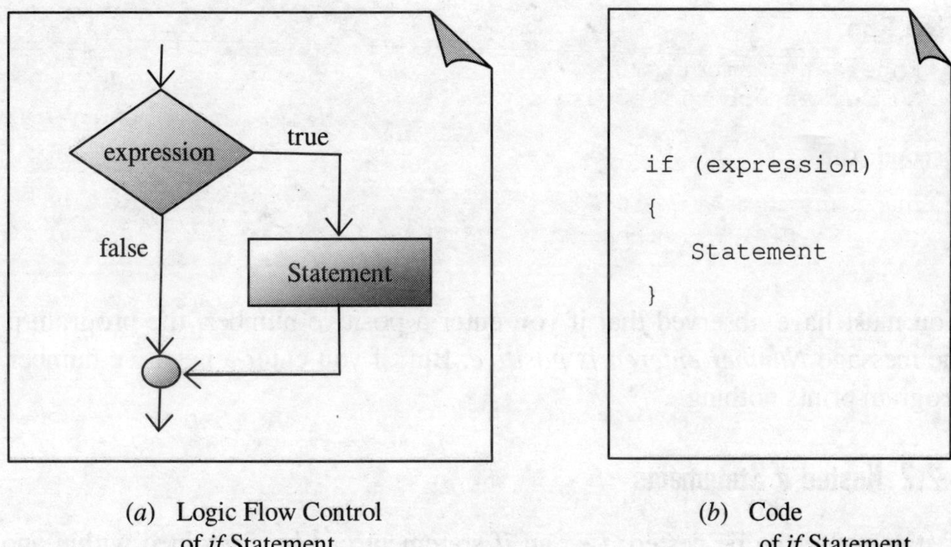

(*a*) Logic Flow Control of *if* Statement

(*b*) Code of *if* Statement

Figure 6.1: Logic flow control and code of *if* statement

The *expression* may represent a relation expression, a logical expression, a numeric variable or a numeric constant. The specified expression may be a simple expression or compound expression.

The expression in C++ evaluates to a *zero* or *non-zero* value. If expression evaluates to a *non-zero* value, then the statements in the statement-block are executed; otherwise they are bypassed.

Listing 6.1

```
/*
*   Program to demonstrate the use of if statement
*/
#include<stdio.h>
void main()
{
   float number;
   printf( "\nEnter any number: " );
   scanf( "%f", &number );
   if ( number > 0 )
      printf ( "Number entered is positive\n" );
}
```

Test Runs

First Run

```
Enter any number: 25
Number entered is positive
```

Second Run

```
Enter any number: -10
```

You must have observed that if you enter a positive number, the program prints the message *Number entered is positive*. But, if you enter a negative number, the program prints nothing.

6.2.2 Nested *if* Statements

If statements can be nested, *i.e.*, an *if* statement can be contained within another *if* statement. The inner *if* statement will be executed if the expression of the outer *if* statement evaluates to *non-zero* value.

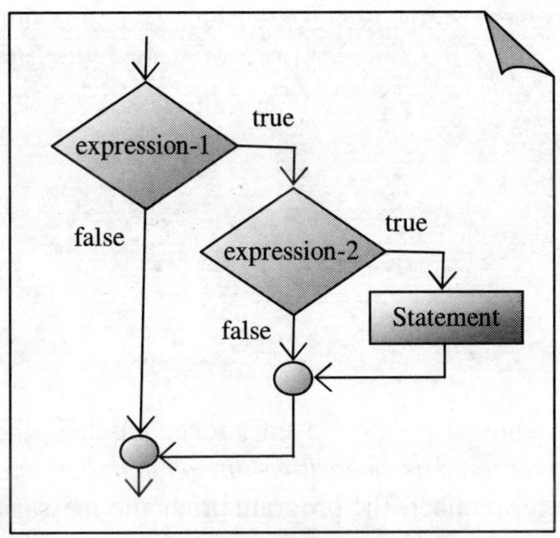

(*a*) Logic Flow Control of nested *if* Statement

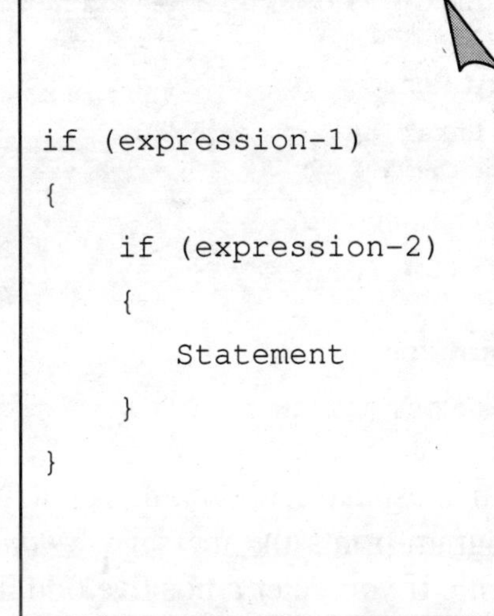

(*b*) Code of nested *if*

Figure 6.2: Logic flow control and code of nested *if* statement

Listing 6.2

```
/*
* Program to demonstrate the use of nested if statements
*/
#include<stdio.h>
void main()
{
   float number;
   printf( "\nEnter any number: " );
   scanf( "%f", &number );
   if ( number > 0 )
   {
      printf( "Number entered is positive" );
      if ( number % 2 == 0 )
         printf( " and even" );
   }
   printf ( "\n" );
}
```

Test Runs

First Run

```
Enter any number: 20
Number entered is a positive integer number and even
```

Second Run

```
Enter any number: 15
Number entered is a positive integer number
```

Third Run

```
Enter any number: -10
```

You must have observed that if you enter a positive even integer number, the program prints the message "*Number entered is a positive integer number and even*". If you enter a positive odd integer number, the program prints the message "*Number entered is positive integer number*". However, if you enter a negative integer number, the program prints nothing.

6.2.3 The *if– else* Statement

The *if* statement executes a single statement (simple or compound), when the specified expression evaluates to a *non-zero* value. It does nothing when it evaluates to a *zero* value. *Is there any way whereby a one statement is executed if the expression evaluates to a non-zero value and another statement if the expression evaluates to a zero value*? The answer is yes. This objective is achieved by using *if – else* statement whose syntax is

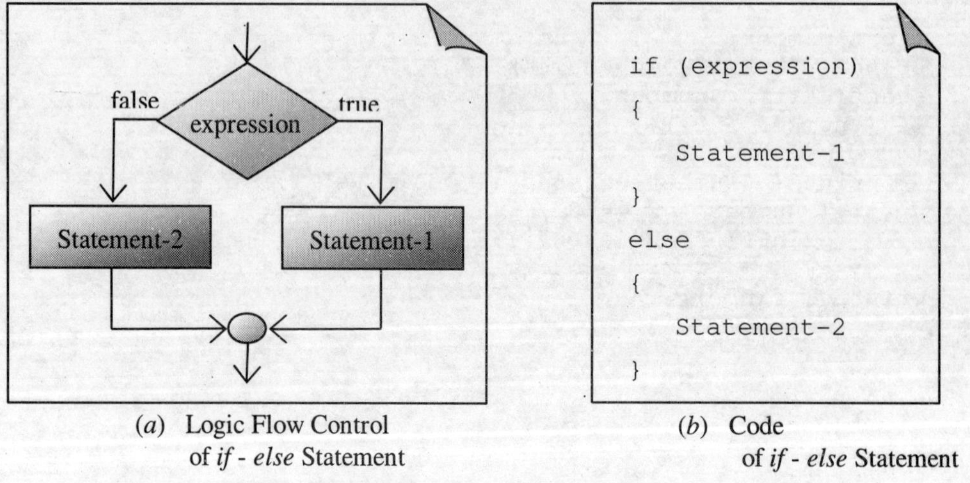

(*a*) Logic Flow Control of *if - else* Statement

(*b*) Code of *if - else* Statement

Figure 6.3: Logic flow control and code of *if-else* statement

If expression evaluates to a non-zero value, the *statement-1* is executed and the *statement-2* is bypassed. However, if the expression evaluates to a zero value, the *statement-1* is bypassed and the *statement-2* is executed.

Listing 6.3

```
/*
*  Program to demonstrate the use of if-else statement
*/

#include<stdio.h>

void main()
{
   float number;

   printf( "\nEnter any number: " );
   scanf( "%f", &number );

   if ( number > 0 )
      printf( "\nNumber entered is positive\n" );
   else
      printf( "\nNumber entered is negative\n" );
}
```

Test Runs

First Run

```
Enter any number: 25
Number entered is positive
```

Second Run

```
Enter any number: -10
Number entered is negative
```

You must have observed that if you enter a positive number, then the program prints the message *Number entered is positive*. If you enter negative number, then the program prints the message *Number entered is negative*.

6.2.4 Nested *if– else* Statements

Like *if* statement, *if-else* statements can also be nested. Here, *if* statement can be nested in *if* part *or else* part. Likewise, *if - else* statement can be nested in *if* part *or else* part. These all situations are shown in following figures.

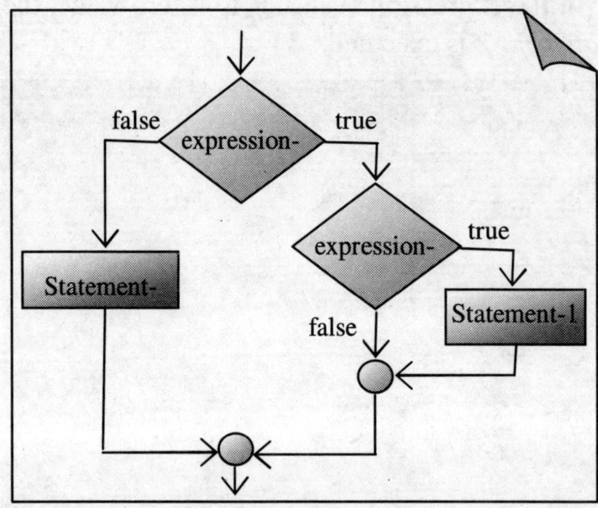

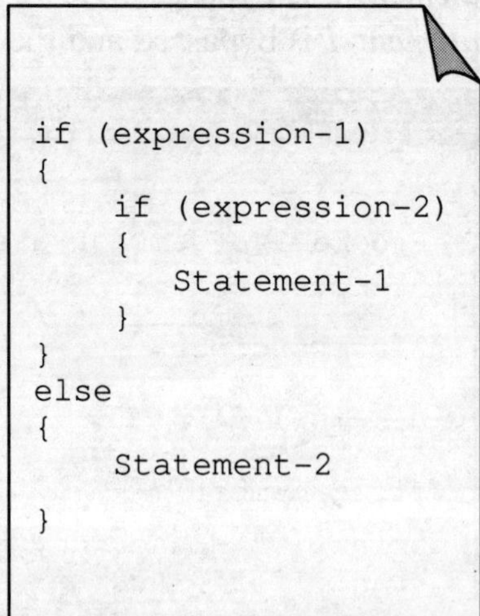

```
if (expression-1)
{
     if (expression-2)
     {
         Statement-1
     }
}
else
{
     Statement-2

}
```

(*a*) Logic Flow Control (*b*) Equivalent Code

Figure 6.4: Logic flow control and code of nested *if-else* statement, when *if* statement is nested in *if* part

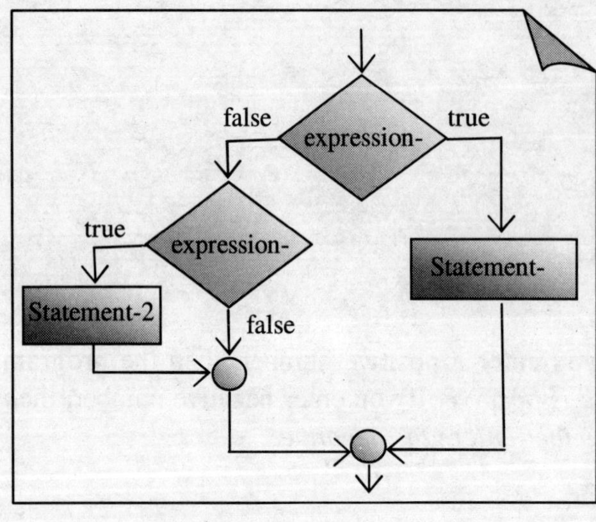

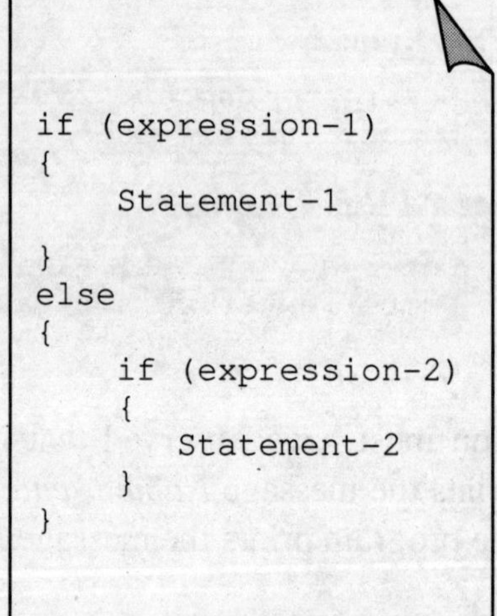

```
if (expression-1)
{
     Statement-1

}
else
{
     if (expression-2)
     {
         Statement-2
     }
}
```

(*a*) Logic Flow Control (*b*) Equivalent

Figure 6.5: Logic flow control and code of nested *if-else* statement, when *if* statement is nested in *else* part

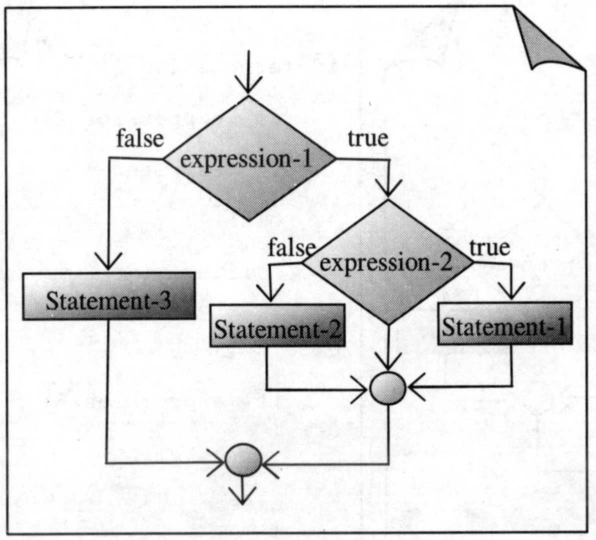

(*a*) Logic Flow Control

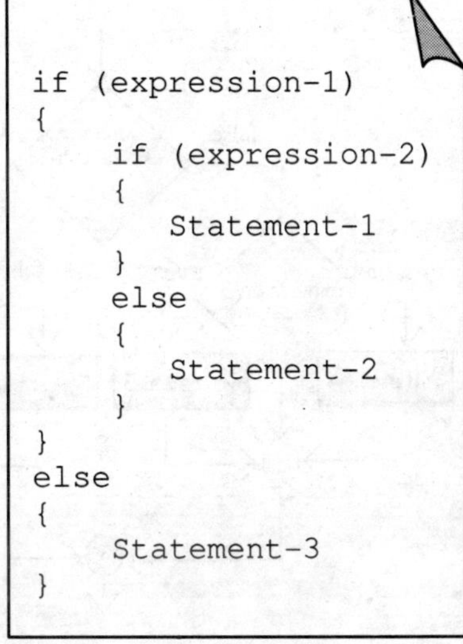

```
if (expression-1)
{
    if (expression-2)
    {
       Statement-1
    }
    else
    {
       Statement-2
    }
}
else
{
    Statement-3
}
```

(*b*) Equivalent Code

Figure 6.6: Logic flow control and code of nested *if-else* statement, when *if-else* statement is nested in *if* part

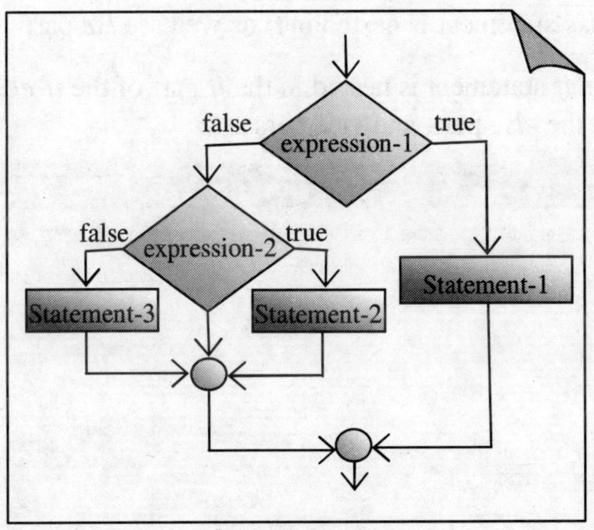

(*a*) Logic Flow Control

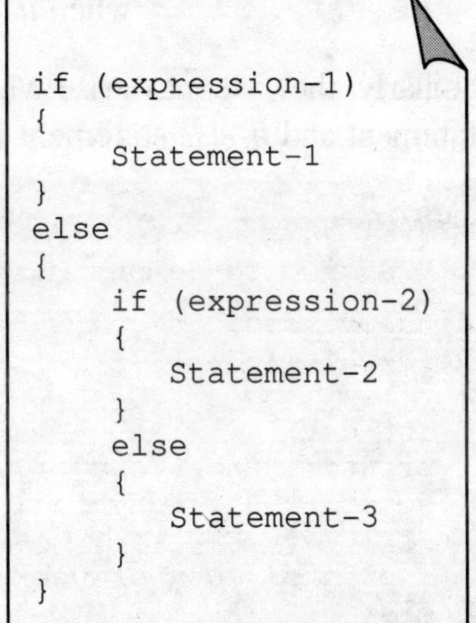

```
if (expression-1)
{
    Statement-1
}
else
{
    if (expression-2)
    {
       Statement-2
    }
    else
    {
       Statement-3
    }
}
```

(*b*) Equivalent Code

Figure 6.7: Logic flow control and code of nested *if-else* statement, when *if-else* statement is nested in *else* part

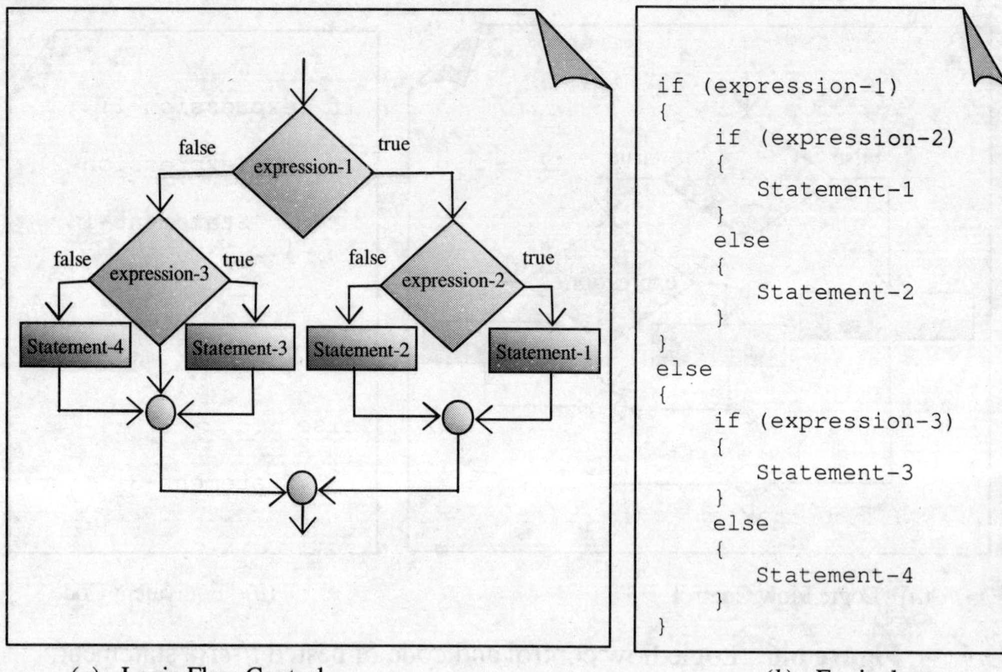

(*a*) Logic Flow Control (*b*) Equivalent

Figure 6.8: Logic flow control and code of nested *if-else* statement, when *if-else* statement is nested in *if* as well as *else* part

Similarly, the case may arise when *if* statement is nested in the *if* part of the *if-else* statement and *if-else* statement in the *else* part, and vice versa.

Listing 6.4

```
/* Program to demonstrate use of nested if-else statements */
#include<stdio.h>
void main()
{
  int day;
  printf( "Enter day of week as number: " );
  scanf( "%d", &day );
  if ( day == 0 )
    printf( "Day of week is Sunday" );
  else
    if ( day == 1 )
      printf( "Day of week is Monday" );
    else
      if ( day == 2 )
        printf( "Day of week is Tuesday" );
      else
        if ( day == 3 )
```

```
          printf( "Day of week is Wednesday" );
        else
          if ( day == 4 )
            printf( "Day of week is Thursday" );
          else
            if ( day == 5 )
              printf( "Day of week is Friday" );
            else
              if ( day == 6 )
                printf( "Day of week is Saturday" );
              else
                printf( "Wrong input" );
  printf( "\n" );
}
```

Test Runs

First Run

```
Enter day week as number: 2
Day of week is Tuesday
```

Second Run

```
Enter day week as number: 7
Wrong input
```

Do you see something wrong with the next program?

Listing 6.5

```
/* Program to demonstrate the use of nested
  if-else statements, which are not properly nested   */
#include<stdio.h>
void main()
{
   int day;
   printf( "Enter day of week as number: " );
   scanf( "%d", &day );
   if ( day == 0 )
   printf( "Day of week is Sunday" );
   else
   if ( day == 1 )
   printf( "Day of week is Monday" );
   else
   if ( day == 2 )
   printf( "Day of week is Tuesday" );
   else
   if ( day == 3 )
   printf( "Day of week is Wednesday" );
```

```
    else
    if ( day == 4 )
    printf( "Day of week is Thursday" );
    else
    if ( day == 5 )
    printf( "Day of week is Friday" );
    else
    if ( day == 6 )
    printf( "Day of week is Saturday" );
    else
    printf( "Wrong input" );
    printf( "\n" );
}
```

Nothing is wrong with this program, and it is functionally equivalent to program listing 6.4. But this style of programming is not recommended specifically in case of nesting of *if* statements. Consider the next program.

Listing 6.6

```
/*Program to demonstrate matching of else with if statement (ver 2)*/
#include<stdio.h>
void main()
{
    int number;
    printf( "Enter any integer number: " );
    scanf( "%d", &number );
    if ( number > 0 )
       if ( number % 2 == 0 )
          printf( "Integer number is positive and even" );
    else
       printf( "Integer number is positive and odd" );
    printf( "\n" );
}
```

Suppose *number* is 15. *What will the output of this program*? You may guess nothing at all. The answer seems reasonable: the first expression (*number* > 0) is *true*, so the second expression (*number* % 2 == 0) is evaluated which is *false*. So at this point it looks that the control may exit from the entire nested *if-else* statement.

However, with the above logic we are mis-lead by the indentation. The program will output the message *Integer number is positive and odd*.

Actually the *else* is associated with the *if* immediately preceding it, not the first *if* as the indentation would lead you to believe. As a rule, an *else* is associated with the last *if* statement that does not have its own *else*. Here is the modified version of the above program, which will not only work correctly but also appears to be.

Listing 6.7

```
/*Program to demonstrate matching of else with if statement (ver 2)*/
#include<stdio.h>
void main()
{
  int number;
  printf( "Enter any integer number: " );
  scanf( "%d", &number );
  if ( number > 0 )
     if ( number % 2 == 0 )
        printf( "Integer number is positive and even" );
     else
        printf( "Integer number is positive and odd"  );

  printf( "\n");
}
```

6.2.5 The *else if* Ladder

Consider the program 6.4, which demonstrates how *if-else* statements are nested. As the resulting indentation gets deep and deep, the program becomes more and more difficult to read. There is another way to write and think about this situation. This is using *else-if* construct whose syntax is

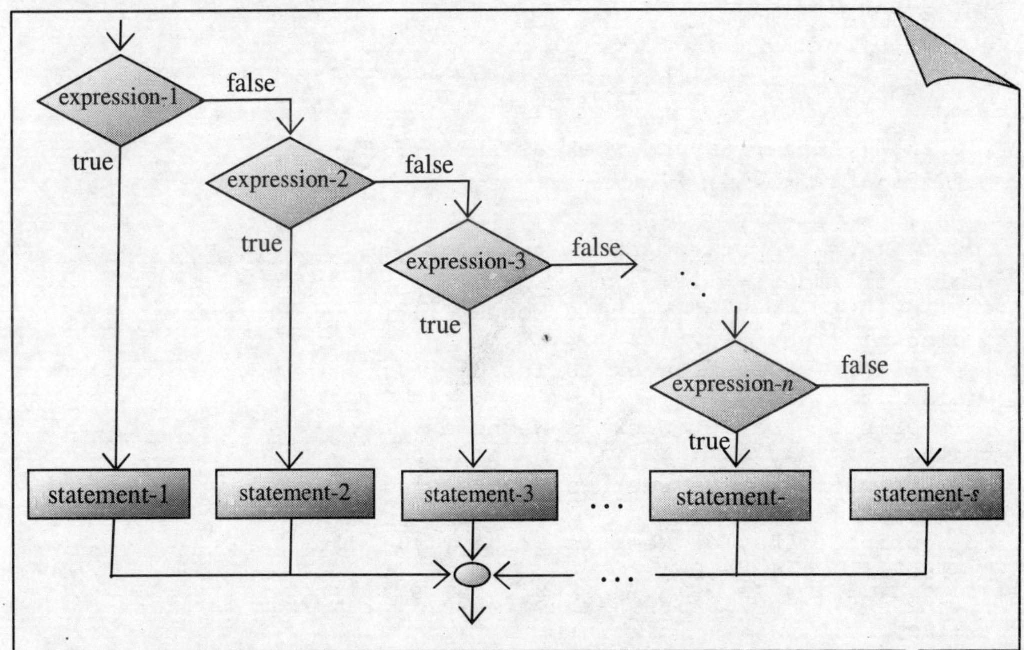

Figure 6.9: Logic Flow Control of *else if* Ladder

The expressions are evaluated in order, and if any expression is true then the statement block associated with it is executed, and this terminates the whole chain. The last *else* part handles *none of the above* or default case where none of the specified expressions are satisfied.

This sequence of *if* statements is the most general way of writing a multi-way decision. The program listing 6.4 can be rewritten using *else if* ladder as shown in program listing 6.8.

```
if ( expression-1 )
   statement-1
else if ( expression-2 )
   statement-2
else if ( expression-3 )
   statement-3
      :
      :
else if ( expression-n )
   statement-n
else
   statement-s
```

Figure 6.10: Code of *else if* Ladder

Listing 6.8

```
/*
*  Program to demonstrate the use of else-if construct
*/
#include<stdio.h>
void main()
{
   int day;
   printf( "Enter day of week as number: " );
   scanf( "%d", &day );
   if ( day == 0 )
      printf( "Day of week is Sunday" );
   else if ( day == 1 )
      printf( "Day of week is Monday" );
   else if ( day == 2 )
      printf( "Day of week is Tuesday" );
   else if ( day == 3 )
      printf( "Day of week is Wednesday" );
   else if ( day == 4 )
      printf( "Day of week is Thursday" );
   else if ( day == 5 )
      printf( "Day of week is Friday" );
   else if ( day == 6 )
      printf( "Day of week is Saturday" );
   else
      printf( "Wrong input");
   printf( "\n" );
}
```

6.2.6 The *switch* Statement

The *switch* statement provides an alternative to *else if* construct. The *switch* statement has more flexibility and a clearer format than *else if* construct. The syntax of *switch* statement is shown in Figure 6.11.

If *expression* takes any value from *val-1*, *val-2*, *val-3*, ..., *val-n*, the control is transferred to that appropriate case. In each case, the statements are executed and then the *break* statement transfers the control out of *switch* statement.

```
switch ( expression )
{
    case val-1 :
                        statement-1
                        break;
    case val-2 :
                        statement-2
                        break;
    case val-3 :
                        statement-3
                        break;
         :
    case val-n :
                statement-n
                break;
    default    :
                statement-d
}
```

Figure 6.11: Code of *switch* Statement

If no *break* statement is used following a case, except the last one in the absence of *default* keyword, the control will fall through to the next case. If the value of the *expression* does not match any of the case values, control goes to the *default* keyword, which is usually at the end of the *switch* statement. The use of the *default* keyword can be of a great convenience. If there is no *default* keyword, the whole *switch* statement simply terminates when there is no match.

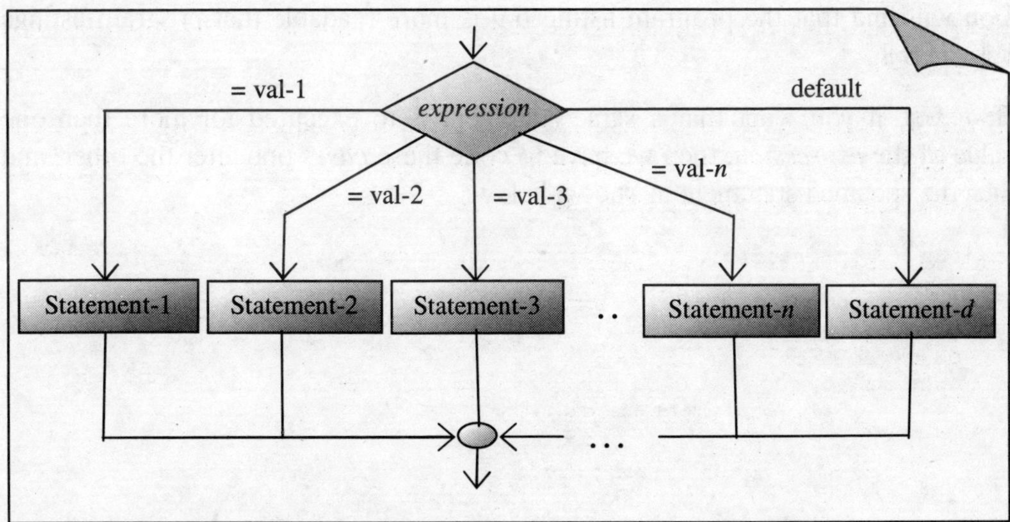

Figure 6.12: Logic Flow Control of *switch* Statement

Listing 6.9

```
/*  Program to demonstrate the use of switch statement  */
#include<stdio.h>
void main()
{
  int day;
  printf( "Enter day of week as number: " );
  scanf( "%d", &day );
  switch ( day )
  {
     case 0   : printf( "Day of week is Sunday" );
                break;
     case 1   : printf( "Day of week is Monday" );
                break;
     case 2   : printf( "Day of week is Tuesday" );
                break;
     case 3   : printf( "Day of week is Wednesday" );
                break;
     case 4   : printf( "Day of week is Thursday" );
                break;
     case 5   : printf( "Day of week is Friday" );
                break;
     case 6   : printf( "Day of week is Saturday" );
                break;
     default  : printf( "Wrong input" );
  }
  printf( "\n" );
}
```

You will find that the program listing 6.9 is more readable that program listings 6.4 and 6.8.

However, if you want that a same statement is to executed for more than one value of the *expression*, then we have to code these *cases* one after the other, and then the specified statement as shown below:

```
switch ( expression )
{
     :
   case val-4 :
   case val-5 :
   case val-6 :
                  statement-block
                  break;
     :
}
```

The *statement-block* will be executed whenever the value of the *expression* is *val-4*, *val-5*, or *val-6*.

6.2.6.1 More About *switch* Statement

Following are some important points about switch statement.

1. The *expression* of switch statement must be of type integer or character type.
2. The *default* case need not be used as the last case. It can be placed at any place.
3. The case values must be integer constants or character constants. These values can also be constant expressions as these are evaluated at compilation time. For example, if expression 5 + 7 appears as case value, it will be evaluated to value 12 at compilation. Similarly, if expression 5 < 7 appears as the case value, it will evaluate to 1 by compiler at compilation time.
4. The case statements can only be used within the scope of switch statement otherwise the compiler will display en error message similar to *"Case outside of switch statement in function ..."*.
5. The case values need not be in any specific order.

6.3 SUPPLEMENTARY PROBLEMS

Let us write a few more C programs to use the features that we have learned in this chapter.

Problem 6.1:

Program to find the roots of a quadratic equation of the type

$ax^2 + bx + c = 0$ provided $a \neq 0$.

The roots of the quadratic equation are given by the formula:

$$x_{1,2} = \frac{-b \pm \sqrt{b^2 - 4ac}}{2a}$$

where the expression $b^2 - 4ac$ is known as the discriminant.

Depending on the sign of the discriminant, there are three possibilities for the roots:

1. If $b^2 - 4ac < 0$, then the root are imaginary, and we can compute real part and imaginary part separately as

$$\text{real part} = -\frac{b}{2a} \qquad \text{imaginary part} = \frac{\sqrt{-(b^2 - 4ac)}}{2a}$$

2. If $b^2 - 4ac = 0$, then the roots are real and equal, and root is simply computed as

$$\text{root} = -\frac{b}{2a}$$

3. If $b^2 - 4ac > 0$, then the roots are real and distinct and are computed as

$$\text{root one} = \frac{-b - \sqrt{b^2 - 4ac}}{2a} \qquad \text{root two} = \frac{-b + \sqrt{b^2 - 4ac}}{2a}$$

The complete program will look like as shown below:

Listing 6.10

```
/*  Program to find the roots of an quadratic equation of type
*   of  type a*x^2+b*x+c = 0, where a is not equal to zero
*/
#include<stdio.h>
#include<math.h>
void main()
{
   float a, b, c, disc, root1, root2, twoA;
   float realPart, imagPart;
   printf( "\nEnter values of a,b,c: " );
   scanf( "%f,%f,%f", &a, &b, &c);
   if ( a == 0 ) {
      printf( "\nIt is not an quadratic equation\n" );
      return;
   }
   disc = b * b - 4.0 * a * c;
   twoA = a + a;
   if ( disc < 0 ) {
      realPart = - b / twoA;
      imagPart = sqrt((double)-disc) / twoA;
      printf( "\nRoots are imaginary" );
      printf( "\nReal part = %.3f", realPart );
      printf( "\nImaginary part = %.3f\n", imagPart );
   } else if ( disc == 0 ) {
      root1 = - b / twoA;
      printf( "\nRoots are real and equal" );
      printf( "\nEach root = %.3f\n", root1 );
   } else {
      root1 = (-b-sqrt((double)disc ))/twoA;
      root2 = (-b+sqrt((double)disc ))/twoA;
      printf( "\nRoots are real and distinct" );
      printf( "\nRoot 1 = %.3f", root1 );
      printf( "\nRoot 2 = %.3f\n", root2 );
   }
}
```

Test Run

```
Enter values of a,b,c: 2,3,5

Roots are imaginary

Real part = -0.750
Imaginary part = 1.392
```

Problem 6.2:

Write a program, which takes two integer operands and one operator form the user, performs the operation and then prints the result. (Consider the operators +, – ,*, /, % and use *switch* statement).

Listing 6.11

```
/*
* Program that takes two integer operands and one operator from
* the user, Performs the operation and then prints the result
*/
#include<stdio.h>
void main()
{
    int operand1, operand2, result1;
    char operator;
    float result2;
    printf("\nEnter expression as operand1 operator operand2: ");
    scanf( "%d %c %d", &operand1, &operator, &operand2);
    switch ( operator )
    {
        case '+': result1 = operand1 + operand2;
                  printf( "\nresult = %d\n", result1 );
                  break;
        case '-': result1 = operand1 - operand2;
                  printf( "\nresult = %d\n", result1 );
                  break;
        case '/': result2 = (float)operand1 / operand2;
                  printf( "\nresult = %f\n", result2 );
                  break;
        case '*': result1 = operand1 * operand2;
                  printf( "\nresult = %d\n", result1 );
                  break;
        case '%': result1 = operand1 % operand2;
                  printf( "\nresult = %d\n", result1 );
                  break;
        default:
                  printf( "\nWrong operator . . .\n" );
    }
}
```

Test Runs

First Run

```
Enter expression as operand1 operator operand2 : 12 + 25
Result = 37
```

Second Run

```
Enter expression as operand1 operator operand2 : 25 / 4
Result = 6.25000
```

Third Run

```
Enter expression as operand1 operator operand2 : 8 ^ 2
Wrong operator . . .
```

Problem 6.3:

Write a program to determine whether the given year is a leap year.

Under the current (Gregorian) calendar, a year is said to be a leap year if it is divisible by 400 or by 4 but not by 100

Listing 6.12

```
/*
*  Program to determine whether the given year is a leap year
*/
#include<stdio.h>
void main()
{
  int year;
  printf("\nEnter any year : ");
  scanf("%d",&year);
  if ((year % 400==0)||((year % 4==0) )&&(year % 100!=0))
     printf("\nYear %d is a leap year.\n", year);
  else
     printf("\nYear %d is not a leap year.\n", year);
}
```

Test Runs

First Run

```
Enter any year : 2000
Year 2000 is a leap year.
```

Second Run

```
Enter any year : 2008
Year 2000 is a leap year.
```

Third Run

```
Enter any year : 2006
Year 2000 is not a leap year.
```

Problem 6.4:

Income tax for individuals is computed on slab rates as follows:

Income	Tax Payable
Upto Rs. 1,00,000/-	Nil
From Rs. 1,00,001/- to Rs. 2,00,000/-	10% of the excess over Rs. 1,00,000/-
From Rs. 2,00,001/- to Rs. 3,00,000/-	20% of the excess over Rs. 2,00,000/-
Above Rs. 3,00,000/-	30% of the excess over Rs. 3,00,000/-

Write a program that reads the income and prints the income tax due.

Listing 6.13

```
/*  Program to compute income tax for given gross income  */
#include<stdio.h>
void main()
{
   float income, tax;
   printf( "\nEnter gross income (in Rs.): " );
   scanf( "%f", &income );
   if ( income <= 100000.0 )
      tax = 0;
   else if ( income <= 200000.0 )
      tax = ( income - 100000.0 ) * 0.1;
   else if ( income <= 300000.0 )
      tax = 10000 + ( income - 200000.0 ) * 0.2;
   else
      tax = 30000 + ( income - 300000.0 ) * 0.3;
   printf( "\nTax due = Rs. %.2f\n", tax );
}
```

Test Runs

First Run

```
Enter gross income : 250000
Tax due = Rs. 20000.00
```

Second Run

```
Enter gross income : 175000
Tax due = Rs. 7500.00
```

Third Run

```
Enter gross income : 320000
Tax due = Rs. 36000.00
```

6.4 QUICK RECAP

In this chapter, we have learnt that

- The control statements allow controlling the order of execution of statements.
- This controlling of statements may involve selecting a statement from the alternate statements or executing some selected statements repeatedly.
- The *if – else* and *switch* statements are known as decision making statement as they allow to select a statement from the alternatives depending upon the outcome of the given condition.
- The *switch* statement work with only those situations where a condition can take integral values.
- When used with the *switch* statement, the *break* statement takes the control outside the scope of the *switch* statement.

6.5 MULTIPLE CHOICE QUESTIONS

1. Consider the following code:

```
switch(ch)
{
   case 'a': printf("a");
   case 'b': printf("b");
   default:  printf("error");
}
```

If value 'a' is given to character variable *ch*, then the output will be

(*a*) a (*b*) ab
(*c*) aberror (*d*) error

2. Consider the following code:

```
int a = 6, b = 6;
if ( b == 6 || --a )
{
   statement1;
   statement2;
}
```

Suppose *statement1* and *statement2* does not modify the value of *a* and *b*, then what is the value of *a* after executing the above code?

(*a*) 6 (*b*) 5
(*c*) 7 (*d*) error

3. Which of the following statement is true about *switch* statement?
(*a*) It may contain zero or more cases.
(*b*) Constant expressions are valid case values.
(*c*) Statement block of every case must have *break* statement as its last statement to avoid the control to fall through the later cases.
(*d*) All of above.

4. If default statement is omitted in *switch* statement and there is no match with case values, then
(*a*) No statement in the switch block is executed.
(*b*) Execute all statements in the switch block.
(*c*) Execute the statements in the last case block only.
(*d*) A run time error occurs.

5. What will be the result of attempting to compile and run the following program?

```
#include <stdio.h>
void main()
{
    int c;
    printf( "\nEnter value of c: " );
    scanf( "%d", &c);
    switch(c);
    {
         case 1 : printf( "\nHello 1\n" );
                  break;
         case 2 : printf( "\nHello 2\n" );
                  break;
       default : printf( "\nInvaild value\n" );
                 break;
         case 3 : printf( "\nHello 3\n" );
                  break;
         case 4 : printf( "\nHello 4\n" );
    }
}
```

(*a*) Program will compile and execute.
(*b*) Program will fail to compile because *default* can only appear at the end after all valid cases.
(*c*) Program will fail to compile and compiler will report the syntax error as *"Case outside of switch statement in function main"* followed *"Misplaced break in function main"* for all cases and the *break* statements.
(*d*) None of above.

6. Consider the following program

```
#include <stdio.h>
void main()
{
    int a, b = 10;
    scanf( "%d", &a );
    if ( a = 0 )
        b *= 2;
    else
        b /= 2;
    printf( "%d  ", b );
}
```

What will be the result of executing the above program with user input of number 6?

(*a*) 20 (*b*) 10
(*c*) 5 (*d*) None

7. Which of the following is not a valid type of expression in the *switch* statement?

(*a*) character (*b*) integer
(*c*) float (*d*) enum

6.6 REVIEW EXERCISES

1. If the *if* statement do not have associated *else*, then what happens if the expression evaluates to zero value?
2. What is the advantage of *switch* statement over *else-if* construct?
3. What does nesting mean?
4. Where the *break* statement is used, and what is its function?

5. Rewrite the following code fragment using the *switch* statement:

```
char code;
code = getchar();

if ( code == 'A' )
   printf("\nAccountant\n");
else if ( code == 'C' || code == 'G' )
   printf("\nGrade IV\n");
else if ( code == 'F' )
   printf("\nFinancial Advisor\n");
else
   printf("\nIncorrect code\n");
```

6. Rewrite the following code fragment using the *if-else* statements:

```
int month;
scanf( "%d", month );
switch ( month )
{
    case 1 :
    case 3 :
    case 5 :
    case 7 :
    case 8 :
    case 10:
    case 12: printf("\nMonth having 31 days\n");
             break;
    case 4 :
    case 6 :
    case 9 :
    case 11: printf("\nMonth having 30 days\n"); break;
    case 2 : printf("\nMonth having 28/29 days\n");
             break;
    default: printf("\nIncorrect month\n");
}
```

7. Rewrite the following code segment using the *switch* statement:

```
if (ch == 'N')
    north++;
if (ch == 'S')
    south++;
if (ch == 'E')
    east++;
if (ch == 'W')
    west++;
else
    unknown++;
```

6.7 PROGRAMMING EXERCISES

1. Given three numbers, determine whether they can form sides of a triangle.
2. The monthly telephone bill is to be computed as follows:

   Minimum Rs. 200 for upto 100 calls
   plus Rs. 0.60 per call for next 50 calls
   plus Rs. 0.50 per call for next 50 calls
   plus Rs. 0.40 per call for any call beyond 200 calls.

   Write a program to compute monthly bill for given number of calls.
3. A department store places an order with a company for *n* pieces of miners, *m* pieces of toasters, and *p* number of fans. Cost of each item is as follows:

Miners	: Rs. 1,500 per piece
Toaster	: Rs. 200 per piece
Fan	: Rs. 450 per piece

   The discount allowed for various items are 5% for miners, 15% for fan, and 10% for toaster. The company charge 10% as sales tax on all items on net value after deducting the discount. Write a program that reads *m*, *n*, and *p* and computes the amount to be paid by the store.
4. Suppose the postal rates for mailing letters are as follows:

   Rs. 0.50 per 10 grams for the first 50 grams,
   Rs. 0.40 per 10 grams for the next 100 grams,
   Rs. 0.25 per 10 grams for the next 250 grams, and
   Rs. 25 per kilogram for letters weighing more than 400 grams.

   Write a program that prompts for weight of a letter and prints the postage to be paid.
5. Given three points $A(x_1, y_1)$, $B(x_2, y_2)$ and $C(x_3, y_3)$, determine whether they are collinear, i.e., lie on the same line.
6. Write a program to determine whether the number is divisible by 2, without performing the division by 2.
7. Given three numbers, determine whether they can form sides of an isosceles triangle.

7 Looping Statements

Learning Objectives

After reading this chapter, students will have the ability to:

- explain the working of *while* statement
- explain the working of *for* statement
- explain the working of *do-while* statement
- explain the nesting of looping statements
- explain the working of *break*, *continue* and *goto* statements
- explain the usefulness of *else if* ladder in multiple alternatives in decision making
- use these statements to write programs to solve problems requiring iteration

7.1 INTRODUCTION

As discussed in the last chapter, a computer program is a set of instructions for a computer that are executed sequentially, *i.e.*, one after the other as they appear in a program.

However, following situations may arise:

- There may be situations when we need to alter this sequence by choosing a particular set of statements (*selection*) among two or more alternatives, based on certain criteria (*i.e.*, when certain conditions are satisfied/not satisfied) is met.
- There may also be situations when we need to repeat (*iteration*) certain group of statements over either fixed number of times or till certain criteria (*i.e.*, when certain conditions are satisfied/not satisfied) is met.
- There may also be situations when we need to transfer the control from one part of the program to another part (*jumping*) in order to skip certain instructions or go back to repeat certain instructions either depending on the satisfaction of certain condition (*conditional transfer*) or without the involvement of any condition (*unconditional transfer*).

This means, we may need to control the execution of the instructions.

In the previous chapter, we had discussed the control statements that allow us to perform the action of selection. This chapter focuses on the control statements that allow us to perform the action of iteration. In addition, the statements that allow us to perform the action of transfer of control within the program conditionally or unconditionally are also discussed.

7.2 THE *while* STATEMENT

The *while* statement is suited for problems where it is not known in advance that how many times a statement or a statement-block will be executed.

Te logic flow and the syntax of the while statement is shown in Figure 7.1. Here *expression* can be a constant, a variable or an expression. The *statement* is executed repeatedly till the *exp* evaluates to a *non-zero* value. Whenever *exp* evaluates to a *zero* value, the execution of *while* statement will terminate and control will pass to a statement immediately following it.

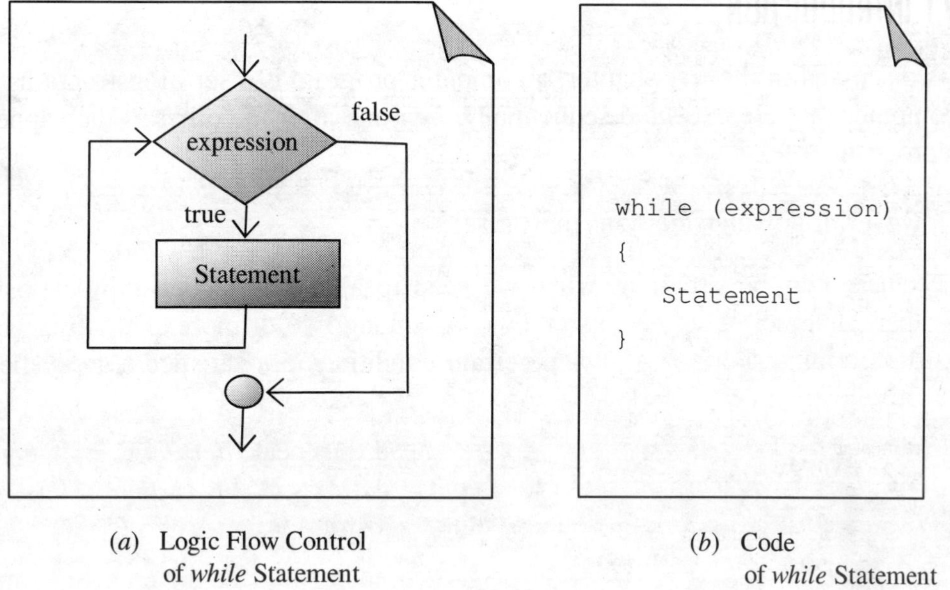

(*a*) Logic Flow Control of *while* Statement

(*b*) Code of *while* Statement

Figure 7.1: Logic flow control and code of *while* statement

Though in C language there are certain exceptions, but in general, the following points must be kept in mind while using the *while* statement:

- There must be a statement prior to *while* statement that initializes the *exp*.
- In the statement-block, there must be a statement that modifies the expression.

To illustrate the use of *while* statement, let us develop some programs.

Listing 7.1

```
/* Program to find sum of first 100 positive integer numbers */
#include <stdio.h>
void main()
{
   int sum = 0, number;
   number = 1;
   while ( number <= 100 )
   {
      sum += number;
      number++;
   }
   printf( "Sum of first 100 positive " );
   printf( "integer numbers = %d\n", sum );
}
```

Test Run

```
Sum of first 100 positive integer numbers = 5050
```

Listing 7.2

```
/* Program to find sum of even and odd numbers from
*  first 100 positive integer numbers    */
#include<stdio.h>
void main()
{
   int sumOdd = 0, sumEven = 0, number;
   number = 1;
   while ( number <= 100 )
   {
      if ( ( number % 2 ) == 0 )
         sumEven += number;
      else
         sumOdd += number;
      number++;
   }
   printf( "Sum of even numbers = %d\n", sumEven );
   printf( "Sum of odd numbers  = %d\n", sumOdd );
}
```

Test Run

```
Sum of even numbers = 2550
Sum of odd numbers  = 2500
```

Listing 7.3

```
/* Program to find sum of digits of a positive
   integer number     */
#include<stdio.h>
void main()
{
   int sum = 0, digit;
   long number, temp;
   printf( "Enter any positive integer number: " );
   scanf( "%ld", &number );
   temp = number;
   while ( temp > 0 )
   {
      digit = temp % 10;
      temp /= 10;
```

```
      sum += digit;
   }
   printf( "\nSum of digits of %ld = %d\n", number, sum );
}
```

Test Run

```
Enter any positive integer number : 3265
Sum of digits of 3265 = 16
```

Listing 7.4

```
/*
* Program to count number of characters, vowels & words
* in a paragraph
*/
#include<stdio.h>
void main()
{
   int vowelCount=0,characterCount=0,wordCount=0;
   char ch;
   printf( "Type in the paragraph and terminate");
   printf( "\nby ENTER key\n\n" );
   while ( ( ch = getche() ) != '\r' )
   {
      characterCount++;
      if ( ( ch == ' ' ) || ( ch == '\t' ) )
         wordCount++;
      if ( (ch=='a')||(ch=='A')||(ch=='e')||
           (ch=='E')||(ch=='i')||(ch=='I')||
           (ch=='o')||(ch=='O')||(ch=='u')||
           (ch == 'U') )
        vowelCount++;
   }
   wordCount++;
   printf( "\nCharacter count = %d", characterCount);
   printf( "\nVowel count = %d", vowelCount);
   printf( "\nWord count = %d\n", wordCount);
}
```

Test Run

```
Type the paragraph and terminate by ENTER key

i enjoy programming in c++ like anything ↵

Character count = 40
Vowel count = 11
Word count = 7
```

7.3 THE *for* STATEMENT

The *for* statement is suited for problems where the number of times a statement or statement-block will be executed is known in advance.

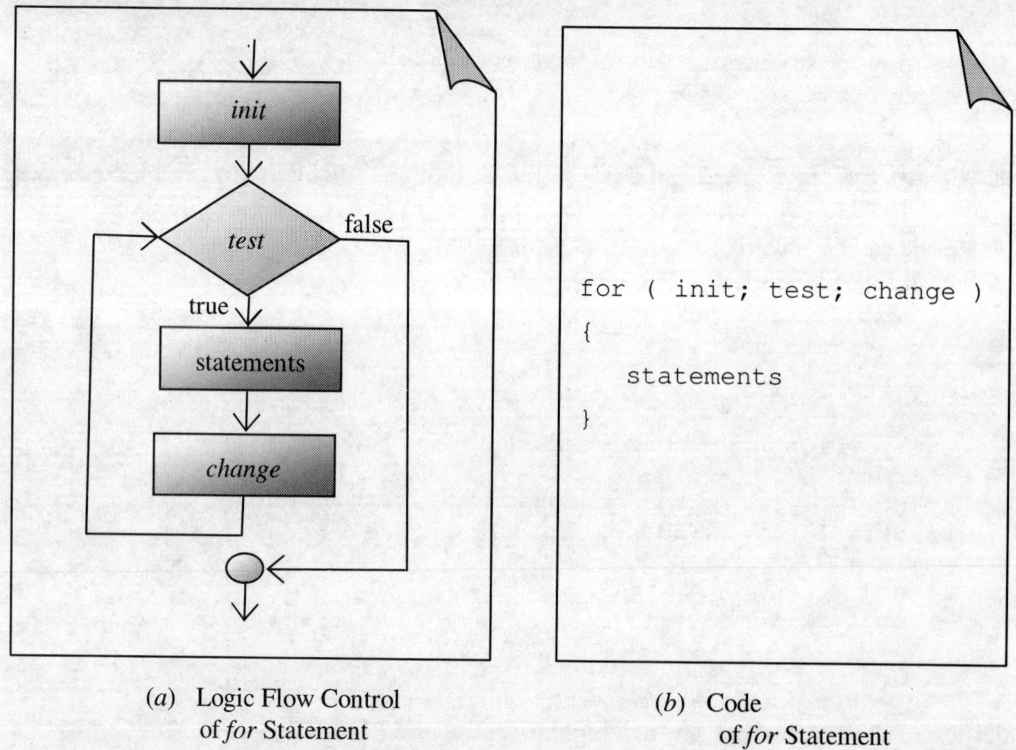

(*a*) Logic Flow Control of *for* Statement

(*b*) Code of *for* Statement

Figure 7.2: Logic flow control and code of *for* statement

where *init* is an expression to initialize the counter, the *test* is an expression to see when to stop iterating, and *change* is an expression to change the counter for each pass of the loop. The *init* and *change* parts can have more than one statement separated by a comma.

Change for the counter can be positive as well as negative, as illustrated below:

```
      :
for ( k = r; k <= s; k += t )
{
    // statements
}
      :
```

```
      :
for ( k = r; k >= s; k -= t )
{
    // statements
}
      :
```

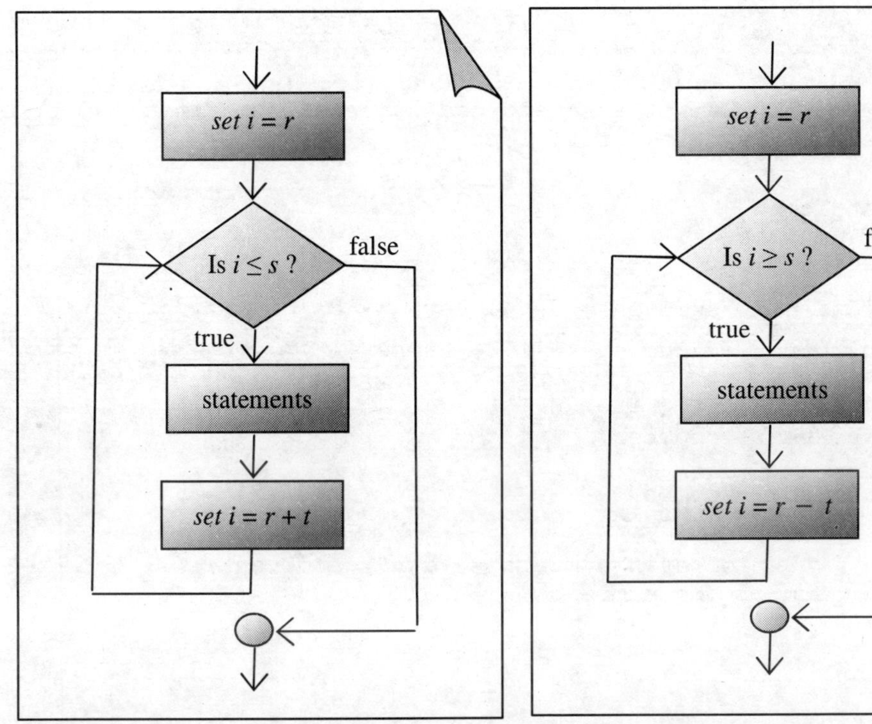

(*a*) When step size *t* is positive (*b*) When step size *t* is negative

Figure 7.3: Working of *for* statement for positive and negative step size

To demonstrate the use of *for* statement, let us develop some program making using of *for* statement.

Listing 7.5

```
/*
*  Program to find sum of first 100 positive numbers
*  using for loop
*/
#include<stdio.h>
void main(void)
{
   int sum = 0, number;
   for ( number = 0; number <= 100; number++ )
   {
     sum += number;
   }
   printf( "\nSum of first 100 positive\n" );
   printf( "integer numbers = %d\n", sum );
}
```

Listing 7.6

```
/*
* Program to find sum of even and odd numbers from first 100
* Positive numbers using 'for' loop
*/
#include<stdio.h>
void main()
{
   int sumOdd = 0, sumEven = 0, number;
   for ( number = 0; number <= 100; number++ )
   {
      if ( ( number % 2 ) == 0 )
         sumEven += number;
      else
         sumOdd += number;
   }
   printf( "\nSum of even numbers = %d\n", sumEven );
   printf( "Sum of odd numbers  = %d\n", sumOdd );
}
```

Listing 7.7

```
/*
*  Program to compute average of 'n' real numbers
*/
#include<stdio.h>
void main()
{
   int i, n;
   float number, sum = 0, average;
   printf( "Enter value of n: " );
   scanf( "%d", &n );
   for ( i = 1; i <= n; i++ )
   {
      printf( "Enter real number %d: ", i );
      scanf ( "%f", &number );
      sum += number;
   }
   average = sum / n;
   printf( "\nAverage of numbers = %.2f\n", average );
}
```

Test Run

```
Enter value of n: 8

Enter real number 1: 2.5
Enter real number 2: 12.0
Enter real number 3: 10.25
Enter real number 4: 8.75
Enter real number 5: 11.0
Enter real number 6: 20.25
Enter real number 7: -7.75
Enter real number 8: 9.0

Average of numbers = 8.25
```

7.4 THE *do – while* STATEMENT

The *do-while* statement, like *while* statement, is also suited for problems where it is not known in advance that how many times a statement will be executed.

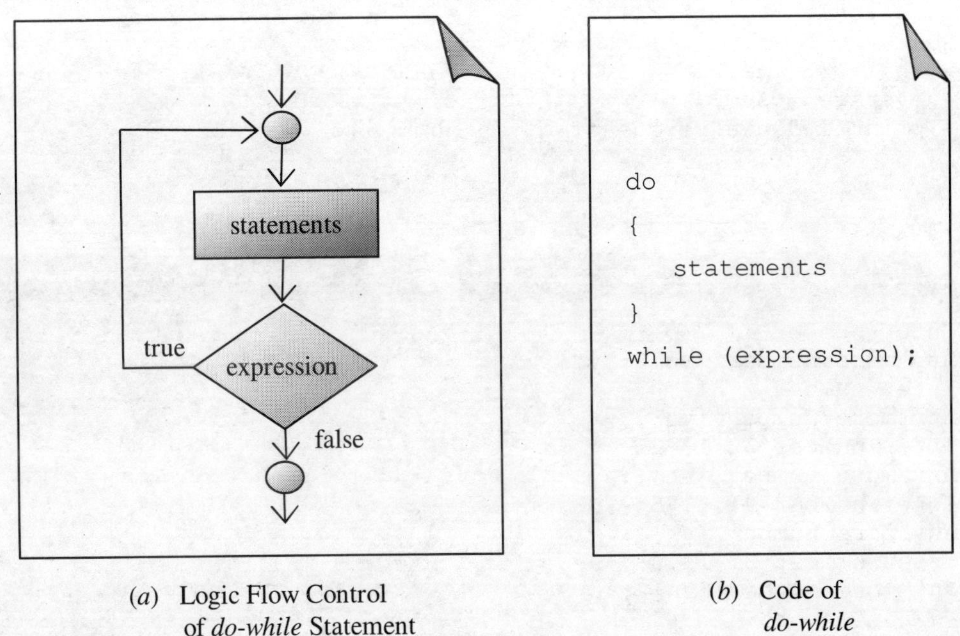

(*a*) Logic Flow Control of *do-while* Statement

(*b*) Code of *do-while*

Figure 7.4: Logic flow control and code of *do-while* statement

where *expression* is a constant, a variable or an expression. The *statement-block* is executed repeatedly till the *exp* evaluates to a *non-zero* value.

To demonstrate the use of *do – while* statement, let us develop a program to find the average of unknown real numbers.

Listing 7.8

```
/*
*  Program to compute average of unknown real numbers
*/

#include<stdio.h>
void main()
{
  int n = 0;
  char yesno;
  float number, sum = 0, average;
  do {
     printf( "\nEnter number %d: ", n+1 );
     scanf( "%f", &number );
     n++;
     sum += number;
     printf( "\nAny more number [yn]?: " );
     yesno = getchar();
  }
  while ( ( yesno == 'y' ) || ( yesno == 'Y' )  );
  average = sum / n;
  printf( "\n\nAverage of given numbers = %.2f\n", average );
}
```

Test Run

```
Enter number 1: 2.5
Any more number [yn]?: y
Enter number 2: 12.0
Any more number [yn]?: y
Enter number 3: 10.25
Any more number [yn]?: y
Enter number 4: 8.75
Any more number [yn]?: y
Enter number 5: 11.0
Any more number [yn]?: n

Average of given numbers = 8.90
```

7.5 NESTED *while*, *for* and *do — while* STATEMENTS

Just as *if* statements can be nested, these statements can also be nested. The inner loop is executed from the beginning for each iteration of the outer loop. The following sections of code show the nesting of looping statements within their own types.

```
for(i=0;i<m;i++)
{
    :
    for(j=0;j<n;j++)
    {
        :
    }
}
```

```
i=0;
while(i<m)
{
    :
    j=0;
    while(j<n)
    {
        :
        j++;
    }
    i++;
}
```

```
i=0;
do
{
    :
    j=0;
    do
    {
        :
        j++;
    } while(j<n);
    i++;
} while(i<m);
```

In general, it is possible to nest while and do-while statements inside *for* statement, *for* statement inside the *while* and *do-while* statements, *i.e.*, all sort of nesting combinations are permitted.

Listing 7.9

```
/*
*  Program to demonstrate the nesting of ‘for’ statements
*/
#include <stdio.h>
#include <ctype.h>
void main()
{
   int j, i, jj;
   for ( i = 2; i <= 10; i++ )
   {
      printf ( "\n\t\t   Table of %d", i );
      printf ( "\n\t\t   ==========\n" );
      for ( j = 1; j <= 10; j++ )
      {
         jj = j + 10;
         printf("\n\t%3d x %2d = %3d\t%3d x %3d = %3d",
                i, j, i*j, i, jj, i*jj );
      }
      printf( "\n\n\tPress any key to continue...");
      getch();
   }
}
```

When you run this program, it will print the tables from 2 to 10, one table per screen. After printing one table, it will ask the user to press any key to continue.

Test Run

```
                Table of 2
                ==========
     2 x  1 =   2  2 x  11 =  22
     2 x  2 =   4  2 x  12 =  24
     2 x  3 =   6  2 x  13 =  26
     2 x  4 =   8  2 x  14 =  28
     2 x  5 =  10  2 x  15 =  30
     2 x  6 =  12  2 x  16 =  32
     2 x  7 =  14  2 x  17 =  34
     2 x  8 =  16  2 x  18 =  36
     2 x  9 =  18  2 x  19 =  38
     2 x 10 =  20  2 x  20 =  40
  Press any key to continue...
```

7.6 JUMPING STATEMENTS

These statements transfer the control from one part of the program to another part. In this section, we will see their working.

7.6.1 The *break* Statement

The *break* statement is always used inside the body of the *switch* statement, and looping statements.

```
switch ( expression )
{
    case val-1 : statement-1
                 break;
    case val-2 : statement-2
                 break;
    case val-3 : statement-3
                 break;
       :
       :
    case val-n : statement-n
                 break;
    default    :
                statement-d
}
```

Figure 7.5: Action of *break* statement in *switch* statement

In *switch* statement, it is used as the last statement of every case except the last one. When executed, it transfers the control out of *switch* statement and the execution of the program continues from the statement following *switch* statement.

In *for*, *while* and *do-while* statements, it is always used in conjunction with *if* statement. Note that it is never used with *if* statement if it is not part of the body of the looping statement. When executed, it transfers the control out of looping statement and the execution of the program continues from the statement following looping statement.

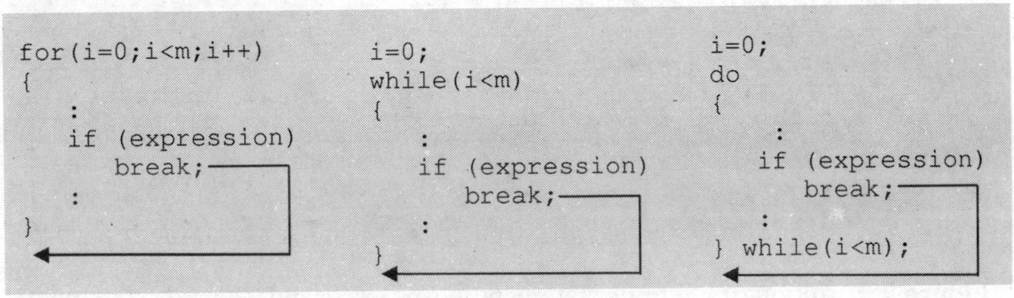

```
for(i=0;i<m;i++)        i=0;                    i=0;
{                       while(i<m)              do
   :                    {                       {
   if (expression)         :                       :
      break;               if (expression)         if (expression)
   :                          break;                  break;
}                          :                       :
                        }                       } while(i<m);
```

Figure 7.6: Action of *break* statement in *for, while* and *do-while* statements

In simple terms, we can say that the *break* when executed terminates the execution of the loop.

Consider the following code segment

```
  :
i = 0;
while ( i <= 100 )
{
    . . . . . .
    scanf("%d", &k);
    if ( k == 0 )
        break;
    m = i / k;
     . . . . . .
}
  :
```

The execution of the *while* loop will be terminated as soon as the user enters value 0 for variable *k* as input or the value of variable *i* exceeds 100, which ever happens earlier.

7.6.2 The *continue* Statement

The *continue* statement is always used inside the body of the looping statements. In looping statements, sometimes a situation may arise where we want that from a given statement onward, the rest of the statement up to the last statement of the loop are to be bypassed. This task is accomplished by using *continue* statement.

The *continue* statement transfers the control to the beginning of the next iteration of the loop thus bypassing the statements which are not yet executed. Note that the *continue* statement is always used in conjunction with the *if* statement.

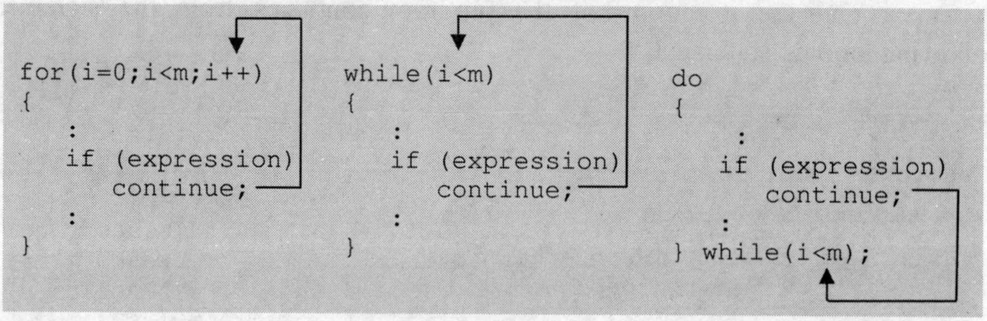

```
for(i=0;i<m;i++)        while(i<m)              do
{                       {                       {
   :                       :                       :
   if (expression)         if (expression)         if (expression)
      continue;               continue;               continue;
   :                       :                       :
}                       }                       } while(i<m);
```

Figure 7.7: Action of *continue* statement in *for, while* and *do-while* statements

In simple terms, we can say that the continue statement when executed terminates the current iteration of the loop.

Consider the following segment

```
   :
i = 0;
while ( i <= 100 )
{
    . . . . . .
    if ( i % 10 == 0 )
       continue;
    . . . . . .
}
   :
```

The use of *continue* statement in conjunction with *if* statement skips the rest of the statements of the *while* loop for values of *i* divisible by 10.

7.6.3 The *goto* Statement

Though in C language, every program can be written without the use of *goto* statement, still a situation may arise where we are forced to use *goto* statement. For example, to transfer a control from deeply nested statements, such as jumping out of two or more loops at once. In that situation, a *break* statement can not be used directly since it exits only from the innermost loop.

The *goto* statement can transfer the control to any part of the program. The target destination of the *goto* statement is marked by a *label*, where a label is any name or integer number followed by colon (character ':'). The syntax for using *goto* statement is

```
    // some statements                        // some statements
       goto label; ──────────┐              label:◄──────────────────┐
                              │                                        │
    // some more statements   │               // some more statements  │
                              │                                        │
label:  ◄─────────────────────┘               goto label; ────────────┘
    // still more statements
                                              // still more statements
```

Figure 7.8: Action of *goto* statement

The code that relies on *goto* statement is generally difficult to understand and hence difficult to maintain than the code written without *goto* statements. Therefore, the use of *goto* statement must be avoided, if possible.

7.7 SUPPLEMENTARY PROBLEMS

Let us write a few more C programs to use the features that we have learned in this chapter.

Problem 7.1:

Program to find whether the given positive number n is a prime number or composite.

I hope you know that a positive integer number is said to be prime if it divisible by 1 and itself only, *i.e.*, it cannot be factorized. In addition, to this definition, an even number except 2, is not a prime number.

Therefore, our test criteria becomes

1. If n is greater than 2 and is even then n is not a prime number.
2. If test at step 1 fails, then we try to divide number n by factors $k = 3, 5, 7, \ldots \sqrt{n}$. Therefore, if n is divisible by any value of k, number n is not a prime number.
3. If test at step 2 also fails, then n is a prime number.

The following program implements this criterion.

Listing 7.10

```
/*
*  Program to find whether given positive number 'n' is prime
*/
#include<stdio.h>
#include<math.h>
void main()
{
  int n, k, m;
  printf( "\nEnter a positive integer number: " );
  scanf("%d", &n);
  if ( ( n > 2 ) && ( ( n % 2 ) == 0 ) )
  {
     printf( "\n%d is not a prime number.\n", n );
  }
  else
  {
     m = sqrt( n );

     for ( k = 3; k <= m; k += 2 )
     {
        if ( ( n % k ) == 0 )
            break;
     }

     if ( k > m )
        printf( "\n%d is a prime number.\n", n );
     else
        printf( "\n%d is not a prime number.\n", n );
  }
}
```

Test Runs

First Run

```
Enter a positive integer number: 43

43 is a prime number.
```

Second Run

```
Enter a positive integer number: 92

92 is not a prime number.
```

Problem 7.2:

Program to find the *n*th prime number.

We know that first prime number is 2, second prime number is 3, fourth prime number is 5, and so on.

Therefore, we start with number 2 and generate the subsequent numbers. On each number we apply primality test, if is passes the test, we count it. After every count, we see do we have reached the desired prime number, if yes we print that number and stop.

The following program implements this criterion.

Listing 7.11

```
/*
*  Program to find the nth prime number
*/
#include<stdio.h>
#include<math.h>
void main()
{
  int n, k, m, count=0, num = 2;
  printf("Program to find nth prime number\n\n");
  printf("Enter positive value for n: ");
  scanf("%d", &n);
  while ( 1 )
  {
      if ( ( num > 2 ) && ( ( num %2 ) == 0 ) ) {
         num++;       /* move to next number, it is even   */
         continue;
      } else {
          m = (int) sqrt ( (double) n );
          for ( k = 3; k <= m; k+= 2 ) {
             if ( ( num % k ) == 0 )
             {
                 num++;              /* move to next number,     */
                 break;              /* as it is divisible by k */
             }
          }
          if ( k > m ) {
             count++;                /*  increase the count     */
             if ( count == n )       /* is it desired number    */
             {
                 printf("\n%dth prime number = %d\n", n, num);
                 return;
             }
```

```
                num++;                  /*  move to next number    */
            }
        }
    }
}
```

Test Run

```
Program to find nth prime number
Enter positive value for n: 10
10th prime number = 29
```

Problem 7.3:

Program to check whether the given positive integer number is an Armstrong number.

Note that a positive integer number is an Armstrong number if the sum of cubes of its digits equals the number itself. For example, number 153 is an Armstrong number as

$$1^3 + 5^3 + 3^3 = 1 + 125 + 27 = 153$$

Listing 7.12

```
/*
*  Program to check whether the given positive integer
*  number is an Armstrong number
*/
#include<stdio.h>
void main()
{
  int intNumber, intTempNumber, intSum = 0, digit;
  printf( "Enter positive integer number : " );
  scanf("%d", &intNumber);
  intTempNumber = intNumber;  /* create copy */
  while ( intTempNumber > 0 ) {
     digit = intTempNumber % 10;
     intTempNumber /= 10;
     intSum += digit * digit * digit;
  }
  if ( intSum == intNumber )
     printf("\n%d is an Armstrong Number\n", intNumber);
  else
     printf( "\n%d is not an Armstrong Number\n", intNumber);
}
```

Test Runs

First Run

```
Enter positive integer number: 153
153 is an Armstrong number
```

Second Run

```
Enter positive integer number: 120
120 is not an Armstrong number
```

Problem 7.4:

A Fibonacci sequence is defined as follows: the first and second terms in the sequence are 0 and 1. Subsequent terms are found by adding the preceding two terms in the sequence. Write a program to generate the first *n* terms of the sequence.

Listing 7.13

```
/*
* Program to generate the first 'n' terms of Fibonacci sequence
*/
#include<stdio.h>
void main()
{
  int previous = 0, current = 1, next, n, count;
  printf( "\nEnter value for n : " );
  scanf( "%d", &n );
  if ( n <= 0 )
  {
     printf( "\nIncorrect value for n, re-run the program" );
     printf( " with correct value for n\n" );
     return;
  }
  if ( n == 1 )
     printf( "%d", previous );
  else if ( n == 2 )
     printf( "%d  %d", previous, current );
  else {
     printf( "%d  %d  ", previous, current );
     count = 2;
     while ( count < n )
     {
```

```
            next = previous + current;
            printf( "%d  ", next );
            count++;
            previous = current;
            current = next;
        }
    }
    printf( "\n" );
}
```

Test Runs

First Run

```
Enter value for n : 0
Incorrect value for n, re-run the program with correct value for n
```

Second Run

```
Enter value for n : 1
0
```

Third Run

```
Enter value for n : 2
0  1
```

Fourth Run

```
Enter value for n : 10
0  1  1  2  3  5  8  13  21  34
```

Problem 7.5:

Write a program to generate all the prime numbers between *m* and *n*, where value of *m* and *n* is supplied by the user.

Listing 7.14

```
/*
* Program to generate all prime numbers between 1 and n, where
* value for n is supplied by the user
*/
#include<stdio.h>
void main()
{
  int i, m, n, k, flag;
  printf( "\nEnter value for m,n : " );
  scanf( "%d,%d", &m, &n );
```

```
    for ( i = m+1; i < n; i++ )
    {
        if ( ( i > 2 ) && ( ( i % 2 ) == 0 ) )
            continue;
        else
        {
            flag = 1;
            m = (int) sqrt ( (double) i );
            for ( k = 3; k <= m; k += 2 )
            {
                if ( ( n % k ) == 0 )
                {
                    flag = 0;
                    break;
                }
            }
            if ( flag == 1 )
                printf( "%d  ", i );
        }
    }
    printf( "\n" );
}
```

Test Runs

First Run

```
Enter value for n : 0
Incorrect value for n, re-run the program with correct value for n
```

Second Run

```
Enter value for n : 10
2  3  5  7  9
```

Problem 7.6:

Write a C program to read in two numbers, *x* and *n*, and then compute the sum of this geometric progression:

$$sum = 1+x+x^2+x^3+\ldots\ldots\ldots\ldots+x^n$$

For example: if *n* is 3 and *x* is 5, then the program computes $1+5+5^2+5^3$.

Print *x*, *n*, the *sum*

Perform error checking. For example, the formula does not make sense for negative exponents – if *n* is less than 0. Have your program print an error message if $n < 0$, then go back and read in the next pair of numbers of without computing the *sum*.

Listing 7.15

```
/*
*  Program to find the sum of geometric progression
*  using straight forward approach
*/
#include<stdio.h>
#include<math.h>
void main()
{
   int x, n, sum, i;
   while(1)
   {
      printf("\nEnter degree of polynomial : ");
      scanf("%d",&n);
      printf("Enter value of x : ");
      scanf("%d",&x);
      if ( n < 0 ) {
         printf("\nWrong value for exponents, re-try!\n");
         continue;
      }
      else
         Break;
   }
   sum = 1;
   for ( i = 1; i <= n; i++ )
   {
     sum = sum + (int)pow((double)x,(double)i);
   }
   printf("\nx = %d, n = %d, sum = %d\n", x, n, sum);
}
```

Test Run

```
Enter degree of polynomial : 3
Enter value of x : 5
x = 5, n = 3, sum = 156
```

The sum of the geometric expression can be computed efficiently by expressing it using Horner's method as shown below:

$$sum = 1+x*(1+x*(1+x*(1+\ldots+x*(1+x))))$$

Listing 7.16

```
/*
*  Program to find the sum of geometric progression by
*  expressing it using Horner's method
*/
#include<stdio.h>
void main()
{
  int x, n, sum, i;
  while(1)
  {
     printf("\nEnter degree of polynomial : ");
     scanf("%d",&n);
     printf("Enter value of x : ");
     scanf("%d",&x);
     if ( n < 0 ) {
        printf("\nWrong value for exponents, re-try!\n");
        continue;
     }
     else
        break;
  }
  sum = 1;
  for ( i = n; i >= 1; i-- ) {
     sum = 1 + sum * x;
  }
  printf("\nx = %d, n = %d, sum = %d\n", x, n, sum);
}
```

Problem 7.7:

Write a program to print a pyramid of numbers with *n* rows. An example pyramid with 5 rows is shown below:

```
                1
             2  3  2
          3  4  5  4  3
       4  5  6  7  6  5  4
    5  6  7  8  9  8  7  6  5
```

Listing 7.17

```
/*  Program to print pyramid of numbers with 'n' rows   */
#include<stdio.h>
void main()
{
   int i, j, k, n;
   printf("\nEnter number of rows for the pyramid (n) : ");
   scanf("%d",&n);
```

```
    printf("\n");

    for ( i = 1; i <= n; i++ )
    {
        for ( j = 1; j <= n-i; j++ )
            printf("    ");
        k = i;

        for ( j = 1; j <= i; j++ )
            printf("%4d", k++);
        k = k-2;

        for ( j = 1; j < i; j++ )
            printf("%4d", k--);
        printf("\n\n");
    }
}
```

Test Run

```
Enter number of rows for the pyramid : 5
                1
            2   3   2
        3   4   5   4   3
    4   5   6   7   6   5   4
5   6   7   8   9   8   7   6   5
```

Problem 7.8:

Write a program to find the greatest common divisor (GCD), of two positive integer *m* and *n*.

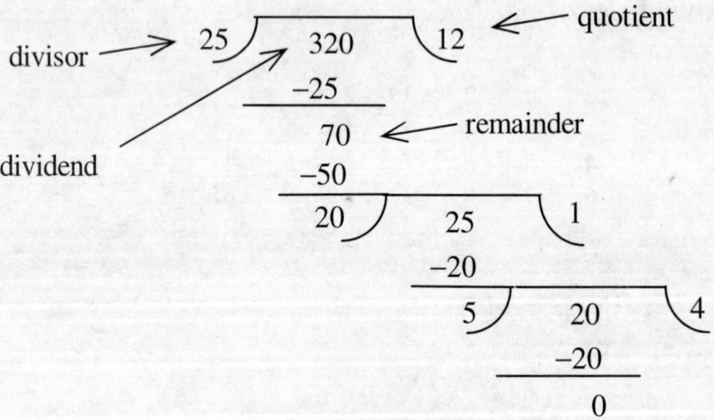

Figure 7.5: Illustration of computational procedure for GCD

From above figure, you must have observed that in successive divisions, the divisor of the previous division becomes dividend, remainder of becomes divisor, and the division is again carried out. This process is carried out till the reminder becomes zero, and the current divisor is taken as GCD of the given integer numbers.

This process can be implemented by using the following steps:

1. Perform division.
2. If remainder is zero, then stop and take the divisor as HCF.
3. Replace dividend by divisor.
4. Replace divisor by remainder.
5. Repeat from step 1.

Listing 7.18

```
/*  Program to compute GCD of two positive Integer numbers  */
#include<stdio.h>
void main()
{
   int m, n, r = 1;
   printf( "\nEnter value for m,n : " );
   scanf( "%d,%d",&m, &n );
   while ( r != 0 )
   {
      r = n % m;
      n = m;
      m = r;
   }
   printf( "\nGCD = %d\n", n );
}
```

Test Run

```
Enter value for m,n : 35,155
GCD = 5
```

Problem 7.9:

The number 1991 is a palindrome because it is the same number when read forward or backward. Write a program to check whether the given number is palindrome or not.

Here, we first find a new number by reversing the digits of a given number and then we compare the given number with reversed number. If they match, then the given number is palindrome otherwise it is not a palindrome.

Listing 7.19

```
/*
* Program to check whether given number is palindrome or not
*/
#include<stdio.h>
void main()
{
  int sum = 0, digit;
  int number, temp;
  printf( "\nEnter any positive integer number: " );
  scanf( "%d", &number );
  temp = number;
  while ( temp > 0 ) {
     digit = temp % 10;
     temp /= 10;
     sum = sum * 10 + digit;
  }
  if ( number == sum )
     printf( "\n%d is a palindrome number.\n", number );
  else
     printf( "\n%d is not a palindrome number.\n", number );
}
```

Test Runs

First Run

```
Enter any positive integer number: 1991

1991 is a palindrome number.
```

Second Run

```
Enter any positive integer number: 1234

1234 is not a palindrome number.
```

Problem 7.10:

The total distance traveled by vehicle in t seconds is given by distance = $ut+1/2at^2$ where u and a are the initial velocity ($m/sec.$) and acceleration (m/sec^2). Write C program to find the distance traveled at regular intervals of time given the values of *u* and *a*. The program should provide the flexibility to the user to select his own time intervals and repeat the calculations for different values of *u* and *a*.

Listing 7.20

```
/*
*  Program to print distance traveled at regular intervals of time
*  for given value of initial velocity (u) and acceleration (a).
*/
#include<stdio.h>
void main(void)
{
   float s, u, a, t, dt, st;
   printf( "\nEnter value initial velocity (u) : ");
   scanf( "%f", &u);
   printf( "Enter value for acceleration (a) : ");
   scanf( "%f", &a);
   printf( "Enter value for time (t) : ");
   scanf( "%f", &t);
   printf( "Enter value for time interval (dt) : ");
   scanf( "%f", &dt );
   st = dt;
   while ( st <= t )
   {
      s = u * st + 0.5 * a * st * st;
      printf("\nDistance traveled after %.2fseconds =%.2f",
             st,s);
      st += dt;
   }
   printf( "\n" );
}
```

Test Run

```
Enter value initial velocity (u) : 0
Enter value for acceleration (a) : 10
Enter value for time (t) : 5
Enter value for time interval (dt) : 0.5

Distance traveled after 0.50 seconds =1.25
Distance traveled after 1.00 seconds =5.00
Distance traveled after 1.50 seconds =11.25
Distance traveled after 2.00 seconds =20.00
Distance traveled after 2.50 seconds =31.25
Distance traveled after 3.00 seconds =45.00
Distance traveled after 3.50 seconds =61.25
Distance traveled after 4.00 seconds =80.00
Distance traveled after 4.50 seconds =101.25
Distance traveled after 5.00 seconds =125.00
```

Problem 7.11:

Write a C program to calculate the following Sum:

$$Sum = 1 - x^2/2! + x^4/4! - x^6/6! + x^8/8! - x^{10}/10!$$

Listing 7.21

```
/* Program to compute the sum of the following series
*         sum = 1 - (x^2)/2! + (x^4)/4! - (x^6)/6! + (x^8)/8! - (x^10)/10!
*/
#include<stdio.h>
#include<math.h>
void main()
{
    int i, j, sign = -1, fact;
    float x, sum = 1.0;
    printf( "\nEnter value for x : " );
    scanf( "%f", &x );
    for ( i = 2; i <= 10; i += 2 ) {
        /*  compute factorial 'i' */
        fact = 1;
        for ( j = 2; i <= i; j++2 )
            fact *= j;
        sum += sign * pow(x,i)/fact;
        sign = -sign;
    }
    printf( "\nSum = %.3f\n", sum );
}
```

Test Run

```
Enter value for x : 2

Sum = -0.474
```

7.8 QUICK RECAP

In this chapter, we have learnt that

- The control statements allow controlling the order of execution of statements.
- This controlling of statements may involve selecting a statement from the alternate statements or executing some selected statements repeatedly.
- The *for*, *while* and *do–while* statements are known as iterative or looping statements as they allow to repeat (iterate) the selected statements.
- The *for* statement is preferred in situations where we known in advance the number of times the statements are to be executed.

- The *while* and *do–while* statements are preferred when the number of times the statements are to be executed depends on the satisfaction of certain conditions.
- The only difference between *while* and *do–while* statements that is *do-while* is always executed at least once whereas *while* loop may or may not be executed at all.
- The *break* statement is used with *switch* and all the looping statements. On its execution, it transfers the control outside the block.
- When used with the *switch* statement, the *break* statement takes the control outside the scope of the *switch* statement.
- When used with looping statement, the *break* statement takes the control outside the loop, *i.e.*, it terminates the execution of the loop.
- The *continue* statement is used only with looping statements. Its execution skips the statements following it', *i.e.*, it terminates the current iteration and the next iteration starts afresh.
- The *goto* statement transferred the control to any labeled part of the program.
- It is recommended to avoid the use of *goto* statement as its makes the program untidy and difficult to understand.

7.9 MULTIPLE CHOICE QUESTIONS

1. Consider the following code:

```
while ( ++i <= n );
```

What will be the value of *i* when the loop completes, initial value of *i* being 1?

(*a*) *n* (*b*) *n*-1
(*c*) *n*+1 (*d*) *n*+2

2. Consider the following code. What is its output?

```
for ( i = 1;i <= 5; i++ ) {
    printf( "%d", i += 2 );
}
```

(*a*) 1 2 3 4 5 (*b*) 3 4 5 6 7
(*c*) 3 5 7 9 11 (*d*) None

3. Which of the following statement is true about *continue* statement?

(*a*) It can be used in conjunction with *switch* statement.
(*b*) It terminates the loop.
(*c*) It terminates the current iteration.
(*d*) None of above.

4. Which of the following statement is true about *switch* statement?
   (*a*) It may contain zero or more cases.
   (*b*) Constant expressions are valid case values.
   (*c*) Statement block of every case must have *break* statement as its last statement to avoid the control to fall through the later cases.
   (*d*) All of above.
5. Which of the following statements are true about *break* statement?
   (*a*) The *break* statement can be used with *if* statement to terminate the execution of its block.
   (*b*) The *break* statement can only be used with loop statements and *switch* statement.
   (*c*) The *break* statement terminates current iteration of the loop.
   (*d*) None of above
6. The *continue* statement is used to
   (*a*) continue the next iteration of the loop statement.
   (*b*) exit the block of loop statement .
   (*c*) exit from the outermost block even it is used in the innermost block.
   (*d*) continue execution of the program even error occurs.
7. Consider the following program

```
#include <stdio.h>
void main()
{
    int i = 3;
    while ( i > 0 ) {
        int i = 75;
        printf( "%d\n", i );
        i--;
    }
}
```

   What will be the result of attempting to compile and execute above program?
   (*a*) Program will fail to compile because variable *i* is duplicated.
   (*b*) Program will fail to compile because variables can only be declared in the beginning of the program.
   (*c*) Program will compile, execute successfully and will print 3, 2, 1 on different lines.
   (*d*) Program will enter into infinite loop. .
8. Consider the following program

```
#include <stdio.h>
void main()
{
```

```
    int k = 0;
    for ( ;; )
    {
        printf( "%d  ", k++ );
        if ( k > 5 )
            break;
    }
}
```

What will be the result of attempting to compile and execute above program?

(*a*) Program will fail to compile because of incorrect use of *for* statement.
(*b*) Program will fail to compile because expression cannot be included in list of variables for the *printf()* function.
(*c*) Program will compile and execute successfully and will print 0 1 2 3 4 5.
(*d*) None of above.

9. Minimum number of times the *do-while* loop will be executed?

(*a*) 0 (*b*) 1
(*c*) Cannot be predicted (*d*) None

10. Consider the following program

```
#include <stdio.h>
void main()
{
    int i, j;
    for ( i = 0; j = 10; i < j;  i++, j-- );
        printf( "x" );
}
```

How many times letter 'x' will be printed?

(*a*) 5 (*b*) 1
(*c*) 10 (*d*) 4

11. Consider the following program

```
#include <stdio.h>
void main()
{
    unsigned char ch;
    for ( ch = 0; ch <= 256; ch++ )
        printf( "%d = %c", ch, ch );
}
```

How many times *for* loop will be executed?

(*a*) 256 (*b*) 255
(*c*) 257 (*d*) Infinitely

12. Consider the following program

```
#include <stdio.h>
void main()
{
    int i;
    for ( i = 1; i <= 10; i++ ) {
       if ( i % 5 )
          continue;
       else
          break;
       printf("\nKeep it up!");
    }
    printf( "%d  ", i );
}
```

How many times the message "Keep it up!" will be printed?

(*a*) 5 times (*b*) 10 times
(*c*) Will not be printed at all (*d*) Once

13. How many times the while loop will be executed in the following program?

```
#include <stdio.h>
void main()
{
    int j = 1;
    while ( j <= 100 );
    {
       printf("\nj = %d, j*j = %d", j, j*j );
       j++;
    }
}
```

(*a*) Infinite times (*b*) 100 times
(*c*) 99 times (*d*) 101 times

7.10 REVIEW EXERCISES

1. What happens if the expression of a *while* statement is initially false?
2. What is the difference between *while* and *do - while* statements?
3. When is the *do - while* statement preferred over *while* statement?
4. Can there be multiple increment expressions in increment part of the *for* statement?
5. When is the *while* statement preferred over a *for* statement?
6. Where the *break* statement is used, and what is its function?
7. What is the action of *continue* statement?
8. What will be the output of the following segment?

```
#include <stdio.h>
void main()
{
    int i;
    printf ( "\n" );
    for ( i = 0; i <= 100; i-- );
        printf ( "i = %d\n", i );
}
```

9. Will the following program compile and execute successfully? If not, give reasons.

```
#include <stdio.h>
void main()
{
    int s1, s2, num;
    s1 = s2 = 0;
    for ( x = 0; x < 11; x++ ) {
        scanf("%d", num);
        if ( num > 0 )
            s1 += num;
        else
            s1 =/ num;
    }
    printf("\ns1 = %d, s2 = %d\n", s1 s2 );;
}
```

10. Rewrite the following program after removing the syntactical error(s), if any. Underline each correction.

```
#include <stdio.h>
const int multiple 3;
void main()
{
    value = 15;
    for ( int counter = 1; counter =< 5; counter++, value -= 2)
    if ( value % multiple == 0 )
        printf("\nvalue * multiple = %d\n", value * multiple);
    else
        printf("\nvalue + multiple = %d\n", value + multiple);
}
```

7.11 PROGRAMMING EXERCISES

1. Write a program to find the sum of *n* integers starting from *m*th integer.
2. Write a program to print first *n* prime numbers.
3. Two prime are said to be twin prime numbers if they differ by 2, such as 11 and 13, 17 and 19, etc. Write a program to print all two digit twin prime numbers.
4. Write a program to find the *n*th number of the following series

   0, 1, 1, 2, 3, 5, 8, 13, 21, 34, 55, . . .

   This series is popularly known as *Fibonacci sequence*.

5. Write a program to sum up the following series:

   $1 - 1/2 + 1/3 - \ldots + 1/n$

6. The number 1991 is a palindrome because it is the same number when read forward or backward. Write a program that finds and prints all palindromes numbers between two numbers *m* and *n*.

7. A factorial chart from 1 to 5 looks like the following:

   1! = 1
   2! = 1×2
   3! = 1×2×3
   4! = 1×2×3×4
   5! = 1×2×3×4×5

   Write a program that will generate a factorial chart from 1 to *n* for any ≤ 9.

8. Suppose an amount (say *amount*) is deposited in a commercial bank, which pays compound interest at the rate of *r%* annually, for *n* years. Write a program that prints the amount in account after each year.

9. A sample inverted pyramid of numbers with 5 rows is shown:

```
5  6  7  8  9  8  7  6  5
   4  5  6  7  6  5  4
      3  4  5  4  3
         2  3  2
            1
```

   Write a program to print a inverted pyramid of numbers with n rows, where the value of *n* will be supplied by the user at execution time.

11. A positive integer number IJK is said to be *well-ordered* if I<J<K. For example, number 138 is called *well-ordered* because the digits in the number (1, 3, 8) increase from left to right, *i.e.*, 1 < 3 < 8. Number 365 is not *well-ordered* because 6 is larger than 5. Write a program that will find and display all possible three digit *well-ordered* numbers. The program should also display the total number of three digit *well-ordered* numbers found.

12. The numbers in the triangles below reveal a pattern for a *number triangle*.

```
1
2  6
3  7  10
4  8  11  13
5  9  12  14  15
```

Discover this pattern and write a program to generate *number triangles* for any size (number of rows) *n* between 1 and 9.

13. Write a program to print all prime numbers between *m* and *n*. The value for *m* and *n* will be supplied by the user.

14. The square arrangement of whole numbers

```
1   2   3   4
2   3   4   1
3   4   1   2
4   1   2   3
```

is called a 4×4 LATIN SQUARE because each whole numbers 1, 2, 3, and 4 appear once and only once in each row and column. There are many ways to arrange the numbers and still make a LATIN SQUARE. Of all the 4×4 LATIN SQUARES, the one above has a simple pattern. We call it a SIMPLE 4×4 LATIN SQUARE. Write a program that will generate a similar SIMPLE *n*×*n* LATIN SQUARE for any whole number *n* between 2 and 9.

15. You know that an even number is a number which is divisible by 2. However there is another approach that can be used to check whether the given number is even or not. The approach is by inspecting the unit digit - *if the unit digit is 0, 2, 4, 6, or 8, the number is even.* So you are required to write a program to check whether the given number is even or not without performing the division by 2.

❑ ❑ ❑

8 Functions

Learning Objectives

After reading this chapter, students will have the ability to:

- explain the concept of top-down design and its advantages
- use structure charts to depict the top-down design of their software solution
- explain the concept of local data and global data
- explain the way functions are declared, defined, and accessed
- explain the different ways in which arguments can be passed to a functions
- explain the use of *return* statement
- explain the concept of recursion, and will be able to write recursive functions
- explain and use command-line arguments
- explain how multiple file programs are handled
- build their own library as per their requirements

8.1 INTRODUCTION

The programs we have discussed so far were very simple and straightforward. They could solve problems that can be understood without much effort. As we move to larger and larger and more complex problems and hence programs, you will discover that it is not possible to understand all aspects of such problems and hence programs without some how reducing them to more elementary parts.

The best way to handle large and complex problems is to split the problem into small problems, called *subproblems* that can be handled easily. This we are used to do in our day-to-day working. Once all these sub problems are solved separately, solutions of these subproblems can be synthesized to generate the solution of the given complex problem.

Like wise, if program to be developed is very large and complex, it is always recommended to break into two or more functions (modules) that can be developed separately, tested separately and then integrated.

The planning for large and complex program starts with understanding the problem as a whole; then breaking it into smaller, simpler and understandable parts. We will call each of these parts of a program a *module* and the process of subdividing a problem into manageable parts *top-down design*.

The principles of top-down design and structured programming dictate that a program should be divided into main module and its related modules. Each module further be divided into submodules and this process should be continued until each submodule performs some specialized task and cannot be further subdivided. This process is known as *factoring*.

In top-down design, a program is divided into a main module and its related modules. Each module, in turn, is divided into submodules until the resulting modules are small enough, specialized and cannot be further subdivided.

Top-down design is usually done using a visual representation of the modules, known as *structure chart*. The structure chart shows the relation between each module and its submodules. The main module represents the entire set of code to solve the problem.

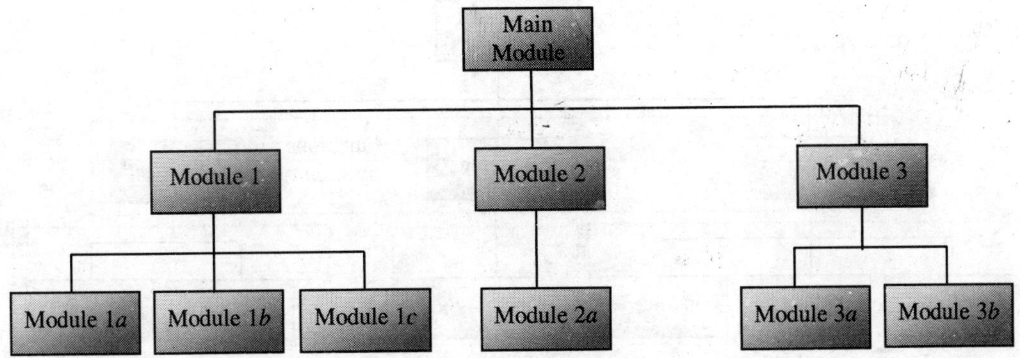

Figure 8.1: Structure Chart

Moving down and left, we then read Module 1. One the same level with Module 1 are Module 2 and Module 3. The main module consists of three submodules. At this point, however, we are dealing only with Module 1. We now note that Module 1 is further subdivided into three modules, Module 1*a*, Module 1*b* and Module 1*c*.

The Main Module is known as the *calling* module because it has submodules. Each of its submodules is known as *called* module. Since Module 1, Module 2 and Module 3 also have submodules, they are also called calling modules; they are both *called* and *calling* modules.

Communication between modules in a structure chart is allowed only through a calling module. If Module 1 needs to send data to Module 2, the data must be passed through the calling module, Main Module. No communication can take place directly between modules that do not have a calling relationship.

The technique used to pass data to a module is known as *argument passing*. The arguments are contained in a list that is a definition of the data passed to the module by the caller. The list serves as the formal declaration of the data types and names.

8.2 FUNCTIONS IN C LANGUAGE

In C language, the idea of top-down design is done using functions. A C program is made of one or more functions, one and only one of which must be named as *main*. The execution of the program always begins and ends with *main*, but it can call other functions to accomplish designated tasks.

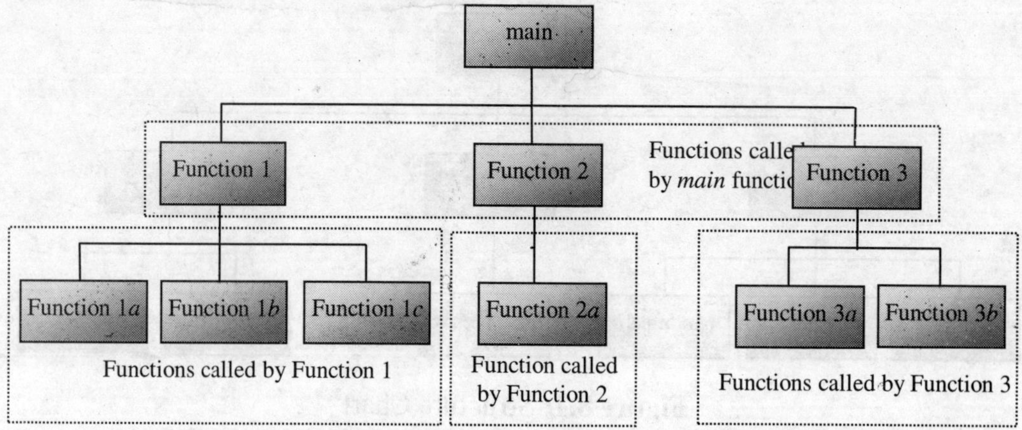

Figure 8.2: Structure Chart for a C Program

A function in C (including *main*) is an independent module that will be called to do a designated task. A *called function* receives control from a *calling function.* When the called function completes its task, it returns control to the calling function. It may or may not return a value to the calling function. The *main* function is called by the operating system; *main* in turn calls other functions, those in turn can call other functions. When the *main* function completes it execution, control returns to the operating system.

In C language, a program is made of one or more functions, one and only one of which must be named as *main*. The execution of the program always begins and ends with *main*, but it can call other functions to accomplish designated tasks.

We had already discussed some library functions in *Chapter 4*. These library functions are actually subprograms, which are written and incorporated into the C compiler because they are used in many situations. Rather than each user writes these subprograms, the C compilers provide these library functions as a convenience. Obviously, the C library cannot contain all the functions used in all application areas. However, it is possible for users to write their own functions whenever such a need arises.

In this chapter, we will study the way functions in C language are declared, defined and accessed, arguments are passed, data types of arguments is specified, the concept of recursion, and building your own library of user-defined functions.

8.3 ADVANTAGES OF USING FUNCTIONS

Several advantages are associated with the use of functions. Some of the major advantages are

1. The use of functions allows managing large and complex problems by factoring them into small, simple and manageable parts.
2. The use of functions provides a way to reuse code that is required n more than one place in a program. As an example, assume that a program requires computing average of series of numbers in five different parts of the program. Each time the data is different. We could write the code to compute the average five times, but this would take a lot of effort. It is much easier to write the code once as a function and then call it whenever we need to compute the average.
3. This advantage of using the functions is closely tied to the reusing the code. Like many language, C language comes with a rich and valuable library. For example, there is a math library that contains almost any mathematical function that we will ever need. These C libraries provide standard functions that make our work as a programmer much easier. We can also create our personal libraries that make developing new systems much easier.
4. The use of functions can protect data. This is done using the concept of *local data*. Local data consist of data described in a function. This data is available only to the function and only while the function is executing. When the function is not executing, the data is not accessible. Data in one function, then, cannot be seen or changed by another function.

8.4 CONCEPT OF LOCAL DATA & GLOBAL DATA

The formal arguments and variables declared in the body of a function are unknown outside the function. The factor that determines which function recognizes a variable and which don't is called the *visibility* of variable. A local variable will be visible to the function in which it is declared, but not to others.

A local variable used in this way in a function is known as *automatic* variable, because it is automatically created when a function is called and destroyed when the function returns except variable having *static* storage class. The length or duration of time a variable lasts is called its *lifetime*.

In contrast to a local variable, a global variable is visible to more functions, and is declared outside all functions. The usual place of declaration of a global variable is in the beginning of the program file, *i.e.*, before all function definitions. In this case, it will be visible to all functions and exists till the program terminates. If the variable is not declared before all the functions, then it will be visible to only those functions following its declaration i.e. global in the restricted sense.

8.5 DECLARING AND DEFINING FUNCTIONS

Like every other data item in C, function also need to declared and defined. The syntax for function declaration and definition is illustrated in Figure 8.3 and Figure 8.4, respectively.

```
returnType functionName(formal argument list);
```

Figure 8.3: Syntax for function declaration

Function Header

```
returnType functionName(formal argument list)
```

```
{
    // Local declarations
    . . .
    // statements
    . . .
}
```

Function Body

Figure 8.4: Syntax for function definition

The function declaration, which needs to be done before the function call, gives the whole picture of the function that needs to be defined later. The declaration mentions the name of the function, the return type, and the type and order of formal arguments. In other words, the declaration uses only the header of the function definition ended in a semicolon. The function definition, which is traditionally coded after the function that makes the call, contains the code needed to complete the task.

8.5.1 Declaring a Function

Function declaration consists only of a function header; it contains no code. Function header consists of three parts: *the return type*, *the function name*, and *the formal argument list*. A semicolon follows the function header.

If the function has no arguments, then write *void* in the parentheses. If the function has two or more arguments, each is separated by comma.

It is not mandatory (essential) to include the names of the arguments in the argument list. The purpose of the argument list is to tell the compiler *the number*, *data type* and *order of arguments*. However, readability and understandability are improved if the names of arguments are used. One point to note, however, is that the names of arguments do not need to be the same in the function declaration and the function definition. On the other hand, if the data types do not match, the compiler will flag an error. The compiler checks the data types of the arguments in the function call to ensure that they are same or at least compatible.

A function declaration statement is also known as *prototype* of the function or as *function prototype*.

The following function declaration

```
int larget(int a, int b, int c);
```

tells the compiler that the return type of the function is *int*, name of the function is *largest*, and it has three argument, all of type *int*. The names of argument are not significant.The following function declaration

```
int larget(int, int, int);
```

is equally good and serves the purpose as earlier declaration

8.5.2 Defining a Function

Function definition consists two parts; *function header* and *function body*.

Function Header

Function header consists of three parts: *the return type*, *the function name*, and *the formal argument list*. A semicolon is not used at the end of function header.

With the implementation of new standard of C (new standard is C99), the return type is mandatory. In the earlier implementations, if the return type was omitted in the function header, it was taken as *int*, by default. When nothing is to be returned, the return type *void* is used in the function header.

The formal argument list declares the variable that will receive the data from the calling function and may also contain variable that can be used to send the data back to the calling function.

Function Body

The function body contains the local declarations and the statements that define the task to be accomplished by the function. The body starts with local declarations that specify the variables needed by the function. After the local declarations, the function statements, followed by the *return* statement, are written.

If the return type of function is *void*, it can be written without *return* statement.

It is recommended that the default statements should be explicitly written for clarity. Therefore, even for a function with *void* as its return type, the return statement must be written.

SOME RULES FOR DEFINING FUNCTIONS

Following are some points to remember while defining functions in C:

- The first statement of the function must be the function defining statement specifying the return type, name and formal arguments.
- If the type of the function is omitted, then it is assumed of type integer (*int*). But it is recommended that the return type must be explicitly specified.
- Rules for naming a function are same as for variable names.
- The formal arguments should neither be constants or expressions.
- If a formal argument is an array name, it must be declared as an array in a type declaration statement before the body of the function starts and its maximum size must be equal to the actual size in the calling function.

As an example, let consider a task where we are concerned to find the largest of three integer numbers.

Listing 8.1

```
/*
   Function that returns largest of three integer numbers (Ver 1)
*/
int largest(int x, int y, int z)
{
   if ( ( x > y ) && ( x > z ) )
      return x;
   else if ( y > z )
      return y;
   else
      return z;
}
```

The logic of the above function can also be written as shown below.

Listing 8.2

```
/*
   Function that returns largest of three integer numbers (Ver 2)
*/
int largest(int x, int y, int z)
{
   int big;
   big = x;
   if ( y > big ) big  = y;
   if ( z > big ) big  = z;
   return big;
}
```

8.6 ACCESSING A FUNCTION

Like library functions, the user-defined functions are accessed from a function simply by its name, including the actual arguments, if any, enclosed within parentheses. However, parentheses must follow the function name even if there is no actual argument to be passed to the function. The actual arguments, if any, must correspond in *number*, *type*, and *order* with formal arguments. The actual arguments can be constants, variable names, subscripted variables, or expressions.

When the name of the function is encountered, the control is transferred to the called function. The formal arguments are replaced by the actual arguments and the execution of the function is carried out. When the *return* statement is executed or last statement has finished its execution, the control is transferred back to the calling function.

The *largest()* function will be accessed/invoked/called using a statement of type

```
big = largest(a, b, c);
```

8.7 THE *return* STATEMENT

The syntax of *return* statement is

```
return;          or      return (exp);
```

where *exp* can be a constant, variable or expression. Use of parentheses around *exp* is optional. The first form is used with functions defined with return type as *void*.

The *return* statement serves two purposes:

- Execution of *return* statement immediately transfers control from the function back to the calling function.
- Whatever is following the *return* statement is returned as a value to the calling function.

In the functions described in Listing 8.2, the statement

```
return big;
```

return the value of variable *big*.

The *return* statement need not be at the end of the function. It can be used any where in the function. As soon as it is executed, the control will return to the calling function. A function can contain any number of *return* statements.

Consider the following function:

Listing 8.3

```
/* Function that returns value 1 if number is even
   else return 0
*/
int oddOrEven( int number )
{
   if ( number % 2 == 0)
      return 1;
   else
      return 0;
}
```

This function returns value 1 if the *number* is not divisible by 2, *i.e.*, *number* is odd; otherwise it returns value 0. So here, different *return* statement will be executed depending on whether the *number* is odd or even.

There is key limitation of *return* statement — it can return only one value. If you want your function to return two or more values to the calling function, you need another mechanism.

8.8 PASSING ARGUMENTS TO A FUNCTION

The mechanism used to pass data to a function is via argument list, where individual arguments are called *actual arguments*. These arguments are enclosed in parentheses after the function name. The actual arguments must correspond in *number*, *type*, and *order* with formal arguments specified in the function definition. The actual arguments can be *constants*, *variables*, *array names*, or *expressions*.

There are two approaches to passing arguments to a function:

- Call by value
- Call by reference

Let us describe these one by one.

8.8.1 Call by Value

In this approach, the actual arguments are used in the function call. The actual argument can be a variable, a constant, or an expression. The values of the actual arguments are passed to the function. When control is transferred to the called function, the values of the actual arguments are substituted to the corresponding formal arguments and the body of the function is executed. If the called function is supposed to return a value, it is returned via *return* statement.

The following points must be noted about passing arguments using call by value mechanism:

1. The actual arguments can be constants, variables, or expressions.
2. When the control is transferred from the calling function to the called function, the memory for formal arguments and local variables is allocated, values of the actual arguments are substituted in the corresponding formal arguments, and the statements in the function body are executed.

3. As soon as the called function finishes its execution, the memory allocated for it is de-allocated, *i.e.*, the values of formal arguments and local variable are destroyed, and finally the control is transferred back to the calling function.
4. Any change made to the formal arguments will have no effect on actual arguments, since the function will only be using the local copy of the arguments.

Following function definition illustrates the mechanism of passing arguments by value.

```
void swap( int a, int b )
{
    int temp;
    temp = a;
    a = b;
    b = temp;
}
```

The above function will be accessed as

```
swap(x,y);
```

where *x* and *y* are actual arguments in the calling function.

Listing 8.4

```
/*
    Program to illustrate the passing of arguments by value.
    It calls a function swap() that interchanges values
    of arguments.
*/
#include <stdio.h>
void swap(int a, int b);      /* declaration of function */
void main()
{
    int x, y;
    printf("\nEnter value for x : ");
    scanf("%d", &x);
    printf("\nEnter value for y : ");
    scanf("%d", &y);
    printf("\nBefore calling swap function\n");
    printf("\nValue of x = %d, Value of y = %d\n", x, y);
    swap(x,y);   /* function call    */
```

```
    printf("\nAfter returning from swap function\n");
    printf("\nValue of x = %d, Value of y = %d\n", x, y);
 }
 void swap( int a, int b )
 {
    int temp;
    temp  = a;
    a = b;
    b = temp;
}
```

Test Run

```
Enter value for x : 10
Enter value for y : 12
Before calling swap function
Value of x = 10, Value of y = 12
After returning from swap function
Value of x = 10, Value of y = 12
```

You must have observed that any change made to the formal arguments have not effect on the actual arguments.

8.8.2 Call by Reference

In this approach the addresses of the actual arguments are used in the function call. In this way the addresses of the actual arguments are passed to the function. When control is transferred to the called function, the addresses of the actual arguments are substituted to corresponding formal arguments and the body of the function is executed. The formal arguments are declared as pointers to *types* that match the data types of the actual arguments. This approach is of practical importance while passing arrays and structures among function, and also for passing back more than one value to the calling functions.

If the called function is supposed to return a value, it is returned via *return* statement. Additional values can be returned to the calling function via formal arguments which will be of pointer type.

Following points must be noted about passing arguments using call by reference mechanism:

1. The actual arguments can only be variables.
2. When the control is transferred from the calling function to the called function, the memory for formal arguments and local variables is allocated, addresses of the actual arguments are substituted in the corresponding formal arguments, and the statements in the function body are executed.
3. As soon as the called function finishes its execution, the memory allocated for it is de-allocated, *i.e.*, the values of formal arguments and local variable are destroyed, and finally the control is transferred back to the calling function.
4. Any change made to the formal arguments will have immediate effect on actual arguments, since function will be working on actual arguments through pointers.

Following function definition illustrates the mechanism of passing arguments by reference (address).

```
void swap( int *a, int *b )
{
   int temp;
   temp  = *a;
   *a = *b;
   *b = temp;
}
```

The above function will be accessed as

```
swap(&x,&y);
```

where *x* and *y* are actual arguments in the calling function.

Listing 8.5

```
/*
   Program to illustrate the passing of arguments by reference
   It calls a function swap() that interchanges values
   of arguments.
*/
#include <stdio.h>
void swap(int *a, int *b);    /* declaration of function */
void main()
{
```

```
  int x, y;
  printf("\nEnter value for x : ");
  scanf("%d", &x);
  printf("\nEnter value for y : ");
  scanf("%d", &y);

  printf("\nBefore calling swap function\n");
  printf("\nValue of x = %d, Value of y = %d\n", x, y);

  swap(&x,&y);  /* function call   */

  printf("\nAfter returning from swap function\n");
  printf("\nValue of x = %d, Value of y = %d\n", x, y);
}
void swap( int *a, int *b )
{
  int temp;
  temp  = *a;
  *a = *b;
  *b = temp;
}
```

Test Run

```
Enter value for x : 10
Enter value for y : 12
Before calling swap function
Value of x = 10, Value of y = 12
After returning from swap function
Value of x = 12, Value of y = 10
```

You must have observed that any change made to the formal arguments is reflected back in the actual arguments.

Next program is another example to demonstrate the passing of arguments using call by reference.

Listing 8.6

```
/* Program that calls function example() to find the average of
   two numbers, largest & smallest of these numbers. The
   average is retuned via return statement while largest and
   smallest numbers are returned via formal arguments
*/
#include <stdio.h>

/* function declaration  */
float example(float x, float y, float *big, float *small);
```

```
void main()
{
   float x, y, avg, larger, smaller;
   printf("\nEnter value for x : ");
   scanf("%f", &x);
   printf("\nEnter value for y : ");
   scanf("%f", &y);
   avg = example(x,y,&larger,&smaller); /*  function call  */
   printf("\nAverage of %.2f and %.2f is %.2f\n", x, y, avg);
   printf("\nLarger number is %.2f\n", larger);
   printf("\nSmaller number is %.2f\n", smaller);
}
/*
   Function to compute the average of two numbers and find the
   largest and smallest of these numbers
*/
float example(float x, float y, float *big, float *small)
{
    float average;
    average = ( x + y ) / 2;
    if ( x > y )
    {
       *big = x;
       *small = y;
    }
    else
    {
       *big = y;
       *small = x;
    }
    return average;
}
```

Test Run

```
Enter value for x : 10.5

Enter value for y : 12.5

Average of 10.50 and 12.50 is 11.50

Larger number is 12.50

Smaller number is 10.50
```

8.8.3 Comparison between Call by Value & Call by Reference

Table 8.1 highlights the key points of differences regarding the prototype, definition and function call.

Table 8.2 highlights the key points of differences regarding the nature of actual arguments, nature of formal arguments and the impact of any change/modification of formal arguments on actual arguments.

Table 8.1

<table>
<tr><th>CALL BY VALUE</th><th>CALL BY REFERENCE</th></tr>
<tr><td>Function Prototype:
<code>void swap(int a, int b);</code></td><td>Function Prototype:
<code>void swap(int *a, int *b);</code></td></tr>
<tr><td>Function Definition:<pre>void swap(int a, int b)
{
    int temp;
    temp = a;
    a = b;
    b = temp;
}</pre></td><td>Function Definition:<pre>void swap(int *a, int *b)
{
    int temp;
    temp = *a;
    *a = *b;
    *b = temp;
}</pre></td></tr>
<tr><td>Function Call:
<code>swap(x, y);</code></td><td>Function Call:
<code>swap(&x, &y);</code></td></tr>
</table>

Table 8.2

CALL BY VALUE	CALL BY REFERENCE
Actual arguments can be constants, variables, or expressions.	Actual arguments can only be variables.
Formal arguments are ordinary variables.	Formal arguments are pointer variables.
Values of actual arguments are substituted in formal arguments.	Addresses of the actual arguments are substituted in formal arguments.
Any change made to formal arguments will have no effect on actual arguments, since the function will only be using the local copy of the arguments.	Any change made to pointer variables will have immediate effect on actual arguments, since the function will be working on actual arguments through address.

8.9 ORGANIZING MULTI-FUNCTION PROGRAMS

There are many situations where the problem to program is quite big and complex. In such cases the entire problem is broken down to small, manageable, and independent modules. Each module is implemented by a C function. So we have collection of functions that are to be integrated together to solve the given problem.

If a single programmer writes all these functions, then one can organize these functions in a single program file in following ways:

1. Declare the prototypes of the various functions to be used in the program, except *main()*, function before the *main()* function. Then, define/write these functions in any order. It is not necessary that the first function should be *main()* function. The system will keep track of the *main()* function as execution of the program begins with *main()* function. Hence, *main()* function acts as driver that drivers the rest of the functions.
2. First define/write other functions and then at the end *main()* function. In this organization, it is very important that function must be defined before its use otherwise compiler will give an error. This situation is same as using a variable before its declaration.

Listing 8.7

```
/*
   Program to find the first 5-digit number that is prime
   and sum of digits of this number is also a prime number
   (Illustrates first organization approach)
*/
#include<stdio.h>
#include<math.h>
int sumOfDigits( unsigned long ); /*  function prototype   */
int isPrime( unsigned long ); /*  function prototype   */
void main()           /*  main function  */
{
   int i;
   unsigned long number = 10000;
   while ( 1 )
   {
      if ( isPrime ( number ) )
      {
         if (isPrime(sumOfDigits(number)))
         {
            printf("\n\n");
            printf("Required 5-digit prime number = %lu\n",
                   number);
```

```
            return:
         }
      }
      number++;
   }
}
/* Function returns 1 if number k is prime else return 0 */
int isPrime ( unsigned long k )
{
   int i, m;
   if ( ( k > 2 ) && ( k % 2 == 0) )
      return 0;
   m = sqrt ( (double) k );
   for ( i = 3; i <= m; i += 2 )
   {
      if ( k % i == 0 )
         return 0;
   }
   return 1;
}
/* Function returns the sum of digits of number 'k' */
int sumOfDigits ( unsigned long k )
{
   int sum = 0;
   while ( k > 0 )
   {
      sum = sum + k % 10;
      k = k / 10;
   }
   return sum;
}
```

Listing 8.8

```
/*
  Program to find the first 5-digit number that is prime
  and sum of digits of this number is also a prime number
  (Illustrates second organization approach)
*/
#include<stdio.h>
#include<math.h>
/* Function returns 1 if number k is prime else return 0 */
int isPrime ( unsigned long k )
{
   int i, m;
   if ( ( k > 2 ) && ( k % 2 == 0) )
      return 0;
   m = sqrt ( (double) k );
   for ( i = 3; i <= m; i += 2 )
   {
```

```
        if ( k % i == 0 )
            return 0;
    }
    return 1;
}
/* Function returns the sum of digits of number 'k' */
int sumOfDigits ( unsigned long k )
{
    int sum = 0;
    while ( k > 0 )
    {
        sum = sum + k % 10;
        k = k / 10;
    }
    return sum;
}
void main()           /*  main function  */
{
    int i;
    unsigned long number = 10000;
    while ( 1 )
    {
        if ( isPrime ( number ) )
        {
            if (isPrime(sumOfDigits(number)))
            {
                printf("\n\n");
                printf("Required 5-digit prime number = %lu\n",
                        number);
                return;
            }
        }
        number++;
    }
}
```

Note: We recommend the use of first approach where all function declarations are placed in global declaration section, i.e., before the *main* function. Placing function declarations in global declaration section serves following purposes:

- It provides a quick reference for the functions used in the program, making them excellent documentation.
- Placing function declarations at the beginning of the program makes them available to all other functions in the program. However, if a particular function declaration is local to a given function, then only the given function can call that particular function. The call to that function by other function will yield a syntax error something like – *"prototype not found"*.

8.10 SUPPLEMENTARY PROBLEMS

To have hands on defining functions, let use consider some examples.

Problem 8.1:

An integer function to compute the factorial of a positive integer number *k*.

Listing 8.9

```
/* Function to compute factorial of a +ve integer number */
int factorial ( int k )
{
   int product = 1, i;
   for ( i = 2; i <= k; i++ )
      product *= i;
   return product;
}
```

Problem 8.2:

Using the definition of factorial function of Example 8.1, let us write a complete program to compute the Binomial coefficient ${}^n c_r$ defined as

$$ {}^n c_r = \frac{n!}{r!(n-r)!} $$

Listing 8.10

```
/*
*    Program to compute Binomial coefficient (Version 1)
*/
#include <stdio.h>
int factorial ( int k );   /*  function prototype   */
void main()
{
    int ncr, n, r;
    printf( "\nEnter value of n: " );
    scanf( "%d", &n );
    printf( "\nEnter value of r: " );
    scanf( "%d", &r );
    ncr = factorial(n)/(factorial(r)*factorial(n-r));
    printf( "\nValue of ncr = %d\n" , ncr);
}
```

This program calls the factorial function thrice with argument *n*, *r*, (*n*–*r*) respectively, and then using these values computes the binomial coefficient.

Problem 8.3:

A function to find highest common factor (HCF), also known as greatest common divisor (GCD), of two positive integers *m* and *n*.

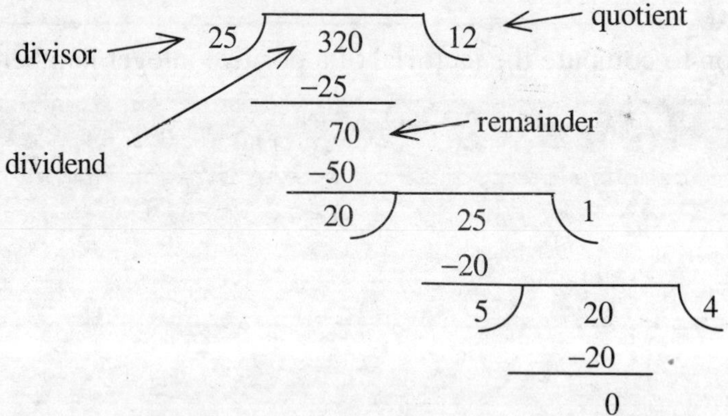

Figure 8.5: Illustration of computational procedure for HCF

From Figure 8.5, you must have observed that in successive divisions, the divisor of the previous division becomes dividend, remainder of becomes divisor, and division is again carried out. This process is carried out till the reminder becomes zero, and the current divisor is taken as HCF of the given integer numbers.

This process can be implemented by using the following steps

1. Perform division.
2. If remainder is zero, then stop and take the divisor as HCF.
3. Replace dividend by divisor.
4. Replace divisor by remainder.
5. Repeat from step 1.

Listing 8.11

```
/*  Function to compute HCF of two +ve integer numbers    */
int computeHCF ( int m, int n )
{
   int k = 1;
   while ( k != 0 )
   {
      k = n % m;
      n = m;
      m = k;
   }
   return n;
}
```

Problem 8.4:

Using the definition of function to compute HCF of Example 8.3, let us write a complete program to compute the HCF of two given integers.

Listing 8.12

```
/* Program to compute HCF of two given integers (m and n)  */
#include <stdio.h>
int computeHCF( int, int );    /*  function declaration  */
void main()
{
    int m, n, r;
    printf( "\nEnter value of m: " );
    scanf( "%d", &m );
    printf( "\nEnter value of n: " );
    scanf( "%d", &n );
    r = computeHCF(m,n);
    printf( "\nValue of HCF = %d\n" , r);
}
```

Test Run

```
Enter value of m: 125
Enter value of n: 35
Value of HCF = 5
```

8.11 RECURSIVE FUNCTIONS

Recursion is an important concept in computer science and is convenient for a variety of problems that would be difficult to solve using *iterative* constructs such as *for, while* and *do* loops. Recursive functions can be directly implemented in C language.

8.11.1 Factorial Function

The factorial of a positive number *n*, written as *n*!, is the product of the positive integers from 1 to *n:*

$$n! = 1.2.3...(n-2).(n-1).n \qquad \text{where as } 0! = 1$$

Thus, definition of the iterative version of the factorial function can be written as

$$n! = \begin{cases} 1 & \text{if } n = 0 \\ \prod_{i=1}^{n} i & \text{if } n > 0 \end{cases}$$

From above definition, we have

0! = 1
1! = 1
2! = 1.2 = 2
3! = 1.2.3 = 6
4! = 1.2.3.4 = 24
5! = 1.2.3.4.5 = 120 and so on.

Observe that

4! = 4.3! = 4.6 = 24 and 5! = 5.4! = 5.24 = 120

And this is true for every positive integer n; that is

$$n! = n.(n-1)!$$

Thus the factorial function can be defined as

$$n! = \begin{cases} 1 & \text{if } n = 0 \\ n(n-1)! & \text{if } n > 0 \end{cases}$$

This definition of $n!$ is recursive, since it refers to itself when it uses $(n-1)!$.

Listing 8.13

```
/*
   Recursive function to compute factorial of a +ve
   integer number
*/
int factorial( int n )
{
  if ( n == 0 )
     return 1;
  else
     return ( n * factorial( n - 1 ) );
}
```

Listing 8.14

```
/*
  Program to print the factorials of first 'n' natural numbers
*/

#include <stdio.h>

int factorial( int n );      /*  function prototype   */

void main()
{
   int i, n;
   printf( "\nEnter value of n: " );
   scanf( "%d", &n );
   for ( i = 1; i <= n; i++ )
   {
       printf( "\n%d! = %d", i, factorial(i) );
   }
}
int factorial( int n )
{
  if ( n == 0 )
     return 1;
  else
     return ( n * factorial( n - 1 ) );
}
```

Test Run

```
Enter value of n: 6

1! = 1
2! = 2
3! = 6
4! = 24
5! = 120
6! = 720
```

8.11.2 Fibonacci Numbers

A very important sequence, *Fibonacci sequence,* usually denoted by F_0, F_1, . . ., F_n, is as follows:

0, 1, 1, 2, 3, 5, 8, 13, . . .

That is, $F_0 = 0$ and $F_1 = 1$ and the subsequent terms are the sum of the two preceding terms.

For example, the next term in the above sequence is

$$8 + 13 = 21$$

A formal definition for Fibonacci number F_n is:

$$fib(n) = \begin{cases} n & \text{if } n \leq 1 \\ fib(n-1) + fib(n-2) & \text{if } n > 1 \end{cases}$$

Notice that the recursive definition of the Fibonacci numbers differs from the recursive definitions of the factorial function and positive exponential power function in the sense that it refers to itself twice.

Listing 8.15

```
/*
*   Recursive function to compute Fibonacci number 'n'
*/
int fibNumber( int n )
{
  if ( n <= 1 )
     return n;
  else
     return ( fibNumber(n-1) + fibNumber(n-2) );
}
```

Listing 8.16

```
/*
  Program to print first 'm' terms of Fibonacci sequence
*/
#include <stdio.h>

int fibNumber( int n );        /*  function prototype   */

void main()
{
   int i, m;
   printf( "\nEnter value of m: " );
   scanf( "%d", &m );
   for ( i = 0; i < m; i++ )
   {
      printf( "%d = %d   ", i, fibNumber(i) );
   }
}
int fibNumber( int n )
{
  if ( n <= 1 )
```

```
        return n;
    else
        return ( fibNumber(n-1) + fibNumber(n-2) );
}
```

Test Run

```
Enter value of m: 8
0   1   1   2   3   5   8   13
```

8.12 COMMAND-LINE ARGUMENTS

To run a program, the name of the program is entered at the operating system's prompt. In addition to entering the name of the program, we can also enter other items, such as the name of the file the program may be using.

For example, you can start Turbo C's IDE in the following ways:

1. By just typing TC at DOS prompt as

   `C:\TC>TC↵`

   In this case, the opening screen will appear, and you can load any file into the environment by using *File* option.

2. By typing TC and the name of the program file, to work on, as

   `C:\TC>TC test↵`

   In this case, if program file *test.c* already exists, it will be loaded into the environment, and the editing session will start. If program file *test.c* does not exist, then the environment will start the edit session to create a new file.

In the later case, the string *test* is used as a *command-line argument — an argument that appears on the command line following the operating system prompt*. We can give multiple arguments on the command line. For example, the COPY command needs two arguments, where first argument is the name of the source file and the second argument is the name of the destination file.

The question here is — *How can these arguments be used in our program*? As you know that the execution of the program always begins with the *main()* function. Accordingly, these arguments can be accessed via arguments in the *main()* function. The C system automatically adds the capability to read these arguments to all C programs. The following program illustrates this.

Listing 8.17

```
/*
*  Program to demonstrate the use of command line arguments
*  filename : cmdline.c
*/
# include <stdio.h>
void main ( int argc, char *argv[] )
{
  int i;
  printf( "\nCommand = %s\n", argv[0] );
  printf( "\nNumber of arguments = %d", argc-1 );
  printf( "\n\nThese are\n\n" );
  for ( i = 1; i < argc; i++ )
  {
      printf( "Argument number %d = %s\n", i, argv[i] );
  }
}
```

Test Run

```
>cmdline first second third fourth↵
Command = C:\TC\CMDLINE.EXE
Number of arguments = 4
These are
Argument number 1 = first
Argument number 2 = second
Argument number 3 = third
Argument number 4 = fourth
```

The two arguments used in the definition of function *main()* are:

- The first argument is *argc* that is of type integer and holds the total number of entries on the command line, including the program name.
- The second argument is **argv[]*, an array of pointers to strings which holds the individual arguments. The argument *argv[0]* holds the name of the program, *argv[1]* holds the first argument, *argv[2]* holds the second argument and so on. These arguments can also be accessed using pointer notation as **(argv+0)*, **(argv+1)*, **(argv+2)* and so on.

If we have written a program that accepts a specified number of command-line arguments, then we must check in the program whether the correct number of arguments is passed to it or not.

For example, suppose we have written a program that emulates DOS COPY command, and is given a name KOPY. Then we can add the following segment in very beginning of the program.

```
if ( argc < 3 )
{
   printf("\nCorrect Usage:>" );
   printf("\nKOPY <sourceFile><destinationFile>\n" );
   return;
}
```

to ensure that the correct number of command-line arguments as expected by the program are specified.

Note that it is not mandatory that names of formal arguments for the main function be *argc* and *argv*, only thing you have to ensure that is — first argument is of type *int* and second argument is array of pointers of type *char*. We will be learning about pointers in *Chapter 12*.

8.13 ORGANIZING MULTI-FILE PROGRAMS

In some situations, a team of programmers is involved to prepare software for big and complex problems. Each programmer will be writing a separate and independent code to handle a particular aspect of the given problem. Therefore he/she will be having his/her own program file. This situation gives rise to a problem of managing these multi-file programs.

The traditional way of managing multi-file programs, as in most high-level languages, is to compile each file separately, and then combine these compiled files using standalone linker.

To illustrate this method, suppose that the program files are *file1.c*, *file2.c*, *file3.c*, and *file4.c*.

In Turbo C, there are two ways to compile a program file. These are:

1. Compiling from within Turbo C's IDE.

   For each file in turn, select *Compile* option from the main menu and then select *Compile to OBJ* option from the *Compile* pull down submenu using up and down arrow keys which have the options shown overleaf.

```
Compile to OBJ
Make EXE file
Link EXE file
Build all
Primary C file
Get info
```

2. Compiling from command-line version.

   Compile each file in turn, by typing following command at the OS prompt as

```
C:\TC>TCC -c file1.c↵      OR      C:\TC>TCC -c file1↵
```

If files are compiled from within Turbo C's IDE, then exit IDE.

Now type the following command to invoke the Turbo linker as

```
C:\TC>TLINK file1+file2+file3+file4↵
```

The final executable file, also called *run file*, is created under the name *file1.exe*. The final run file is always given the name of the first file in the command. You can execute the program by typing the name of the run file at the DOS prompt.

So while managing large number of files in a complex problem, mostly referred to as a project, we have to keep track of each file. Whenever any file is updated, we have to compile it again and using linker create a new run file. However this process can be automated using Turbo C's project facility. This feature of Turbo C's development environment is explained in the next section.

In Turbo C's IDE, there is a project facility which facilitates the management of multi-file programs. To use project facility, select *Project* option form Turbo C's IDE main menu. The *Project* pull down submenu appears as

```
Project name
Break make on        Errors
Auto dependencies    Off
Clear project
Remove message
```

Using up and down arrow keys, select *Project name* option, and give name to the current project and then create this project file and type here the name of all program files.

Suppose, we give name *sample* to our project, project file gets extension *.PRJ*.

Now type in the following contents

```
file1
file2
file3
file4
```

in file *sample.prj* using Turbo C's built-in editor.

In Turbo C++'s IDE, there is a project facility that facilitates the management of multi-file programs. To use project facility, select *Project* option form Turbo C++'s IDE main menu.

The *Project* pull down submenu appears as

```
Open Project
Close Project
Add item ...
Delete item ...
Local Options ...
Include files ...
```

Give name to the project, and then using *Add item ...* option, add the following

```
file1
file2
file3
file4
```

And when this project file is active, all the files are automatically compiled and linked (for the first time) when we use *Make* option from the compile submenu or we press hot key F9.

Do remember that whenever you want to work on a particular project, activate a particular project file. For the first time, when you create a project file, it is active by default.

Whenever, any source file is updated, we rebuild the project. The Turbo C/C++'s project facility automatically checks for the source file that has been changed, and compile them and creates a new run file.

When you have finished working on a particular project, clear the active project by selecting *Clear project* from *Project* pull down submenu.

8.14 BUILDING YOUR OWN MODULES/LIBRARY

Turbo C/C++'s development environment provides the facility to build your own library of user-defined functions. You can compile user-defined functions and then combine them with system library using TLIB utility. Thereafter, you don't need to include the source code of the user-defined function in the program or explicitly link the object code of the user-defined function with your program. The linker will automatically link it with your program code as it does with built-in library functions.

Suppose, the user-defined function under question is stored in the disk file named *sample.c*. The process of adding this user-defined function to the system library is shown below.

1. Compile the source file *sample.c* to produce *sample.obj* file either using *Compile* option from within the IDE or command line version.
2. From the OS prompt, enter the following command

```
C:\TC>TLIB \TC\LIB\CS.LIB+\TC\SAMPLE.OBJ
```

The source object code of the user-defined function contained in the disk file *sample.obj* will be combined with system library file CS.LIB.

8.15 STORAGE CLASSES

Every variable in C language possesses a characteristic called its *storage class*. The storage class defines two main characteristics of the variable, apart from the place of storage and the initial value. These are

- Lifetime
- Visibility or scope

Lifetime — *Lifetime* of a variable is the length of time it retains a particular value.

Visibility — *Visibility* or *scope* of a variable refers to those parts of a program that will be able to recognize it.

At first instance, a question arises: *why are storage classes necessary*? The answer is that by using variables with the appropriate lifetime and visibility, we can write programs that use memory more efficiently, run faster, and are less prone to programming errors. The correct use of storage class is especially important in large programs.

The storage class precedes the variable's declaration and tells the compiler regarding where the variable should be stored, what should be its initial value, what will be its scope, and for how much time it will be available for use.

The C language supports following four storage classes:

- auto
- static
- extern
- register

If the storage class in the variable declaration is omitted, it is assumed of type *auto*, *i.e.*, storage class is *auto* by default. Let us examine these storage classes one by one.

8.15.1 The *auto* Storage Class

The variables declared with *auto* storage class, which is the storage class by default, have following features:

- Stored in memory.
- If not initialized in the declaration statement, their initial value is unpredictable, which is often called *garbage value*.
- Local (visible) to the block in which the variable is declared. If the variable is declared within a function, then it is only visible to that function. But if the variable is declared outside the function, then it is visible to all the functions following its declaration.
- It retains its value till the control remains in the block in which the variable is declared. For example, if the variable is declared within a function, it will retain its value till the control is within that function. As the execution of the function terminates, it is cleared/destroyed.

The following examples illustrate these features.

Listing 8.18

```
/* Program to illustrate the auto storage class  */
#include <stdio.h>
void main()
{
   auto int i, j = 10;
   printf( "Value of i = %d\n", i );
   printf( "Value of j = %d\n", j );
}
```

This example program shows how an automatic storage class is declared, and the fact that if the variable is not initialized, it contains a garbage value.

Test Run

```
Value of i = 1250
Value of j = 10
```

Next time you run this program you may get different value of *i*. The reason is that we have not initialized variable *i* prior to outputting it, so it can be assigned any garbage value depending on the storage location set aside for it. Most of the times, for un-initialized variables, we will be getting value zero. I would suggest our readers to check this fact. Consider the following program.

Listing 8.19

```
/*
*   Program to illustrate the auto storage class
*   when variable is declared outside all the blocks
*/
#include<stdio.h>
void main()
{
   auto int j = 10;
   {
      {
         {
            printf( "Value of auto variable j in" );
            printf( " innermost block = %d\n", j );
         }
         printf( "Value of auto variable j in" );
         printf( " next innermost block = %d\n", j );
      }
      printf( "Value of auto variable j in" );
      printf( " outermost block = %d\n", j );
   }
}
```

Test Run

```
Value of auto variable j in innermost block = 10
Value of auto variable j in next innermost block = 10
Value of auto variable j in outermost block = 10
```

In this program, all the *printf()* statements output value 10, the reason being that all the *printf()* statements occur within the outermost block in which the variable *j* is declared.

Consider the following program.

Listing 8.20

```
/*
*   Program to illustrate the auto storage class
*   when variable is declared in different blocks
*/

#include <stdio.h>
void main()
{
  auto int j = 10;
  {
     {
        auto int j = 50;
        printf( "Value of auto variable j in" );
        printf( " innermost block = %d\n", j );
     }
     printf( "Value of auto variable j in" );
     printf( " outer block = %d\n", j );
  }
}
```

Test Run

```
Value of auto variable j in inner block = 50
Value of auto variable j in outer block = 10
```

Note that the compiler treats these *j*s as different variables, since they are defined in different blocks, although, within the same function (main function in this case). As soon as the execution of the innermost block is complete, the variable *j* loses its value 50. And in the outer loop the variable *j* refers to value 10. And finally, when the execution of the function terminates, the variable *j* also loses its value.

8.15.2 The *static* Storage Class

The variables declared with *static* storage class have the following features:

- Stored in memory.
- If not initialized in the declaration statement, their initial value is zero.
- Local (visible) to the block in which the variable is declared. If the variable is declared within a function, then it is only visible to that function. But if the variable is declared outside the function, then it is visible to all the functions following its declaration.

- It retains its value between different function calls. That is, when for the first time a function is called, a static variable is created with initial value zero, and in subsequent calls it retains its present value.

Consider the following program.

Listing 8.21

```
/*
 *  Program to illustrate the auto storage class
 *  when variable is declared in different blocks
 */
#include <stdio.h>
void main()
{
   int sumOfDigits(int);
   int a, b;
   a = sumOfDigits(125);
   b = sumOfDigits(125);
   printf("%d, %d", a, b);
}
int sumOfDigits(int n)
{
  static int sum = 0;
  while ( n > 0 )
  {
     sum = sum + n % 10;
     n = n / 10;
  }
  return sum;
}
```

Test Run

```
8, 16
```

You may be expecting answer "8, 8" since we are attempting to find the sum of digits of the same number 125.

The local variable *sum* is declared with *static* storage class. Further, lifetime of a static variable is program execution time, hence a static variable is able to retain its existing value between different calls. Therefore, on the first call, the *sum* variable is initialized to 0 and at return time has value 8. In the second call, the initial value of *sum* is 8, and further 8 (sum of digits of 125) is added thus giving value 16.

8.15.3 The *register* Storage Class

Register storage class is like *auto* in the sense that the visibility and lifetime of the variable is limited to the block in which it is declared. The difference is that the compiler, if possible, will assign a register variable to one of the processor's register instead of storing it in the memory. Value stored in register can be accessed much faster than the value stored in memory. But do remember that there is limited number of registers in a processor, and secondly not all variables can be register variables. Most of the compilers (especially Turbo C compiler) only guarantee registers storage of type *int* and pointer types.

Now the question arises, *what variables should be made register variables*? The obvious candidates are those variables on which the program spends most of its time to process them such as index variables used of *for loop*.

The variables declared with *register* storage class have the following features:

- Stored in processor registers, if a register is available. If no register is available the variable is stored in memory, and works as if its storage class is *auto*. As soon as register becomes available, the storage class of that variable is converted to register type.
- If not initialized in the declaration statement, their initial value is unpredictable i.e. *garbage*.
- Local (visible) to the block in which the variable is declared. If the variable is declared within a function, then it is only visible to that function. But if the variable is declared outside the function, then it is visible to all the functions following its declaration.
- It retains its value till the control remains in the block in which the variable is declared. For example, if the variable is declared within a function, it will retain its value till the control is within that function. As the execution of the function terminates, it is cleared/destroyed.

8.15.4 The *extern* Storage Class

The scope of external variables is global. External variables are declared outside all functions, *i.e.*, in the beginning of the program file. As all the function will be defined after this variable declaration, so these variables are visible to all functions in a program file. However, if we have written our functions in separate program files, then we have to declare that variable again with *extern* storage class to tell the compiler that this variable or these variables are external variables and are defined in other source file(s).

The variables declared outside all the functions (if all functions are in single file) or declared with *extern* storage class (if you have multi-file programs) have the following features:

- Stored in memory.
- If not initialized in the declaration statement, their initial value is zero.
- Global, *i.e.*, visible to all functions.
- Retains its values till the program execution terminates.

Consider the following programs stored in separate files as shown:

Listing 8.22

```
/* file : extern1.c
*  Program to illustrate the extern storage class.
*  A global variable is defined here.  */
#include <stdio.h>
int commonVariable = 10;     /* definition of global variable */
void main()
{
   void sample();               /* prototype of function  */
   printf("\nValue of global variable in main function=");
   printf("%d\n", commonVariable);
   sample();
}
```

Listing 8.23

```
/* file : extern2.cpp
*  Function that uses global variable declared in other file.
*  A global variable is defined here.   */
#include <stdio.h>
extern int commonVariable; /* declaration of global variable */
void sample()
{
   printf("\nValue of global variable in sample function=");
   printf("%d\n", commonVariable);
}
```

Test Run

```
Value of global variable in main function = 10
Value of global variable in sample function = 10
```

Table 8.3 summarizes lifetime and visibility of various types of variables. The first three types are local; those defined within a function. Their visibility is confined to that function, and their lifetime — except for static variables — is also the same as that of the functions. These first three types of variables can also be defined within a block (a pair of braces); in this case, they will only be visible within block.

Table 8.3: Lifetime and visibility of various types of variables.

Place of Declaration	Storage class	Lifetime	Visibility
Function	auto	Function	function
function	register	function	function
function	static	program	function
file	static	program	one file
file	not specified	program	one file
file	extern	program	multi-file

The next three types are defined in the beginning of the file, *i.e.*, external to any function. In the first case, the variable is confined to a single file. The *extern* keyword cannot be used to reference it from other files. We use this storage class when we wish to hide the variables in one file.

In second case, which is most common, the variable is defined externally but is not declared in any other files. The visibility of such variables is confined to a single file. In this case the variable is visible only from the place in the file where it is defined to the end of the file. It is invisible to functions occurring before it even in the same program file.

In third case, a variable is defined in one file, but also declared in other files. In this case, its visibility will extend to the appropriate parts of all the files in which it is declared.

8.15.5 Advantages of Storage Classes

By using the appropriate storage class for a variable, the programmer can economize on memory requirements by restricting the lifetime of the variables. It will also help to maintain a modular, well-structured program by allowing access to variables only to those files and functions that need it. The number of ways in which the visibility and lifetime of variables can be restricted is an important reason for C's popularity with developers of large programs and systems.

8.16 MORE SUPPLEMENTARY PROBLEMS

In this section, we will take some more programming problems to illustrate the development and use of functions.

Problem 8.5:

Write a function, say *int smallestDigit(int x)*, that returns the smallest digit in number *x*. Use minimum number of variables and minimum number of statements. Don't use array at all. Use this function in a program to demonstrate its use.

The procedure to find the smallest digit is as follows: We know that the largest digit is 9 and the smallest digit is 0. We start with taking 9 as the current smallest digit. In each iteration, we separate a digit and compare it with current smallest digit. If the digit under consideration is less than the current smallest digit, we take digit under consideration as the current smallest digit. This process is repeated till all digits in a number have been examined.

Listing 8.24

```
/*
* Program to find smallest digit in a positive integer number
*/
#include <stdio.h>
int smallestDigit(int); /* prototype   */
void main()
{
    long int number;
    printf( "\nEnter positive integer number : " );
    scanf( "%ld", &number);
    printf( "\nSmallest digit in %ld is %d\n", number,
            smallestDigit(number));
}
/* function that returns smallest digit in a +ve integer number  */
int smallestDigit(int k)
{
    int smallDigit = 9;
    int digit;
    while ( k > 0 ) {
       digit = k % 10;
       k /= 10;
       if ( digit < smallDigit )
          smallDigit = digit;
    }
    return smallDigit;
}
```

Test Run

```
Enter positive integer number : 23145
Smallest digit in 23145 is 1
```

Problem 8.6:

Write a function, say *int IsPrime(int n)*, that returns the value 1 if integer argument n represents a prime number else returns value 0. Use this function in a program to print all three digit prime numbers.

The procedure to be followed is as follows: We start with number 100 (the smallest three digit number) and continue upto 999 (the largest three digit number). For each number, we call function *IsPrime()* to test the number to see whether it is prime or not which will be indicated by value 1 or 0, respectively. If the number is prime, we will send the number to output and continue with the next number. However, if the current number is not prime, we will not send it to the output, and we proceed with the next number. This process is repeated till all three digit numbers are examined.

Listing 8.25

```
/*  Program to print all three digit prime numbers  */
#include <stdio.h>
#include <math.h>
int IsPrime(int);    /* prototype  */
void main()
{
    int i;
    printf( "\nAll three digit prime numbers are\n\n");
    for ( i = 100; i <= 999; i++ ) {
       if ( IsPrime(i) ) /* it is same as (IsPrime(i) == 1) */
          printf( "%4d", i);
    }
    printf( "\n");
}
/* function that returns value 1 if its argument represents
   a prime number else returns value 0
*/
int IsPrime(int n)
{
   int m, k;
   if ( ( n > 2 ) && ( ( n % 2 ) == 0 ) ) {
      return 0;
   }
   else {
      m = sqrt(n);
      for ( k = 3; k <= m; k+= 2 ) {
```

```
            if ( ( n % k ) == 0 )
                return 0;
        }
    }
    return 1;
}
```

Test Run

```
All three digit prime numbers are
101 103 107 109 113 127 131 137 139 149 151 157 163 167 173 179
181 191 193 197 199 211 223 227 229 233 239 241 251 257 263 269
271 277 281 283 293 307 311 313 317 331 337 347 349 353 359 367
373 379 383 389 397 401 409 419 421 431 433 439 443 449 457 461
463 467 479 487 491 499 503 509 521 523 541 547 557 563 569 571
577 587 593 599 601 607 613 617 619 631 641 643 647 653 659 661
673 677 683 691 701 709 719 727 733 739 743 751 757 761 769 773
787 797 809 811 821 823 827 829 839 853 857 859 863 877 881 883
887 907 911 919 929 937 941 947 953 967 971 977 983 991 997
```

Problem 8.7:

Write a program that takes a list of numbers as its command line arguments, and prints the sum of these numbers.

The procedure to be followed is as follows: The command line arguments are received by the *main()* function as string. Since the command line arguments are just numbers, therefore the string are made up of only letters 0-9 and decimal point '.'. We use here a library function *atof()* to convert a string of representing a number to numeric value. Then we add these numeric values one by one after conversion. We need to include *stdlib.h* header file in order to use *atof()* library function.

Listing 8.26

```
/*  Program to add list of integer numbers given as
    command line arguments
    filename : sum.c
*/
# include <stdio.h>
# include <stdlib.h>
void main ( int argc, char *argv[] )
{
    int i;
    float sum = 0;
    for ( i = 1; i < argc; i++ )
    {
```

```
        sum = sum + atof( argv[i] );
    }
    printf("\nSum of numbers on command line = %.2f\n", sum);
}
```

Test Run

```
>sum 1 2 3 4 5 6 7 8 9 10
Sum of numbers on command line = 55.00
```

8.17 QUCK RECAP

In this chapter, we have learnt that

- Many problems that arise because of the size and complexity of software can be handled efficiently using modular design approach.
- Each function is complete and independent in its own.
- Each function handled one aspect of the complex problem.
- Value can be returned from a function using *return* statement.
- A Function can return any type of value. This includes pointers as well.
- Arguments can be passed to a function either using call by value approach or call by reference approach.
- A function prototype, like variable declaration, is a declaration that specifies the return type, name, and type of formal arguments.
- A function can also be accessed/invoked using a pointer to a function.
- A recursive function is one that calls itself directly or indirectly.
- Main function can accept arguments given on the command-line.
- You can build own library.
- Storage class determines the lifetime and visibility of the variables. It also determines that where the variables will be stored, what will be their initial value if they are not initialized.
- The different storage classes are auto, static, register, and extern.

8.18 MULTIPLE CHOICE QUESTIONS

1. Which of the following statement about functions is false?
   (*a*) More than one function is allowed in a program unit.
   (*b*) A function can call another function.
   (*c*) A function can call itself.
   (*d*) Constants can appear in the formal argument list.

2. Which of the following is not a valid reason for using functions?
   (*a*) They use less memory than repeating the same code.
   (*b*) They keep different program activities separate.
   (*c*) They run faster.
   (*d*) They keep variables safe from other parts of the program
3. What is the default return type of a function?
   (*a*) void (*b*) int
   (*c*) float (*d*) char
4. The program execution starts from the
   (*a*) *main()* function (*b*) function which is defined first
   (*c*) function that is defined last (*d*) None of above
5. The C language allow arguments to be passed
   (*a*) only call by value (*b*) only call by reference
   (*c*) both *a* & *b* (*d*) None of above
6. Identify the correct statement
   (*a*) A function can be defined more than once in a program.
   (*b*) One function cannot be defined within another function definition.
   (*c*) All functions must be in the same file.
   (*d*) Function should appear in the order they are called in the main function.
7. Consider the following program

```
#include <stdio.h>
void main()
{
    int i = 5, j = 10;
    swap(i, j);
    printf( "\n%d, %d", i, j );
}
swap(int i, int j)
{
   i = i + j; j= i - j; i = i - j;
}
```

   What will happen when we attempt to compile & run the program?
   (*a*) Program will fail to compile because same variable names cannot be used in *main()* and *swap()* functions.
   (*b*) Program will fail to compile because return type of the swap function is not specified.
   (*c*) Program will compile and execute giving output as 5, 10.
   (*d*) Program will compile and execute giving output as 10, 5.

8. Consider the following function definition, and identify the correct statement

```
myFunction( a + b, c, d, 5 )
int a, b, c, d;
{
     int sum;
     sum = a + b +  c + d + 5;
     return sum;
}
```

   (*a*) Function will fail to compile because expression is not permitted as formal argument.
   (*b*) Function will fail to compile because constant is not permitted as formal argument.
   (*c*) Function will fail to compile because return type of the function is omitted.
   (*d*) Both (*a*) and (*b*).

9. The process of dividing a program into functions which in turn are further divided into function until they consists of elementary operations and cannot be further divided is known as
   (*a*) Structuring (*b*) Charting (*c*) Factoring (*d*) Splitting

10. Which of the following is not a valid definitions for the *main()* function so that it can compile and execute successfully?
   (*a*) `main(void)  { /* . . .  body . . .   */ }`
   (*b*) `void main(int count, char *args[] )`
   `{  /* . . .  body  . . .   */  }`
   (*c*) `void main(void)  {  /*  . . .  body  . . .   */  }`
   (*d*) `int main(float count, char *argv[])`
   `{  /* . . .  body  . . .   */  }`

11. Which of the following is a part of the function header?
   (*a*) Function name (*b*) Return type
   (*c*) Argument list (*d*) All

12. Consider the following declaration statement

```
extern int a;
```

   What information does it convey?
   (*a*) Variable *a* is declared in some other source file.
   (*b*) Variable *a* has its initial value as 0.
   (*c*) Variable a can retain its value during different function calls.
   (*d*) None of above.

13. Which of the following statement is true about *register* storage class?
   (*a*) Variable always stored in processor registers.
   (*b*) Can only be used with integral data types and pointers.

(*c*) Variable takes initial value 0 if not initialized.
(*d*) None of above.

14. Find the output of the following program.

```
void main()
{
    f();
    f();
    f();
}
void f(void)
{
    static int x =0;
    printf("%d ", ++x);
}
```

(*a*) 0 1 2 (*b*) 1 1 1 (*c*) 1 2 3 (*d*) 3 3 3

15. Find the output of the following program.

```
void main()
{
    static int i =0;
    i++;
    if ( i <= 5 ) {
        printf("%d ",i);
        main();
    } else {
        return;
    }
}
```

(*a*) 5 4 3 2 1 (*b*) 1 2 3 4 5 (*c*) 1 1 1 1 1 (*d*) None

8.19 REVIEW EXERCISES

1. What is the difference between a user-defined function and library function?
2. When is the execution of the function terminated?
3. How many arguments can be passed to a function?
4. What are the rules regarding the relationship between formal arguments and actual arguments?
5. How is a function invoked?
6. How many times can a function be called?
7. What is wrong with the following function definition?

```
testFunction( int k )
{
    float temp = 5.25;
    temp = k / 2.0;
    return temp;
}
```

8. **Find the errors, if any, in the following function definition**

```
void fun( int x, int y )
{
   int z;
   /*  some statement   */
   return z;
}
```

9. **Find the errors, if any, in the following function definition**

```
void fun( int x, y )
{
   int z;
   /*  some statement   */
   return;
}
```

10. **Find the errors, if any, in the following function definition**

```
int fun1( int x, int y )
{
   int z;
   /*  some statement   */
   int fun2( int t )
   {
      return (t-2);
   }
   /*  some more statements   */
   return z;
}
```

12. **What will be the output of the following program?**

```
void main()
{
   float r = 5.0, c;
   float func( float t );      /* function prototype   */
   c = func( r );
   printf( "\nValue returned by function" );
   printf( " = %d\n", c);
}
float func( float t )
{
   float temp;
   temp = t * t / 2;
   return 5.0;
}
```

13. **What will be the output of the following program?**

```
int sum ( int, int, int );   /*  function prototype  */
void main()
{
   int a = 10;
   printf( "\nValue returned by function" );
   printf( " = %d\n", sum(a++,++a,++a) );
}
int sum ( int a, int b, int c )
{
   return (a+b+c);
}
```

14. Find the errors, if any, in the following function declarations:

    (*a*) `int diff(int x, y);` (*b*) `void fun(void, void);`

    (*c*) `float diff(float, float);` (*d*) `int test(float x, int y)`

8.20 PROGRAMMING EXERCISES

1. Write a function, say *int sumOfDigits(int number)*, that returns the sum of digits of a positive integer number.
2. Write a function, say *float absValue(float value)*, that returns the absolute value of a number of type *float*.
3. Write a function, say *int round(float x)*, that returns rounded value of *x* to nearest integer value.
4. Give recursive definition of the function to compute the greatest common divisor of the two positive integer numbers. Also show its implementation.
5. Write a function, say *int sumOfN(int n, int m)*, which computes the sum of *n* integers starting with *m*th integer, *i.e.*,

   $m + (m + 1) + (m + 2) + . . . + (m + n - 1)$
6. The combination function *C(n, r)* can be defined recursively as *C(n–1,r)* + *C(n–1,r–1)*. What is the base case? Write a recursive program to compute *C(n, r)*.
7. Write a function, say *int isPrime (int n)*, that returns 1 if number *n* is prime else return 0.
8. A number is a palindrome if it is the same number when read forward or backward. For example, numbers 1991, 1001 and 1221 palindrome numbers. Write a function, say *int isPalindrome(unsigned int k)*, that returns value 1 if the number k is palindrome else returns value 0.
9. A positive integer number IJK is said to be *well-ordered* if I < J < K. For example, number 138 is called *well-ordered* because the digits in the number (1, 3, 8) increase from left to right, *i.e.*, 1 < 3 < 8. Number 365 is not *well-ordered* because 6 is larger than 5. Write a function, say *int isWellordered(unsigned int k)*, that returns value 1 if the *k* is a *well-ordered* number else returns 0.
10. Write a function, say *int largestDigit(int x)*, that returns the largest digit in number *x*. Use minimum number of variables and minimum number of statements. Don't use array at all.
11. Write a function, say *int unitDigit(int n)*, that returns the unit digit of a number represented in argument *n*.
12. Write a function, say *int IsLeapYear(int year)*, that returns value 1 if the argument *year* represents a leap year else return value 0.

❑ ❑ ❑

9 Arrays

Learning Objectives

After reading this chapter, students will have the ability to:

- explain the concept of arrays
- explain the usefulness of arrays in handling class of related problems
- declare, initialize and do input/output of arrays
- explain the way arrays are passed as arguments to functions
- write efficient programs using arrays to solve variety of problems

9.1 INTRODUCTION

The variables used so for are also called *scalar* variables or *non-subscripted* variables. Each such variable represents a memory cell/location in which a single value can be stored. However, there are many situations in which it is necessary to process a collection of identical/homogeneous values. To illustrate this, consider that, for a class of 50 students, we have with us score of each student in final exam, and we are interested in having the following information:

- maximum score,
- average score of the class, and
- number of students whose score is greater than class's average score

One way of solving the above problem is

- use 50 variables, where each variable represents individual score,
- input these 50 scores,
- use about 50 *if* statements to find the maximum of these scores,
- add these 50 variables scores to find the total score of the class
- divide the total score by 50 to get the average score
- use another set of about 50 *if* statements to compare the individual scores with the average score to find the scores greater than average score and count such scores
- output the results

If at later stage, we want to process the scores of students of another class with number of students less or more than 50, the above program have to be modified as the number of variables will vary in the resulting program. This change in number of variables will affect the other parts of the program. The readers must find out themselves those parts that are affected.

Thus the above approach of processing a collection of homogeneous data is too cumbersome and not flexible enough to handle the collection of data of varying size.

The C language, like other high-level languages, provides a convenient way of processing such collections of homogeneous data. This is using *arrays* or *subscripted* variables.

In this chapter, we describe the processing of arrays.

9.2 ARRAY DEFINED

An *array* is a collection of homogeneous data elements (i.e. of same data type) described by a single name, and each individual element of an array is referenced by a *subscripted* variable, formed by affixing to the array name a *subscript* or *index* enclosed in brackets. The term subscript has the same meaning as in the mathematical notation. If single subscript is required to refer to an element of an array, the array is known as *one-dimensional* or *linear array*, and if two subscripts are required to refer to an element of an array, the array is known as *two-dimensional* array, and so on. Analogously, the arrays whose elements are referred by two or more subscripts are called *multi-dimensional* arrays.

9.3 ONE-DIMENSIONAL ARRAYS

A list of items can be given a common name and the individual items can be referenced using only one subscript. Such variables are referred to a *single-subscripted* variable or a *one-dimensional* array.

In mathematics, we often deal with variables that are single-subscripted. For instance, we use the equation

$$\overline{x} = \frac{\sum_{i=1}^{n} x_i}{n}$$

to calculate the average of n values of a list named x. The subscripted variable x_i refers to the ith element of x.

In C language, single subscripted variable is referred as $x[i]$.

For illustration, let us consider a list of 10 scores. The array named *scores* can be visualized as shown in Figure 9.1.

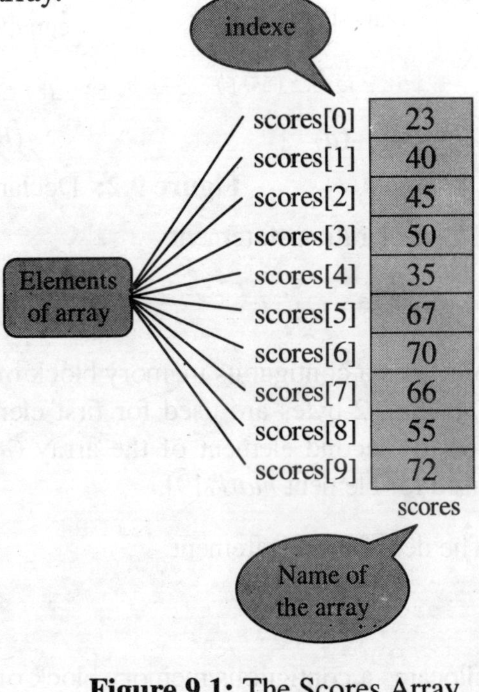

Figure 9.1: The Scores Array

9.3.1 Declaration and Definition

An array must be declared and defined before it can be used. Array declaration and definition tell the compiler *the name of the array, the type of its elements*, and *the size or number of elements in the array*. The size of the array is a constant and must have a value at compilation time.

The syntax for declaration of one-dimensional array is

```
type arrayName[arraySize];
```

Figure 9.2 shows three different array declarations, one for integers, one for floating-point numbers, and one for characters.

marks[0]	56
marks[1]	76
marks[2]	54
marks[3]	77
marks[4]	50
marks[5]	88
marks[6]	68
marks[7]	43
marks[8]	69
marks[9]	80

`int marks[10];`

(*a*)

cgpa[0]	5.0
cgpa[1]	4.5
cgpa[2]	7.0
cgpa[3]	8.0
cgpa[4]	6.5
cgpa[5]	7.0
cgpa[6]	5.5
cgpa[7]	6.0
cgpa[8]	8.5
cgpa[9]	9.0

`float cgpa[10];`

(*b*)

name[0]	A
name[1]	n
name[2]	n
name[3]	i
name[4]	
name[5]	S
name[6]	o
name[7]	o
name[8]	d
name[9]	

`char name[10];`

(*c*)

Figure 9.2: Declaring and defining arrays

The declaration statement

```
int marks[10];
```

allocates a contiguous memory block of 20 bytes, 2-bytes for each element of type *int*. First 2-bytes are used for first element of the array (*marks*[0]), next 2-bytes for the second element of the array (*marks*[1]), and so on. The last 2-bytes are used for element *marks*[9].

The declaration statement

```
float cgpa[10];
```

allocates a contiguous memory block of 40 bytes, 4-bytes for each element of type *float*. First 4-bytes are used for first element of the array (*cgpa*[0]), next 4-bytes for the second element of the array (*cgpa*[1]), and so on. The last 4-bytes are used for element *cgpa*[9].

The declaration statement

```
char name[10];
```

allocates a contiguous memory block of 10 bytes, 1-byte for each element of type *char*. First byte is used for first element of the array (*name*[0]), next byte for the second element of the array (*name*[1]), and so on. The last byte is used for element *name*[9].

9.3.2 Accessing Elements

The C language uses single *index* to access individual elements in a one-dimensional array. The index must be an integral value or an expression that evaluates to an integral value.

For example, given the *marks* array in Figure 9.2 (*a*), we would access the first element as

```
marks[0]
```

To process all the elements in *marks*, a loop similar to the following code is used:

```
for (i = 0; i < 10; i++ ) {
   process ( marks[i] );
}
```

One very interesting point that you may be keen to know is that how the C system knows where an individual element is located in memory. In *marks* one-dimensional array, there are ten elements. *How does it find just one of them*? The answer is simple – the array's name is a symbolic reference for the address to the first byte of the block of memory allocated for the array. The address of the first byte for the array is also known as *base address* of the array. Whenever we use the array's name, we actually refer to the first byte of the array. The index represents an offset from the beginning of the array to the element being referenced. With these two facts of information, the C system can calculate the address of any element in the array using the following simple formula:

```
element address = base address + ( sizeof(element) * index )
```

or simply as

```
address(marks[i]) = base address + ( sizeof(element) * i )
```

For example, assume that the base address for array *marks* is 1000. Since the elements of the array *marks* are of type *int*, the size of one element is the size of *int*, *i.e.*, 2 bytes. The address of an element at index 3 is

```
address(marks[3]) = 1000 + ( 2 * 3 ) = 1006
```

In C language, there is no built-in facility to ensure that while accessing array elements, the subscript is within the permissible range. For example, the declaration statement is *int a[10]*, and even if we attempt to access the 16th element as *a*[15], which of course is not a valid array element, in our program, the C system will not flag any error at any stage. It will just pick up a garbage value from the accessed memory location. The programmer must take care of this problem. Further, *i*th element of above array can also be accessed as *i*[*a*], in addition to normal way as *a*[*i*].

9.3.3 Storing Values

Declaration and definition only reserve space for the elements of the array. No values are stored in the array at this moment. To store values in the array, we must initialize the elements, read values from the keyboard, or assign values to each individual element.

9.3.3.1 Initialization

Just as simple variables can be initialized along with declaration and definition, the elements of the arrays can also be initialized. For each element in the array, we provide a value. The only difference is that the values must be enclosed in braces, and if there is more than one, separated by comma. The following examples provide all possible ways of initializing one-dimensional array. The following statement

```
int b[10]={12, 0, 14, -4, 7, 8, 10, 11, 9, 15};
```

initializes element *b*[0] to 12, *b*[1] to 0, *b*[2] to 14, *b*[3] to –4, *b*[4] to 7, *b*[5] to 8, *b*[6] to 10, *b*[7] to 11, *b*[8] to 9, *b*[9] to 15.

What you can expect from the following declaration statement?

```
int b[10] = {12, 0, 14, -4, 7};
```

The first five elements get values 12, 0, 14, –5, and 7 respectively; the remaining elements gets value 0, *i.e.*, remaining elements of a partially initialized array are always initialized to value 0.

What you can expect from the following declaration statement?

```
int b[] = {12, 0, 14, -4, 7};
```

In this declaration statement, no number is supplied for the size of the array. In this case, the compiler counts the number of elements in the initialization list and fixes that as the array size.

What you can expect from the following declaration statement?

```
int b[10] = {0};
```

It initializes all elements of array *b* to 0.

What you can expect from the following declaration statement?

```
int a[6]={12, 0, 14, -4, 7, 15, -20, 22, 25};
```

The compiler will flag an error message as the initialization list contains more elements than the declared size.

9.3.3.2 Inputting Values

The second way to fill the array with values is to read the values from the keyboard or a data file. This method of inputting values is done using a loop. The following segment shows the way data is entered into one-dimensional array.

```
for ( i = 0; i < 10; i++ )
{
   scanf( "%d", &marks[i] );
}
```

```
for ( i = 0; i <= 9; i++ )
{
   scanf( "%d", &marks[i] );
}
```

Observe the following things:

1. We start the index, *i*, at 0. Since the array has 10 elements, we must store the values from index location 0 through 9. The limit test, therefore, is set at $i < 10$ or $i <= 9$, which conveniently is the number of elements in an array.
2. Even though, we are dealing with array elements, the *address of* operator (&) is still necessary in the *scanf()* function call.

9.3.3.3 Assigning Values

The third way to fill the array with values is to assign the values to the individual elements using the assignment operator. Any value that is compatible can be assigned to the individual array element.

A simple assignment statement for *marks* is given below:

```
marks[3] = 45;
```

We can also assign the elements of one array to second array provided they match fully in type and size. Suppose that two arrays named *first* and *second* are compatible, and size of each array is 25, and we want to copy the elements of array *first* to *second*, the following loop will serve the purpose:

```
for ( i = 0; i < 25; i++ ) {
  second[i] = first[i];
}
```

If the values of elements of an array follow a certain pattern, we can use a loop to assign values. For example, the following loop assigns a value to the element that is twice of its index:

```
for ( i = 0; i < 10; i++ ) {
  a[i] = 2 * i;
}
```

The following loop assigns value 0 to elements at even index and value 1 to elements at odd index:

```
for ( i = 0; i < 10; i++ ) {
   if ( i % 2 == 0 )
      a[i] = 0;
   else
      a[i] = 1;
}
```

One array cannot be copied to another using assignment. For instance, if *a* and *b* are two arrays that match fully in type and size, the statement "a = b;" is not acceptable.

9.3.4 Outputting Values

To output values of elements of an array, we use the loop as follows:

```
for ( i = 0; i < n; i++ ) {
   printf( "%d  ", a[i] );
}
printf( "\n" );
```

All the values are displayed on one line. However, if all the values cannot be displayed in one line either because of their magnitude of values or number of values, they are displayed in subsequent lines. After, the *for* loop completes, a final call to *printf()* function advances the cursor to the next line.

The following *for* loop display one value per line:

```
for ( i = 0; i < n; i++ ) {
    printf( "\n%d", a[i] );
}
printf( "\n" );
```

However, if the values are more than 25, these values will scroll up. However, we can set up some of counter to control the display so that we able to view all the values.

Having understood the various aspects of the one-dimensional arrays, let us write some C functions and complete programs to demonstrate the power of one-dimensional arrays to handle complex problems.

Example 9.1:

Given an array, named *x*, of size (≤ 50) whose elements are of type *int*. Write a program that reads the actual size 'n' of the array, assigns array elements with value that is square of its index, and finally prints the elements of array such that maximum of 5 elements are printed on one line.

Listing 9.1

```
/*
* Program that assigns elements of the array with square of
* its index, and then prints the array such that maximum
* of 5 elements on one line
*/

#include<stdio.h>

void main()
{
  int x[50], i, n, counter = 0;
  printf("\nEnter actual size of array (<=50) : ");
  scanf("%d", &n);
  for ( i = 0; i < n; i++ )
     x[i] = i  * i;

  for ( i = 0; i < n; i++ )
  {
     printf("%d  ", x[i]);
```

```
    counter++;
    if ( counter == 5 )
    {
       printf("\n");
       counter = 0;
    }
  }
}
```

Test Run

```
Enter actual size of array (<=50) : 18
  0    1    4    9   16
 25   36   49   64   81
100  121  144  169  196
255  256  289
```

Example 9.2:

Let us consider that for a class of *n* students, we have with us score of each student in final exam, and we are interested in generating the following information

- maximum score of the class,
- average score of the class, and
- number of students whose score is greater than class's average score

The following program accomplishes this task.

Listing 9.2

```
/*
*  Program to find the maximum score, average score, and the
*  number of students whose score is greater than class average
*/
#include<stdio.h>
void main()
{
   float score[SIZE], maximumScore, averageScore;
   float totalScore;
   int i, n, noOfStudents = 0;
     printf("\nEnter number of students in class: ");
   scanf( "%d", &n );
   printf( "\nEnter %d scores\n\n", n );
   for ( i = 0; i < n; i++ )
     scanf( "%f", &score[i] );
```

```
    totalScore = 0;
    for ( i = 0; i < n; i++ )
        totalScore += score[i];
    averageScore = totalScore / n;
    maximumScore = score[0];
    for ( i = 1; i < n; i++ ) {
        if ( score[i] > maximumScore )
            maximumScore = score[i];
    }
    for ( i = 0; i < n; i++ ) {
        if ( score[i] > averageScore )
            noOfStudents++;
    }
    printf( "\nMaximum score of class = %.2f", maximumScore );
    printf( "\nAverage score of class = %.2f", averageScore );
    printf( "\nNo. of students with score > %.2f = %d\n",
               averageScore, noOfStudents );
}
```

Test Run

```
Enter number of students in class: 10
Enter 10 scores
75.25
80
65.5
59.5
72.25
35.5
55.75
69
43
85
Maximum score of class = 85.00
Average score of class = 63.58
No. of students with score > 63.58 = 6
```

Example 9.3:

Program to find the range of a set of value collected from some experiment or survey.

The *range* is defined as difference between the smallest and largest element of the given set of values. In order to find the range, first we have to find the largest and smallest element of the set. The following program accomplishes this task.

Listing 9.3

```
/* Program to find the range from a set of values    */
#include<stdio.h>
void main()
{
   float a[50], smallest, largest, range;
   int i, n;
   printf( "\nEnter size of array: " );
   scanf( "%d", &n );
   printf("Enter %d elements of the array\n",n);
   for ( i = 0; i < n; i++ )
     scanf( "%f", &a[i] );
   smallest = largest = a[0];
   for ( i = 1; i < n; i++ ) {
      if ( a[i] > largest ) largest = a[i];
      if ( a[i] < smallest ) smallest = a[i];
   }
   range = largest - smallest;
   printf( "\nRange of set of value = %.2f\n", range );
}
```

Test Run

```
Enter size of array: 10
Enter 10 elements of the array
75.25
80
65.5
59.5
72.25
35.5
55.75
69
43
85

Range of set of value = 49.50
```

Example 9.4:

Program to find standard deviation (σ) for a given set of data, say X ($x_0, x_1, x_2, \ldots, x_{n-1}$). Standard deviation is a valuable statistics that measures the dispersion of data, *i.e.*, how the data is dispersed (scattered) about the mean ($\bar{x}$) of data.

The formula for computing standard deviation is

$$\text{standard deviation } (\sigma) = \sqrt{\frac{\sum_{i=0}^{n-1} \left(x_i - \bar{x}\right)^2}{n}}, \text{ where mean } (\bar{x}) = \frac{\sum_{i=0}^{n-1} x_i}{n}$$

Listing 9.4

```
/*
*  Program to find standard deviation for a given set of data
*/

#include<stdio.h>

#include<math.h>
void main()
{
   float x[50], average, sum, stdDeviation, temp;
   int i, n;

   printf("\nProgram to compute standard deviation for" );
   printf(" a given set of data\n\n");

   printf("\nEnter number of elements in data set (n): ");
   scanf( "%d", &n );
   printf("\n\n");   /*  insert two blank lines */
   for ( i = 0; i < n; i++ )
   {
      printf( "Enter data element #%d : ", i+1 );
      scanf( "%f", &x[i] );
   }
   for ( sum = 0.0, i = 0; i < n; i++ )
      sum += x[i];

   average = sum / n;

   for (sum = 0.0, i = 0; i < n; i++ )
   {
      temp = x[i] - average;
      sum += temp * temp;
   }

   stdDeviation = sqrt( (double) sum / n );
   printf( "\nStandard deviation = %.3f", stdDeviation );
   printf( " (rounded to three decimal digits)\n" );
}
```

Test Run

```
Program to compute standard deviation for a given set of data

Enter number of elements in data set (n): 5
Enter data element #1: 1
Enter data element #2: 2
Enter data element #3: 3
Enter data element #4: 4
Enter data element #5: 5

Standard deviation = 1.414 (rounded to three decimal digits)
```

Example 9.5:

Program to sort a linear array *a* with *n* elements in ascending order. The elements of *a* are indexed from 0 to (*n*–1).

In order to sort the above array, we will use one very important method known as Bubble sort.

Before writing a program to sort the given array, let us first understand the working of Bubble sort method. Bubble sort requires (*n*–1) passes to sort an array with *n* elements. In each pass, every element *a*[*i*] is compared with *a*[*i*+1], for *i* = 0 to (*n*–*k*–1), where *k* is the pass number and if they are out of order, *i.e.* if *a*[*i*] > *a*[*i*+1], they are swapped. This will cause the largest element to move or bubble up. Thus, after the end of first pass, the largest element in the array will be placed at index (*n*–1). Further, on each successive pass, the next largest element is placed at indices (*n*–2), (*n*–3), ..., 1, respectively.

For more clarity, carefully examine the following steps.

Pass 1.

Step 1. If *a*[0] > *a*[1] then swap *a*[0] and *a*[1].
Step 2. If *a*[1] > *a*[2] then swap *a*[1] and *a*[2].
:
Step *n*–1. If *a*[*n*–2] > *a*[*n*–1] then swap *a*[*n*–2] and *a*[*n*–1].

Pass 2.

Step 1. If *a*[0] > *a*[1] then swap *a*[0] and *a*[1].
Step 2. If *a*[1] > *a*[2] then swap *a*[1] and *a*[2].
:
Step *n*–2. If *a*[*n*–3] > *a*[*n*–2] then swap *a*[*n*–3] and *a*[*n*–2].

:

Pass *K*.

Step 1. If $a[0] > a[1]$ then swap $a[0]$ and $a[1]$.
Step 2. If $a[1] > a[2]$ then swap $a[1]$ and $a[2]$.
:
Step $n-k$. If $a[n-k-1] > a[n-k]$ then swap $a[n-k-1]$ and $a[n-k]$.

:

Pass *n*−1.

Step 1. If $a[0] > a[1]$ then swap $a[0]$ and $a[1]$.

To illustrate the working of bubble sort method, consider the sorting of the following array in ascending order.

12 40 3 2 15

Note that, the output of a given pass becomes the input for the next pass.

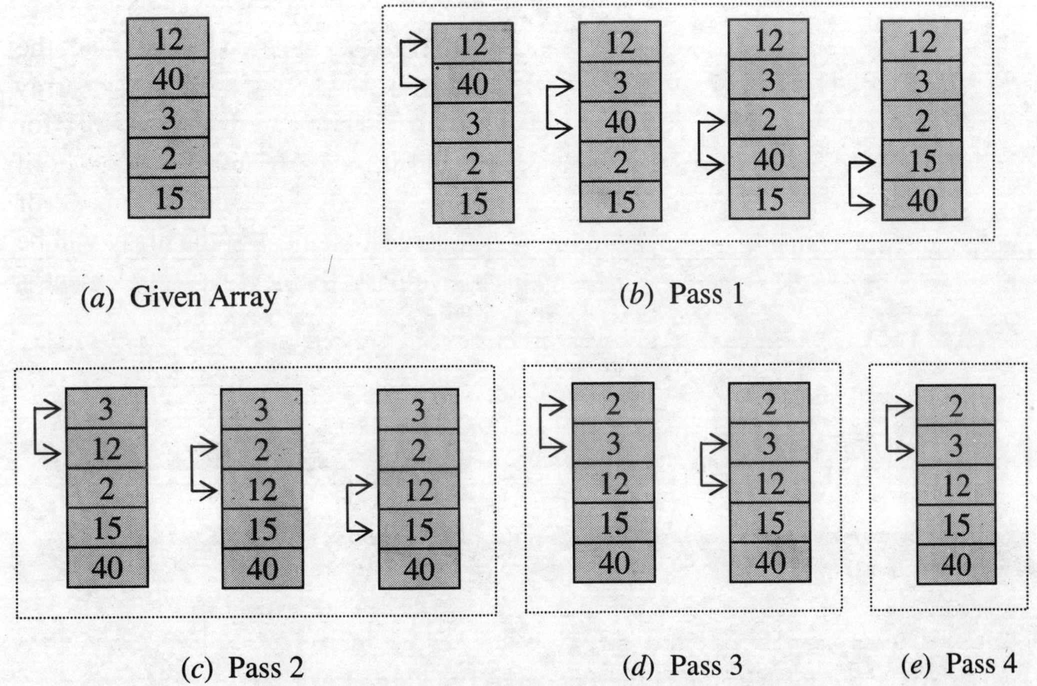

Figure 9.3: Illustration of Bubble sort method

The following listing shows the implementation of bubble sort method to sort an array in ascending order.

Listing 9.5

```
/*
*  Program to sort an array of integers in ascending order
*  using Bubble sort method
*/

#include<stdio.h>

void main(void)
{
    int a[50], i, n, k, temp;

    printf( "\nEnter size of array: " );
    scanf( "%d", &n );
    printf("\nEnter %d elements of the array\n",n);

    for ( i = 0; i < n; i++ )
       scanf ( "%d", &a[i] );
    for ( k = 0;  k < n-1;  k++ )
    {
       for ( i = 0; i < n-k-1; i++ )
       {
           if ( a[i] > a[i+1] )
           {
              temp = a[i];
              a[i] = a[i+1];
              a[i+1] = temp;
           }
       }
    }

    printf( "\nArray elements after sorting\n" );
    for ( i = 0; i < n; i++ )
        printf ( "%d  ", a[i] );
    printf( "\n" );
}
```

Test Run

```
Enter size of array: 10
Enter 10 elements of the array
75 80 65 59 72 35 55 69 43 85

Array elements after sorting
35  43  55  59  65  69  70  72  80  85
```

9.3.5 Passing One-Dimensional Array as Argument

Note that instead of passing values of all elements of an array to a function, only address of the array is passed. As you know, in C, the name of an array is a primary expression whose value is the address of the first element of the array.

```
/*  main function    */
#include <stdio.h>
void fun( int x[], int m );
void main()
{
   int a[10], n;
   /*  other local declarations */

   func(a, n); /* function call */
   /*   other statements         */
}
```

```
/*  function definition    */
void fun( int x[], int m )
{
   /*  local declarations */
   /*  other statements   */
}
```

Figure 9.4: Passing one-dimensional array as an argument to a function

Since, indexed references are simply calculated addresses, all we need to refer to any of the elements of the array is the address of the array, *i.e.*, address of the first element.

Because the name of the array is in fact its address, therefore, passing the array name allows called function to refer to the array back in the calling function.

Listing 9.6

```
/*
*  Program to demonstrate the passing of an array as an argument
*/
#include <stdio.h>
int largest( int x[], int size );  /*  function prototype */
void main(void)
{
   int a[50]={12,15,20,17,25,50,11,10,8,13};
   int i;
   printf( "Largest of the array element is %d\n",
   largest(a,50));
}
/* function that returns largest element of the array   */
int largest( const int x[], int size )
{
   int big, i;
```

```
   big = x[0];
   for ( i = 1; i < size; i++ ) {
      if ( x[i] > big )
         big = x[i];
   }
   return big;
}
```

Test Run

```
Largest of the array element is 50
```

Listing 9.7

```
/*
*  Program to swap elements of the first half of the array
*  with elements of the second half of the array
*/
#include <stdio.h>
void swapHalves(int a[], int n);  /* function prototype */
void main()
{
    int a[50];
    int n, i;
    printf("\nEnter even value for n as size of array : ");
    scanf("%d", &n);
    printf("Enter %d elements of array A\n", n);
    for ( i = 0; i < n; i++ )
      scanf("%d", &a[i]);
    swapHalves(a,n);   /*  call function   */
    printf("\nElements of array after swapping elements of the");
    printf(" first half with elements of the second half\n\n");
    for ( i = 0; i < n; i++ )
      printf("%d  ", a[i]);
}

/*
*  function that swaps elements of first half with elements
*  of the second half of a given array
*/
void swapHalves(int a[], int n)
{
    int i, j, temp;
    j = n/2;
```

```
    for ( i = 0; i < j; i++ )
    {
        temp = a[i];
        a[i] = a[i+j];
        a[i+j] = temp;
    }
}
```

If the value of *n* is even, the index set for the elements of the first half will 0..((*n*/2)-1) and the index set for the elements of the second half will be (*n*/2)..(*n*-1). To accomplish the above task, we use a loop to vary the index *i* from 0 to ((*n*/2)-1), and for each value of index *i*, elements at index *i* at index (*i*+*n*/2) are swapped. The function *swapHalves()* implements the above logic.

9.4 TWO-DIMENSIONAL ARRAYS

The array we have discussed for far are known as one-dimensional arrays because the data are organized linearly only in one direction (dimension). Many applications require that data be organized in more than one dimension. One common example is a matrix (a table), which is an array that consists of rows and columns.

Figure 9.5 shows a matrix (table) with 4 rows and 4 columns which is commonly used as a two-dimensional array.

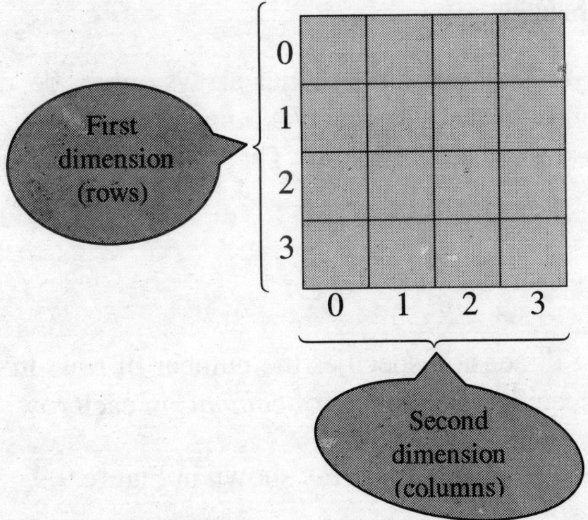

Figure 9.5: Two-dimensional array

Although two-dimensional array is exactly what is shown in Figure 9.5, C language looks at it in a different way. It looks at the two-dimensional array as am array of arrays. In other words, a two-dimensional array in C language is an array of one-dimensional arrays. This concept is shown in Figure 9.6.

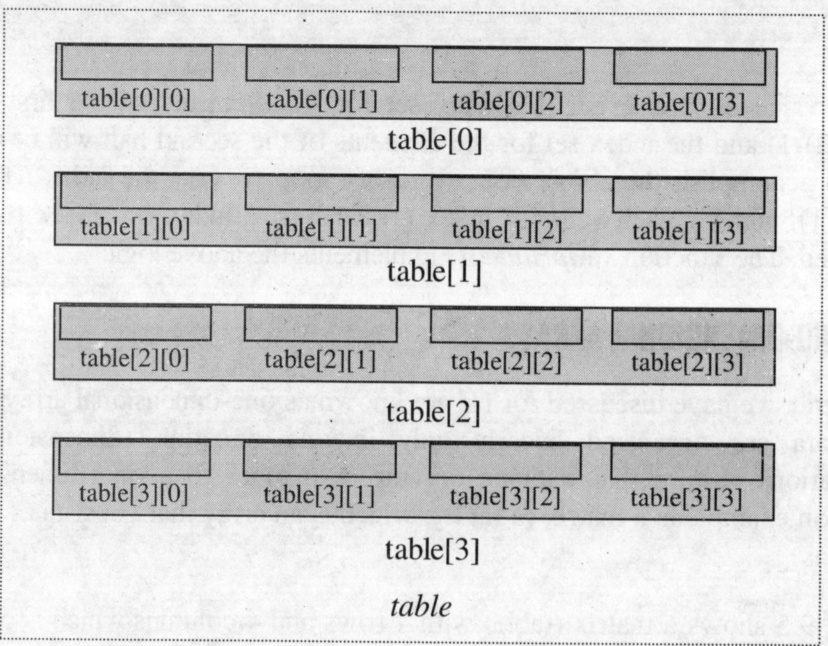

Figure 9.6: Array of arrays

9.4.1 Declaration and Definition

Two-dimensional arrays, like one-dimensional arrays, must be declared before being used. Declaration tells the compiler *the name of the array*, *the type of its elements*, and *the size of each dimension*. The syntax for declaration of two-dimensional array is

```
type arrayName[sizeOfDimension1][sizeOfDimension2];
```

By convention, the first dimension specifies the number of *rows* in the array while the second dimension specifies the number of *columns* in each row.

The declaration statement, declares the array shown in Figure 9.9

```
int table[4][4];
```

This declarations statement allocates a contiguous memory block of 32 bytes, 8-bytes for each row. First set of 8-bytes are used to store elements of first row, second set of 8-bytes are used to store elements of second row, third set of 8-bytes are used to store elements of third row and the last set of 8-bytes are used to store elements of the fourth (last) row. Within in each row, first set of 2-bytes are used to store element of the first column, next set of 2-bytes are used to store element of second column, next set of 2-bytes are used to store elements of the third column, and final set of 2-bytes are used to store element of the fourth (last) column.

Elements of two-dimensional array are stored row-wise, *i.e.*, in the allocated contiguous block of memory, first elements of first row are stored, then elements of third row, then elements of third row, and so on.

9.4.2 Accessing Elements

The C language uses two *indexes* to access individual elements in a two-dimensional array. These indices must be integral values or expressions that evaluates to an integral value. The first index is used to denote the row and the second index to denote the column.

Therefore, to access *j*th element of the *i*th row, we write

```
table[i][j]
```

To process all the elements row-wise of *table*, nested loops similar to the following code will be used:

```
for (i = 0; i < 4; i++ )
{
    for (j = 0; j < 4; j++ )
    {
        process ( table[i][j] );
    }
}
```

9.4.3 Storing Values

Like one-dimensional array, the declaration and definition of two-dimensional array also only reserve space for the elements of the array. No values are stored in the array at this moment. To store values in the array, we must initialize the elements, read values from keyboard, or assign values to each individual element.

9.4.3.1 Initialization

One way to initialize two-dimensional arrays is as shown below:

```
int table[4][4] = { 0, 0, 0, 0, 1, 1, 1, 1,
                    2, 2, 2, 2, 3, 3, 3, 3 };
```

It will initialize all the elements of the first row with value 0, elements of the second row with value 1, elements of the third row with 2 and elements of the fourth row with value 3.

Though, the above initialization has no problems, it highly recommended that nest braces be used to show the exact nature of the two-dimensional array. The array *table* is better initialized as shown below:

```
int table[4][4] = { { 0, 0, 0, 0 },
                    { 1, 1, 1, 1 },
                    { 2, 2, 2, 2 },
                    { 3, 3, 3, 3 },
                  };
```

In above way of initialization, we initialize each row as a one-dimensional array of four elements enclosed in braces. The array of four rows also has its set of braces. Note that we use commas between the elements in the columns and also commas between the rows.

As we have seen with the initialization with one-dimensional arrays that if the array is completely initialized, we need not specify the size of the array. The C system will assume the size of the array same as the number of elements in the initialization list. The same concept is carried forward to multi-dimensional arrays, except that only the first dimension can be omitted. All other dimensions must be specified. This concept is illustrated below:

```
int table[][4] = { {  0,  1,  2,  3 },
                   {  4,  5,  6,  7 },
                   {  8,  9, 10, 11 },
                   { 12, 13, 14, 15 },
                 };
```

To initialize the entire two-dimensional array to zeros, we can do by specifying the zero as the value for the first element only as shown below:

```
int table[][4]={ 0 };
```

9.4.3.2 Inputting Values

The second way to fill the array with values is to read the values from the keyboard or a data file. This method of inputting values is done using nested loops. Following segment shows the way elements can be read row-wise using nested for loops:

```
for (i = 0; i < 4; i++ )   {
    for (j = 0; j < 4; j++ ) {
        scanf( "%d", &table[i][j] );
    }
}
```

In general, if the one-dimensional array is of size $m \times n$, the first loop varies from 0 to $(m-1)$ and the second loop varies from 0 to $(n-1)$.

9.4.3.3 Assigning Values

The third way to fill the array with values is to assign the values to the individual elements using the assignment operator. Any value that is compatible can be assigned to the individual array element. A simple assignment statement for *table* is given below:

```
table[1][2] = 40;
```

We can also assign the elements of one array to second array provided they match fully in type and size. Suppose that two arrays named *a* and *b* are compatible, and size of each array is 4×4, and we want to copy the elements of array *a* to *b*, the following loop will serve the purpose:

```
for (i = 0; i < 4; i++ ) {
     for (j = 0; j < 4; j++ ) {
         b[i][j] = a[i][j];
     }
}
```

If the values of elements of an array follow a certain pattern, we can use nested loops to assign values. For example, if we want to initialize a 4×4 two-dimensional array to represent an identity matrix, this can be done using following nested loops as shown:

```
for (i = 0; i < 4; i++ )   {
     for (j = 0; j < 4; j++ )   {
         if ( i == j )
             a[][] = 1;
         else
             a[i][j] = 0
     }
}
```

$$\begin{pmatrix} 1 & 0 & 0 & 0 \\ 0 & 1 & 0 & 0 \\ 0 & 0 & 1 & 0 \\ 0 & 0 & 0 & 1 \end{pmatrix}$$

Figure 9.7: Identity matrix

9.4.4 Outputting Values

To output values of elements of two-dimensional array, we use the nested loops as follows:

```
for ( i = 0; i < 4; i++ )
{
    for ( j = 0; j < 4; j++ ) {
       printf( "%d", a[i][j] );
    }
    printf( "\n" );
}
```

The elements of the two-dimensional array will be output row-wise by the above segment. The first loop controls the rows while the second loop controls the columns.

Example 9.6:

Program to compute the transpose of a matrix *A* of order *m*×*n*.

We know that if we interchange the rows with columns, we get transpose of a given matrix, say B of order *n*×*m*, *i.e.*,

$$b_{ji} = a_{ij}$$

Listing 9.8

```
/*  Program to compute transpose of matrix A of size mxn  */
#include<stdio.h>
void main()
{
    int a[10][10], b[10][10];
    int n, m, i, j;
    printf( "Enter size of matrix A as m,n: " );
    scanf( "%d,%d", &m, &n);
    printf("\nEnter %d elements of matrix A row-wise\n",m*n);
    for ( i = 0 ; i < m; i++ )
    {
        for ( j = 0; j < n; j++ )
        {
           scanf( "%d", &a[i][j] );
        }
    }
    for ( i = 0 ; i < m ; i++ )
    {
        for ( j = 0 ; j < n ; j++ )
        {
```

```
            b[j][i] = a[i][j];
        }
    }
    printf( "\nTranspose is\n\n" );
    for ( i = 0 ; i < n; i++ )
    {
        for ( j = 0; j < m; j++ )
        {
            printf( "%5d", b[i][j] );
        }
        printf ( "\n" );
    }
}
```

Test Run

```
Enter size of matrix A as m,n: 3,3

Enter 9 elements of matrix A row-wise
1 2 3
4 5 6
7 8 9

Transpose is

   1    4    7
   2    5    8
   3    6    9
```

Example 9.7:

Program to add two matrices *A* and *B*, each of order $m \times n$.

We know that if to add to matrices, we add corresponding elements to get the element of a resultant matrix, i.e.,

$$c_{ij} = a_{ij} + b_{ij}$$

Listing 9.9

```
/*  Program to add matrix A and B, each of order mxn  */
#include<stdio.h>
void main()
{
    float a[10][10], b[10][10], c[10][10];
    int n, m, i, j;
    printf( "Enter size of matrices as m,n: " );
    scanf( "%d,%d", &m, &n);
```

```
    printf( "Enter %d elements of matrix A row-wise\n", m*n );
    for ( i = 0 ; i < m; i++ )
    {
        for ( j = 0; j < n; j++ ) {
            scanf( "%f", &a[i][j] );
        }
    }
    printf( "Enter %d elements of matrix B row-wise\n", m*n );
    for ( i = 0 ; i < m; i++ )
    {
        for ( j = 0; j < n; j++ ) {
            scanf( "%f", &b[i][j] );
        }
    }
    for ( i = 0 ; i < m ; i++ ) {
       for ( j = 0 ; j < n ; j++ ) {
          c[i][j] = a[i][j] + b[i][j];
       }
    }
    printf( "\nSum A+B is\n\n" );
    for ( i = 0 ; i < m; i++ ) {
        for ( j = 0; j < n; j++ ) {
          printf( "%7.2f", c[i][j] );
        }
        printf ( "\n" );
    }
}
```

Test Run

```
Enter size of matrices as m,n: 3,3
Enter 9 elements of matrix A row-wise
1 1 1
1 1 1
1 1 1
Enter 9 elements of matrix B row-wise
2 2 2
2 2 2
2 2 2

Sum A+B is

  3.00  3.00  3.00
  3.00  3.00  3.00
  3.00  3.00  3.00
```

Example 9.8:

Program to multiply two matrices A and B. The matrix A is of order $m \times n$ matrix and the matrix B is of order $p \times q$ matrix, provided $n = p$.

As we want to multiply two matrices A and B, where the matrix A is of order $m \times n$ and the matrix B is of order $p \times q$, the product matrix, say matrix C, then will be of order $m \times p$ with entry c_{ij}, which appears in the ith row and jth column is given as:

$$
\begin{aligned}
c_{ij} &= \text{sum of the products of the entries in the } i\text{th row of matrix } A \text{ with} \\
&\quad \text{the corresponding entries in the } j\text{th column of matrix } B \\
&= a_{i0} \times b_{0j} + a_{i1} \times b_{1j} + a_{i2} \times b_{2j} + \ldots + a_{i(n-1)} \times b_{(n-1)j} \\
&= \sum_{k=0}^{n-1} a_{ik} b_{kj}
\end{aligned}
$$

Listing 9.10

```
/*
*  Program to multiply matrix A of size mxn by matrix B of
*  size pxq. Program also checks for feasibility of product.
*/
#include<stdio.h>
void main()
{
    float a[10][10], b[10][10], c[10][10];
    int n, m, p, q, i, j, k;
    printf( "Enter size of matrix A as m,n: " );
    scanf( "%d,%d", &m, &n);
    printf( "Enter size of matrix B as p,q: " );
    scanf( "%d,%d", &p, &q);
    if ( n != p ) {
        printf( "\nMatrix Product AxB is not feasible\n" );
        return;
    }
    printf("\nEnter %d elements of matrix A row-wise\n", m*n);
    for ( i = 0 ; i < m; i++ )
    {
       for ( j = 0; j < n; j++ )
       {
          scanf( "%f", &a[i][j] );
       }
    }
    printf("\nEnter %d elements of matrix B row-wise\n", p*q);
    for ( i = 0 ; i < p; i++ )
    {
       for ( j = 0; j < q; j++ )
       {
          scanf( "%f", &b[i][j] );
       }
    }
    for ( i = 0 ; i < m ; i++ )
    {
```

```
        for ( j = 0 ; j < q ; j++ )
        {
            c[i][j] = 0;
            for ( k = 0; k < n; k++ )
            {
                c[i][j] += a[i][k] * b[k][j];
            }
        }
    }
    printf( "\nProduct AxB is\n\n" );
    for ( i = 0 ; i < m; i++ )
    {
        for ( j = 0; j < q; j++ )
        {
            printf( "%7.2f\t", c[i][j] );
        }
        printf ( "\n" );
    }
}
```

Test Run

```
Enter size of matrix A as m,n: 3,3
Enter size of matrix B as p,q: 3,3

Enter 9 elements of matrix A row-wise
1 1 1
1 1 1
1 1 1

Enter 9 elements of matrix B row-wise
2 2 2
2 2 2
2 2 2

Product AxB is

 6.00  6.00  6.00
 6.00  6.00  6.00
 6.00  6.00  6.00
```

9.4.5 Passing Two-Dimensional Array as Arguments

When we pass two-dimensional array to a function, we use the array name as we did with one-dimensional array. The formal argument in the argument list in the called function header must indicate the array has two dimensions. This is done by including two sets of brackets, one for each dimension. During function call, only the base address of the array is passed.

```
/*  main function    */
#include <stdio.h>
void fun(int x[][], int m, int n);
void main()
{
   int a[4][4];
   /*  other local declarations
*/

   func(a,m,n); /* function call
*/
   /*  other statements
*/
```

```
/*  function definition    */
void fun(int x[][], int m, int
n)
{
   /*  local declarations  */
   /*  other statement     */
}
```

Figure 9.8: Passing entire two-dimensional array

The following program illustrates the passing of entire two-dimensional array as argument. The program multiplies two compatible matrices. It uses functions to read, multiply and display matrices.

Listing 9.11

```
/*
*  Program to multiply matrix A of size mxn by matrix B of size
*  pxq. Program also checks for feasibility of product. This
*  program uses function to read, multiply and display matrices
*/
#include<stdio.h>
/*    function declarations    */
void readMatrix(float a[][], int m, int n);
void displayMatrix(float a[][], int m, int n);
void multiplyMatrix(float a[][],b[][],c[][],int m,int n,int q);
void main()
{
   float a[10][10], b[10][10], c[10][10];
   int n, m, p, q;
   printf( "Enter size of matrix A as m,n: " );
   scanf( "%d,%d", &m, &n);
   printf( "Enter size of matrix B as p,q: " );
   scanf( "%d,%d", &p, &q);
   if ( n != p )
   {
      printf( "\nMatrix Product AxB is not feasible\n" );
      return;
   }
   readMatrix(a,m,n);              /* input matrix 'a'  */
   readMatrix(b,p,q);              /* input matrix 'b'  */
   multiplyMatrix(a,b,c,m,n,q); /* multiply matrix a by matrix 'b'*/
```

```
    printf( "\nProduct AxB is\n\n" );
    displayMatrix(c,m,q);           /* output matrix 'c' */
}

/*  function that reads a matrix 'a' of order mxn  */
void readMatrix(float a[][], int m, int n)
{
   int i, j;
   printf("\nEnter %d elements of matrix A row-wise\n", m*n );
   for ( i = 0 ; i < m; i++ )
   {
      for ( j = 0; j < n; j++ )
      {
         scanf( "%f", &a[i][j] );
      }
   }
}

/*  function that displays a matrix 'a' of order mxn  */
void displayMatrix(float a[][], int m, int n)
{
    int i, j;
    for ( i = 0 ; i < m; i++ )
    {
       for ( j = 0; j < n; j++ )
       {
          printf( "%7.3f\t", c[i][j] );
       }
       printf ( "\n" );
    }
}

/*  function that multiplies matrices 'a' and 'b' and
   stores the product in matrix 'c' */
void multiplyMatrix(float a[][],b[][],c[][],int m,int n,int q)
{
    int i, j, k;
    float temp;
    for ( i = 0 ; i < m ; i++ )
    {
        for ( j = 0 ; j < q ; j++ )
        {
           for ( temp = 0, k = 0; k < n; k++ )
           {
              temp += a[i][k] * b[k][j];
           }
           c[i][j] = temp;
        }
    }
}
```

9.5 MULTI-DIMENSIONAL ARRAYS

Multi-dimensional arrays can have three, four, or more dimensions. The terminology used to describe the three-dimensional array is *planes*, *rows*, and *columns*. The first dimension is called a plane, which consists of rows and columns. Arrays of four or more dimensions can be created and used, but they are difficult to draw and visualize.

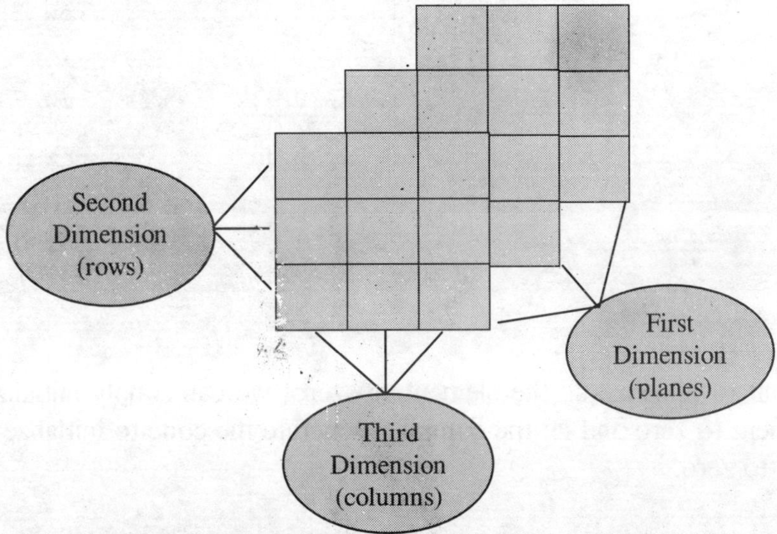

Figure 9.9: A three-dimensional array (3×3×3)

Although a three-dimensional array is exactly what is shown in Figure 9.15, the C language looks at it in a different way. It takes a three-dimensional array to be an array of two-dimensional arrays. It considers the two-dimensional array to be an array of one-dimensional arrays. In other words, a three-dimensional array in C is an array of arrays of arrays. This concept also holds true for arrays of more than three dimensions.

9.5.1 Declaration and Definition

Multi-dimensional arrays like one-dimensional and two-dimensional arrays must be declared before being used. The declaration tells the compiler the name of the array, the type of each element, and the size for each dimension. The three-dimensional array shown in Figure 9.15 will be declared as

```
int table[3][3][3];
```

9.5.2 Initialization

The three-dimensional array is initialized as follows. Comments are added to make the reading of the values easier.

```
int table[3][3][3] = { {  /*  plane 0  */
                        { 0, 1, 2, 3 },          /*  row 0  */
                        { 1, 0, 3, 2 },          /*  row 1  */
                        { 2, 1, 0, 3 }           /*  row 2  */
                      },
                      {  /*  plane 1  */
                        { 5, 1, 3, 0 },          /*  row 0  */
                        { 1, 5, 1, 2 },          /*  row 1  */
                        { 0, 1, 4, 2 }           /*  row 2  */
                      },
                      {  /*  plane 2  */
                        { 7, 2, 4, 8 },          /*  row 0  */
                        { 3, 4, 5, 9 },          /*  row 1  */
                        { 2, 3, 1, 0 }           /*  row 2  */
                      } };
```

If we want to initialize all the elements to zero, we can simply initialize only the first element to zero and let the compiler generate the code to initialize the rest of the array to zero.

```
int table[3][3][3] = { 0 };
```

Since, most of the problems of the engineering, business, and industry can be solved using one-dimensional and two-dimensional array, and multi-dimensional arrays are just introduced for academic interest.

S9.6 SUPPLEMENTARY PROBLEMS

Problem 9.1:

Write a function that takes an array of *n* integer numbers as its argument, and reverses the order of its elements without using any other array. For example, if the elements of the array are

2 4 1 6 7 9 15 12

The function should rearrange the array as

12 15 9 7 6 1 4 2

Solution: To accomplish the above task, we use two index variables *i* and *j*, where index variable *i* is initialized with the index of the first element, and index variable *j* is initialized with the index of the last element. Now elements at index *i* and at index *j* are swapped. Then index variable *i* is incremented and index variable *j* is decremented, and this is continued till $i \leq j$. The function *reverseElements()* implements the above logic. Following is the complete listing for the program to accomplish above task.

Listing 9.12

```
/*
 *  Program to reverse the order of elements of the array
 */
#include <stdio.h>
void reverseElements(int a[], int n);  /* function prototype */
void main()
{
    int a[100];
    int n, i;
    printf("\nEnter even value for n as size of array : ");
    scanf("%d", &n);
    printf("Enter %d elements of array A\n", n);
    for ( i = 0; i < n; i++ )
        scanf("%d", &a[i]);
    reverseElements(a,n);          /*  call function    */
    printf("\nElements of array after reversing the order of ");
    printf(" elements of a given array\n\n");
    for ( i = 0; i < n; i++)
        printf("%d  ", a[i]);
}

/* function that reverses the order of elements of an array  */
void reverseElements(int a[], int n)
{
   int i, j, temp;
   i = 0;
   j = n-1;
   while ( i <= j )
   {
      temp = a[i];
      a[i] = a[j];
      a[j] = temp;
      i++;
      j--;
   }
}
```

Problem 9.2:

Write a function that takes an array of *n* (where *n* is even) integer numbers as its argument, and rearrange its elements in such a way that values of alternate locations of the array are exchanged. For example, if the elements of the array are

2 4 1 6 7 9 15 12

The function should rearrange the array as

4 2 6 1 9 7 12 15

Solution: To accomplish the above task, we use index variable *i* and vary it from 0 to (*n*-1) in steps of 2. In each iteration, element at index *i* and at index (*i*+1) are swapped. The function *rearrangeElements()* implements the above logic.

Listing 9.13

```
/*
*  Program to rearrange the elements of array in such a way
*  that values of alternate locations of the array are exchanged.
*/
#include <stdio.h>
void rearrangeElements(int a[],int n); /* function prototype */
void main()
{
    int a[100];
    int n, i;
    printf("\nEnter even value for n as size of array : ");
      scanf("%d", &n);
    printf("Enter %d elements of array A\n", n);
    for ( i = 0; i < n; i++ )
       scanf("%d", &a[i]);
    rearrangeElements(a,n);    /*  call function    */
    printf("\nElements of array after swapping the alternate");
    printf(" elements of a given array\n\n");
    for ( i = 0; i < n; i++ )
       printf("%d  ", a[i]);
}
/* function that swaps alternate elements of the array   */
void rearrangeElements(int a[], int n)
{
    int i, temp;
    for ( i = 0; i < n; i += 2 )
    {
       temp = a[i];
       a[i] = a[i+1];
       a[i+1] = temp;
    }
}
```

Problem 9.3:

Write a program that read a matrix of size *m*×*n*, computes sum of its rows and columns and prints the output in the following format.

```
12   9  10  13  | 44
 7  11  22   5  | 45   <------  row sums
 6  25  21  15  | 67
20   8  33  16  | 77
----------------------
 45  53  86  49  <------  column sums
```

Solution: To accomplish the above task, we create two one-dimensional arrays named *colSum* and *rowSum* to store the sum of elements of respective rows and columns. Once these sums are computed, we print the elements of the array *rowSum* as the last column after printing all elements of a given row of the given matrix. After printing all the rows of the given matrix, we print the elements of the array *colSum* as the last row.

The following program implements the details.

Listing 9.14

```
/*
* Program to find row sums and column sums of the given matrix
*/
#include<stdio.h>
void main()
{
    int a[10][10], rowSum[10] = {0}, colSum[10] = {0};
    int i, j, n, m;
    printf( "Enter size of matrix A as m,n: " );
    scanf( "%d,%d", &m, &n);
    for ( i = 0 ; i < m; i++ ) {
       for ( j = 0; j < n; j++ ) {
          scanf( "%d", &a[i][j] );
      }
    }
    /*   compute the sum of elements of rows    */
    for ( i = 0 ; i < m; i++ ) {
       for ( j = 0; j < n; j++ ) {
          rowSum[i] += a[i][j];
      }
    }
    /*   compute the sum of elements of columns    */
    for ( j = 0 ; j < n; j++ ) {
       for ( i = 0; i < m; i++ ) {
```

```
            colSum[j] += a[i][j];
        }
    }
    /*   print the output    */
    for ( i = 0 ; i < m; i++ ) {
        for ( j = 0; j < n; j++ ) {
            printf("%5d", a[i][j]);
        }
        printf("  |%5d\n", rowSum[i]);
    }
    for ( j = 0; j < n; j++ )
        printf("-----");
    for ( j = 0; j < n; j++ ) {
        printf("%5d", colSum[j]);
    }
    printf("\n");
}
```

9.7 QUICK RECAP

In this chapter, we have learnt that

- An array is a data structure to store collections of similar values under a given name.
- Elements of an array stored in contiguous memory locations.
- Elements of an array are accessed by name of the array followed by index within brackets. One pair of brackets is used for each dimension.
- An array must be declared and defined before being used. Declaration and definition tells the compiler about the name of the array, type of each element and the size for each dimension.
- Arrays can be initialized at the time of declaration and definition.
- If one-dimensional array is completely initialized, then it is not necessary to specify the size, however it is recommended.
- The C language does not provide boundary check on the elements of an array.
- When an array is partially initialized, the rest of the elements are set to zero.
- Individual elements of an array can be passed to a function by value of by address.
- Entire array can also be passed to a function as argument. In this case, only the address of the array is passed. The called function has access to all its elements.
- Two-dimensional array is a representation of a table (matrix) with rows & columns.
- We can pass a single element, a row or whole two-dimensional array to a function.
- A multi-dimensional array is an extension of a two-dimensional array to three, four, or more dimensions.

9.8 MULTIPLE CHOICE QUESTIONS

1. Elements of two-dimensional array are stored in
   (*a*) column major order (*b*) row major order
   (*c*) random order (*d*) None
2. The value within [] in an array declaration specifies
   (*a*) size of the array (*b*) largest permitted subscript value
   (*c*) both (*a*) & (*b*) (*d*) None
3. Consider the following program in C language

```
#include <stdio.h>
void main()
{
   int i;
   int a[] = { 5, 7, 9, 11, 13 };
   for ( i = 0; i <=4; i++ ) {
     if ( i )
       continue;
     else
       printf( "%5d", i[a] );
   }
}
```

   What will be result of attempting to compile and run the above program?
   (*a*) Program will fail to compile because accessing *i*th element of array *a* as *i*[*a*] is not permitted in C.
   (*b*) The program will output: 5 7 9 11 13
   (*c*) The program will output: 5
   (*d*) Program will fail to compile because in array declaration, size of the array is not specified.
4. Given the declaration "int a[10];" Identify the which of the following is wrong?
   (*a*) *a*[–1] (*b*) *a*[0]
   (*c*) *a*[10] (*d*) ++a
5. Consider the following program in C language.

```
#include <stdio.h>
void main()
{
   int i;
   int a[] = { 5, 8, 9, 10, 13 };
   for ( i = 0; i <=4; i++ ) {
      if ( a[i] % 2 != 0 )
         a[i] /= 2;
      else
         a[i] *= 2;
```

```
        if ( a[i] % 2 == 0 )
            a[i] *= 2;
        else
            a[i] /= 2;
        printf( "    %d", a[i] );
    }
}
```

What will be its output?

(*a*) 5 8 9 10 13 (*b*) 10 16 18 20 36

(*c*) 4 32 8 40 12 (*d*) 2 4 4 5 6

6. When we should use an array?
   (*a*) When we need to hold constants.
   (*b*) When we need to hold data of same type.
   (*c*) When we need to hold data of different type.
   (*d*) When we need to obtain automatic memory cleanup functionality.
7. The use of arrays makes a program ------ .
   (*a*) general and capable of handling class of problems.
   (*b*) difficult to understand.
   (*c*) compact and efficient.
   (*d*) both *a* & *c*.
8. The maximum number of dimensions an array can have is ________ .
   (*a*) 3 (*b*) 4
   (*c*) user-defined (*d*) compiler dependent
9. What is the difference between the 5's in the below expressions?

```
int num[5];
num[5]=10;
```

   (*a*) First specifies the array size, the second one specifies individual element.
   (*b*) First specifies the individual element, the second one specifies the size.
   (*c*) Both specify array size.
   (*d*) None.
10. What would be the output of the following program if the array begins at 65486 address location?

```
#include <stdio.h>
void main()
{
    int a[6]={ 12,14,15,17,19 };
    printf("%u, %u ", arr, &arr );
}
```

   (*a*) 65486, 65488 (*b*) 65488, 65486
   (*c*) 65486, 65486 (*d*) 65488, 65488

11. What would be the output of the program, if the array begins at address 1200?

```
#include <stdio.h>
void main()
{
    int a[5]={ 2,4,6,8,10 };
    printf("%u, %d ", a, sizeof(a) );
}
```

(*a*) 1202, 10 (*b*) 10, 1202
(*c*) 10, 1200 (*d*) 1200, 10

12. A two dimensional array is called as a ____________ .

(*a*) Matrix (*b*) Vector
(*c*) Stack (*d*) queue

9. The number of passes required in Bubble sort for an array of size *n* is ______ .

(*a*) *n* (*b*) *n*-1
(*c*) > *n*-1 (*d*) < *n*-1

14. What will be the output of the following program?

```
#include <stdio.h>
void main()
{
    void fun(int x[]);
    int a[] = {1, 2, 3, 4, 5 };
    fun(a);
    printf("\n%d,%d", a[0], a[1]);
    printf("%d,%d,%d\n", a[2], a[3], a[4]);
}
void fun(int x[])
{
    x[2] = x[2] + 2;
    x[4] = x[4] + 4;
}
```

(*a*) 5,6,7,8,9 (*b*) 2,4,6,8,10
(*c*) 3,4,5,6,7 (*d*) None

15. Which would be the output of the following program?

```
#include <stdio.h>
void main()
{
    int a[5] = { 1, 2 };
    printf("\n%d,%d,%d\n", a[2], a[3], a[4]);
}
```

(*a*) 0, 0, 0 (*b*) 2, 2, 2
(*c*) 1, 1, 1 (*d*) Garbage

16. What will happen if in a C program, you assign a value to an array element whose subscript exceeds the size of the array?

(*a*) Nothing will happen, and the element will get a given value.

(*b*) Compiler will flag a syntax error.

(*c*) Memory location immediately after the last memory location of the array will be overwritten, and this may cause system to crash.

(*d*) The array size will automatically be increased to accommodate the new value.

17. Which of the following is a correct output of the program?

```
#include <stdio.h>
void main()
{
    int i, j, m;
    int a[5] = { 5, 1, 15, 20, 25 };
    i = ++a[1];
    j = a[1]++;
    m = a[i++];
    printf("\n%d, %d, %d\n", i, j, m);
}
```

(*a*) 2, 1, 15 (*b*) 3, 2, 15

(*c*) 1, 15, 20 (*d*) 1, 2, 15

18. When an array is passed as an argument, what actually get passed?

(*a*) All the elements.

(*b*) Only the first element.

(*c*) The base address of the array, *i.e.*, address of the first element.

(*d*) Addresses of all the elements.

19. In which of the following cases mentioning the name of the array does not yield the base address?

(*a*) When the array name is passed to *scanf()* function.

(*b*) When the array name is used with the *sizeof* operator.

(*c*) When the array name is operand of the *addressof* (&) operator.

(*d*) All of above.

20. Which of the following is a correct output of the program?

```
#include <stdio.h>
void main()
{
    int a[] = { 11 };
    printf("\n%d", 0[a]);
}
```

(*a*) 0 (*b*) 1

(*c*) 11 (*d*) Syntax error

9.9 REVIEW EXERCISES

1. What is an array?
2. Is it possible to declare and initialize an array in C simultaneously? If yes, how?
3. What are the rules for naming an array?
4. What is the subscript of the first element of the array?
5. How a real array named *data* with 100 elements will be declared? What will be the subscript of the last element?
6. Is it possible to declare more than one array in the same declaration statement?
8. What happens if the number of values in the initialization list is less than the size of the array?
9. What happens if number of values in initialization list is more than size of array?
10. Is the following array declaration is correct? If not, why?

```
int a(50);
```

11. If the declaration segment is

```
#define ROWS  100
float height[ROWS];
```

Is the following segment to enter data in array is correct?

```
for ( i = 0; i <= ROWS; i++ )
    scanf ( "%f", height[i] );
```

12. When an array is passed as an argument to a function, what is actually passed?
13. When an entire array is passed as an argument to a function, the function can alter the values of the elements of the array. We want to prevent the function from doing so, how this task can be accomplished?
14. Is any thing wrong with the following declaration? Explain.

```
int a[3][] = { { 1, 2, 3 }, { 3, 2, 1 }, { 4, 5, 2 } };
```

9.10 PROGRAMMING EXERCISES

1. Write a program that accepts an array, interchanges the first element with the last element, second element with the second last element, and so on, and finally prints the new array.
2. Write a function, say *void transpose(float a[][], int n)*, that computes the transpose of a square matrix *A* of size $n \times n$. Note that the transpose of the matrix is to be stored in the original matrix itself not in a separate matrix.

3. Write a program to pre-multiply a matrix by its transpose.
4. There are *n* students in a class. The name and his/her score in a class test are given. Write a program to print name of a student who topped the class test.
5. Write a program to read a set of *n* integers between 1 and 10 and count the number of times each integer appears in the set. Print the integers in order of frequency, the number occurring the highest number of times first.
6. A department store chain has *m* (≤10) stores, and each store has the same *n* (≤15) departments. The weekly sales of the chain are stored in *m*×*n* array *SALES* (say). Write down the program which

   (*a*) Prints the total weekly sales of each store.
   (*b*) Prints the total weekly sales of each department.
   (*c*) Prints the total weekly sales of the chain.
7. Write a program which inserts an element *d* in *k*th position of an array *a* of size *n*.

13. Given a matrix *A* of order *m*×*n*, write a program to find the sum of squares of the reciprocal of each row and store it in one-dimensional array and print the largest of the sums.

14. Given a matrix *A* of order *m*×*n*, write a program to find the row having the maximum number of negative elements.

10. A square matrix *A* of size *nxn* is said to be symmetric if element $a_{ij} = a_{ji}$ for all values of *i* and *j*. Write a function, say *int isSymmetric(int a[][], int n)* that returns value 1 if the input matrix is symmetric else returns value 0.

11. Write a program that fills a 5×5 array as follows:

   (*a*) Elements above diagonal are assigned value 1.
   (*b*) Elements on the diagonal are assigned value 0.
   (*c*) Elements below diagonal are assigned value −1.

   Display the contents of the array.

12. Suppose you are given a sample of *n* (≤100) values between 1 and 10. Write a program that builds the frequency array and prints it in the form of a histogram.

13. Given a matrix *A* of order *m*×*n*, write a program to sort the even rows in ascending order and odd rows in descending order

❑ ❑ ❑

10 Strings

Learning Objectives

After reading this chapter, students will have the ability to:

- comprehend the handling of string as array of characters
- declare, initialize and perform input/output of string data
- explain the use of various library function for manipulating strings
- explain the way strings are passed to functions as arguments
- write efficient programs for manipulating strings as a part of overall problem

10.1 INTRODUCTION

Each of the arrays, illustrated in *Chapter 9*, so far contained numeric elements. We can also have array of characters. Using array of characters, we can store string data. But do remember that as such strings are not directly supported in C language, though sometimes loosely we refer to array of characters as strings.

A string in C language is a variable length array of characters that is delimited by null character ('\0'). Generally, characters comprising a string are selected only from printable characters; however, C language does permit the use of any character except the null character. In fact, it is common to use formatting characters, such as tabs, format specifiers, etc., in strings.

In this chapter, we will discuss the various aspects related to handling of strings in C language.

The C language uses variable length, delimited strings. The null character '\0' is used as the delimiting character. Though the null character '\0' looks like a sequence of two characters, '\' and '0', but in C language it is treated as single character.

10.2 STORING STRINGS

In C language, a string is stored in an array of characters. It is terminated by the null ('\0') character. Figure 10.1 shows how a string "Hello" is stored in memory. Because a string is stored in an array, the name of the array, and hence string, is a pointer to the beginning of the string.

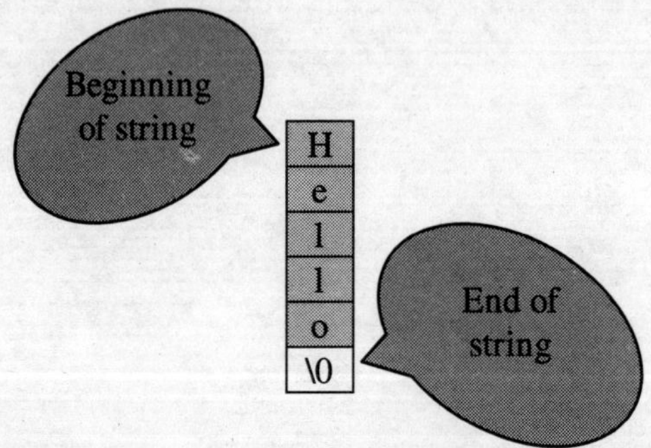

Figure 10.1: Storing a string in memory

Figure 10.2 shows the difference between the storage of a character and a one character string. The character required only one storage location (of 1-byte) whereas one character string requires two storage location (of 1-byte each); one for the character and one for the delimiter. The figure also shows how an empty string is stored. The empty string consists of null character only.

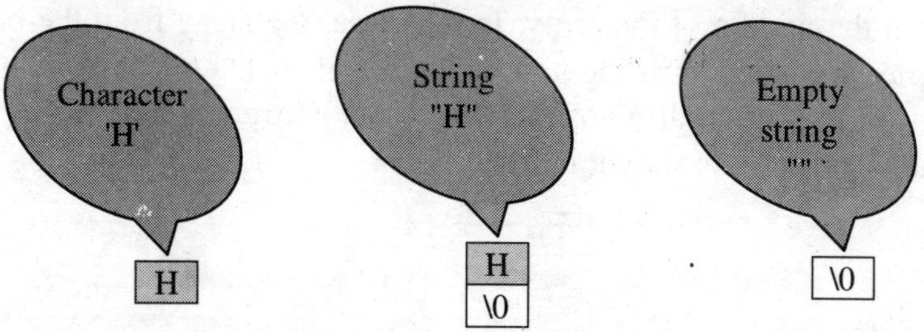

Figure 10.2: Difference in storage of characters and strings

10.3 NEED OF STRING DELIMITER

The question – *Why actually we need a null character to terminate a string*? - may be coming in your mind. The answer to this question is that a string is not a data type; it is data structure – *an array*. Therefore, implementation of string is logical not physical. The physical structure is the array in which string is stored. Since, strings are of varying length, there is a need to identify the logical end of data within physical structure.

Let look at the need of string delimiter from another point of view. If the data is of fixed length, then we don't need string data structure to store them rather it can easily be stored in an array. When data is stored in an array, the end of the data is always indicated by the last element of the array. But, if the data is not of fixed length (*i.e.*, varying length), then we need some other way to determine the end of the data.

The null character is used to mark the end of the string data.

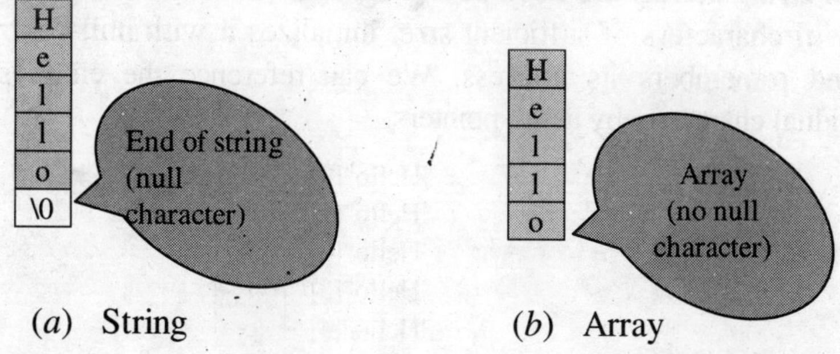

(*a*) String (*b*) Array

Figure 10.3: Difference between a string and an array of characters

Because strings are variable-length structures, enough space for the maximum-length string that we have to store plus one for the null character (delimiter) be reserved. In many situations it may be possible that the entire array is not filled and we may have null character in the middle of the array. In that case, the array from the beginning to the null character is treated as string and remaining elements of the array are ignored. This means that a part of an array of characters can be treated as a string provided it ends with a null character, as shown in Figure 10.4.

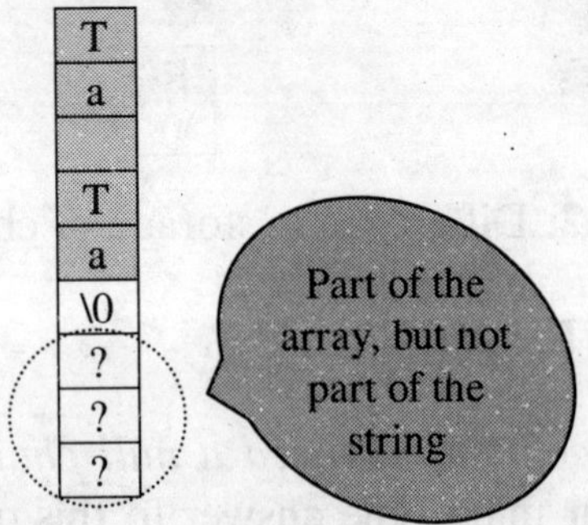

Figure 10.4: String stored in part of array

10.4 STRING LITERALS

A *string literal*, also known as *string constant*, is a sequence of characters enclosed in double quotes. The following are examples of some string literals:

```
"Hello! you are wel come"
"Hari\'s Book"
""
"A"
```

Note that embedded spaces are significant. And if quotes, single (') or double ("), are part of the string, they must be used with the escape sequence.

When string literals are used in a program, the C system automatically creates an array of characters of sufficient size, initializes it with null-delimited string, stores it, and remembers its address. We can reference the entire string literal or its individual characters by using pointers.

"Hello"[0]	H	← "Hello"
"Hello"[1]	e	
"Hello"[2]	l	
"Hello"[3]	l	
"Hello"[4]	o	
"Hello"[5]	\0	

Figure 10.5: Referencing string literals

Let us have a look at addressing s string literal. A string literal, being an array of characters, is itself a pointer constant to the first character of the string. Generally, we will be referring to the entire string literal, however, it is possible to refer to any character of the string literal by suffixing the index of the character as shown in Figure 10.5.

Listing 10.1

```
/* Program to demonstrate the referencing of string literals */
#include<stdio.h>
void main()
{
    printf( "\n%c\n", "Hello"[4] );
}
```

Test Run

```
o
```

10.5 STRING VARIABLES

A string variable is actually an array of characters.

10.5.1 Declaring String Variables

String variables are declared as shown in the following statement

```
char str[20];
```

This statement declares string variable *str* of length 20. In fact, the maximum characters that can be stored are 19 as last character is always the null character. In fact, the above declarations reserves a memory block of 20 bytes, with the array name *str* representing the address of the first element of the array.

10.5.2 Initializing String Variables

String variable can alsc be initialized during declaration. The following declaration illustrates one such approach.

```
char mess[] = {'Y', 'o', 'u', ' ', 'a', 'r', 'e', ' ',
               'w', 'e', 'l', ' ', 'c', 'o', 'm', 'e', '\0'};
```

Here string variable *mess* is initialized as sequence of character constants. In this style it is programmer's job to specify the null character as the last character. In addition to this, as you can see, the size of the array is not specified. *Can you guess what will be the size of mess*? In fact it is the number of character constants specified, including the null character.

Since strings will be used very often, the C language provides a short and efficient approach for initializing strings.

For example, the task of above statement can also be accomplished as

```
char mess[] = "You are wel come";
```

Note that in this approach, the compiler automatically appends the null character.

10.6 STRINGS AND THE ASIGNMENT OPERATOR

Since a string is an array of characters, therefore, the name of the array (string) is a pointer constant. As a pointer constant, it is an *rvalue*, and therefore cannot be used as the left operand of the assignment operator.

The next example, demonstrates this

```
char str1[] = "Hello";
char str2[20];

str2 = str1;     /*  compile time error  */
```

As mentioned earlier in *Chapter 13*, if we want to copy elements of one array to another array, it is possible only by setting up loops to assign element by element. The same can be done by writing a loop to assign character individually, but there is a better way.

The C language provides a rich library of function to manipulate strings, including moving one string to another. We will learn about these library functions in coming sections.

10.7 INPUT/OUTPUT OF STRINGS

A string can be read and written. The C language provides several functions for input and output of string data. There are two approaches to perform input/output of string data.

These are

- Using unformatted I/O functions (*getchar()*, *getche()*, *getch()*, *putchar()*, *gets()*, *puts()*)
- Using formatted I/O functions (*scanf()*, *printf()*)

10.7.1 Input/Output of Strings Using Unformatted I/O Functions

The input/output of string data can be performed using character I/O functions – *getche()* and *putchar()* functions,as illustrated in the following program.

Listing 10.2

```
/*
*  Program to perform input/output of string
*  data with character I/O functions
*/
#include<stdio.h>
void main()
{
 char str[30];
 int i, n = 0;
 printf( "\nEnter string of length <= 29" );
 printf( "\nand terminate with ENTER key\n\n" );
 while ( ( str[n] = getche() ) != '\r' )
    n++;
 str[n] = '\0';
 printf( "\nYou have entered\n\n" );
 for ( i = 0; i < n; i++ )
    putchar ( str[i] );
}
```

Test Run

```
Enter string of length <= 29
and terminate with ENTER key

Enjoy working with string.↵

You have entered

Enjoy working with string.
```

Input/output of strings using *getche()* character input function is very handy, when security features, such as user authentication is done using *login ids*, are incorporated in the programs as demonstrated in Listing 10.3.

Listing 10.3

```
/*
*  Program to demonstrate the handling of password type input
*  using getche() character input function
*/
#include<stdio.h>
void main()
{
   char str[2], ch;
   int i, n = 0;
   printf( "\nEnter password : " );
   while ( ( ch = getche() ) != '\r' ) {
      printf("\b*");
      str[n++] = ch;
   }
   str[n] = '\0';
   printf( "\n\nPassword provided by you is " );
   for ( i = 0; i < n; i++ )
      putchar ( str[i] );
   printf( "\n" );
}
```

Test Run

```
Enter password : ******

Password provided by you is guess
```

The input/output of string data can be performed using string I/O functions (*gets()* and *puts()*) as illustrated in the following program.

Listing 10.4

```
/*
*  Program to perform input/output of string
*  data with string I/O functions
*/
#include<stdio.h>
#include<string.h>
void main()
{
   char str[30];
   printf( "\nEnter string of length <= 29" );
   printf( "\nand terminate with ENTER key\n\n" );
   gets( str );
   printf( "\nYou have entered\n\n" );
   puts( str );
}
```

Test Run

```
Enter string of length <= 29
and terminate with ENTER key
There is no substitute of hard work.↲
You have entered
There is no substitute of hard work.
```

10.7.2 Input/Output of Strings Using Formatted I/O Functions

The input/output of string data can be performed using formatted I/O functions – *scanf()* and *printf()* functions.

10.7.2.1 Formatted String Input

We can read strings using formatted input function – *scanf()*. The format specifier for a string is "s". The *scanf()* function ignores the any occurrences of leading whitespace characters. Once it finds a character, all are read until they find a whitespace, putting each character in the array in order, followed by the null character. All trailing whitespace characters are left in the input stream, which can be flushed before subsequent read operation, of any data.

Format specifier can use the following fields – *flag, maximum field size*, and *size*.

Flag

The only flag that can be used is asterisk (*), which discards the data read.

Maximum Field Size

Maximum field size, when present, specifies the maximum numbers characters that can be read.

Size

Normal characters are read if no size option is used. In order to read wide characters (as per new standard C99), we use size *l* (alphabet letter l - ell).

Consider following declaration for string

```
char str[10];
```

To read string from the keyboard, we can simply write

```
scanf("%s", str);
```

An address of operator is not required for *str* since itself is a address (pointer constant). However, the use of it will result in an error.

The only thing that we must take care is to ensure that we reserve sufficient space to store all the characters of the string including the null character. If it is not done, then we overwrite the memory that follows the array.

Therefore, we must ensure that we don't exceed the size of the array. We can provide the protection against the maximize size of the data that the user can enter, as illustrated below:

```
scanf("%9s", str);
```

Here we set the maximum number of characters to nine while the array size is ten. This is because *scanf()* function will read up to maximum of nine characters and then insert the null character. Now, if the user enters more than nine characters, the extra characters will be left in the input stream. But this can cause a problem subsequently.

Listing 10.5

```
/*
*  Program to perform I/O of string data with scanf() &
*  prinft() functions
*/
#include<stdio.h>
void main()
{
 char str[20];
 printf( "\nEnter string of length <= 19" );
 printf( "\nand terminate with ENTER key\n" );
 scanf( "%19s", str );
 printf( "\nYou have entered\n\n" );
 printf( "%s", str );
}
```

From the user point of view, the working of the abovc programs will be same as shown the following test run.

Test Run

```
Enter string of length <= 19
and terminate with ENTER key
I love programming.↵
You have entered
I love programming.
```

10.7.2.2 Formatted String Output

We can write strings using formatted output function – *printf()*. It uses the same format specifier that was used with *scanf()* function. The format specifier can use the following fields – *the left-justify flag, width, precision*, and *size*.

Justification Flag

The justification flag (-) is used to left justify the output. It has meaning only when the width is also specified, and the length of the string is less than the width. If no flag is used, the justification is right, by default.

The following call to *printf()* function demonstrates the use of justification flag.

```
printf("\n|%-30s\n", "String is left justified.");
```

Output:

```
|String is left justified.     |
```

Minimum Width

The width set the minimum size of the string for output. If it is used without a justification flag, the string is printed right justified as shown below:

```
printf("\n|%30s\n", "String is left justified.");
```

Output:

```
|     String is left justified.|
```

Precision

Strings can be long sometimes. Because the width specifies the minimum size for the string, a long string can destroy the formatting.

To provide a safe guard against this, the C language uses the precision option to set the maximum number of characters tat will be printed, as shown below:

```
printf("\n|%-20.14s\n", "String is left justified.");
```

Output:

```
|String is left      |
```

Size

Normal characters are written if no size option is used. In order to write wide characters (as per new standard C99), we use size l (alphabet letter l - *ell*).

Listing 10.6

```
/*
*   Program to perform input/output
*   of string data with scanf()
*   prinft() functions
*/
#include<stdio.h>
void main()
{
 char str[] = "C Programming";
 int i, j;
 printf( "\n\n" );
 for ( i = 0; i <= 12; i++ )
 {
    printf("%13.*s\n", i, str);
 }
 for ( i = 11; i >= 0; i-- )
 {
    printf("%13.*s\n", i, str);
 }
}
```

Test Run

```
            C
            C
          C P
         C Pr
        C Pro
       C Prog
      C Progr
     C Progra
    C Program
   C Programm
  C Programmi
 C Programmin
C Programming
 C Programmin
  C Programmi
   C Programm
    C Program
     C Progra
      C Progr
       C Prog
        C Pro
         C Pr
          C P
            C
            C
```

In the above program, the precision is used dynamically. Basically, in the format specifier for *printf()* function, "%*" uses the value of the corresponding item in list of items.

For example, in the following statement

```
printf( "\n%*.*s\n"", 16, 12, str );
```

will use 16 as the width and 12 as the precision.

10.8 STRING MANIPULATION FUNCTIONS

Almost every C compiler provides a large number of library functions for manipulating strings. Table 10.1 lists some frequently used string functions.

Table 10.1: Frequently Used String Functions

String Function	Operation Performed
`strcat`	Appends the characters of second argument at the end of first string variable.
`strncat`	Appends first *n* characters of second argument at the end of first string variable.
`strcmp`	Compares two strings (comparison is case sensitive).
`strcmp`	Compares two strings (comparison is case sensitive).
`strncmp`	Compares first *n* characters of two strings (comparison is case sensitive).
`strcmpi`	Compares two strings without regard to case (comparison is case insensitive).
`strcmp`	Compares two strings (comparison is case sensitive).
`strcpy`	Copies the character of source string constant or variable to destination string variable.
`strncpy`	Copies first *n* characters of source string constant or variable to destination string variable.
`strlen`	Finds length of a string.
`strlwr`	Converts a string to lowercase.
`strrev`	Reverses the string. Only supported by Turbo C.
`strupr`	Converts a string to uppercase.
`strset`	Sets all characters of a string to a given character.
`strstr`	Finds first occurrence of a given string in another string.

Let us discuss some of these string functions one by one.

10.8.1 The *strlen()* Function

This function takes one argument that can be a string constant or a variable. It counts the number of character present in the string. Do remember that null character '\0' is not a part of the character; it is merely used to mark the end of the string, so it is not counted.

Listing 10.7

```
/*  Program to illustrate the use of strlen()function  */
#include <stdio.h>
#include <string.h>
void main()
{
   char str[30];
   int len;
   printf( "\nEnter a string of length <= 29" );
   printf( "\nand terminate with ENTER key" );
   gets (str);
   len = strlen ( str );
   printf( "Number of characters in %s = %d\n", str, len );
}
```

Test Run

```
Enter string of length <= 29
and terminate with ENTER key
Turbo↵
Number of characters in Turbo = 5
```

10.8.2 The *strcat()* Function

This function takes two arguments, of which first is a string variable and second can be a string constant or a variable. It appends the character(s) of the second arguments at the end of the first argument. There must be sufficient space available to accommodate the incoming characters from destination string, otherwise overflow occurs.

Listing 10.8

```
/*  Program to illustrate the use of strcat()function  */
#include <stdio.h>
#include <string.h>
void main()
```

```
{
   char str1[30] = "Wel", str2[30] = " Come";
   printf( "\nFirst string is %s\n", str1 );
   printf( "Second string is %s\n", str2 );
   strcat( str1, str2 );
   printf( "First string after appending\n" );
   printf( "second one: %s\n", str1 );
}
```

Test Run

```
First string is Wel
Second string is Come
First string after appending
second one: Wel Come
```

10.8.3 The *strcpy()* Function

This function takes two arguments, of which first is a string variable and second can be a string constant or a variable. It copies the character(s) of the second arguments to the first argument.

The following program illustrates its use.

Listing 10.9

```
/* Program to illustrate the use of strcpy()function */
#include <stdio.h>
#include <string.h>
void main()
{
  char str1[30] = "Wel", str2[30] = " Come";
  printf( "\nFirst string is %s\n", str1 );
  printf( "Second string is %s\n", str2 );
  strcpy( str1, str2 );
  printf( "First string after copying\n" );
  printf( "second one: %s\n", str1 );
}
```

Test Run

```
First string is Wel
Second string is Come
First string after copying
second one: Come
```

10.8.4 The *strcmp()* Function

This function takes two arguments, of which both can be string variables or constants. It compares the characters of each but one at a time and returns a value indicating the result of the comparison. For example, in the statement

```
strcmp ( str1, str2 );
```

value returned will have the following meanings:

Table 10.2: Interpretation of value returned *by strcmp()* function

Value Returned	Meaning
Less than zero	*str1* is less than *str2*, *i.e.*, *str1* comes first *str2* in dictionary order.
Zero	*str1* is identical to *str2*.
Greater than zero	*str1* is greater *str2* i.e. *str1* comes after *str2* in dictionary order.

The following program illustrates its use.

Listing 10.10

```
/*  Program to illustrate the use of strcmp()function  */
#include <stdio.h>
#include <string.h>
void main()
{
    char str1[31], str2[31];
    int value;
    printf( "Enter first  string: " );
    gets(str1);
    printf( "\nEnter second string: " );
    gets( str2 );
    value = strcmp( str1, str2 );
    if ( value > 0 )
    {
       printf("\n%s comes after %s", str1, str2);
       printf(" in dictionary order\n" );
    } else if ( value < 0 ) {
       printf("\n%s comes before %s", str1, str2);
       printf(" in dictionary order\n" );
    } else
       printf("\nBoth strings are same\n"  );
}
```

Test Run

```
Enter first string: software
Enter first string: hardware
hardware comes before software in dictionary order
```

10.8.5 The *strrev()* Function

This function takes string variable as its single argument. It reverses the string i.e. the last character becomes the first one, the second last becomes the second one, and so on. To illustrate its use, let us consider an interesting problem. A word is said to be a palindrome if it remains same after reversing, such as *radar*, *i.e.*, its first character is same as last character, second character is same as second last character, and so on.

The *strrev()* function is not supported by C compilers on Linux and Unix based systems.

Listing 10.11

```
/*
*  Program to illustrate the use of strrev()function
*/
#include <stdio.h>
#include <string.h>
void main()
{
 char str1[31], str2[31];
 printf( "Enter any string of length <= 30: " );
 gets (str1);
 strcpy ( str2, str1 );
 strrev ( str2 );
 if ( ( strcmp ( str1, str2 ) ) == 0 )
    printf( "\n%s is a palindrome\n", str1 );
 else
    printf( "\n%s is not a palindrome\n", str1 );
}
```

Test Run

```
Enter any string of length <= 30: adda
adda is a palindrome
```

10.8.6 The *strlwr()* Function

This function takes string variable as its single argument and returns a pointer to converted string. It converts uppercase alphabet letters of the string to lower case letters.

Listing 10.12

```
/* Program to illustrate the use of strlwr()function   */

#include <stdio.h>
#include <string.h>

void main()
{
   char str1[31];
   printf( "Enter any string of length <= 30: " );
   gets (str1);
   printf( "\nString after conversion: %s\n",  strlwr(str1) );
}
```

Test Run

```
Enter any string of length <= 30: TURBO C

String after conversion: turbo c
```

10.8.7 The *strupr()* Function

This function takes string variable as its single argument and returns a pointer to converted string. It converts lowercase alphabet letters of the string to uppercase letters.

Listing 10.13

```
/*
*  Program to illustrate the use of strupr()function
*/

#include <stdio.h>
#include <string.h>

void main()
{
   char str1[31];
   printf( "Enter any string of length <= 30: " );
   gets (str1);
   printf( "\nString after conversion: %s\n",  strupr(str1) );
}
```

Test Run

```
Enter any string of length <= 30: Turbo c
String after conversion: TURBO C
```

10.9 PASSING STRINGS TO A FUNCTION

A string can be passed as an argument to a function using subscripted notation for arrays. In a function definition, the formal parameter is declared as an array of characters. The following program illustrates the passing of a string to a function.

Listing 10.14

```
/*
*  Program to illustrates passing of a string to a function
*/
#include<stdio.h>
#include<string.h>

void func( char [] );    /*  function prototype  */

void main()
{
   char str1[] = "Sample string";
   func( str1 );
}

void func( char temp[] )
{
   printf( "String passed to it: " );
   puts( temp );
   printf( "\nand its length is: %d\n", strlen( temp ) );
}
```

Test Run

```
String passed to it: Sample string
and its length is: 13
```

10.10 ARRAY OF STRINGS

In the last section, we discussed string variables that can store one string value at a time. Suppose we want to handle list (array) of such strings, then *what is the solution*? The answer to this question can be found by using two-dimensional array of characters. In two-dimensional arrays, the first row stores the first string, the second row stores the second string, and so on.

Suppose, we want to handle a list of names of 4 persons, where the name of each person can be maximum of 30 characters long. The following will be the declaration

```
char names[4][31];
```

The following statement shows the way list of strings can be initialized.

```
char names[4][31] = { "Ram Parkash",
                      "Inder Mohan Singh Sidhu",
                      "Amanpreet",
                      "Rajan"
                    };
```

The next program illustrates the input/output of list of strings represented as a two-dimensional array of characters.

Listing 10.15

```
/*
* Program to illustrates the input/output of array of strings
* represented as two-dimensional array of characters
*/
#include <stdio.h>
#include <string.h>
void main()
{
   char names[50][31];
   int i, n;
   printf( "Enter number of strings: " );
   scanf( "%d", &n );
    for ( i = 0; i < n; ++i ) {
       printf( "Enter string number %d: ", i+1 );
       gets( names[i] );
    }
    printf( "\nList of given strings\n\n" );
    for ( i = 0; i < n; ++i )
       puts ( names[i] );
}
```

But this scheme of representing list of strings has one serious problem. The problem is of memory wastage. As in the above example, we assumed that the name could be up to 30 characters long, so we have declared the string length equal to 30. In fact, some names may be of few characters long while others roughly half of the declared length. So, on average, half of the allocated space is not utilized at all. Using array of pointers to strings can solve this problem of memory wastage. We will discuss this aspect in *Chapter 12*.

10.11 QUICK RECAP

In this chapter, we have learnt that

- As such, C language does not support string data type however strings are handled as an array of characters.
- The C language uses null-terminated variable length strings.
- A string constant in C language is a sequence of characters enclosed in double quotes.
- When string constants are used in a program, C automatically creates an array of characters, initializes it to a null-terminated string, stores it, and remembers its address.
- To store a string, we need an array of characters with size one plus than the maximum length string.
- The difference between a character and a string is that later one is a data type while former one is a data structure. String uses array of character as its basic type.
- The input/output of string data can be performed using unformatted and formatted I/O function.
- Strings can be passed as arguments just like any other one-dimensional array. The only difference is that string arrays we don't need to pass the size of the array where as for other arrays we have to that.
- List of strings are handled by using two-dimensional array of characters.
- There is rich library of functions for manipulating strings.

10.12 MULTIPLE CHOICE QUESTIONS

1. If the declaration is "`char sample[80];`", what is the length of string that can be correctly represented by *sample*?

   (*a*) 80 (*b*) 79 (*c*) 81 (*d*) None

2. Which of the following statement is true about strings in C?

   (*a*) Every string must be terminated by null character ('\0').
   (*b*) String is a primitive data type in C.
   (*c*) String can be assigned to another string using assignment operator '='.
   (*d*) All of above.

3. Which of the following function is not supported in C on Unix/Linux operating system?

   (*a*) strlen (*b*) strcat (*c*) strcmp (*d*) strrev()

4. What will be the output of the following program?

```
#include <stdio.h>
void main()
{
    printf(5+"Fascimile");
}
```

(*a*) Error (*b*) Fascimile (*c*) mile (*d*) Fasci

5. What will be the output of the following program?

```
#include <stdio.h>
void main()
{
    char str1[] = "Hello", str2[] = "Hello";
    if ( str1 == str2 )
        printf("Equal");
    else
        printf("Unequal");
}
```

(*a*) Equal (*b*) Unequal (*c*) Error (*d*) None

6. What will be the output of the following program?

```
#include <stdio.h>
void main()
{
    char a[] = "Visual C++", *b = "Visual C++";
    printf("%d,%d", sizeof(a), sizeof(b));
}
```

(*a*) 11, 2 (*b*) 2, 11 (*c*) 11, 11 (*d*) None

7. Which of the following is not a correct way of creating and initializing a *char* array named *vowels* with string value "aeiou"?

(*a*) char vowels[] = { 'a', 'e', 'i', 'o', 'u', '\0' };
(*b*) char vowels[] = { 'a', 'e', 'i', 'o', 'u', '\n' };
(*c*) char vowels[] = "aeiou";
(*d*) None of above

8. Consider the following statements

```
char *ptr = "abba";
putchar(*ptr);
```

What will be printed?

(*a*) first letter (*b*) entire string
(*c*) it is a syntax error (*d*) last letter

9. If two strings *str1* and *str2* are identical, then the value *y* in the following code segment will be

```
int y;
y = strcmp(str, str2);
```

(*a*) 1 (*b*) -1 (*c*) 0 (*d*) None

10. Which of the following is a correct output of the following program?

```
#include <stdio.h>
void main()
{
    char str[] = { "\0" };
    if ( printf("%s", str) )
        printf("\nString is not empty\n");
    else
        printf("\nString is empty\n");
}
```

(*a*) String is empty (*b*) String is not empty
(*c*) Syntax error (*d*) None of above

11. Which of the following is a correct output of the following program?

```
#include <stdio.h>
void main()
{
    printf("Touch me, ""Touch me!");
}
```

(*a*) Touch me, (*b*) Touch me!
(*c*) Touch me, Touch me! (*d*) Compile time error

12. Which of the following is a correct output of the following program?

```
#include <stdio.h>
#include <string.h>
void main()
{
    char str[] = "Spider\0man\0";
    printf("%d", strlen(str));
}
```

(*a*) 6 (*b*) 10 (*c*) 11 (*d*) 13

13. Which of the following is a correct output of the following program?

```
#include <stdio.h>
void main()
{
    char str[] = "Sales\0man";
    puts(str);
}
```

(*a*) Sales (*b*) man (*c*) Salesman (*d*) Error

10.13 REVIEW EXERCISES

1. How a string is stored in C language?
2. What will be the declaration for array named *str* in which string "*C is just like sea*" is to be stored?
3. What is the difference between "A" and 'A'?
4. Name the function which is more appropriate to input multiword string.

5. Consider the following declaration
```
char name[20];
```
What is the maximum length of string which can be stored correctly in name?

6. Consider the following declaration
```
char name[20];
```
Is following the correct way of assigning string "*Rajan Mehta*" to *name*?
```
name = "Rajan Mehta";
```

7. Name the library function to find the length of the string.
8. What are the different ways of initializing of strings?
9. List various I/O functions that be used to perform the I/O of string data.

10.14 PROGRAMMING EXERCISES

1. Write a program to that produce the output as shown in Figure 10.6.
2. Write a program that asks the user to enter a sentence and then splits out the words in the sentence and puts them in a table.
3. Write a program that asks the user for a list of words and prints the list in reverse order.
4. Suppose you translate a number into a string of digits spelled out, one word for each digit, followed by a single space. For example, the number 407 become the digit string: "*Four Zero Seven*". If the number 407.8, then its digit string is "*Four Zero Seven Point Eight*". Write a program to accept a positive number and print out its digit string.
5. Write a program that accepts an amount in figures and prints that in words. For example, for an amount of Rs. 12, 500.25 it should output the string *Rs. Twelve Thousand Five Hundred and paise Twenty Five only*.

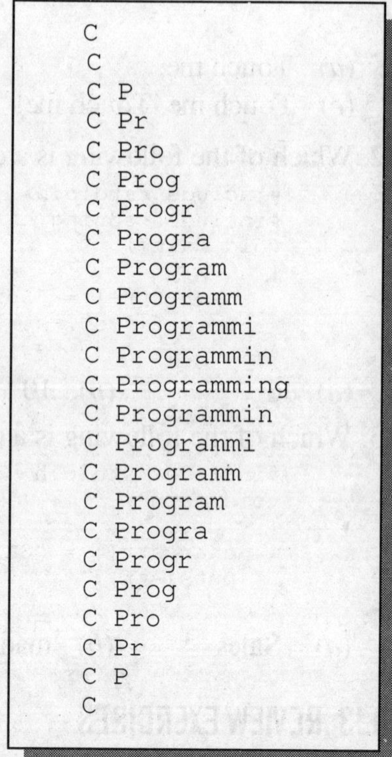

Figure 10.6

11 Structures and Unions

Learning Objectives

After reading this chapter, students will have the ability to:

- explain the concept of structure
- explain how a structure is different from an array
- declare, initialize and do input/output of structures
- explain the way array of structures are handled
- explain the way structures are passed as arguments to functions
- write efficient programs using structures to solve variety of problems
- explain the concept of union
- declare and initialize unions

11.1 INTRODUCTION

This chapter describes two important C constructs, the *structure* and the *union*. You can think of a structure as an array of closely related items. However, unlike an array, a structure permits the data items to be of different data types. These data items occupy contiguous memory locations. Unions, which are in some way similar to a structure, but in other ways are completely different, allow you to store data items of different data types. But these data items are stored in same memory, and store one value of given type at one time and another value at different time. The size of memory allocated depends on the data item whose memory requirements are more. These two data structures are the foundation of most database and spreadsheet programs.

A structure and a union are a type defined by the users as per their requirements. This way a user creates a new data type. These newly created data types are known as *user-defined data types*.

This chapter describes how to build structures, access structure elements, create arrays of structures, nested structures, self-referential structures, pass structures as arguments to a function, and finally about unions.

11.2 STRUCTURES

We have seen how a simple variable can hold one value at a time and how arrays can hold a number of values of the same data type. These two data storage mechanisms can handle a wide variety of problems. But we often want to process data items of different types together as a unit. In this case, neither the scalar variable nor the array is adequate.

Suppose we want to store information of employees in an organization. This information may include employee's name (character array), department code (integer number), salary (floating point number), and so forth. And we want our program to deal with them as elements of an array.

One possible approach is to use several arrays — a character array for names, an integer array for department code, a floating point array for salary, and so forth. And using common index we can access the information for a particular employee, but this approach obscures the fact that we are dealing with data items related to a single entity, *an employee* in our example.

To solve this sort of problem, C language provides a special data type: *the structure*. You can think of a structure as group of data items of different data types held together in a single unit. In our example, structure would consist of employee's name, department number, salary, and so forth.

11.2.1 Declaring a Structure

The fundamental data types, such as *integer*, *real* or *character*, are pre-defined by the compiler. Thus when we use an *integer* variable, we know it always occupies two bytes, and the compiler will interpret the contents of these two bytes in a certain way. This is not true for structures. The reason being that a structure can contain any number of data items and that can be of different data types. So the programmer must tell the compiler how the structure will look like before using variables of that type.

The C language has two ways to declare a structure: *tagged structure* and *type-defined structure*.

Tagged Structure

The first way to declare a structure is to use tagged structure. A tagged structure can be used to define variables, arguments, and return types. The syntax for declaring a tagged structure is

```
struct STUDENT
{
   . . .
   Field list
   . . .
};
```

(*a*) Format

```
struct STUDENT
{
   int rollNo;
   char name[20];
   char fname[20];
   char grade;
};
```

(*b*) Example

Figure 11.1: Declaring a tagged structure

The tagged structure starts with the keyword *struct*. The next element in the declaration is *tag*. The tag is the identifier for the structure, and will be used to declare variable, arguments of the functions, and return types for the functions.

If we conclude the structure declaration with semicolon after the closing brace, no variables are defined. In this case, the structure is simply a type template with no associated storage.

Type-defined Structure

The more powerful way to declare a structure is by using type definition *typedef*. The syntax for declaring a type-defined structure is

```
typedef struct
{
    . . .
   Field list
    . . .
} TYPE;
```

(*a*) Format

```
typedef struct
{
   int rollNo;
   char name[20];
   char fname[20];
   char grade;
} STUDENT;
```

(*b*) Example

Figure 11.2: Declaring a type-defined structure

Type-defined structure differs from tagged structure in following aspects:

1. The keyword *typedef* is used before the *struct* keyword.
2. Identifier after the *struct* keyword is not mandatory as is the case with tagged structure.
3. Identifier is required after the closing brace and before the semicolon.
4. As we will see later, the variable can be declared with the declaration of tagged structure whereas it cannot be with type-defined structures.

A type definition, *typedef*, gives a name to a data type by creating a new type that can be used anywhere a type is permitted. Syntax for type definition is

```
typedef dataType IDENTIFIER;
```

where *dataType* is either built-in data type or user-defined data type, and *IDENTIFIER*, usually in uppercase, is the new and convenient name for the *dataType*. The *typedef* keyword tells the compiler to recognize the *IDENTIFIER* as synonymous of *dataType*.

11.2.2 Declaring Structure Variables

Once a structure is declared, we can declare variables using these declarations. Usually, the declaration is placed in the global area of the program, *i.e.*, before the *main()* function, so that it is visible to all the functions in the program. The variables, on the other hand, are usually declared in the local area of the functions or in the argument list in the functions headers. Following statements shows the way structure variables are declared.

For tagged structure, the variable is declared as

```
struct STUDENT aStudent;
```

For type-defined structure, the variable is declared as

```
STUDENT bStudent;
```

By comparing both the declarations, you will find the type-defined structure is handier in the declarations of the variable because you don't need to use the *struct* keyword. This can be quite time and effort saving if the variable declarations are required at many placed in the program.

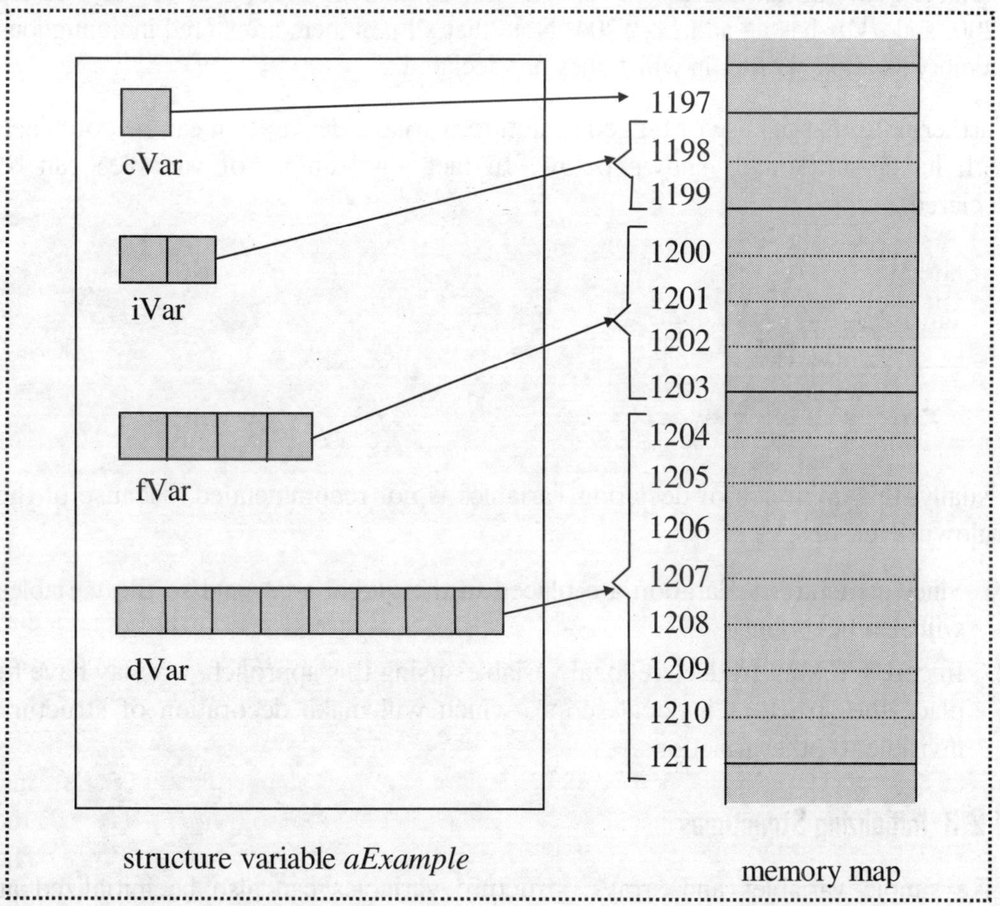

Figure 11.3: Memory layout for structure variable *aExample*

To understand how the elements of a structure variable are stored in memory, consider the following declarations.

```
struct EXAMPLE {
    char   cVar;
    int    iVar;
    float  fVar;
    double dVar;
};
EXAMPLE aExample;
```

Figure 11.3 shows a conceptual view of the memory layout for variable *aExample*, describing how the fields (members) of the structure are stored in memory.

Variable *cVar* has an address 1197, *iVar* has an address 1198, *fVar* has an address 1200, and *dVar* has an address 1204. Note that all members are stored in contiguous memory location in order in which they are declared.

Further note that in case of tagged structure, variable declaration can be combined with its declaration as shown below. In fact any number of variables can be declared.

```
struct EMPLOYEE {
  int   code;
  char  name[25];
  char  department[15];
  float salary;
} aEmployee, bEmployee;
```

Usually, this approach of declaring variables is not recommended, because of the following reasons:

1. Since structure declaration are placed in the global area, and so the variables will also be global.
2. In case we want to declare local variables using this approach, we may have to place the structure in local scope, which will make decoration of structure invisible to other functions.

11.2.3 Initializing Structures

Like simple variables and arrays, structure variables can also be initialized at declaration time. The format used is quite similar to that used to initialize arrays.

The following segment illustrates this

```
typedef struct
{
  int   rollno;
  char  name[25];
  int   age;
  float height;
} STUDENT;

STUDENT aStudent = { 1000, "Surbhi", 18, 5.6 };
```

Like partially initialized arrays, if a structure variable is partially initialized, the remaining numeric fields will be initialized to zero and the string fields will be initialized to null.

11.2.4 Accessing Structures

We have seen how to declare structures, declare variables and initialize them. Now is the time to see how we can use them in our program.

Each element in a structure can be accessed and manipulated using operators and expressions. Anything which we can do with individual variables (simple variable) can be done with structure elements. The only thing required is to identify individual elements of the structure in which we are interested.

To reference an element in a structure, we need to refer to both the structure and the element. The C language uses hierarchical naming conventions that first use the structure variable-identifier and the element-identifier. The structure variable-identifier is separated from element-identifier by a dot (.). The dot here is known as the direct selection operator, which is a postfix operator at precedence level 1 in the precedence table.

Again consider the following statements

```
typedef struct
{
  int   rollno;
  char  name[25];
  int   age;
  float height;
} STUDENT;

STUDENT aStudent;
```

We refer to the individual elements of structure variable *aStudent* as shown below:

```
aStudent.rollno    /* reference to element rollno */
aStudent.name      /* reference to element name   */
aStudent.age       /* reference to element age    */
aStudent.height    /* reference to element height */
```

11.2.5 Reading and Writing Structures

We can also read into and write data from a structure element in the same manner as we do with simple variables. For example, the elements of *aStudent* structure, we can read data, interactively, from the keyboard and place in the *aStudent* structure using following statements

```
printf("\nEnter roll number of the student : ");
scanf("%d", &aStudent.rollno);
printf("\nEnter name of the student : ");
scanf("%d", aStudent.name);
printf("\nEnter age of the student : ");
scanf("%d", &aStudent.age);
printf("\nEnter height of the student : ");
scanf("%d", &aStudent.height);
```

Note that in the *scanf()* function, the expression

```
&aStudent.rollno
```

is interpreted by the compiler as

```
&(aStudent.rollno)
```

because of higher precedence of direct selection operator over *addressof* operator (&), and that is what exactly is required.

Listing 11.1

```
/* Program to illustrate way data is entered into structures */
#include<stdio.h>
#include<sting.h>
struct EMPLOYEE  {
 int code;
 char name[25];
 char department[15];
 float salary;
};
```

```
void main()
{
  struct EMPLOYEE aEmployee;
  printf("Enter employee's code: " );
  scanf( "%d", &aEmployee.code );
  fflush(stdin);
  printf("Enter employee's name: " );
  gets( aEmployee.name );
  printf("Enter employee's department: " );
  gets( aEmployee.department );
  printf("Enter employee's salary: " );
  scanf("%f", &aEmployee.salary );
  printf("\n\nParticulars of employee as" );
  printf(" entered by user\n" );
  printf("\nEmployee's code: %d", aEmployee.code );
  printf("\nEmployee's name: %s", aEmployee.name );
  printf("\nEmployee's department: %s",aEmployee.department);
  printf("\nEmployee's salary: %.2f\n", aEmployee.salary );
}
```

Test Run

```
Enter employee's code: 826
Enter employee's name: Rajesh Kumar
Enter employee's department: Computer Science
Enter employee's salary: 20000

Particulars of employee as entered by user

Employee's code: 826
Employee's name: Rajesh Kumar
Employee's department: Computer Science
Employee's salary: 20000.00
```

Following is a program that uses structures and direct selection operator. It multiplies two fractions and prints the result. For example, if the fractions are 2/5 and 3/5, it prints the result as 6/25.

Listing 11.2

```
/*   Program to multiply two fractions     */
#include<stdio.h>
struct FRACTION
{
  int nom;        /*   nominator    */
  int denom;      /*   denominator */
};
void main()
```

```
{
   struct FRACTION aFraction, bFraction, cFraction;
   printf( "Enter first fraction as x/y : " );
   scanf( "%d%*c%d",&aFraction.nom, &aFraction.denom);
   printf( "Enter second fraction as x/y : " );
   scanf( "%d%*c%d",&bFraction.nom, &bFraction.denom);
   cFraction.nom = aFraction.nom * bFraction.nom;
   cFraction.denom = aFraction.denom * bFraction.denom;
   printf( "\nResult of (%d/%d) x (%d/%d) = (%d/%d)\n",
            aFraction.nom, aFraction.denom,
            bFraction.nom, bFraction.denom,
            cFraction.nom, cFraction.denom );
}
```

Test Run

```
Enter first fraction as x/y : 2/5
Enter second fraction also as x/y : 3/5
Result of (2/5) x (3/5) = (6/25)
```

11.2.6 Operations on Structures

A structure is an entity that can be treated as a whole. There is only one operation that can be performed on the structure as a whole is that a structure can be copied into another structure of the same type using the assignment operator.

Again consider the following statements

```
typedef struct
{
  int   rollno;
  char  name[25];
  int   age;
  float height;
} STUDENT;
STUDENT aStudent, bStudent;
```

The following assignment statement

```
aStudent = bStudent;
```

assigns the contents of structure *bStudent* to *aStudent*.

It is a unique feature of structures as compared to arrays, where in order to copy one array to another array of same type, we have to set up a loop to copy element-by-element.

This is rather an amazing capability when you think about it. When you assign one structure to another, all the values in the structure are assigned to corresponding structure elements. Simple assignment statement cannot be used this way for arrays. That is, to assign one array to another, we have to assign element by element.

11.2.7 Arrays of Structures

In many practical situations, we need to create an array of structures. As an example, we need to create an array of students to work with a group of students in a class. By putting the data of students in an array of structures, we can quickly and efficiently process the student's data.

An array of structures to store the data of students will be declared as

```
STUDENT students[50];
```

11.2.7.1 Accessing Elements of Array of Structures

Individual elements of a structure in an array of structures are accessed by referring to structure variable name, followed by index, followed by direct selection operator, and ending with the structure element desired.

In our example of students of a class, the name of the ith student can be accessed as follows:

```
students[i].name;
```

11.2.7.2 Initializing Array of Structures

Like any other array, an array of structures can also be initialized. Since each element of array structures is a different structure, we need to include elements of each structure in a separate set of braces as shown:

```
STUDENT students[50] = {
                       { 1000, "Monika",{56,76,85,69}, 'A' },
                       { 1001, "Ram", {50,66,70,60}, 'B' },
                                  :
                       { 1049, "Raju", {65,62,68,59}, 'B' },
                     };
```

Following program illustrates input, processing and output of array of structures.

Listing 11.3

```
/*
* Program to illustrate processing of array of structures by
* storing list of students in memory, and computes their grades
*/

#include <stdio.h>

typedef struct
{
   int  rollno;
   char sname[25];
   int  marks[4];
   char grade;
} STUDENT;

void main()
{
   STUDENT students[50];
   int totalMarks, i, j, n;

   printf( "\n\nEnter number of students in a class : " );
   scanf( "%d", &n );

   for ( i = 0; i < n; i++ )
   {
      printf("\nParticulars of student #%d\n\n", i+1);
      printf( "Enter students' roll number : " );
      scanf("%d", &students[i].rollno );
      printf( "\nEnter students' name : " );
      gets( students[i].sname );
      printf( "\nEnter students marks in four subjects\n\n" );
      for ( j = 0; j < 4; j++ ) {
         scanf("%d", &students[i].marks[j] );
      }
   }
   for ( i = 0; i < n; i++ ) {
      totalMarks = 0;
      for ( j = 0; j < 4; j++ ) {
          totalMarks += students[i].marks[j];
      }
      if ( totalMarks > 75 )
          students[i].grade = 'A';
      else if ( totalMarks > 60 )
          students[i].grade = 'B';
      else if ( totalMarks > 50 )
          students[i].grade = 'C';
      else if ( totalMarks > 40 )
          students[i].grade = 'D';
      else
          students[i].grade = 'F';
```

```
    }
    printf("\nPerformance of students\n\n");
    printf("%-10s", "Roll No.");
    printf("%-30s", "Name");
    printf("%6s\n", "Grade");
    for ( i = 0; i < n; i++ )
    {
        printf("%-10d", students[i].rollno);
        printf("%-30s", students[i].sname);
        printf("%4c\n", students[i].grade);
    }
}
```

11.2.8 Nested Structures

Just as there can be arrays of arrays, there can also be structures that contain other structures as its elements. This can be a powerful way to create complex data types. The only restriction on nesting of structures is that a structure cannot contain a member that is itself a structure of the same type (*i.e.*, with the same *tag*) as the outer structure.

As an example, suppose we want to include additional information regarding date of joining of an employee in the *EMPLOYEE* structure, one way of doing so is as shown below:

```
struct DATE
{
    int day;
    int month;
    int year;
};
struct EMPLOYEE
{
    int code;
    char name[25];
    struct DATE dateOfJoining;
    char department[15];
    float salary;
};
struct EMPLOYEE aEmployee;
```

Here structure *EMPOLYEE* contains a data member named *dateOfJoining,* which is a variable of structure type *DATE*. The structure *EMPLOYEE* is acting as a container structure, Container in the sense that it holds a variable of another structure type.

The second way is as shown below:

```
struct EMPLOYEE {
    int code;
    char name[25];
    struct DATE {
        int day;
        int month;
        int year;
    } dateOfJoining;
    char department[15];
    float salary;
};
struct EMPLOYEE aEmployee;
```

Here structure *EMPLOYEE* is acting as a *nesting structure* (outer structure), whereas structure *DATE* is acting as *nested structure* (inner structure). The *DATE* structure don't have its independent existence, it exists only in the scope of *EMPLOYEE* structure.

11.2.8.1 Accessing Elements of Nested Structures

Individual elements of a nested structure are accessed by referring to outer structure variable name, followed by direct selection operator (.), followed by inner structure variable name, followed by direct selection operator, and ending with the desired member of the structure.

In our example, suppose we want to access the year of joining of an employee, we can do so by writing

```
aEmployee.dateOfJoining.year;
```

The nesting process need not stop at this level; we can nest a structure within a structure within a structure.

11.2.8.2 Initialization of Nested Structures

Initialization of nested structures follows the rules of simple structures. Each structure must be initialized Individual separately before preceding to the next element. Each structure is enclosed in a set of braces. The following code demonstrates this.

```
struct EMPLOYEE aEmployee = { 1256,
                              "Rakesh Bahl",
                              { 12, 06, 1962 },
                              "Finance",
                              40000
                            };
```

11.2.9 Structures and Functions

In order to be fully useful, we must be able to pass structures to functions as arguments and returning them from functions. Structure can be passed by value as well as by reference. In this section, we will consider passing a structure by value only. Passing structure by reference, we will consider in the *Chapter 12*.

```
typedef struct {
   int day;
   int month;
   int year;
} DATE;
void printDate(DATE);
void main()
{
   DATE aDate = { 10, 6, 2008 };
   int x;
   printDate(aDate);
   /*  more statements    */
}
```

```
/*  function definition   */
void printDate(DATE tDate )
{

   /*  local declarations */
   /*  other statements   */

}
```

Figure 11.4: Passing structure by value

Listing 11.4

```
/*  Program to illustrate passing of a structure by value   */
#include <stdio.h>
typedef struct {
   int day;
   int month;
   int year;
} DATE;
void printDate( DATE aDate );   /*  function declaration   */
void main()
{
   DATE tDate = { 10, 6, 2008 }; /* initialize a structure  */
   printDate( tDate );            /*  function call          */
}
void printDate( DATE aDate )
{
  printf( "\nDate in format dd/mm/yy: %02d/%02d/%2d\n",
           aDate.day, aDate.month, aDate.year );
}
```

Test Run

```
Date in format dd/mm/yy: 10/06/2008
```

A function can also return a value of structure type as well via *return* statement as illustrated below.

```
typedef struct
{
   int day;
   int month;
   int year;
} DATE;
DATE getDate(void);
void main()
{
   DATE aDate;
   int x;
   aDate = getDate();
   /*  more statement   */
}
```

```
/*  function definition    */
DATE getDate(void)
{
   DATE tDate;
   /*  local declarations */
   /*  more statements    */
   return tDate;
}
```

Figure 11.5: Function returning a structure

Listing 11.5

```
/* Program to illustrate function returning a structure  */
#include <stdio.h>
typedef struct {
   int day;
   int month;
   int year;
} DATE;
DATE getDate( void );         /*  function declaration   */
void main()
{
   DATE tDate;
   printf( "Enter date in format dd/mm/yyyy : " );
   tDate = getDate();
   printf( "\nDate entered by you: %02d/%02d/%2d\n",
         tDate.day, tDate.month, tDate.year );
}
DATE getDate( void )
{
   DATE xDate;
   scanf( "%d/%d/%d", &xDate.day, &xDate.month, &xDate.year );
   return xDate;
}
```

Test Run

```
Enter date in format dd/mm/yy: 10/6/2008

Date entered by you: 10/06/2008
```

11.3 UNIONS

As mentioned in the very beginning of this chapter, both structures and unions are used to group a number of variables of different type in single unit. While a structure enables us to treat this unit as a number of different variables stored at different places in memory, a union enables us to treat the same space in memory as a number of different variables. That is, a union permits a section of memory to be treated as a variable of one type on one occasion, and as a different variable of a different type on another occasion.

If two or more variables are mutually exclusive, unions provides an opportunity to the programmer to economize the usage of memory by sharing memory among those variables by declaring them members of a union.

The syntax for declaring a union, declaring variables of union type, accessing elements of a union, is identical to that of structures, except for storage of members of union and their initialization.

11.3.1 Declaring a Union

Like structures, the C language also provides two ways to declare a union: *tagged union* and *type-defined union*.

Tagged Union

The first way to declare a union is to use tagged union. A tagged union can be used to define variables, arguments, and return types. The syntax for declaring a tagged union is

```
union MIXTYPES
{
   . . .
   Field list
   . . .
};
```

(*a*) Format

```
union MIXTYPES
{
     char   cVar;
     int    iVar;
     flota  fVar;
     double dVar;
};
```

(*b*) Example

Figure 11.6: Declaring a tagged union

The tagged union starts with the keyword *union*. The next element in the declaration is *tag*. The tag is the identifier for the union, and will be used to declare variable, arguments of the functions, and return types for the functions.

If we conclude the union declaration with semicolon after the closing brace, no variables are defined. In this case, the union is simply a type template with no associated storage.

Type-defined Union

The more powerful way to declare a union is by using type definition *typedef*. The syntax for declaring a type-defined union is

```
typedef union
{
   . . .
   Field list
   . . .
} TYPE;
```

(*a*) Format

```
typedef union
{
   char   cVar;
   int    iVar;
   flota  fVar;
   double dVar;
} MIXTYPES;
```

(*b*) Example

Figure 11.7: Declaring a type-defined union

Type-defined union differs from tagged union in following aspects:

1. The keyword *typedef* is used before the *union* keyword.
2. Identifier after *union* keyword is not mandatory as is the case with tagged union.
3. Identifier is required after the closing brace and before the semicolon.
4. As we will see later, the variable can be declared with the declaration of tagged union whereas it cannot be with type-defined unions.

To understand how the elements of a union variable are stored in memory, consider the following declarations.

```
typedef union {
   char   cVar;
   int    iVar;
   float  fVar;
   double dVar;
} EXAMPLE;
EXAMPLE bExample;
```

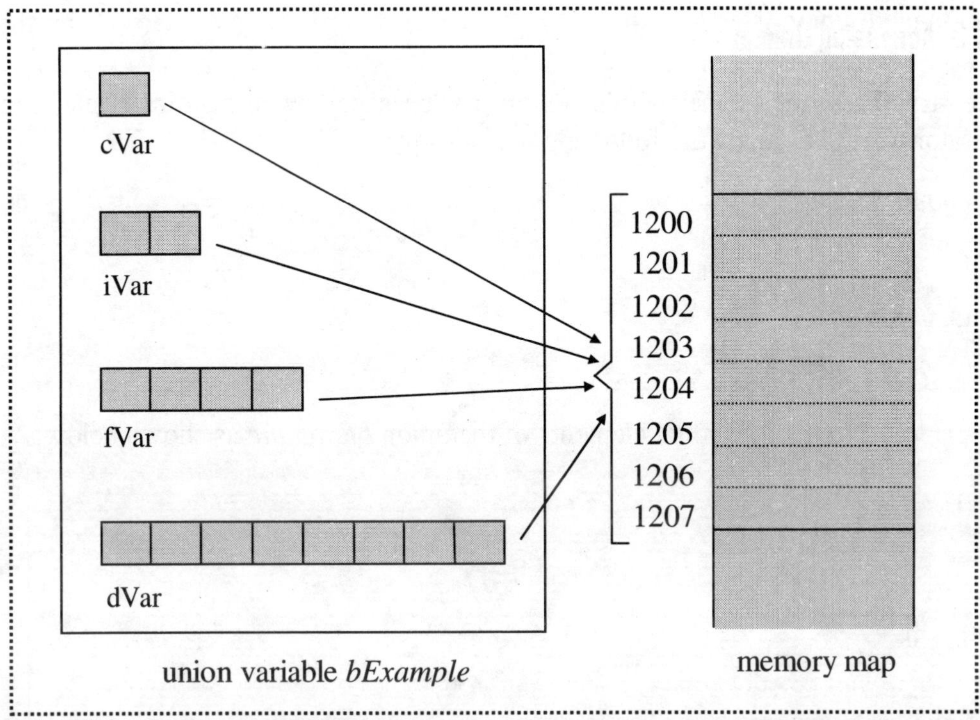

Figure 11.8: Memory layout for union variable *bExample*

Figure 11.8 shows a conceptual view of the union variable *bExample* and its relationship to memory, *i.e.*, how its members are stored in memory. Each variable has an address 1200. However, the character value is stored in first byte, integer value in first two bytes, float value in first four bytes, and double value in all the eight bytes.

11.3.2 Initializing a Union

Like structures, the unions cannot be initialized at the declaration time. Consider the following type-defined union declaration

```
typedef union  {
   char   cVar;
   int    iVar;
   float  fVar;
} EXAMPLE;
```

then the declaration statement

```
EXAMPLE bExample = { 'A', 300, 250.25 };
```

will not be acceptable.

11.3.3 Accessing Unions

Like structures, the elements of a union can be accessed using direct selection operator. Consider again the following declarations

```
typedef union {
    char   cVar;
    int    iVar;
    float  fVar;
} EXAMPLE;

EXAMPLE bExample = { 'A', 300, 250.25 };
```

We can refer to the individual elements of the union *bExample* as shown below:

```
bExample.cVar
bExample.iVar
bExample.fVar
```

Listing 11.6

```
/*  Program to illustrate the use of a union   */
#include <stdio.h>
typedef union {
   char   cVar;
   int    iVar;
   float  fVar;
} EXAMPLE;
void main()
{
   EXAMPLE bExample;
   printf( "\nSize of EXAMPLE = %d\n", sizeof(EXAMPLE) );
   bExample.cVar = 'A';
   printf( "\nbExample.cVar = %c\n", bExample.cVar );
   bExample.iVar = 300;
   printf( "\nbExample.iVar = %d\n", bExample.iVar );
   bExample.fVar = 250.25;
   printf( "\nbExample.fVar = %.2f\n", bExample.fVar );
}
```

Test Run

```
Size of EXAMPLE = 4

bExample.cVar = A

bExample.iVar = 300

bExample.fVar = 250.25
```

11.4 UNIONS AND STRUCTURES

Just as there can be arrays within structures, structures within structures, array of structures, there can be structures within unions, and unions within structures. In this section, we will consider a case of union of structures. Consider following structure declarations

```
typedef struct
{
   int code;
   char name[25];
   char department[15];
   float salary;
} EMPLOYEE;
```

```
typedef struct
{
   int  rollno;
   char name[25];
   int  MARKS[4];
   char grade;
} STUDENT;
```

Union of these two structures will be declared as

```
typedef union  {
   EMPLOYEE aEmployee;
   STUDENT  aStudent;
} COMMON;
COMMON example;
```

The elements of this union of structures are accessed using direct selection operator twice as we do with nested structures. For example

```
example.aStudent.rollno
```

refer to element *rollno* in the structure *aStudent* in union *ex*, where as

```
example.aEmployee.code
```

refer to element *code* in the structure *aEmployee* in union *ex*.

11.5 BIT FIELDS

Structures can contain special members called *fields* or *bit fields*. The data type of these members is *int*, *unsigned int* or *unsigned*. The length of bit fields is specified in terms of bits rather than bytes. For example, a member declared as

```
unsigned int threeBitField : 3;
```

is treated as a variable made up of only three bits. The non-negative integer number (in the range 1 to 16) following the colon specifies the number of bits to be used for the declared variable.

If the field is *signed*, which by default, the minimum number of bits is 2 (one bit for sign). If the bit-field length is *n*, the range of values is -2^{n-1} to $-2^{n-1}-1$ for signed, and 0 to 2^n-1 for unsigned.

We know that an integer value takes 2-bytes of memory. There may be many occasions where the integer values to be stored needs less than 2-bytes. In such cases, there is wastage of memory. For example, if know that value of an integer variable will be less than 15, it can be stored in 4-bits rather than 16-bits. By using bit fields, we can save lot of memory. There can be unnamed fields declared with size, such as

```
unsigned : bit-length
```

Such fields provide padding within the words, but cannot be accessed because they don't have name.

To illustrate the use of bit fields, let us suppose to create a database of employees in an organization. Further suppose that information to be recorded about each employee consists of employee code (in the range of 1 to 9999), name (maximum of 25 characters), sex, number of children (not more than 2-digit number), age (less than 60), and salary per month (maximum of 20,000).

The following declaration of structure will serve the purpose

```
struct EMPLOYEE {
    unsigned int employee_code : 14;
    char name[26];
    unsigned int sex : 1;
    unsigned int children : 4;
    unsigned int age : 6;
    unsigned int salary;
};
```

As bit fields provide a way to avoid memory wastage, they have some limitations as well. Some of these are enumerated below:

1. The address of bit fields cannot be obtained, and hence the input of bit fields cannot be performed with *scanf()* function. Thus, input of bit fields can only be performed indirectly.
2. A pointer cannot be used to access bit fields.
3. The *sizeof* operator cannot be applied on bit fields.
4. Array of bit fields is not permitted.

11.6 SUPPLEMENTARY PROBLEMS

Let us consider some more problems to illustration to use of structures.

Problem 11.1:

Given the following declaration

```
struct STUDENT {
  int  rollNo;
  char name[31];
  int   marks;
};
```

to represent the information of a student.

Using this structure, write a function that takes list of students, in the form of an array, as its argument, and sorts them in the descending order of the marks secured by the students.

Using the above structure and function, write a program that reads the data for *n* students and displays them in descending order of marks secure by the students.

Listing 11.6

```
/*
*  Program to the given information of students in
*  Descending order of the marks secured by them
*/
typedef struct {
  int  rollno;
  char name[20];
  int  marks;
} STUDENT;
void arrangeBubble(STUDENT students[], int n);
void main()
{
  STUDENT students[50];
  int i, n;
  printf( "\n\nEnter number of students : " );
  scanf( "%d", &n );
  for ( i = 0; i < n; i++ )
  {
     printf("\nParticulars of student #%d\n\n", i+1);
     printf( "Enter students' roll number : " );
     scanf("%d", &students[i].rollno );
     printf( "Enter students' name : " );
     gets(students[i].name );
     printf( "Enter students' marks : " );
```

```
      scanf("%d", &students[i].marks );
   }
   arrangeBubble(students,n);    /*  function call  */
   printf("\nStudent's Information after sorting\n\n");
   printf("%-10s", "Roll No.");
   printf("%-20s", "Name");
   printf("%6s\n\n", "Marks");
   for ( i = 0; i < n; i++ )
   {
      printf("%-10d", students[i].rollno);
      printf("%-20s", students[i].name);
      printf("%4d\n", students[i].marks);
   }
}
void arrangeBubble(STUDENT st[], int n)
{
    int i, j, k;
    STUDENT temp;
    for ( i = 1; i < n; i++ )
    {
       k = n-i;
       for ( j = 0; j < k; j++ )
       {
          if ( st[j].marks < st[j+1].marks )
           {
              temp = students[j];
               st[j] = st[j+1];
               st[j+1] = temp;
           }
       }
    }
}
```

Test Run

```
Enter number of students : 5

Particulars of student #1

Enter students' roll number : 1000
Enter students' name : Ravi
Enter students' marks : 80

Particulars of student #2

Enter students' roll number : 1001
Enter students' name : Shankar
Enter students' marks : 79

Particulars of student #3

Enter students' roll number : 1002
Enter students' name : Ankit
```

```
Enter students' marks : 65

Particulars of student #4

Enter students' roll number : 1003
Enter students' name : Rupinder
Enter students' marks : 75

Particulars of student #5

Enter students' roll number : 1004
Enter students' name : Mehak
Enter students' marks : 88

Student's Information after sorting

Roll No.  Name                Marks

 1004     Mehak                88
 1000     Ravi                 80
 1001     Shankar              79
 1003     Rupinder             75
 1002     Ankita               65
```

Problem 11.2:

Use a structure to model a complex number. Using this structure write functions to accomplish the following tasks:

- Function that returns the structure read from the keyboard.
- Function that takes two structures using call be value mechanism as its arguments and return their sum.
- Function that takes single structure using call be value mechanism as its arguments and prints it.

Use these functions in the program to demonstrate their working.

Listing 11.7

```
/*
* Program to demonstrate passing structure to a function using
* call by value mechanism and function returning a structure
*/

#include <stdio.h>
typedef struct {
   float real;
   float imag;
} COMPLEX;
COMPLEX input(void);  /*  function declarations   */
void output(COMPLEX);
COMPLEX add(COMPLEX, COMPLEX);
```

```
COMPLEX multiply(COMPLEX, COMPLEX);
void main()
{
   COMPLEX n1, n2, n3, n4;
   printf("\nProgram to add two complex numbers\n\n");

   printf("\nEnter first complex number\n");
   n1 = input();

   printf("\nEnter second complex number\n");
   n2 = input();
   n3 = add(n1,n2);

   printf("\nSum of given complex numbers\n\n");
   output(n3);

   n4 = multiply(n1,n2);
   printf("\nProduct of given complex numbers\n\n");
   output(n4);
}
/* function to read a complex number    */
COMPLEX input(void)
{
   COMPLEX t;
   printf("\nEnter real part : ");
   scanf("%f", &t.real);
   printf("Enter imaginary part : ");
   scanf("%f", &t.imag);
   return t;
}
/* function to output a complex number    */
void output(COMPLEX t)
{
   printf("Real part : %.2f", t.real);
   printf("\nImaginary part : %.2f", t.imag);
}
/*function to add two complex numbers*/
COMPLEX add(COMPLEX a, COMPLEX b)
{
   COMPLEX t;
   t.real = a.real + b.real;
   t.imag = a.imag + b.imag;
   return t;
}
/*function to multipliy two complex numbers*/
COMPLEX multiply(COMPLEX a, COMPLEX b)
{
   COMPLEX t;
   t.real = a.real * b.real - a.imag * b.imag;
   t.imag = a.real * b.imag + a.imag * b.real;
   return t;
}
```

Test Run

```
Program to add two complex numbers

Enter first complex number

Enter real part : 1.0
Enter imaginary part : 2.5
Enter second complex number
Enter real part : 2.5
Enter imaginary part : -1.5
Sum of given complex numbers

Real part : 3.50
Imaginary part : 1.00

Product of given complex numbers

Real part : 6.25
Imaginary part : 4.75
```

11.7 QUICK RECAP

In this chapter, we have learnt that

- A structure is a collection of related elements, which can be of different types, having a single name.
- Each element of the structure is called a field.
- There are two ways to declare a structure: *tagged structure* and *type defined structure*.
- A structure can be initialized when it is declared and defined. The list of comma separated values is enclosed in pair of braces.
- We can access the fields of the structure using direct selection, dot operator (.).
- Unlike arrays and string, a structure can be assigned to another structure using assignment operator.
- The data of the structure can be send to the function using one of the following ways:
  - Passing individual fields by value as well as by reference.
  - Passing entire structure by value.
  - Passing entire structure by address (reference).
- Structures can be nested. In this case one dot operator is used for each level of nesting.

- Union is a data structure that is also used to group elements of different types. But these elements share same memory. The memory requirements for a union variable are equal to memory requirements of a field that requires more memory than others.
- At a given time, only one element of a union variable can be assigned a value.
- Bit fields can be used in structures to save memory.

11.8 MULTIPLE CHOICE QUESTIONS

1. A structure is

   (*a*) Scalar data type (*b*) Derived data type
   (*c*) Primitive data type (*d*) None of above

2. Which of the following statement is true about structures?

   (*a*) The elements of the structure must be of different type.
   (*b*) Structure tag is mandatory in all cases.
   (*c*) While declaring a variable of structure type, you need to prefix keyword *struct* before tag name.
   (*d*) Structure element are accessed using star (*) operator.

3. A structure is a data type in which

   (*a*) Each element must have the same type.
   (*b*) Elements can be of different type.
   (*c*) Each element must be of pointer type.
   (*d*) None

4. Consider the following declaration

```
struct ex
{
    char cVvar;
    int iVar;
    long lVar;
};
```

   What value will be returned by the *sizeof* operator called on *ex*?

   (*a*) 4 (*b*) 7
   (*c*) 1 (*d*) 6

5. If the elements of a union are *var1* of type integer, *var2* also of type integer, *var3* of the real (single precision), then memory allocated to a variable of above union type is ____.

   (*a*) 8 (*b*) 2
   (*c*) 4 (*d*) None

6. Keyword used to create a structured data type is

   (*a*) structure (*b*) structr
   (*c*) struct (*d*) struc

7. The operator used to access the structure member is

   (*a*) * (*b*) .
   (*c*) & (*d*) []

8. If one or more members of a structure are other structures, then the structure is known as

   (*a*) Nested structure (*b*) Structured structure
   (*c*) Invalid structure (*d*) Self-referential structure

9. Identify the wrong statement

   (*a*) Structure variable can be passed as an argument.
   (*b*) Member of a structure can be passed as an argument.
   (*c*) More than one structure variable can be declared in a single declaration statement.
   (*d*) None of above.

10. Consider the statement: "The size of a *struct* is always equal to the sum of its members."

    (*a*) Valid (*b*) Can't say
    (*c*) Invalid (*d*) None

11. Consider the following statement

```
honda.engine.bolt = 20;
```

    Which of the following statement is correct?

    (*a*) Structure *bolt* is nested within structure *engine*.
    (*b*) Structure *engine* is nested within structure *honda*.
    (*c*) Structure *honda* is nested within structure *engine*.
    (*d*) Structure *bolt* is nested within structure *honda*.

12. Consider the following code segment

```
strcut Date {
    int day, month, year;
};
struct Date dt, *pdt;
pdt = &dt;
```

    Which of the following statement assigns value 11 to month?

    (*a*) pdt.month = 11;. (*b*) &pdt.month = 11;
    (*c*) pdt->month = 11; (*d*) None of above

13. Union differs from structure in the following way

    (*a*) All members are used at a time.
    (*b*) Only one member can be used at a time.
    (*c*) Unions cannot have more than two members.
    (*d*) Union initializes all members as structure.

14. A bit-field is a

    (*a*) Pointer variable in a structure.
    (*b*) Member of a structure can be passed as an argument.
    (*c*) One or more adjacent bits within a word.
    (*d*) None of above.

15. A bit-field can be of _______ type.

    (*a*) int (*b*) float
    (*c*) double (*d*) All of above

16. Consider the following segment:

```
union
{
   int x;
   char y;
   struct
   {
      char x;
      char y;
      int xy;
   } p;
} q;
```

What is the size of *q*?

(*a*) 7 (*b*) 6
(*c*) 5 (*d*) 4

11.9 REVIEW EXERCISES

1. What is the main reason for using structures?
2. How a structure is different from an array?
3. What is a structure template?
4. What is the structure tag and what is its purpose?
5. What are different ways of declaring a structure variable?
6. In what sense a structure can be recursive?

7. Is any there thing wrong with the following?

```
struct Time
{
    int hrs;
    int mts;
    int secs;
}
time t1;
```

8. What is wrong with the following, if any?

```
struct Time
{
    int hrs =10;
    int mts = 20;
    int secs = 35;
} t1, t2, t3;
```

9. Identify the errors, if any, in the following

```
struct {
    int hrs;
    int mts;
    int secs;
} time;
time t1, t2, t3;
```

10. Give the output of the following program:

```
#include <stdio.h>
struct Point
{
    int X, Y;
};
void Show( Point P )
{
    printf("\n%d:%d\n", P.x, P.y);
}
void main()
{
    Point U = { 10, 20 }, V, W;
    V = U;
    V.Y -= 10;
    W = V;
    U.Y -= 5;
    U.X += 5;
    W.y -= 5;
    Show(U);
    Show(V);
    Show(W);
}
```

11. Give the output of the following program:

```
#include <stdio.h>
struct MyBox {
    int Length, Breadth, Height;
};
void Dimension( MyBox M )
{
    printf("\n%d x %d x %d\n",M.Length,M.Breadth,M.Height);
}
void main()
{
    MyBox B1 = { 12, 20, 8 }, B2, B3;
    ++B1.Height;
    Dimension(B1);
    B3 = B1;
    ++B3.Length;
    B3.Breadth++;
    Dimension(B3);
    B2 = B3;
    B2.Height += 5;
    B2.Length--;
    Dimension(B2);
}
```

11.10 PROGRAMMING EXERCISES

1. Design a structure named *distance* to store a length in *yards*, *feets* and *inches*. Using this structure, write a program that accepts two measurements from the user as represented by these structures and prints the absolute difference between these measurements.
2. Design a structure named *student* to store data about a student which contains following elements — *rollno* of type *int*, *name* an array of type *char* of size 20, *college* an array of type *char* of size 40, and *score* of type *float*. Assume that there are not more than 100 students. Write a program to input the data about students, and output the stored data according to the merit of the students.
3. A car manufacturing company records the following information about their cars — *engineNo* an array of type *char* of size 12, *chasyNo* an array of type *char* of size 15, *YearOfManufacturing* type *int*, and *horsePower* of type *float*. Assume that there are not more than 100 cars. Design a structure to store data about a car, and using this structure, write a program that accepts the data about cars from the user and retrieves the data about a car whose *engineNo* is given.
4. Design a structure to store information about employees of an organisation consisting of following elements — *code* an array of type *char* of size 5, *name* an array of type *char* of size 30, *department* an array of type *char* of size 20, and *joiningDate* of type *date*, where *date* is also a structure with *day*, *month* and *year*

as its members and all of type *int*. Assume that there are not more than 100 employees. Write a program to print the names of those employees who have completed at least one year of service.

5. Consider the following declaration:

```
struct EMPLOYEE
{
    int code;
    char name[31];
    float salary;
};
```

Given that there are *n* (≤50) employees in an organization. Write a program that output the details of the employee having highest salary.

6. Create a structure named *Time* to model a time in 12 hour system having three fields as *hours*, *minutes* and *seconds*. Write a function called *elapsedTime* that takes two arguments, the start time and the end time. The function should return a *Time* structure containing the time elapsed between the two arguments. Write a program to test the above function.

7. A point in plane in Cartesian system can be represented by its coordinates *x* and *y*. We can create a structure to represent a point in plane as shown below:

```
typedef struct
{
    int x;
    int y;
} POINT;
```

Write a function that accepts the structure representing a point and returns an integer value 1, 2, 3 or 4 indicating the quadrant in which the point is located. Write a program to test the above function.

8. A straight line is a geometric object connecting two points, therefore, it can be represented by a nested structure having two structures of POINT type

```
typedef struct
{
    POINT beg;
    POINT end;
} LINE;
```

Write a function that accepts two argument of POINT type and returns a structure of type LINE representing the line connecting the two points Write a program to test the above function.

9. Write a function that accepts a structure type LINE as its argument and return an integer (1,2,3), where 1 means line is vertical, 2 means line is horizontal, and 3 means line is oblique. Write a program to test the above function.

[**Hint:** A vertical line is line whose *x*-coordinates are the same. Horizontal line is a line whose *y*-coordinates are the same. An oblique line is a line which is neither vertical nor horizontal]

10. Define a structure that contains three members – name of country, name of the capital, and per capita income. Using this structure, write a program to list the countries along with their capitals in the decreasing order of their per capita income.

11. A landline telephone number, such as (0181) 223 2353 can be thought of as having three parts – *the area code (0181)*, *the exchange code (233)*, and *the phone number (2353)*. Define a structure named, *phone* to, store these three parts of a telephone number. Using this structure definition, define another structure that contains its members as *name*, *address* and *phone number* of above type. Write a program that displays entire information area wise.

12. Consider the following structure definition:

```
struct BOX
{
    char make[25];
    float length, breadth, height;
};
```

Write a function that takes the address of the *BOX* structure and returns its volume.

14. Consider the following declaration:

```
struct EMPLOYEE
{
    int code;
    char name[31];
    float salary;
};
```

Given that there are *n* (≤50) employees in an organization. Write a program, using pointer notation to access the data of an employee that output the details of the employee having highest salary.

❑ ❑ ❑

12 Pointers

Learning Objectives

After reading this chapter, students will have the ability to:

- comprehend the world of pointers, one of the richest feature of C language
- explain how main memory is organized and addresses are assigned to each memory location
- declare, initialize and access through pointer
- explain the usefulness of pointers in passing arguments to a function
- explain the permissible operations on pointers
- explain the concept of memory allocation
- distinguish between static allocation and dynamic allocation
- comprehend and use various memory management functions for dynamic memory management
- explain what possible problems can occur while working with pointers
- write efficient programs using pointers to solve variety of problems

12.1 INTRODUCTION

Pointers are one of the most important features of C language. Pointers, by most people, are regarded as one of the most difficult topics in C. Let me tell you frankly, it is more a myth rather a fact. I would prefer to say that pointers are one of the most delicate aspects of C language, and you know delicate things need very careful handling. Therefore, pointers need very careful handling.

There are many reasons for using pointers, some of them are enumerated below:

- A pointer allows a function or a program to access a variable (better we say memory location) outside the preview of function or a program. In fact, using a pointer, your program can access any memory location in the computer's memory.
- Since using *return* statement, a function can only pass back a single value to the calling function, pointers allows a function to pass back more than one value by writing them into memory locations that are accessible to the calling function.
- Use of pointers makes the program execute faster.
- Using pointers, arrays and structures can be handled in more efficient way.
- Without pointers, it will be impossible to create complex data structures, such as *linked lists*, *trees* and *graphs*.
- To communicate with operating system about memory. For example, the operator *new* returns the location of free memory block by using a pointer and the operator *delete* returns the memory block pointed to by a pointer to the operating system.

In totality, we can say that the real power of C language lies in the judicious use of pointers. Therefore, every reader of C must learn and master the art of using pointers.

In this chapter our goal is to explain the pointers as clearly as possible. In an attempt to achieve our goal, we ensure that the groundwork is laid carefully before we move on to use pointers in more advanced situations.

12.2 UNDERSTANDING POINTERS

Computer's memory is organized as a linear collection of bytes or words. For Intel processors, memory is byte-organized whereas for most of the non-Intel processors, memory is word-organized. In byte-organized memory, each memory location is of one byte, whereas in word-organized, each memory location is of one word. Each memory location is assigned a unique number called *location number* or *address*. Figure 12.1 shows the schematic of memory organization.

Figure 12.1: Memory Organization

We know that one byte is equal to 8 bits, whereas one word may be made up of two or more bytes. A word is a measure of the capacity of processor in terms of the size of operands that it can process (*i.e.* add, subtract, multiply, divide, compare, etc.) in single operation. When we say that a processor is a 16-bit processor, it means that its word size is 16-bits (2 bytes) and it can process 16-bit operands in single operations. For large size operands, it needs more operations.

A *memory cell* is either of one byte/word or more contiguous bytes/words. Each cell can store one value at a given time. The address of a cell is always the address of the first byte/word.

When you give a command to run a program, the operating system first finds a free block of requisite size from computer (main) memory, and then loads the program into that block. Even in that block, usually, the program's code is loaded in one part and the program's data in another part of the block. Each of the data operand is stored in a cell and the system associates each of the variables with these addresses. This is illustrated in Figure 12.2.

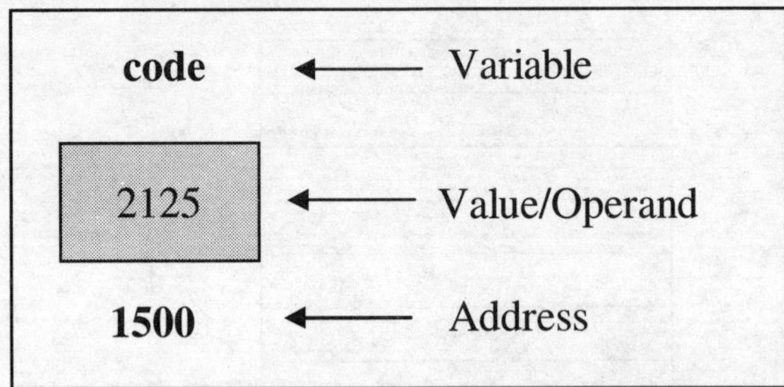

Figure 12.2: Representation of a Variable in Memory

In order to access the data operand either we use either variable name or we can use address of the memory cell. Since these addresses are simply positive integer numbers, they can also be assigned to some variables and stored in memory, like any other variable. Such variables that hold addresses are known as a *pointer*. A pointer is, therefore, nothing but a variable that contains address of another variable in memory.

Since pointer is a variable, its value is also stored in memory in another address. Suppose we assign the address of variable *code* to a variable *ptr*. The link between the variable *ptr* and *code* can be visualized as shown in Figure 12.3.

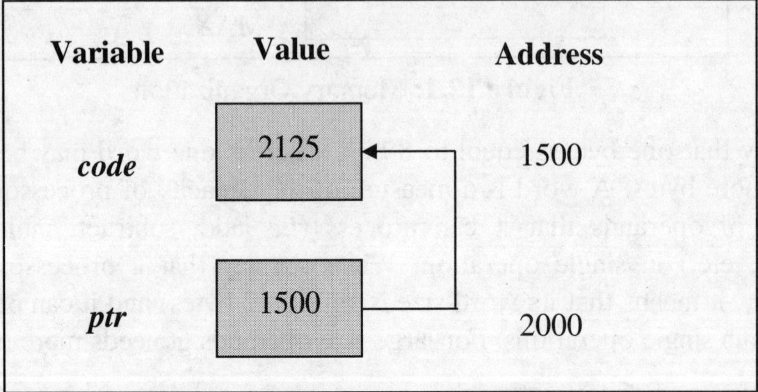

Figure 12.3: Pointer as a Variable

Since the value of the variable *ptr* is the address of the variable *code*, we can access the value of variable *code* by using the value of variable *ptr* and therefore, we say that the variable *ptr* points to the variable *code*, and hence *ptr* gets the name pointer.

12.3 ACCESSING ADDRESS OF A VARIABLE

The actual address of a variable is a system dependent. During compilation and linking, addresses are assumed to be relative to some base address, usually 0. When the operating system loads the program in a free block, all the address are transformed with relative to address of the first memory location of the free block. Hence, we do not know the address of a variable. Therefore, a question arises — *how can we determine the address of a variable*? This is done with the help of *address of* operator (&).

Consider the following statement

```
ptr = &code;
```

It will assign the number 1500 (address of variable *code*) to the variable *ptr*.

The following restrictions must be observed carefully:

1. The address of operator can only be used with variables or an array element. The following are illegal use of *address of* operator:

   (*a*) `&1200` (pointing at constant expression)
   (*b*) `&(a/b)` (pointing at expression)

2. Pointer variable can be initialized only with the use of *address of* operator or by assigning the value of another compatible pointer variable. The following way of initializing a pointer variable *ptr* is illegal:

   ```
   ptr  = 1500;
   ```

   Though, the number 1500 happen to be the address of variable code.

12.4 DECLARING AND INITIALIZING POINTERS

Like other variables, the pointer variables are to be declared first in the declaration block to tell the compiler that to which kind of values these variables will be pointing. The syntax for declaring pointer variable is

```
type *ptr_name;
```

where *type* is a *pre-defined* or *user-defined* data types and indicates that the pointer will point to the variables of that specific data type, and character '*' indicates that variable is a pointer variable.

For example, the statement

```
int *ptr1;
```

declares a pointer variable *ptr1* that can point to an integer type variable.

For example, the statement

```
float *ptr2;
```

declares a pointer variable *ptr2* that can point to a float type variable.

The pointer variable(s) declaration can also be combined with the declaration of other variables, provided they are of same type. For example, the statement

```
int x, *ptrX;
```

declares an integer variable *x* and a pointer variable *ptrX*.

Once a pointer has been declared, it must be initialized prior to its use. It is important to note here that like other variables, a pointer variable will take a garbage value, which can be an address of any storage location. Therefore, if not properly initialized, a pointer may point to any location in memory including those locations where operating system is running, and your system may hang-up i.e. stop responding. Such un-initialized pointers are sometimes referred to as *dangling/wild pointers*.

12.5 ACCESSING A VARIABLE THROUGH ITS POINTER

Once a pointer has been assigned the address of a variable, the question remains as how to access the value of the variable using the pointer. This is done using indirection operator (*). Consider the following statements

```
int *ptrX, x = 10, y;
ptrX = &x;
y = *ptrX;
printf("Value of variable x = %d\n", x );
printf("Value of variable pointed to by ptrX = %d\n",*ptrX );
printf("Address of variable x = %u\n", ptrX );
printf("Value of variable y  = %d\n",  y );
```

The declaration statement tells the compiler that *ptrX* is pointer variable that will point to an integer value, *x* is an integer variable and it also initializes the variable *x* with value 10, and *y* is another integer variable.

And suppose that during the execution of the above segment, a memory location with address 1098 is set aside for variable *x*.

The output of the above segment will look like:

```
Value of variable x = 10
Value of variable pointed to by ptrX = 10
Address of variable x = 1098
Value of variable y = 10
```

Note that writing the statements

```
ptrX = &x;
y = *ptrX
```

is equivalent to writing

```
y = *&x;
```

or for more clarity as

```
y = *(&x);
```

which in turn is equivalent to writing

```
y = x;
```

It is important to note that assignment of pointers and addresses is always done symbolically, by means of symbolic names. You cannot access the value stored at address 1098 by writing *1098. It will not work.

Listing 12.1

```
/* Program to illustrate use of address of & indirection operators*/
#include<stdio.h>
void main()
{
    int *ptrX, x = 10, y;
    ptrX = &x;
    y = *ptrX
    printf( "Value of variable x = %d\n", x );
    printf( "Value of variable pointed to by ptrX = %d\n", *ptrX );
    printf( "Address of variable x = %u\n", ptrX );
    printf( "Value of variable y  = %d\n",  y );
}
```

12.6 POINTER ARITHMETIC

The C language is very consistent in its approach to pointer arithmetic. The integration of pointers, arrays, and pointer arithmetic is one of the strengths of the C language. In this section, we will briefly describe the various operations permissible on pointers.

The following operations are permitted on pointers.

1. **Addition of a number to a pointer variable.**

   Suppose *p* is a pointer variable pointing to an element of integer type, then the statement

   ```
   p++;      or   ++p;
   ```

   increments the value of *p* by a factor of 2, so that it points to the next location that holds another value of integer type. This increment factor will be 1 for *character*, 4 for *long integer* and *float*, and 8 for *long float*. The statement

   ```
   p += i;
   ```

   where *i* is either a positive integer constant or an integer variable having positive value, increments *p* such that it points to the *i*th location beyond the location to which it is currently pointing.

2. **Subtraction of a number from a pointer variable.**

   Suppose *p* is a pointer variable pointing to an element of integer type, then the statement

   ```
   p—;      or   —p;
   ```

   decrements the value of *p* by a factor of 2, so that it now points to the location preceding the current location. The statement

   ```
   p —= i;
   ```

   where *i* is either a positive integer constant or an integer variable having positive value, decrements *p* such that it points to the *i*th location before the location to which it is currently pointing.

3. **Subtraction of one pointer variable from another.**

   One pointer variable can be subtracted from another provided both point to the same data type. The difference of the two indicates the number of bytes separating the corresponding elements.

In addition to these arithmetic operations, pointer variables can be compared with one another, provided they are compatible, *i.e.*, point to variables of same data type.

The following arithmetic operations on pointers are not permitted.

- Addition of two pointer variables.
- Multiplication of a pointer variable by a number.
- Division of a pointer variable by a number.

12.7 POINTER TO A POINTER

As mentioned, a pointer is variable that holds the address of another variable. This concept can be further extended. We can have a variable that hold an address of a variable that in turn holds an address of another variable. This type of variable will be known as *pointer to a pointer*. The underlying concept is known as *double indirection*. This concept can be further extended to triple level, fourth level, and so on.

A pointer to a pointer will be declared as

```
int **ptr;
```

The value pointed to by a pointer to another pointer will be accessed as

```
**ptr;
```

Listing 12.2

```
/*  Program to illustrate the use of double indirection  */
#include<stdio.h>
void main()
{
   int a = 5, *ptrA, **ptrPtrA;
   ptrA = &a;
   ptrPtrA = &ptrA;
   printf( "\nAddress of a = %u", &a );
   printf( "\nValue of a = %d", a );
   printf( "\nAddress of ptrA = %u", &ptrA );
   printf( "\nValue of ptrA = %u", ptrA );
   printf( "\nValue pointed to by ptrA = %d", *ptrA );
   printf( "\nAddress of ptrPtrA = %u", &ptrPtrA );
   printf( "\nValue of ptrPtrA = %u", ptrPtrA);
   printf( "\nValue pointed to by ptrPtrA = %d", **ptrPtrA);
}
```

Test Run

```
Address of a = 65524
Value of a = 5
Address of ptrA = 65522
Value of ptrA = 65524
Value pointed to by ptrA = 5
Address of ptrPtrA = 65520
Value of ptrPtrA = 65522
Value pointed to by ptrPtrA = 5
```

A practical example of using pointers to pointers is when pointers are passed by address to a calling function. The following skeleton of code demonstrates this:

```
void main()
{
   int *ptr1;
   // . . .
   func1( &ptr1, . . . );
   // . . .
}
void func1( int **ptr2, . . . )
{
   // . . .
   func2( &ptr2 );
   // . . .
}
void func2( int ***ptr3, . . .)
{
   // . . .
   // . . .
}
```

In the rest of the sections, we will extensively demonstrate the of use pointers. This is the area that is given a secondary treatment in most of the textbooks on C language. It is important to remember that pointers are the backbone of C language. Therefore every reader of C language must master them.

12.8 MEMORY ALLOCATION

It is important to note that anything that needs to be executed (programs) or processed (data) must be loaded into memory before it can be executed or processed. Therefore, for every program to be executed or data to be processed, some memory must be allocated for them. The memory allocation can be done in two ways – *statically* and *dynamically*. Let us look at both the ways.

12.8.1 Static Memory Allocation

When you give a command to run your program, the operating system allocates a block of memory for your program, loads it from the secondary storage (Floppy disk, hard disk, CD or DVD, etc.) into that block and then initiates its execution. When the program finishes its execution, the memory occupied by the program is automatically released. It means that the memory requirements are determined prior to execution of your program, and thereafter your program neither can acquire more memory nor can release the free memory, if not required.

The above situations depicts a situation where the amount of memory required is known before hand, and the compiler then can determine the memory requirements for the data as well as the instructions. In such a situation, memory allocation is known as *static memory allocation*.

12.8.2 Dynamic Memory Allocation

Further, it is important to note that the memory requirements for the instructions are always fixed. However, there may be situation when the exact memory requirements for the data may not be known in advance or the data requirements may vary from one program execution to another program execution, *i.e.*, memory requirements for the data are dynamic.

Therefore, when the amount of memory is not known before hand for a particular data item(s), then it is allocated at the execution time, *i.e.*, when the program is running. In such a situation, memory allocation is known as *dynamic memory allocation*.

12.8.3 Heap/Free Store

As mentioned earlier, every program is provided with a pool of unallocated memory that it can utilize during execution. This pool of unallocated memory is known as *heap* or *free store*. Therefore, whenever the memory of requisite size (amount) is required by the program, it is taken from the free store, and when the previously allocated memory is not required further, it is returned back to the free store.

The memory requirements for the instructions (program code) are always fixed, whereas the memory requirements for data may change when your program is dealing with dynamic structures.

12.9 DYNAMIC MEMORY MANAGEMENT

As mentioned earlier, when you give a command to run your program, the operating system allocates a block of memory for your program, loads it from the disk into that block and then initiates its execution. When the program finishes its execution, the memory occupied by the program is automatically released. It means that the memory requirements are determined prior to execution of your program, and there after your program can neither acquire more memory nor can release the free memory, if not required.

However, C language provides a set of library functions (listed in Table 12.1), called *dynamic memory management functions*, to allocate and de-allocate memory at execution time, *i.e.*, dynamically. By allocation, we mean that your program can obtain as much memory as required by your program even during execution of your program. By de-allocation, we mean that the memory acquired dynamically can be released at any time during your program execution. It is important to note that memory allocated dynamically, must be de-allocated before your program finishes its execution. Otherwise, even if your program terminates, memory allocated dynamically is never released automatically, and from operating system point of view that memory is still in use. Therefore, if you run the same program many times, many users are using your program concurrently, the operating system may run out of memory.

Table 12.1: Memory Management Functions

Function Name	Description
malloc	Allocates memory from heap.
calloc	Allocates memory from heap and initializes the allocated memory to zeroes.
realloc	Readjusts the existing block and copies the contents to the new location.
free	Deallocates a block allocated by *malloc*, *calloc* and *realloc* functions.
coreleft	Returns a measure of unused memory.

Each of these memory management functions is described below:

The *malloc()* function dynamically allocates memory from heap. The prototype for *malloc()* function is

```
void *malloc(size_t size);
```

It takes one argument that specifies the size of the block in bytes. The function returns a pointer to the allocated memory on success or a null pointer (0) in case of failure.

The *calloc()* function dynamically allocates memory and automatically initializes the memory to zeroes. The prototype for *calloc()* function is

```
void *calloc(size_t nitems, size_t size);
```

It takes two arguments. The first argument is the number of elements and the second argument is the size of each element. The function returns a pointer to the allocated memory on success or a null pointer (0) in case of failure.

The *realloc()* function changes the size of previously dynamically allocated memory with *malloc()*, *calloc()* or *realloc()* functions. The original contents held in the previously allocated memory are not changed provided the memory allocated is larger than the amount of memory previously allocated otherwise the contents are unchanged upto the size of new object. The prototype for *realloc()* function is

```
void *realloc(void *block, size_t size);
```

It takes two arguments. The first argument is the pointer to the original object and the second argument is the new size of the object.

Depending on the values of these arguments, following things can happen

- If the pointer to the original object is 0 (NULL), the *realloc()* function works identical to *malloc()* function.
- If size of new object is 0 and pointer is not 0, the memory of the object is freed.
- If the pointer is not 0 and the size of the new object is greater than zero, *realloc()* function tries to allocate new block of memory. If new space cannot be allocated, the object pointed to by the pointer is unchanged.

The *realloc()* function returns either a pointer to reallocated block or a null pointer.

The *free()* function deallocates a memory block previously allocated with *malloc()*, *calloc()* or *realloc()* functions. The prototype for *free()* function is

```
void free(void *block);
```

It takes one argument that specifies the pointer to the allocated block. But it is important to note that only the allocated block is deallocated, the pointer variable is not deleted.

The *coreleft()* function returns amount of free memory in the heap. Its protypes is

```
unsigned long coreleft(void);
```

12.10 POINTERS AND ARRAYS

When we declare an array, the compiler allocates a block of memory of appropriate size so that all the elements of an array can be stored in contiguous memory locations. The address of the first memory location (also the address of the first element of the array) of allocated block is known as the *base address*, and is assigned to the array name. Thus, array name behaves as a pointer variable.

12.10.1 Pointers and One-dimensional Arrays

Consider the following declaration statement

```
float a[9] = { 0, 1, 2, 3, 4, 5, 6, 7, 8 };
```

This statement set aside a contiguous block of 9 memory locations for the array named *a*. Here the array named *a* holds the address of the first element of the array i.e. base address of the array. The memory map of the array *a* is shown in Figure 12.4. By adding offset (index of the element) to this base address, the other elements of the array can also be accessed. For example, using pointer notation, elements of array *a* can be accessed as

```
*(a+0),  *(a+1),  *(a+2), ..., *(a+8)
```

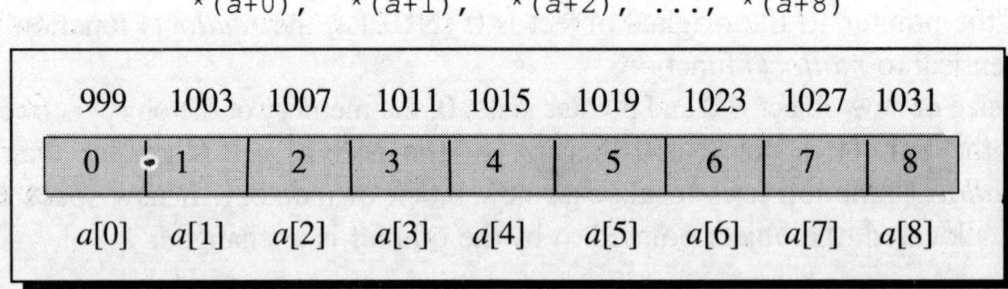

Figure 12.4: Memory map of one-dimensional array *a* with a base address 999

Listing 12.3

```
/*
*  Program to demonstrate the way elements of one dimensional
*   array are accessed using pointer notation
*/
#include<stdio.h>
void main()
{
   int arr[10]={12,15,20,17,25,50,11,10,8,13};
   int i, count, *ptr;
   float sum, average;
   ptr = arr;
   for ( sum = 0, i = 0; i < 10; i++ )
      sum += *(ptr+i);
   average = sum / 10;
   for ( count = 0, i = 0; i < 10; i++ )
   {
      if ( *(ptr + i ) > average )
         count++;
   }
   printf( "\nNo. of elements > average = %d\n", count);
}
```

12.10.2 Pointers and Two-dimensional Arrays

Consider the following declaration statement

```
float a[3][3] = {{1,2,3},{4,6,9},{3,2,7}};
```

This statement set aside a contiguous block of 9 memory locations for the array named *a*. Here the array named *a* holds the address of the first element of the array, *i.e.*, base address of the array. As we know that there is no concept of rows and columns in memory. The elements of the array, irrespective of that whether it is one-dimensional, two-dimensional or three-dimensional, are stored in a continuous chain, *i.e.*, one after the other.

	Col #0	Col #1	Col #2
Row #0	1	2	3
Row #1	4	6	9
Row #2	3	2	7

999	1003	1007	1011	1015	1019	1023	1027	1031
1	2	3	4	6	9	3	2	7
a[0][0]	*a*[0][1]	*a*[0][2]	*a*[1][0]	*a*[1][1]	*a*[1][2]	*a*[2][0]	*a*[2][1]	*a*[2][2]

Figure 12.5: Memory map of two-dimensional array *a* with base address 999

Now let us see how we can access individual elements of the above two-dimensional array using pointers. The procedure is slightly difficult. As mentioned earlier that two-dimensional array can be treated as an array of arrays, where each element of the array is one-dimensional array. For example, above array can be visualized as

a[0]	1	2	3
a[1]	4	6	9
a[2]	3	2	7

Figure 12.6: Two-dimensional array *a* as array of one-dimensional arrays

We can refer to individual elements as *a*[0], *a*[1], and *a*[2]. More specifically, *a*[0] gives the address of the first one-dimensional array, *a*[1] gives the address of the second one-dimensional array, *a*[2] gives the address of the third one-dimensional array.

Listing 12.4

```
/*  Program to illustrate 2D array as array of 1D arrays  */
#include<stdio.h>
void main()
{
   int a[3][3] = { { 1, 2, 3 }, { 4, 6, 9 }, { 3, 2, 7 } };
   int i;
   for ( i = 0; i < 3; i++ ) {
      printf("\nAddress of  1D array number %d = %u",
              i+1, a[i]);
   }
   printf( "\n" );
}
```

Now the question is — *how can we access the individual elements of these arrays*? Suppose we want to access the *j*th element of the *i*th row. We know that *a*[*i*] will give address of the *i*th one-dimensional array (i.e. *i*th row). And we also know from our knowledge of one-dimensional arrays that writing *a*[*i*] in subscript notation is equivalent to *(*a*+*i*). Further if *a*[*i*] is the address of the *i*th row, the address of the *j*th element of *i*th row will be (*a*[*i*]+*j*), and thus the element can be accessed as *(*a*[*i*]+*j*), which on replacing *a*[*i*] by *(*a*+*i*) becomes *(*(*a*+*i*)+*j*). Thus, all of the following expressions refer to element a_{ij}.

```
a[i][j]
*(a[i]+j)
*(*(a+i)+j)
```

Listing 12.5

```
/* Program to print elements of the 2D array using
   pointer notation  */
#include<stdio.h>
void main()
{
   int a[3][3] = { { 1, 2, 3 }, { 4, 6, 9 }, { 3, 2, 7 } };
   int i, j;
   printf("\nElements of two-dimensional array are\n\n");
   for ( i = 0; i < 3; i++ ) {
      for ( j = 0; j < 3; j++ )
          printf ( "%4df\t", *(*(a+i)+j) );
      printf ( "\n" );
   }
}
```

12.10.3 Dynamic Arrays

The declaration of arrays at the compilation time (i.e. using subscripted notation) has one major limitation. The memory is allocated during the compilation time. If the number of actual data elements is very less as compared to the declared size, then a lot of memory is wasted. On the other hand, if the number of actual data elements is more than the declared size then we have to modify the source code. However, this limitation can be overcome if the memory is allocated at the execution time. The next program illustrates this concept.

Listing 12.6

```
/*
 *  Program to illustrate the allocation of memory
 *  for one-dimensional array at execution time
 */

#include<stdio.h>
#include<alloc.h>

void main()
{
    int  *a, n, i, big;
    printf( "Enter size of one-dimensional array: "  );
    scanf( "%d", &n );

    /* allocate memory for array */
    a = (int *) malloc(n*sizeof(int));
    if ( a == NULL )
    {
        printf ( "\nUnable to allocate memory\n" );
        return;
    }
    printf( "Enter %d elements of array\n", n );
    for ( i = 0 ; i < n ; i++)
        scanf( "%d", a+i );

    for ( big = *a, i = 1 ; i < n ; i++ )
    {
        if ( *(a+i ) > big )
            big = *(a+i);
    }
    printf( "\nLargest element of the array = %d\n", big );

    /* release the memory held by array */
    free ( a );
}
```

12.11 POINTERS AND FUNCTIONS

12.11.1 Pointers as Function Arguments

If you remember, in *Chapter 8*, we had mentioned that the arguments to a function could be passed using either *call by value* or *call by address* mechanism. When we use call by value mechanism, the formal arguments of the function are declared as simple variable, and at execution time the values of the actual arguments are copied into formal arguments (formal arguments are local to the function), and the execution of the function begins.

However, when we use call by reference mechanism, the formal arguments are declared as pointers, and at execution time, the addresses of the actual arguments are copied into formal arguments and the execution of the function begins.

Listing 12.7

```
/*
*  Program to illustrate pointers as function arguments
*/
#include<stdio.h>
void main()
{
  int a = 10, b = 20;
  void interchange( int *, int *);  /* function prototype */
  printf( "\nValue of a = %d and b = %d", a, b );
  printf( " before function call\n"  );
  interchange ( &a, &b);    /*   function call   */
  printf( "\nValue of a = %d and b = %d", a, b );
  printf( " after function call\n"  );
}
void interchange( int *x, int *y )  /* function definition */
{
  int temp;
  temp = *x;
  *x = *y;
  *y = temp;
}
```

Test Run

```
Value of a = 10 and b = 20 before function call
Value of a = 20 and b = 10 after function call
```

Consider the following program listing.

Listing 12.8

```
/*
 *  Program to illustrate non-pointer variables
 *  as function arguments
 */
#include<stdio.h>
void main()
{
    int a = 10, b = 20;
    void interchange( int, int );    /* function prototype */
    printf( "\nValue of a = %d and b = %d", a, b );
    printf( " before function call\n"  );
    interchange ( &a, &b);           /* function call       */
    printf( "\nValue of a = %d and b = %d", a, b );
    printf( " after function call\n"  );
}
void interchange ( int x, int y )   /* function definition */
{
    int temp;
    temp = x;
    x = y;
    y = temp;
}
```

Test Run

```
Value of a = 10 and b = 20 before function call
Value of a = 10 and b = 20 after function call
```

Why this version of the program could not complete the task of interchanging the values of the arguments. In this version, values of the *a* and *b* are copied into *x* and *y*, which act as local variables. Thus the values, in fact, of *x* and *y* are interchanged in the workspace of the *interchange()* function, but as soon as the function completes its execution, these variables are destroyed. Thus, the values of the variables remain un-effected. However, in the first version of the program, the addresses of variables *a* and *b* are copied into pointer variables *x* and *y*. These pointer variables, though local to the function *interchange()*, interchanges the values of *a* and *b* indirectly in the work space of the *main()* function, with the help of a local variable *temp*. When the function *interchange()* completes its execution, the variables *x*, and *y* along with temp are destroyed, but the task has been accomplished.

12.11.2 Function Returning a Pointer

Like any type of value, a function can also return a pointer pointing to an appropriate type of values. The syntax for declaring a function that return a pointer is

```
type *fun_name( args )
{
   /* . . . */
}
```

The following program listing illustrates the various steps.

Listing 12.9

```
/* Program to illustrate passing of array of strings to a function */
#include<stdio.h>
void main()
{
   int x = 20;
   int *address( int );    /*   function prototype   */
   printf( "\nAddress of %d in main function is %u", x, &x );
   printf( "\nand in function it is copied in address %u\n",
           address(x) );
}
int *address( int y )
{
   return &y;
}
```

12.12 POINTERS AND STRINGS

As we know that a string is an array of characters, terminated with a null character '\0'. Therefore, like one-dimensional arrays, we can use individual characters in a string.

Listing 12.10

```
/* Program to illustrate access of individual characters in a string  */
#include<stdio.h>
void main()
{
   char city[]= "Chandigarh is a beautiful city";
   char *ptr;
   ptr = city;
   printf( "Individual characters of the strings are" );
   printf( "\n\n" );
   while ( *ptr != '\0' )
```

```
    {
        printf ( "\n%c is stored is address %u", *ptr, ptr );
        ptr++;
    }
    printf ( "\n"  );
}
```

As mentioned earlier, storing a table of strings (list of strings) using a two-dimensional array is not an efficient way. We will take up that issue here again.

Consider the following declaration

```
char names[4][12] = { "Ram",
                      "Inder Mohan",
                      "Amanpreet",
                      "Rajan"
                    };
```

Where we have considered that each string can be of 20 characters, at maximum excluding the null character. This list of strings will be represented in memory as shown below:

R	a	m	'\0'								
I	n	d	e	r		M	o	h	a	n	'\0'
A	m	a	n	p	r	e	e	t	'\0'		
R	a	j	a	n	'\0'						

Total memory requirements are 48 bytes. However, if we count, first string requires 4 bytes, second string requires 12 bytes, third string requires 10 bytes, and the fourth string requires 6 bytes. Thus total memory requirements come out to be 32, wastage of 16 bytes. In practice, it has been shown that, on average, half of the allocated space is mere wastage.

However, this kind of representation of list of strings can be practical only if all strings are of equal length, but this happens rarely in practice.

Therefore, more practical and efficient way of storing a list of strings is using array of pointers to strings. The following declaration illustrates this point

```
char *names[4] = { "Ram",
                   "Inder Mohan",
                   "Amanpreet",
                   "Rajan"
                 };
```

This will be represented in memory as

R	a	m	'\0'								
I	n	d	e	r		M	o	h	a	n	'\0'
A	m	a	n	p	r	e	e	t	'\0'		
R	a	j	a	n	'\0'						

This declaration allocates only 32 bytes of memory, *i.e.*, what is actually needed.

Listing 10.11

```
/*
*  Program to illustrate input/output of strings
*  represented using array of pointer
*/

#include<stdio.h>
#include<string.h>

void main()
{
   char *names[30];
   int i, n;
   printf( "\nEnter number of strings : " );
   scanf( "%d", &n);
   for ( i = 0; i < n; i++ ) {
      printf ( "\nEnter string #%d : ", i+1 );
      gets(names[i]);
   }
   printf( "\nYou have entered following strings\n\n" );
   for ( i = 0; i < n; i++ )
      puts(names[i]);
}
```

Limitations of Array of Pointer to Strings

Though, it is an efficient way to represent list of strings using array of pointers to strings as compared to the representation using two-dimensional array of characters. But this approach also suffers from one limitation. That limitation is that we cannot input a string using *scanf()* function, because we have to pass the address of the variable in which input value is to be stored. As we know that when an array is declared, its elements contain garbage value. So, in case of array of pointers to strings, the garbage values do not represent a valid addresses to be sent to the *scanf()* function.

12.13 POINTERS AND STRUCTURES

As we can use pointers with other data types, we can also use pointers for structure variables. Consider the following declarations

```
typedef struct
{
   int code;
   char name[20];
   int  dept_code;
   float  salary;
} EMPLOYEE;
EMPLOYEE empl, *ptr;
```

These declarations create an user-defined data type and given it name *EMPLOYEE* and declares *empl* as variable of type employee and *ptr* as pointer variable to type employee.

Now the following statement

```
ptr = &empl;
```

can be used to assign the address of variable *empl* to pointer variable *ptr*. Now, we can access the members of the structure variable *empl* using pointer variable *ptr*. You may expect that the elements can be accessed as shown below:

```
*ptr.code     *ptr.name     *ptr.dept_code     *ptr.salary
```

But this approach will not work as the *dot operator* '.' has higher priority than the *indirection operator* '*'. The correct way is to write as

```
(*ptr).code   (*ptr).name  (*ptr).dept_code   (*ptr).salary
```

There is another approach that is more elegant and simple. In this approach, the elements of structure are accessed using *arrow operator* '–>' which is a combination of two characters, *i.e.*, hyphen '–' and greater-than '>'.

The syntax for accessing members of structure using arrow operator is:

```
ptr->vname
```

where *ptr is* pointer variable pointing to a structure, and *vname* is the name of element of the structure.

Using arrow operator, the elements of structure of type *employee* pointed to by pointer variable *ptr* can be accessed as

```
ptr->code     ptr->name     ptr->dept_code     ptr->salary
```

Listing 12.12

```
/*  Program to illustrate I/O of structure using pointers  */

#include<stdio.h>
#include<string.h>

typedef struct
{
   int code;
   char name[20];
   int dept_code;
   float salary;
} EMPLOYEE;

void main()
{
   EMPLOYEE empl, *ptr;
   ptr = &empl;

   printf("\nEnter employee code as integer number: ");
   scanf( "%d", &(ptr->code));
   printf( "\nEnter name of employee : " );
   gets(ptr->name);
   printf("\nEnter department code as integer number: ");
   scanf( "%d", &(ptr->dept_code) );
   printf( "\nEnter Salary: " );
   scanf( "%f", &(ptr->salary) );

   printf( "Particulars of employee as entered by" );
   printf( "you are\n\n" );
   printf( "\nEmployee code : %d", ptr->code );
   printf( "\nEmployee name : %s", ptr->name );
   printf( "\nDepartment code : %d", ptr->dept_code );
   printf( "\nEmployee salary : %.2f", ptr->salary );
}
```

12.13.1 Self-referential Structures

The self-referential structures are structures that include an element that is a pointer to another structure of the same type. These structures find their application in building complex data structure such as *linked lists*, *trees* and *graphs*.

Following are some examples of self-referential structures.

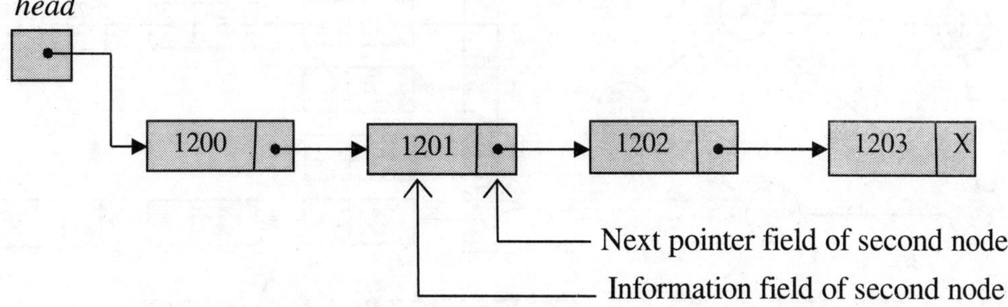

Figure 12.6: Linear linked list of integer values with nodes 4

To represent the above linear linked list in memory, we need following declarations

```
typedef struct nodeType
{
   int info;
   struct nodeType *next;
} NODE;
NODE *start;
```

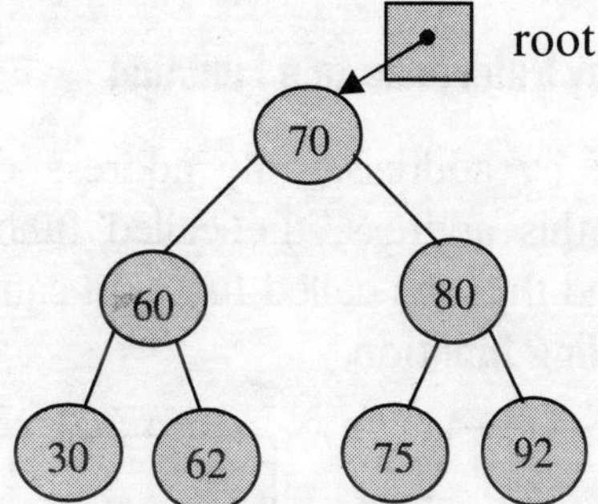

Figure 12.7: Binary tree

To represent a binary tree in memory, we need following declarations

```
typedef struct nodeType
{
   struct nodeType *left;
   int info;
   struct nodeType *right;
}  BNODE;
BNODE *root;
```

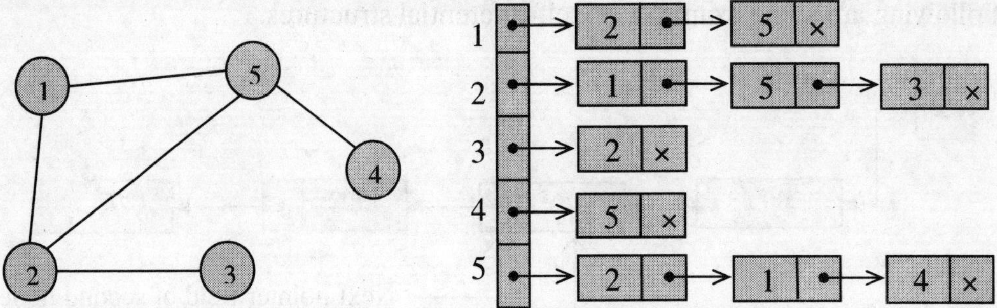

Figure 12.8: Undirected graph **Figure 12.9:** Adjacency list for graph

To represent a graph in memory, one of the best representation schemes is adjacency list as shown in Figure 12.9. Therefore, for a graph with maximum of 50 vertices/nodes, we need following declarations

```
#define MAX 50
typedef struct nodeType  {
   int vertex;
   struct nodeType *link;
} node;

node *adj[MAX];
```

12.13.2 Passing Structures by Reference to a Function

When we pass a structure by address, only address of the first byte of the structure is passed. Using this address, the called function can access all the elements of the structure, and thus the called function can process the structure in the memory space of the calling function.

```
typedef struct {
   int day;
   int month;
   int year;
} DATE;
void printDate(DATE *);
void main()
{
   DATE aDate = { 10, 6, 2008 };
   int x;
   printDate(&aDate);
   /*  more statements    */
}
```

```
/*  function definition    */
void printDate(DATE *tDate )
{

   /*  local declarations */
   /*  other statements   */

}
```

Figure 12.10: Passing entire structure by address

Listing 12.13

```
/*
*   Program to illustrate the passing of a structure by address
*/
#include <stdio.h>
typedef struct
{
   int day;
   int month;
   int year;
} DATE;
void printDate( DATE *aDate );      /* function declaration  */

void main()
{
   DATE tDate = { 10, 6, 2008 };   /* initialize a structure */
   printDate( &tDate );             /* function call           */
}

void printDate( DATE *aDate )
{
   printf( "\nDate in format dd/mm/yy: %02d/%02d/%2d\n",
           aDate->day, aDate->month, aDate.->year );
}
```

12.14 POSSIBLE PROBLEMS WITH THE USE OF POINTERS

Pointers can be the source of mysterious and catastrophic program bugs. Common bugs related to pointers and memory management is *dangling/wild pointers*, *memory leaks*, and *allocation failures*. Each of these problems is discussed next.

12.14.1 Problem of Dangling/Wild Pointers

The most common problem with pointers is that the programmer fails to initialize a pointer with a valid address. Such an initialized pointer, referred to as *dangling/wild pointer*, can end up pointing anywhere in memory that may include the program code itself or to the code of the operating system. If the programmer assign a value to such pointer, the value will overwrite the program or operating system instructions, and the computer program may show undesirable behaviour or may even crash, *i.e.*, stop responding. When the system stop responding, we say the system has hanged up and the only option left is to reboot the system. Therefore, care must be taken to initialize pointers with valid address.

12.14.2 Problem of Null Pointer Assignment

One particular situation that happens is when the pointer points to address 0, which is called NULL. For example, this may happen that if the pointer variable is declared as global since global variables are initialized to 0. Likewise, this can also happen for a local un-initialized pointer variable, particularly for local static variables, they are also initialized to 0.

When it happens, and no catastrophic situations had occurred, then the system will display a message "*Null pointer assignment*" on termination of the program.

12.14.3 Problem of Memory Leak

Another very serious problem with pointers is that of *memory leak.* Memory leak is a situation where the programmer fails to release the memory allocated at run time in a module. Note that when memory is allocated, a pointer variable is used to hold the address of the allocated block, however, when the module completes its execution, the pointer variable goes out of scope and there will be no way to reach that memory block. Therefore, care must be taken to release the allocated memory block in a module where memory was allocated.

Listing 12.14

```
/*  Program to illustrate the cause of memory leak   */
#include<stdio.h>
void main()
{
   . . . . .
   fun(); //  invoke function named 'fun'
   . . . . .
}
void fun()
{
   int *intPtr;
   . . . . .
   /*  allocate memory for 'n' integer numbers
   intPtr = ( int * ) malloc(n*sizeof(int));
   /*   work on the allocated block    */
}
```

12.14.4 Problem of Allocation Failures

Allocation failure is a situation when the program through *malloc()*, *calloc()*, *realloc(),* function request for a block of memory, and the operating could not fulfill the request of the program because the sufficient memory may not be available in the free pool of memory. In that case, these functions return a NULL pointer indicating the allocation failure.

Therefore, the programmer should take care of allocation failures and provide a safe exit in their programs on such failures.

Listing 12.15

```
/*
*  Program to illustrates the allocation failure, and
*  the way it should be handled
*/
#include<stdio.h>
void main()
{
   int *intPtr;
   . . . . .
   /*  allocate memory for 'n' integer numbers
   intPtr = ( int * ) malloc(n*sizeof(int));

   if ( intPtr == NULL )
   {
       printf("\nUnable to allocate memory . . .\n");
       return;
   }

   /*   work on the allocated block    */
   . . . . .
   free(intPtr);    // release the memory
}
```

12.15 SUPPLEMENTARY PROBLEMS

Problem 12.1:

Write a program that takes a list of numbers as its command line arguments, and prints the sum of these numbers.

The procedure to be followed is as follows:

The command line arguments are received by the *main()* function as string. Since the command line arguments are just numbers, therefore the string are made up of only letters 0-9 and decimal point '.'. We use here a library function *atof()* to convert a string of representing a number to numeric value. Then we add these numeric values one by one after conversion. We need to include *stdlib.h* header file in order to use *atof()* library function.

Listing 12.16

```
/* Program to add list of integer numbers given as
*  command line arguments
*  filename : sum.c
*/

# include <stdio.h>
# include <stdlib.h>

void main( int argc, char *argv[] )
{
   int i;
   float sum = 0;
   for ( i = 1; i < argc; i++ )
   {
      sum += atof( argv[i] );
   }
   printf("\nSum of numbers on command line = %.2f\n", sum);
}
```

Test Run

```
>sum 1 2 3 4 5 6 7 8 9 10

Sum of numbers on command line = 55.00
```

Problem 12.2:

Consider the following declaration:

```
char *names[]={"Vimal", "Amit", "Anuj", "Rohit", "Abhijit"};
```

Write a program to produce the following output:

```
tijihbA, tihoR, junA, timA, lamiV
```

Listing 12.17

```
/*  Program to reverse each string of array of strings  */

# include <stdio.h>
# include <stdlib.h>

void reverseString(char *p);

void main()
{
   int i;
   char *names[] = {"Vimal", "Amit", "Anuj", "Rohit", "Abhijit"};
   printf( "\n" );
   for ( i = 4; i >= 1; i-- )
```

```
    {
        reverseString(names[i]);
        printf( "%s,", names[i]);
    }
    reverseString(names[i]);
    printf( "%s,", names[i]);
    printf( "\n" );
}
void reverseString(char *p)
{
    char t;
    char *sStr, *eStr;
    sStr = p;
    eStr = p + strlen(p) - 1;
    while ( eStr > sStr ) {
        t = *sStr;
        *sStr = *eStr;
        *eStr = t;
        sStr++;
        eStr--;
    }
}
```

Test Run

```
tijihbA, tihoR, junA, timA, lamiV
```

Problem 12.3:

Write a function that takes an array as its argument and returns the largest, smallest and range of its elements. Using this function, write a program using pointers to find the largest, smallest and range of elements of the array.

Listing 12.18

```
/* Program to find the largest, smallest, and range of elements
*  using pointer notation only  */
#include<stdio.h>
#include<alloc.h>
void compute(int *,int,int *,int *,int); /*function declaration*/
void main()
{
    int *a, i, n, largest, smallest, range;
    printf( "\nEnter size of array: "  );
    scanf( "%d", &n );
    /* allocate memory for array */
    a = (int *) malloc(n*sizeof(int));
```

```
    if ( a == NULL )
    {
       printf ( "\nUnable to allocate memory\n" );
       return;
    }
    printf( "\nEnter %d elements of array\n\n", n );
    for ( i = 0 ; i < n ; i++ )
       scanf( "%d", a+i );
    compute(a, n, &largest, &smallest, &range); /*function call*/
    printf( "\nLargest element of the array   = %d", largest );
    printf( "\nSmallest element of the array  = %d", smallest );
    printf( "\nRange of elements of the array = %d\n", range );
    free ( a );      /* release the memory held by array */
}
/* function definition */
void compute(int *a, int n, int *big, int *small, int *range)
{
    int i;
    *big = *small = *a;
    for ( i = 1; i < n; i++ )
    {
       if ( *(a+i) > *big ) *big = *(a+i);
       if ( *(a+i) < *small ) *small = *(a+i);
    }
    *range = *big - *small;
}
```

Test Run

```
Enter size of array: 10

Enter 10 elements of array

12 30 21 34 9 59 70 54 44 33

Largest element of the array   = 70
Smallest element of the array  = 9
Range of elements of the array = 61
```

12.16 QUICK RECAP

In this chapter, we have learnt that

- Pointer is a variable that holds an address of an operand.
- Pointers offers many advantages such as returning more than one value from a function, building complex data structures, communicating with the H/W, etc.

- An addition operation on pointers is permitted. A subtraction operation is permitted in the restricted sense that it must give positive difference. Multiplication and division operation is not permitted.
- Memory allocation can be done in two ways – *statically* and *dynamically*.
- Static memory allocation is that which is done at compilation time.
- Dynamic memory allocation is that which is done at compilation time.
- Every program is provided with a pool of unallocated memory that it can utilize during execution. This pool of unallocated memory is known as *heap* or *free store*.
- The process of managing the memory at execution time is known as *dynamic memory management*.
- In C language, *malloc()*, *calloc()*, *realloc()* and *free()* functions are used for dynamic memory management.
- The *malloc()*, *calloc()* and *realloc()* functions allocates the requisite amount of memory while the *free()* function deallocates the memory.
- Pointers are used to pass arguments by address.
- Arrays, strings and structures can be efficiently passed as arguments to a function.
- A function can return a pointer.
- A self-referential structure is a structure that includes at least one element that is a pointer to itself.
- An initialized pointer is referred to as *dangling/wild pointer*, as it can end up pointing anywhere in memory.
- Whenever there is attempt to write on zero address (also known as *Null pointer*) or the system will flag and a message "*Null pointer assignment*" on termination of the program.
- Memory leak is a kind of situation when memory is allocated in a called function but it is not deallocated in that function after it use. As a result, when the called function completes its execution, the pointer variable is destroyed and there is no means to reach that allocated memory block.
- Allocation failure is a situation when the system is not able to find a requisite block of free memory. The system indicates this situation by returning a *NULL* pointer.

12.17 MULTIPLE CHOICE QUESTIONS

1. The address of a variable can be obtained using ___ operator.
   (*a*) * (*b*) &
   (*c*) ? (*d*) ->
2. Which of the following operator is known as *indirection* (*dereference*) operator?
   (*a*) & (*b*) <<
   (*c*) ^ (*d*) *
3. Which of the following operator is known as *address of* operator?
   (*a*) & (*b*) *
   (*c*) -> (*d*) **
4. Identify the correct declarations of pointer variables *ptr1*, *ptr2*.
   (*a*) `int ptr1, *ptr2;` (*b*) `int *ptr1, ptr2;`
   (*c*) `int ptr1, ptr2;` (*d*) `int *ptr1, *ptr2;`
5. The operators exclusively used with pointers are
   (*a*) * and / (*b*) & and *
   (*c*) & and ^ (*d*) * and +
6. The operand of *addressof* operator can be a/an
   (*a*) constant (*b*) array element
   (*c*) expression (*d*) None
7. Pointer variables may be assigned
   (*a*) address value represented in hexadecimal notation
   (*b*) address value represented in octal notation
   (*c*) address of another variable
   (*d*) address value represented in binary notation
8. Operand of *indirection* (*dereference*) operator is
   (*a*) pointer variable (*b*) ordinary variable
   (*c*) integer constant (*d*) none of above
9. Identify the operator that is not used with pointers
   (*a*) -> (*b*) &
   (*c*) * (*d*) >>

10. The function used for dynamic memory allocation is

(*a*) `memalloc()` (*b*) `blockalloc()`
(*c*) `malloc()` (*d*) `mcalloc()`

11. Pointer can be used to achieve

(*a*) call by function (*b*) call by name
(*c*) call by reference (*d*) call by procedure

12. Which of the following statements about functions is not correct?

(*a*) function can return a pointer
(*b*) function cannot return a pointer
(*c*) function can have its formal arguments declared as pointer
(*d*) function can be called using a pointer to a function

13. Which of the following operation is not permitted on pointers?

(*a*) incrementing a pointer variable
(*b*) adding a number to a pointer variable
(*c*) division of a pointer variable by a number
(*d*) difference of two pointer variables

14. When *addressof* operator (&) is prefixed to a variable, it yields

(*a*) variable's value (*b*) variables data type
(*c*) variable's address (*d*) none of above

15. Consider the following statements

```
char *ptr;
ptr = "abba";
putchar(*ptr);
```

What will be printed?

(*a*) first letter (*b*) entire string
(*c*) it is a syntax error (*d*) last letter

16. What does the following declaration mean?

```
int (*ptr)[10];
```

(*a*) *ptr* is a pointer to 10 arrays (*b*) *ptr* is a pointer to array of 10 integers
(*c*) *ptr* is a pointer to a function (*d*) *ptr* is a generic pointer

17. What will be the output of the following program?

```
#include <stdio.h>
void change (int *, int);    /* function declaration  */
void main()
{
```

```
    int  i, a[5]={3,4,5,6,7};
    change(a,5);
    for(i=0 ; i<5 ; i++)
       printf("%3d",a[i]);
}
void change (int *p, int n)
{
    int i;
    for ( i = 0 ; i < n ; i++ )
        *(p+i) += i+1;
}
```

(*a*) 3 5 7 9 11 (*b*) 4 6 8 10 12
(*c*) 7 8 9 10 11 (*d*) 3 4 5 6 7

18. What is the difference between the following declarations?

```
const int *intptr;
int *const intptr;
```

(*a*) First statement declares pointer to integer constant while the second declares constant pointer to an integer.
(*b*) First statement declares constant pointer to an integer while the second declares pointer constant to an integer.
(*c*) Both declares pointer to an integer.
(*d*) Both declares constant pointer to an integer.

19. What is the difference between the following declarations?

```
int *ptr(int arg);
int (*ptr)(int arg);
```

(*a*) First declares a function that returns a pointer to an integer, the second one declares a pointer to a function.
(*b*) First declares a pointer to a function, the second one declares a function that returns a pointer.
(*c*) Both declares function that return a pointer to an integer.
(*d*) Both declares pointer to a function.

20. What is the difference between the following declarations?

```
int (*a)[];
int *a[];
```

(*a*) First declares a pointer an integer array, the second one declares array of integer pointers.
(*b*) First declares array of integer pointer, the second one declares a pointer an array.
(*c*) Both declares pointer to an array.
(*d*) Both declares array of pointers.

21. What is the value of *x* after executing the following segment?

```
int x = 5, *p;
p = &x;
*p = 7;
```

(*a*) 5 (*b*) 7
(*c*) Undefined (*d*) None

22. What will be the output of the following segment?

```
int a[5] = {1,2,3,4};
int *p = a;
printf("%d",*(p+2));
```

(*a*) 4 (*b*) 0
(*c*) 3 (*d*) 2

23. Consider the following statement

```
int p= 20, *q=&p, **k = &q;
```

then the variable *k* is called __________.

(*a*) pointer to an integer (*b*) pointer to pointer to an integer
(*c*) pointer to pointer to an integer pointer (*d*) just double pointer

24. Consider the following program segment:

```
int *p, a[] = { 1, 2, 3, 4, 5 };
p = &a[2];
printf("%d", p[-1]);
```

Which of the following is correct about above program segment?

(*a*) Compiler time error because *p* is not an array
(*b*) Output will be 2
(*c*) Compiler time error because subscript cannot be negative
(*d*) None of above

25. Consider the following program segment:

```
const int i = 5;
int *p;
i = 20;
p = &i;
printf("\n%d, %d\n", *p, i);
```

Which of the following is correct about above program segment?

(*a*) Output will be 20, 20 (*b*) Output will be 5, 20
(*c*) Output will be 20, 5
(*d*) Compile time error because the value of variable *i* cannot be changed.

26. Consider the following program segment:

```
char *s1 = "Mumbai";
char *s2 = "Delhi";
char *ps1 = s1, *ps2 = s2;
while ( *ps1++ = *ps2++ ) ;
puts(s1);
```

Which of the following is correct about above program segment?

(*a*) Mumbai (*b*) Delhi
(*c*) MumbaiDelhi (*d*) None

12.18 REVIEW EXERCISES

1. How can we get the address of a variable?
2. What is a pointer variable?
3. How is a pointer variable declared?
4. How can the values pointed to by a pointer variable be accessed?
5. What are the various types of pointers?
6. Pointers are double-edged weapons. Comment.
7. What are the operations permissible on pointers?
8. What are the operations, which are not permissible on pointers?
9. What is the difference between *static* and *dynamic* memory allocation?
10. Predict the output and explain the working of the following program, and identify the error, if any?

```
#include <stdio.h>
void main()
{
    int i = 6, j = 4;
    void kudo( int, int * );  /* function prototype */
    kudo(j, &i);
    printf("\ni = %d, j = %d\n", i, j);
}
void kudo( int x, int *y )  /* function definition  */
{
    x = *y * x;
    *y = x * *y;
}
```

11. Predict the output and explain the working of the following program, and identify the error, if any?

```
#include <stdio.h>
void main()
{
    int i = 156;
```

```
    int *j, *k;
    j = &i;
    k = j;
    printf("\ni = %d, *(&i) = %d, *j = %d, *k = %d\n",
           i, *(&i), *j, *k);
}
```

12. Identify the error, if any, in the following program, and explain the reason.

```
#include <stdio.h>
void main()
{
    int x[6] = { 1, 2, 3, 4, 5, 6 };
    int *r, *s;
    r = x;
    s = x + 4;
    r *= 2;
    s /= 2
    printf("\n*r = %d, *s = %d\n", *r, *s);
}
```

13. Identify the error, if any, in the following program, and explain the reason.

```
#include <stdio.h>
void main()
{
    int x[6] = { 1, 2, 3, 4, 5, 6 };
    int i = 0;
    while ( i < 6 ) {
        printf("\nx[%d] = %d\n", i, *x);
        ++i;
        x++;
    }
    printf("\nThe End\n");
}
```

14. Predict and explain the output of the following program.

```
#include <stdio.h>
void func(int, int *); // prototype
void main()
{
    int x[] = { 2, 4, 6, 8 };
    int i = 0, b = 6;
    while ( i < 4 ) {
        func(x[i],&b);
        printf("x[%d] = %d, b = %d\n", i, x[i], b);
        i++;
    }
}

void func(int a, int *p)
{
    a = *p += 2;
    printf("\na = %d, ", a);
}
```

15. What do you mean by a *dangling/wild pointer*? What type of problems it may cause?

16. What is a NULL pointer assignment?

17. What is a memory leak? What can be the possible reason for it? How can memory leaks be avoided?

18. What is an allocation failure?

19. What is the difference between the following declarations?

```
const int *intptr;      and      int *const intptr;
```

20. Identify the errors, if any, in following program and also give appropriate reasons.

```
#include <stdio.h>
void main()
{
    int i = 5;
    const int j = 100;
    int * const ptr = &j;
    *ptr++;
    ptr = &i;
    printf("\n%d,%d,%d\n", *ptr, i, j);
}
```

21. What will be the output of the following program?

```
#include <stdio.h>
void main()
{
   float a[3][4] = { { 1, 2, 3, 5 },
                     { 6, 7, 8, 9 },
                     { 10, 11, 12, 13 }
                   };
   float *p;
   p = &a[0][0];
   printf( "\n1.   *(*(a+2)+0)  = %d", *(*(a+2)+0) );
   printf( "\n2.   *(*a+2)+3    = %d", *(*a+2)+3 );
   printf( "\n3.   *(1+*(a+2))  = %d", *(1+*(a+2)) );
   printf( "\n4.   *(*(a)+2)+3  = %d", *(*(a)+2)+3 );
   printf( "\n5.   *p           = %d", *p );
   printf( "\n6.   *(p+2)       = %d", *(p+2) );
   printf( "\n7.   (*(p+1)+2)   = %d", (*(p+1)+2) );
   printf( "\n8.   ++ *p        = %d", ++ *p );
   printf( "\n9.   *p ++        = %d", *p++ );
}
```

12.19 PROGRAMMING EXERCISES

1. Write a function that takes an array as its argument and returns the largest, smallest and range of its elements.
2. Write a function to compute the roots of a quadratic equation by using call by reference mechanism to pass computed roots to calling function.
3. Write a program that dynamically allocates memory for an array of size *n*, reads elements of array and sorts them in ascending order.
4. Write a function *substr()* whose prototype is given as

```
char *substr(char *str1, char *str2);
```

that scan the first string for the occurrence of a second string, and returns a pointer to the element in the first string where the second string begins. However, if the second string does not occur in the first string, the function should return NULL. Write a program to test the above function.

5. Write a function *replace()* whose prototype is given as

```
int replace(char *str, char c1, char c2);
```

that replace every occurrence of character c1 with character c2, and returns the total replacements made. Write a program to test the above function.

6. Consider the following structure definition:

```
struct BOX {
   char make[25];
   float length, breadth, height;
};
```

Write a function that takes address of the *BOX* structure and returns its volume.

7. Consider the following declaration:

```
struct EMPLOYEE {
   int code;
   char name[31];
   float salary;
};
```

Given that there are *n* (≤50) employees in an organization. Write a program, using pointer notation to access the data of an employee that output the details of the employee having highest salary.

8. "Little Endian" means that the low-order byte of the number is stored in memory at the lowest address, and the high-order byte at the highest address. (The little end comes first.)

For example, a 4 byte *long int*

```
Byte3 Byte2 Byte1 Byte0
```

will be arranged in memory as follows:

```
Base Address+0   Byte0
Base Address+1   Byte1
Base Address+2   Byte2
Base Address+3   Byte3
```

Intel processors (those used in PC's) use "Little Endian" byte order.

"Big Endian" means that the high-order byte of the number is stored in memory at the lowest address, and the low-order byte at the highest address. (The big end comes first.)

Our *long int*, would then be stored as:

```
Base Address+0   Byte3
Base Address+1   Byte2
Base Address+2   Byte1
Base Address+3   Byte0
```

Motorola processors (those used in Mac's) use "Big Endian" byte order.

Write a program in C language to check that whether the computer on which you are working is *little endian* or *big endian*.

9. Consider the following declaration:

```
char *names[]={ "Vimal","Amit","Anuj","Rohit","Abhijit" };
```

Write a program to produce the following output:

```
char *names[]={ "tijihbA","tihoR","junA","timA","lamiV" };
```

10. Write a function *substr()* whose prototype is given as

```
char *substr(char *str1, char *str2);
```

that scan the first string for the occurrence of a second string, and returns a pointer to the element in the first string where the second string begins. However, if the second string does not occur in the first string, the function should return NULL. Write a program to test the above function.

11. Write a function *replace()* whose prototype is given as

```
int replace(char *str, char c1, char c2);
```

that replace every occurrence of character c1 with character c2, and returns the total replacements made. Write a program to test the above function.

❑ ❑ ❑

13 File Handling

Learning Objectives

After reading this chapter, students will have the ability to:

- comprehend the concept of data file and its usefulness
- distinguish between a text file and a binary file
- explain the different steps in processing a file
- explain the opening, reading and writing of files
- describe the variety of library functions available for doing input/ output on files
- write efficient programs for file handling

13.1 INTRODUCTION

The programs described so far, accepts the input data from the keyboard at the time of execution. The main limitation of this approach is that it is very difficult to handle large volume of data. As an example, suppose there are about 100 data items to enter. Some of the problems that may arise are enumerated below:

- It takes lot of time to enter the entire data.
- If the user makes a mistake while entering the data, he has to start from the beginning.
- If the same data is to be processed again at some later stage, again we have to enter it again. That is, for every program run, we have to enter the same data again and again.

Therefore, if the data is entered in computer's memory, checked for its correctness, and finally stored in a disk file, a program can read it directly from the disk and that too at very high speed.

In addition, the output of one program may become input for another program. In such a situation, it is more efficient to store the output of a program in a disk file, which can subsequently be read by other program(s).

A program developed in C language can read and write files in a variety of ways. Each of these ways is described in this chapter in a very simple manner and illustrated with well-designed programming examples.

13.2 STANDARD I/O VERSUS SYSTEM-LEVEL I/O

The are two different ways of file processing. These are known as *standard* I/O (also called *stream* I/O or *high-level* I/O), and *system-level* I/O (also called *low-level* I/O). Though either one of these can handle most of the tasks, still there are many important differences between the two.

The *Standard I/O* is the easiest and most commonly used way of performing file I/O in C programs. The standard I/O system provides a wide variety of operations. A programmer need not be bothered about the details of I/O operations such as buffering, data conversions etc., as all of these operations takes place automatically. It is important to mention here that if a particular version of C language has only one system available for file I/O, then it will be *Standard I/O*.

The *System-level I/O* matches the way the operating system uses for reading and writing files. In system-level I/O, the data cannot be written as individual *characters*, *strings*, or as *formatted data* as is possible using *standard I/O*. In this approach, data can only be written as a buffer full of bytes. Writing a buffer full of data resembles *record I/O* in the *standard I/O* package. However, unlike *standard I/O*, the programmer must set up the buffer for the data, place the appropriate data in the buffer before writing and take it out from the buffer after reading.

In this chapter, we will restrict our discussion to *standard I/O*.

13.3 TEXT MODE VERSUS BINARY MODE

Depending on the way a file is opened for processing, a file can be classified as a *text file* or a *binary file*.

The mode of opening a particular file determines how various details of the file are handled. For example, how *newline character* ('\n') is stored and how *end-of-file* (*EOF*) is indicated. In addition, the numbers in the text format are stored as string of characters, whereas in binary format they are stored the same way as they are stored in computer's main memory.

Newline Character - In C language, the end of a line is signaled by a single character; the *newline character* '\n' with ASCII value 10 decimal. Whereas for storage in the disk, the end of line is marked by two characters, the *carriage return* (CR) with ASCII value 13 decimal and the *linefeed* (LF) with ASCII value 10 decimal which is same as of C's *newline* character.

In a text mode, *newline* character is automatically translated into CR/LF combination before writing to the file. Similarly, while reading a file, the CR/LF combination on the disk is automatically translated back into a *newline* character.

However, in a binary mode, this translation will not take place. Therefore, the *newline character* '\n' will be written as only *linefeed* (LF) character. Similarly, while reading, the combination of CR/LF will be treated as two separate characters as '\r' and '\n' characters.

End-of-File - It is important to understand that *EOF* is not a character. It is actually an integer value sent to the program by the operating system, and is defined in a header file *stdio.h* to have a value of –1. No character with this value is stored in a file on the disk. While creating a file, when the operating system finds the last character to the file has been sent, it transmits the *EOF* signal.

Both in text as well as in binary mode, the system keeps track of the total length of the file and will signal an *EOF* when this length has been reached.

However, in a text mode, a special character, 1A hex (decimal 26) is inserted after the last character in the file. This character can also be used to indicate *EOF*. A character 1A hex can be generated by holding down *Ctrl* and *Z* keys simultaneously (often represented as ^Z) or by typing key F6. If this character is encountered at any point in the file, the read function will return the *EOF* signal to the program.

But in a binary mode, the numbers are stored in binary format. Therefore a number stored in memory may happen to be 1A hex. Thus, if a file is created in binary mode, and your program opens it in text mode for reading, the reading may terminate prematurely.

In text mode, character 1A hex indicates end-of-file, where as in binary mode, it is just as another number.

DIFFERENCES BETWEEN A TEXT FILE AND A BINARY FILE

Text File	Binary File
1. Data is stored using human readable characters.	1. Data is stored in the same format as it is stored in memory.
2. Each line of data ends with a *newline* character.	2. There are no lines or *newline* character.
3. There is a special character called end-of-file (EOF) marker at the end of the file.	3. There is an end-of-file marker at the end of the file, which is usually implementation dependent.

```
int x = 255; char ch = 'A'
```

Text File:

2	5	5	A
00110010	00110101	00110101	01000001
← 255		→	← A →

Binary File:

00000000	11111111	01000001
← 255	→	← A →

Figure 13.1: Text and Binary Files

13.4 STEPS IN PROCESSING A FILE

The processing of a file involves following steps:

1. **Opening a file** — First step in file processing is to open the file in appropriate mode. If you want to read from a file in your program, the file must be opened in the read/input mode. Similarly, if you want to write the output of your program to a file, the file must be opened in the write/output mode. However, there may be cases when you want to read from and also write onto the same file, then file must be opened in read-write mode.
2. **Reading from or writing onto a file** — Once a file is opened successfully, data can be read from a file or written to a file in a variety of ways that are described in next sections.
3. **Closing the file** — This is the final step in file processing. Once we have completed the reading and writing of the files, each file must be closed.

13.4.1 Opening a File

Before a program can write to a file or read from a file, the program must open it. Opening a file establishes an understanding between the program and the operating system. This provides the operating system with the *name* of the file and the *mode* in which the file is to be opened, *i.e.*, whether for reading or writing and that too in text mode or binary mode. Communication areas are set up between the file and the program. One of these areas is a structure of type *FILE*, declared in header file named *stdio.h* that holds information about the file.

For example, the statement

```
fptr = fopen( "test.dat", "w" );
```

request the operating system to open a file named *test.dat* in text mode and prepare it for writing.

Table 13.1: File Opening Modes

Mode	Purpose
rt	Open a text file for reading. The file must already exist.
wt	Open a text file for writing. If the file already exists, its contents will be discarded. If it does not exist, it will be created.
at	Open a text file for extending. Data will be added to the end of the existing file, if file already exists. If it does not exist, it will be created.
rb	Open a binary file for reading. The file must already exist.

Table 13.1: File Opening Modes *contd.*

Mode	Purpose
wb	Open binary file for writing. If the file already exists, its contents will be overwritten. If it does not exist, it will be created.
ab	Open binary file for extending. Data will be added to the end of the existing file, if file already exists. If it does not exist, it will be created.
rt+ or *r+t*	Open a text file for both reading and writing. The file must already exist.
wt+ or *w+t*	Open a text file for both reading and writing. If it does not exist, it will be created.
at+ or *a+t*	Open a text file for both reading and appending. If the file does not exist, it will be created.
rb+ or *r+b*	Open a binary file for both reading and writing. The file must already exist.
wb+ or *w+b*	Open a binary file for both reading and writing. If it does not exist, it will be created.
ab+ or *a+b*	Open a binary file for both reading and appending. If the file does not exist, it will be created.

If text or binary mode is not specified while opening a file, it will be opened in text mode by default.

When the program makes a request to open a file, it receives back a pointer to this particular structure, if the request is granted; otherwise it receives a sentinel value, such as a *NULL* value defined *stdio.h*. Each file opened will have its own *FILE* structure, with a pointer to it. Any program can open any number of files.

Possible Trouble with Opening a File

As mentioned earlier, the request for opening a file may be granted or rejected. In case of rejection, the program will not run and will terminate abnormally. There may be many reasons for the rejection of program request. For example

- Trying to open a file for reading that does not exist.
- Trying to open a file for writing, but sufficient space is not available on the disk.
- Trying to open a file that has been corrupted, etc.

Thus, it is important for the program that uses a disk file to check whether a file has been opened successfully before trying to read from or write onto the file. If the file cannot be opened, *fopen()* function returns a NULL value.

Therefore, a program can check the value returned by the *fopen()* function to determine whether the file is opened successfully or not. Hence, it is always better to write program segment responsible for opening a file as

```
fptr = fopen ( "test.dat", "w" );
if ( fptr == NULL )   {
   printf ( "\nCan't open file test.dat.\n" );
   exit ( 1 );
}
```

In more professional way, the above segment can also be written as

```
if ( ( fptr = fopen( "test.dat", "w" ) ) == NULL ) {
   printf ( "\nCan't open file test.dat.\n" );
   exit ( 1 );
}
```

In the second segment, the *fopen()* function is enclosed in an *if* statement. In above segments, if the function returns NULL, then the message "*Can't open file test.dat*" is printed and the *exit()* function is executed, causing the program to terminate immediately, and avoid the situation of trying to read from or write onto a non-existent file.

13.4.2 Closing a File

When a program has finished with reading/writing of a file, it must be closed. This task is carried out by using *fclose()* library function, whose syntax is

```
fclose( fptr );
```

where *fptr* is a file pointer associated with a file which is to be closed.

Closing a file explicitly has two effects. These are

- Any data remaining in the buffer is written to the file. It may be noted that the buffer used is invisible to the programmer.
- Frees the communication areas used by the particular file so that they are available for other files. These areas include the *FILE* structure and the buffer itself.

For all possible ways of reading & writing, way of opening and closing a file is same.

Why buffer is required?

A *buffer* is a temporary storage area in main memory. A buffer is necessary even if it is invisible. To visualize its importance, let us consider a particular example. Suppose our program accesses the disk to read/write one character at a time. The disk system takes some time to position the head on the correct track and then further waits for the correct sector of the track to come around. For every read/write operation, the motor that rotates the disk actually has to start from a stand still. If you type several characters repeatedly, and each one requires a separate disk access, some of the characters would probably be lost. So this approach will be inefficient. To solve this problem, the buffer is used.

When a program writes data to a file, it is actually stored in a buffer rather than being written immediately to the disk. When the buffer is full, its contents are written to the disk all at once, and subsequent writes continue onto the buffer. Similarly, when a program reads data from a file, a block of data, equal to the size of buffer except the last block, is read from the disk file and is placed in the buffer. The input functions subsequently read data from a buffer. When a program attempts to read a data item that is not in buffer, it forces to read another block of data containing the requested data item.

13.4.3 Reading and Writing of Files

There is a variety of ways of reading data from a file and writing data to a file. These are enumerated below:

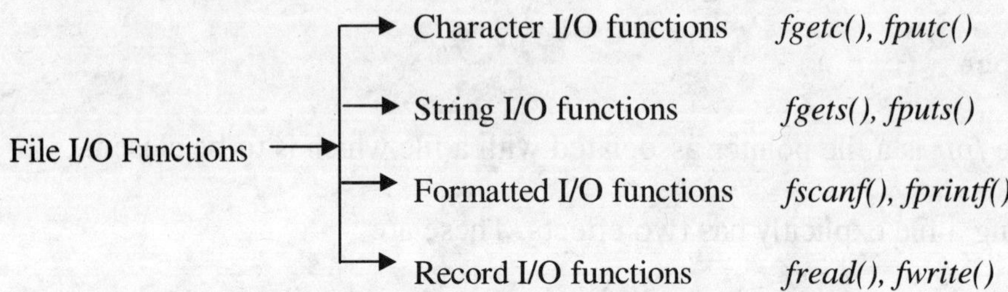

13.4.3.1 Reading and Writing using Character I/O Functions

Using character I/O functions, data can be read or written one character at a time. This is analogous to the way functions *putchar()* and *getchar()* write data to screen and read data from the keyboard.

Writing to a file

Once the program has established a line of communication with a particular file by opening it, then it can write to the file. The syntax of function that writes one character at a time is

```
fputc( ch, fptr );
```

where *ch* is a character variable or constant, and *fptr* is a file pointer.

The *fputc()* function is similar to *putchar()* function, the only difference is that a *putchar()* function always writes to screen unless redirection is employed. The following listing shows the example of a program that accepts a line of text from keyboard, one character at a time, and writes into disk file named *file1.dat*.

Listing 13.1

```
/*
 * Program to demonstrate writing of one character at a time to
file
 */
#include<stdio.h>
void main()
{
   FILE *fptr;
   char ch;
   fptr = fopen( "file1.dat", "w" );
   if ( fptr == NULL )
   {
      printf( "\nUnable to open file1.dat\n" );
      return;
   }
   printf( "\nType a line of text, when finished" );
   printf( ", when finished hit Enter key\n" );
   while ( ( ch = getche() ) != '\r' )
      fputc ( ch, fptr );
   fclose( fptr );
}
```

When the above program is executed, it prompts the user to type a line of text. When you have finished, you hit the Enter (↵) key to terminate the program.

Test Run

```
C is a powerful procedural language. It provides both low-level
as well as high level features. ↵
```

Reading from a file

If the program can write to a file, it should also be able to read from a file. The syntax of the function that reads and returns one character at a time is

```
ch = fgetc( fptr );
```

where *ch* is a character variable, and *fptr* is a file pointer.

The *fgetc()* function returns the character read from the file or the end-of-file (EOF) character if it has reached the end of the file. The *fgetc()* function is similar to *getchar()* function, the only difference is that the later functions always read from the keyboard unless redirection is employed. The following listing shows the example of a program that reads one character at a time from file, and writes onto the screen.

Listing 13.2

```
/*
 * Program to demonstrate reading of character at a time from a
file
 */
#include<stdio.h>
#include<stdlib.h>
void main()
{
   FILE *fptr;
   char ch;
   fptr = fopen( "file1.dat", "r" );
   if ( fptr == NULL ) {
      printf( "\nUnable to open file1.dat\n" );
      return;
   }
   printf( "\nContens of file are:\n\n" );
   while ( ( ch = fgetc (fptr) ) != EOF )
      putchar( ch );
   fclose( fptr );
}
```

When the above program is executed, it reads the contents of file *file1.dat*, one character at a time and writes onto screen till it encounters the end-of-file (EOF).

Test Run

```
Contents of file are:

C is a powerful procedural language. It provides both low-level
as well as high level features.
```

13.4.3.2 Reading and Writing using String I/O functions

Using string I/O functions, data can be read or written in the form of string of characters. Reading and writing strings of characters is as easy as individual characters. This is analogous to *puts()* and *gets()* functions that write data to screen and read data from the keyboard.

Writing to a file

The syntax of the function that writes a string of characters at a time is

```
fputs( str, fptr );
```

where *str* is a array of characters or a string constant, and *fptr* is a file pointer.

The *fputs()* function is similar to *puts()* function, the only difference is that the *puts()* function always writes to the screen unless redirection is employed. The following listing shows the example of a program that accepts a series of strings from keyboard, and writes them onto a disk file.

Listing 13.3

```
/*
*  Program to demonstrate writing of strings to a file
*/
#include<stdio.h>
#include<string.h>
void main()
{
   FILE *fptr;
   char str[81];
   fptr = fopen( "file2.dat", "w" );
   if ( fptr == NULL )
   {
      printf( "\nUnable to open file2.dat\n" );
      return;
   }
   printf( "\nEnter a set of strings, press just" );
   printf( " Enter key to finish\n" );
   while ( strlen( gets( str ) ) > 0 ) {
      fputs( str, fptr );
      fputs( "\n", fptr );
   }
   fclose( fptr );
}
```

Test Run

```
C is a powerful procedural language.↵
It is a middle level language.↵
All Programs are tested using Turbo C Compiler.↵
↵
```

When the above program is executed, it accepts set of strings terminated by hitting *Enter* key. When you have finished, hit the *Enter* key in the beginning without entering anything, which is taken as string of length 0 i.e. *null string*, to terminate the program.

In the above program, we have set up an array of characters to store the string. The *fputs()* function then writes the contents of the array to the disk. Since *fputs()* function does not add a *newline* character automatically to the end of the string, we must do this explicitly to make it easier to read the string back from the file.

Reading from a file

The syntax of the function that reads strings from a file is

```
fgets( str, n, fptr );
```

where *str* is an array of characters and specifies the address where the string is to be stored, *n* is the maximum length of the input string, and *fptr* is a file pointer.

The *fgets()* function is similar to *gets()* function, the only difference is that the *gets()* function always reads from keyboard unless redirection is employed. The *fgets()* function returns a *NULL* value when it reads end-of-file *EOF*. The following listing shows the example of a program that reads one string at a time from a file, and writes onto the screen.

Listing 13.4

```
/*
*  Program to demonstrate reading of strings from a file
*/
#include<stdio.h>
#include<string.h>
void main()
{
   FILE *fptr;
   char str[81];
   fptr = fopen( "file2.dat", "r" );
   if ( fptr == NULL ) {
      printf( "\nUnable to open file2.dat\n" );
```

```
        return;
    }
    printf( "\nContens of file are:\n\n" );
    while ( fgets( str, 80, fptr ) != NULL )
        puts( str );
    fclose( fptr );
}
```

When the above program is executed, it reads the contents of *file3.dat* one string at a time and writes them onto the screen till it encounters EOF.

Test Run

```
Contents of file are:

C is a powerful procedural language.
It is a middle level language.
All Programs are tested using Turbo C Compiler.
```

13.4.3.3 Reading and Writing using Formatted I/O functions

So far we have considered reading and writing of characters, strings, and integer numbers. *What about the real numbers*? and *What about the mixed type of data*? For example, suppose that we want to store information about an agent comprising his name (a string), code number (an integer number), and height (a real number). We want to create a data file for a given list of agents. This can be done using formatted I/O functions.

Writing to a file

The syntax of the function that writes formatted data to a file is

```
fprintf( fptr, "format-string" , ditems );
```

where *fptr* is a file pointer, and *ditems* is a lists of variables to be written to a file. The *fprintf()* is similar to *printf()* function, the only difference is that *printf()* function writes formatted data onto the screen.

Listing 13.5

```
/*
*  Program to demonstrate writing of formatted
*  data to a file
*/
#include<stdio.h>
void main()
```

```
{
   FILE *fptr;
   char yes_no;
   char name[41];
   int code;
   float height;
   fptr = fopen( "file3.dat", "w" );
   if ( fptr == NULL )
   {
      printf( "\nUnable to open file3.dat\n" );
      return;
   }
   while ( 1 )
   {
      printf( "\nEnter name, code number, height" );
      scanf( "%s,%d,%f", name, &code, &height );
      fprintf( fptr,"%s,%d,%f", name, code, height );
      printf( "Any more input y/n?: " );
      yes_no = tolower( getche() );
      fflush ( stdin );
      if ( yes_no == 'n' )
         break;
   }
   fclose( fptr );
}
```

Test Run

```
Enter name, code number, height
Geetu, 10, 160.25
Any more input y/n?: y
Enter name, code number, height
Shivani, 11, 158.5
Any more input y/n?: y
Enter name, code number, height
Vijay, 12, 165.5
Any more input y/n?: y
Enter name, code number, height
Gurpreet, 13, 166.25
Any more input y/n?: n
```

The above information is now in a file named *file3.dat*. If we attempt to look at it using TYPE command, the entire output will be on the same line as there are no *newlines* in the data. To format the output more conveniently, we can write a program specifically to read the above file using formatted input.

Reading from a file

The syntax of the function that reads formatted data to a file is

```
fscanf( fptr, "format-string" , ditems );
```

where *fptr* is a file pointer, and *ditems* is a lists of address where the values read from a file are to be stored.

The *fscanf()* is similar to *scanf()* function, the only difference is that *scanf()* function reads formatted data from the keyboard.

Listing 13.6

```
/* Program to demonstrate writing of formatted from a file  */
#include<stdio.h>
void main()
{
   FILE *fptr;
   char yes_no;
   char name[41];
   int code;
   float height;
   fptr = fopen( "file3.dat", "r" );
   if ( fptr == NULL )
   {
      printf( "\nUnable to open file3.dat\n" );
      return;
   }
   printf( "\nContens of file are:\n\n" );
   while(fscanf(fptr,"%s,%d %f", name, &code, &height) != EOF)
   {
      printf( "%s %d %f\n", name, code, height );
   }
   fclose( fptr );
}
```

Test Run

```
Contents of file are:

Geetu 10 160.25
Shivani 11 158.5
Vijay 12 165.5
Gurpreet 13 166.25
```

13.4.3.4 Reading and Writing using Record I/O functions

We have seen that *character I/O* and *string I/O* permits reading and writing of character data only, whereas the *formatted I/O* permit reading and writing of character data as well as numeric data. However, the numbers are stored as sequence of characters, not the way they are stored in memory.

This way of storing numbers takes lot of disk space. In addition to that, these methods provide no direct way to read and write complex data types such as arrays and structures. Though, the arrays and structures can be handled by reading and writing each array element one at a time, but this approach is very inefficient.

Solution to these problems is *record I/O*, sometimes called *block* I/O. Record I/O writes numbers to disk files in binary format, so that integers are stored in two bytes, long integers are stored in four bytes, single precision floating point numbers in four bytes, and double precision floating point numbers in eight bytes — *the same format used to store numeric data in memory.*

Record I/O also permits reading and writing of data at once; the process is not limited to a single character or string or the few values. In fact, arrays, structures, array of structures can be read and written as a unit.

Writing to a file

The syntax of the function that writes block of data at a time is

```
fwrite( ptr, m, n, fptr );
```

where *ptr* is an address of an array or a structure to be written, *m* is the size of an array or a structure, *n* is the number of such arrays or structures to be written, and *fptr* is a file pointer of a opened in binary mode for writing. After writing the block, *fwrite()* function returns the number of data items actually written. If the number of items written is less than requested, it means some error has occurred. The usage of *fwrite()* function is illustrated in the following programs.

Writing Arrays

Suppose we want to store an integer array *a* having 10 elements to a file named *file4.dat.*

Listing 13.7

```
/* Program to demonstrate writing of an entire array to a file */
# include <stdio.h>
```

```
void main()
{
   FILE *fptr;
   int i, a[10];
   fptr = fopen( "file4.dat", "wb" );
   if ( fptr == NULL ) {
      printf( "\nUnable to open file4.dat\n" );
      return;
   }
   printf( "\nEnter ten values, one per line\n" );
   for ( i = 0; i <= 10; i++ )
      scanf( "%d", &a[i] );
   fwrite(a, sizeof(a), 1, fptr); /* write entire array to file */
   fclose( fptr );
}
```

When executed, this program will prompt the user to enter ten integer values, and then writes the entire array to the disk file named *file4.dat*.

Writing Structures

Suppose, we want to write a structure named *agent* whose elements are — *name* (maximum of 40 characters), *code* (maximum of 5 characters), and *height* (a real number) to a disk file named *file5.dat*.

Listing 13.8

```
/* Program to demonstrate writing of an entire structure to a file */
#include<stdio.h>
struct
{
   char name[41];
   char code[6];
   float height;
} agent;
void main()
{
   FILE *fptr;
   char yes_no, numstr[40];
   fptr = fopen( "file5.dat", "wb" );
   if ( fptr == NULL ) {
      printf( "\nUnable to open file5.dat\n" );
      return;
   }
   while ( 1 ) {
      printf( "\nEnter name : " );
      gets( agent.name );
      printf( "\nEnter code number : " );
      gets( agent.code );
```

```
        printf( "\nEnter height : " );
        gets( numstr );
        agent.height = atof ( numstr );
        fwrite( &agent, sizeof(agent), 1, fptr );
        printf( "Any more input y/n?: " );
        yes_no = tolower( getche() );
        fflush( stdin );
        if ( yes_no == 'n' )
            break;
    }
    fclose( fptr );
}
```

When executed, this program will prompt the user to enter the particulars of an agent, stores them in a structure and then writes this structure to the disk file named *file5.dat* in a single write operation.

Suppose *agent*, instead of a structure variable is an array of structures with *n* elements, and we want to write the entire array in a single write operation.

This task can be accomplished by writing the *fwrite()* function as

```
fwrite( agent, sizeof(agent[0]), n, fptr );
```

The above program demonstrates another way of performing input of numeric data. The numeric data can also read as a string and converted later on to the appropriate value. The library function *atoi()* converts a integer string to integer value, where as the function *atof()* converts a real string to real number. There counter parts are *itoa()* and *fcvt()* which converts an integer value and a real value to the appropriate string, respectively. These functions are defined in header files *stdlib.h*. The question may arise — *Why these conversions are required*?

There are two reasons for this.

- Some times we may need to combine a numeric value with a string, and this will be possible only if the numeric value is converted into a string.
- The C system is very inconsistent with the input of real numbers with *scanf()* function. Sometimes it gives error message — *floating point format not linked.*

Another function used in the above program is *fflush()* function. This function is used to flush the undesired data that may be left in keyboard buffer. You may have observed that sometimes the system did not stop for a particular input in response to a call to some input function. This is because of some undesired data that is left in the keyboard buffer. So we can flush it before taking next input using the *fflush()* function.

Reading from a file

The syntax of the function that reads a block from a file is

```
fread( ptr, m, n, fptr );
```

where *ptr* is an address of an array or a structure where block will be stored after reading, *m* is the size of an array or a structure to be read, *n* is the number of such arrays or structures to be read, and *fptr* is a file pointer of a file opened in binary mode for reading. The *fread()* function returns the number of actual data items read. The usage of this function is illustrated in next program.

Listing 13.9

```
/* Program to demonstrate reading of entire structure from a file */
#include<stdio.h>
struct
{
   char name[41];
   char code[6];
   float height;
} agent;
void main()
{
   FILE *fptr;
   int record_no = 0;
   fptr = fopen( "file5.dat", "rb" );
   if ( fptr == NULL )
   {
      printf( "\nUnable to open file5.dat\n" );
      return;
   }
   while ( fread(&agent,sizeof(agent),1,fptr) > 0 )
   {
      printf( "\nRecord #%d\n", record_no );
      printf( "\nName : %s", agent.name );
      printf( "\nCode number : %s", agent.code );
      printf( "\nHeight : %.2f", agent.height );
      record_no++;
      printf("\n\nPress any key to see next record..." );
      getch();
   }
   fclose( fptr );
}
```

The above program reads the data file created by the program listing 13.8. It reads one structure at a time and display onto the screen. The *while* loop will terminate when *fread()* function returns value 0, which means it is not able to read a block. This indicates end of file.

13.5 FILE STATUS FUNCTIONS

The C language provides following three functions to handle file status queries:

- Function *eof()* to test end of file.
- Function *ferror()* to test error.
- Function *clearerr()* to clear error.

13.5.1 Test End of File: *feof()* Function

The *feof()* function is used to check if the end of file has been reached. If the file pointer is at the end, *i.e.*, all data have been read, the function returns 1. If the end of file is not reached, it returns value 0. The prototype for *feof()* is

```
int feof(FILE *stream);
```

where *stream* is a file pointer for the currently opened file.

13.5.2 Test Error: *ferror()* Function

The *ferror()* function is used to test the error status of file. As mentioned earlier, errors can be created for many reasons, ranging from bad media (disk, CD, etc.) to illegal operations such as trying to read a file in the write state. If the *ferror()* function returns 1 if an error has occurred after a file operation. If no error has occurred, the file ferror() returns value 0. The prototype for *ferror()* is

```
int ferror(FILE *stream);
```

where *stream* is a file pointer for the currently opened file.

It is important to note here that testing for an error does not reset the error condition. Once an error has occurred, it can only return to normal read or write state after clearing the error state using *clearer()* function, described next.

13.5.3 Clear Error: *clearerr()* Function

When an error occurs, the subsequent calls to the *ferror()* function return 1, until the error status of the file is reset. The *clearerr()* function is used for this purpose.

The prototype for *clearerr()* is

```
void clearerr(FILE *stream);
```

where *stream* is a file pointer for the currently opened file.

It is important to note here that even though we have cleared the error, we have not necessarily cured the problem. We may find that subsequent read or write operation may return to error state.

13.6 FILE POSITIONING FUNCTIONS

The C language provides following three functions to handle file positioning operations:

- Function *rewind()* to set the file pointer to the beginning of the file.
- Function *ftell()* to know the current position of the file pointer in the file.
- Function *seek()* to change the position of the file pointer in the file.

13.6.1 Rewind File: *rewind()* Function

One way of positioning the file pointer to the beginning of the file is to close the file and then re-open it again. However, we can accomplish the same task without closing the file using *rewind()* function. This function positions the file pointer in the beginning of the file. This function sounds very much like rewinding the audio or video cassette in order to listen or watch the cassette from the beginning.

The prototype of *rewind()* function is

```
void rewind(FILE *stream);
```

where *stream* is a file pointer for the currently opened file.

13.6.2 Current Location: *ftell()* Function

In some situations, it may be required to find the current location of the file pointer within the file. The *ftell()* function lets us know the current position of the file pointer.

The prototype of the *ftell()* function is

```
long int ftell(FILE *stream);
```

where *stream* is a file pointer for the currently opened file. Note that the *ftell()* function returns a long integer. This is necessary because many files may have more that 32, 767 bytes of data.

Recall that the C I/O system considers files as streams of bytes of data. It measures the position in the file by the number of bytes, relative to zero, *i.e.*, from the beginning of the file. When file pointer is at the beginning of the file, the *ftell()* function returns 0. If the file pointer is at the second byte, the *ftell()* function returns value 1.

13.6.3 Set Position: *fseek()* Function

In order to read a data item from anywhere in a file, we have to move the file pointer to the beginning of that data item. To accomplish this task, we can use *fseek()* function. The syntax of using *fseek()* function is

```
int fseek(file *stream, long offset, int wherefrom );
```

The *fseek()* function takes three arguments, where the first argument *stream* is a file pointer, the second argument *offset* is variable of type *long integer* that specifies the number of bytes by which file pointer is to moved, and third argument *wherefrom* specifies from which position the *offset* is measured. The various values for argument *wherefrom* are listed in Table 13.2.

Table 13.2: Various Values of *wherefrom* for *fseek()* function

Mode	Offset is measured from
0	Beginning of the file
1	Current position of the file
2	End of the file

Table 13.3: Some examples illustrating the use of *fseek()* functions

Seek Call	Action performed
`fseek(fptr, 0, 0);`	Moves the file pointer *fptr* to the beginning of the file. If file pointer is currently at beginning of file, it results in no action.
`fseek(fptr, n, 0);`	Moves the file pointer *fptr* forward by *n* bytes, *i.e.*, move the file pointer to (*n*+1)th bytes in the file.
`fseek(fptr, -n, 1);`	Moves the file pointer *fptr* backward by *n* bytes from current position.
`fseek(fptr, 0, 2);`	Moves the file pointer *fptr* to the end of the file. If file pointer is currently at end of file, it results in no action.

Table 13.3: Some examples illustrating the use of *fseek()* functions *contd*

Seek Call	Action performed
`fseek(fptr, 0, 2);`	Moves the file pointer *fptr* to the end of the file. If file pointer is currently at end of file, it results in no action.
`fseek(fptr, n, 1);`	Moves the file pointer *fptr* forward by *n* bytes from the current position.
`fseek(fptr, 1, 1);`	Moves the file pointer *fptr* to the next byte.
`fseek(fptr, -1, 1);`	Moves the file pointer *fptr* to the previous byte.
`fseek(fptr, m, 2);`	Moves the file pointer *fptr* backward by *m* bytes from end of the file.

13.7 DIRECT/RANDOM ACCESS

In all the previous programs, the reading and writing has been sequential. While writing to a file, data items (which may be a character, a string, an array or a structure) are placed one after the other in a sequence. Similarly, while reading from a file, the data items are read from the beginning of the file in sequence until we came to the end of the file is reached.

It is also possible to access a particular data item that may be in the middle of the file. This way of accessing a file is called *direct accessing* or *random accessing*. The only restriction for direct/random addressing is that all the data items must be of same size, *i.e.*, record length must be of fixed size.

File Pointer

Before going ahead with direct accessing, let us first familiarize ourselves with the file pointers. A *file pointer* is a pointer to a particular byte in a file. Every time, when we write to a file, the file pointer moves to the end of the data item written so that writing can continue from that point. When a file is closed, and subsequently opened for reading, the file pointer is set to the beginning of the file. So we can read the file from beginning. After reading a data item, the file pointer moves to the beginning of the next data item, which can be subsequently be read. However, if the file is opened in append mode, then the file pointer will be positioned at the end of the exiting file, so that new data items can be written from there onwards.

Listing 13.10

```
/* Program to demonstrate reading data randomly from a file */

#include<stdio.h>
struct {
   char name[41];
   char code[6];
```

```
   float height;
} agent;
void main()
{
   FILE *fptr;
   char yes_no, numstr[40];
   long offset;
   int record_no = 0;
   fptr = fopen( "file12.dat", "wb" );
   if ( fptr == NULL ) {
       printf( "\nUnable to open file12.dat\n" );
       return;
   }
   printf( "\nEnter some records of agents," );
   printf( "\nwhich can be accessed later" );
   printf( "\non by their record number." );
   printf( "\n\nRemember that records are numbered" );
   printf( " from 0 onwards" );
   while ( 1 )
   {
       printf( "\n\nRecord #%d", record_no );
       printf( "\n\nEnter name : " );
       gets( agent.name );
       printf("Enter code number (5 character): ");
       gets( agent.code );
       printf( "Enter height : " );
       scanf( "%f", &agent.height );
       if ( fwrite(&agent,sizeof(agent),1,fptr) <= 0 ) {
           printf( "\nDisk write error\n" );
           return;
       }
       printf( "\nAny more input y/n?: " );
       yes_no = tolower( getche() );
       fflush ( stdin );
       if ( yes_no == 'n' )
           break;
       record_no++;
   }
   fclose( fptr );
   fptr = fopen( "file12.dat", "rb" );
   if ( fptr == NULL ) {
       printf( "\nUnable to open file12.dat\n" );
       return;
   }
   while ( 1 )
   {
      printf( "\nEnter the record to accessed: " );
      scanf( "%d", &record_no );
      offset = ( long ) record_no * sizeof(agent);
      fseek( fptr, offset, 0 );
      if ( fread(&agent,sizeof(agent),1,fptr) == 0 ) {
          printf( "\nDisk read error or record#" );
          printf( " out of range\n" );
          return;
      }
```

```
        printf( "\nThe Particulars of the agent are\n" );
        printf( "\nName : %s", agent.name );
        printf( "\nCode number : %s", agent.code );
        printf( "\nHeight : %.2f", agent.height );
        printf( "\n\nAny more record to access y/n?: " );
        yes_no = tolower( getche() );
        fflush ( stdin );
        if ( yes_no == 'n' )
            break;
        rewind( fptr );
    }
    fclose( fptr );
}
```

The program first permits the user to create a binary file with some records. Then, the user can access any record by giving the record number of that particular record.

13.8 FILE UPDATION

The most usual way of updating a sequential file is to read data items from one file, update the required data items and write onto a new file. This is illustrated below by an example. We have with us a file containing students' awards in five subjects namely *English*, *Maths*, *Physics*, and *Chemistry*. It is decided that those students who had secured less than 50 marks in English are to be given 5 grace marks.

Listing 13.11

```
/* Program to demonstrate updation of a file while
   creating a new file  */
#include<stdio.h>
struct  {
   int roll_no;
   float eng_marks;
   float math_marks;
   float phy_marks;
   float chem_marks;
} student;
void main()
{
   FILE *fptr1, *fptr2;
   fptr1 = fopen ( "oldfile.dat", "rb" );
   if ( fptr1 == NULL ) {
      printf ( "\nUnable to open oldfile.dat\n" );
      return;
   }
   fptr2 = fopen ( "newfile.dat", "wb" );
   if ( fptr2 == NULL ) {
      printf ( "\nUnable to open newfile.dat\n" );
      return;
   }
```

```
    while ( ( fread(&student, sizeof (student), 1, fptr1 ) > 0 ) )
    {
        if ( student.eng_marks < 50 )
            student.eng_marks += 5;
        fwrite (&student,sizeof(student),1,fptr2);
    }
    fclose ( fptr1 );    /*  close files    */
    fclose ( fptr2 );
}
```

Since C language permits reading and writing of files at the same time, so instead of creating a new updated file, the data items can be updated in the original file.

Listing 13.12

```
/*  Program to demonstrate updation of a file without
    creating a new file */
#include<stdio.h>
struct {
    int roll_no;
    float eng_marks;
    float math_marks;
    float phy_marks;
    float chem_marks;
} student;
void main()
{
    FILE *fptr;
    fptr = fopen ( "datafile.dat", "rb+" );
    if ( fptr == NULL ) {
       printf ( "\nUnable to open datafile.dat\n" );
       return;
    }
    while ( (fread( &student, sizeof(student), 1, fptr ) ) > 0 ) {
        if ( student.eng_marks < 50 ) {
            student.eng_marks += 5;
            fseek ( fptr, -(long)sizeof(student),1 );
            fwrite(&student,sizeof(student),1,fptr);
        }
    }
    fclose( fptr );
}
```

We have used the *fseek()* with second argument as a long negative number, which requests the operating system that file pointer is to moved in the backward direction. We know that after reading the current data item, the file pointer is moved to the beginning of the next data item. Since we want to update the current data item, therefore we have to bring back the file pointer to the beginning of the data item to be updated. Thus after modifying the data item in memory, the *fwrite()* function overwrites the existing data item with the modified one.

In C language, files can also be updated in a random manner. The only thing required is that we must know the record number of the data item(s) to be updated. If we know the record number of the data item, we can access it directly, and after modifying the data item, we can write it back.

Deletion of a data item(s) in the file itself is not possible. To delete a data item, we have to create a new file that contains all the data items of the original file except the data item to be deleted.

13.9 WORKING WITH STANDARD FILES

In standard I/O, to perform reading or writing on a file, we use *fopen()*, which sets up a file pointer to the file in question. Under DOS environment, there are five predefined pointers for five standard files. These standard file pointer are defined in header file *stdio.h*. To access these files, there is no need to use *fopen()* function to set up pointers for them. These standard file pointers are shown in Table 13.4.

Table 13.4: Standard File Pointers for DOS Environment

Standard File Pointer	Description
`stdin`	Standard input device (keyboard)
`stdout`	Standard output device (VDU)
`stderr`	Standard error device (VDU)
`stdaux`	Standard auxiliary device (serial port)
`stdprn`	Standard printing device (parallel printer)

Thus, the following statement

```
ch = fgetc ( stdin )
```

will read a character from the keyboard rather than from a file.

Similarly, the following statement

```
fputc ( ch, stdprn )
```

will print the character on printer rather writing to a file. The following program reads the contents of a file and prints on the printer connected to the parallel port.

Listing 13.13

```
/* Program to illustrate the use of standard file pointers by
*  printing a text file on a parallel printer   */
#include <stdio.h>
void main()
{
```

```
    FILE *fp;
    char ch;
    if ( ( fp = fopen ( "sample.txt", "r" ) ) == NULL ) {
       printf ( "\nUnable to open file sample.txt\n" );
       return;
    }
    while ( ( ch = fgetc ( fp ) ) != EOF )
       fputc ( stdprn );
    fclose ( fp );
}
```

13.10 SUPPLEMENTARY PROBLEMS

Problem 13.1:

Program to find the size of a given file, where the name of the file is given as the command-line argument.

To know the seize of the specified file, position the file pointer at the end of the file using *fseek()* function, and access the value of the file pointer using *ftell()* function that gives the size of the file.

Listing 13.14

```
/* Program to find the size of a given file
   filename : fsize.c    */
#include <stdio.h>
void main ( int argc, char *argv[] )
{
   FILE *fptr;
   fptr = fopen(argv[1], "r");
   if (!fptr)  {
      printf("\nFile %s does not exist\n",   argv[1]);
      return;
   }
   fseek(fptr, 0L, 2);
   printf("\nSize of file = %ld bytes.\n", ftell(fptr));
   fclose(fptr);
}
```

Test Run

```
>fszie fsize.c↵
Size of file = 387 bytes.
```

The above test run shows that the size of the program file (source code) created in Listing 13.14 is 387 bytes.

Problem 13.2:

Write a program that read some text from the keyboard and write it into a file named TEXT. Program then reads this file and displays its contents on screen.

Listing 13.15

```
/* Program that creates a file and then reads its contents and
*  display them on the computer screen  */
#include <stdio.h>
void main()
{
   char ch;
   FILE *fp1;
   fp1 = fopen("TEXT", "w");     /*  open file for writing  */
   if ( fp1 == NULL ) {
      printf("\nUnable to open file TEXT for writing\n");
      return;
   }
   printf("\nType some text and terminate");
   printf(" the input by Enter key\n\n");
   while ( ( ch = getche() ) != '\r' )
      fputc(ch, fp1);
   fclose(fp1);    /*  close file  */
   fp1 = fopen("TEXT", "r");     /*  open file for reading  */
   if ( fp1 == NULL )
   {
      printf("\nUnable to open file TEXT for reading\n");
      return;
   }
   printf("\n\nContents of file TEXT are\n\n");
   while ( !feof(fp1) )
   {
      ch = fgetc(fp1);
      putchar(ch);
   }
   fclose(fp1);
}
```

Test Run

```
Type some text and terminate the input by Enter key

Don't do any thing with others which you wish other should not
do with you.↵

Contents of file TEXT are

Don't do any thing with others which you wish other should not
do with you.
```

Problem 13.3:

Write a program to copy the contents of one file to another file byte-by-byte. The names of the files are taken as command line arguments.

Listing 13.16

```
/* Program to copy the contents of a given file to another file.
   filename : kopy1.c    */
#include <stdio.h>
void main(int argc, char *argv[])
{
   char ch;
   FILE *fp1, *fp2;
   fp1 = fopen(argv[1], "r");
   if ( fp1 == NULL ) {
      printf("\nUnable to open file: %s for reading\n", argv[1]);
      return;
   }
   fp2 = fopen(argv[2], "w");
   if ( fp2 == NULL ) {
      printf("\nUnable to open file: %s for writing\n", argv[2]);
      return;
   }
   while ( !feof(fp1) ) {
      ch = fgetc(fp1);
      fputc(ch, fp2);
   }
   fclose(fp1);
   fclose(fp2);
}
```

Test Run

```
>kopy1 kopy1.c kk
>
```

You can verify that the contents of file *kk* will be same as that of *kopy1.c*.

Problem 13.4:

Write a C program to reverse the first *n* characters in a file. The *file name* and *n* are specified on the command line.

Listing 13.17

```
/* Program to copy contents of a given file to another file.
  filename : kopy2.c    */
```

```
#include <stdio.h>
void main(int argc, char *argv[])
{
   char *str, ch;
   int i, n;
   FILE *fp1;
   fp1 = fopen(argv[1], "r+");
   if ( fp1 == NULL ) {
      printf("\nUnable to open file: %s for reading\n", argv[1]);
      return;
   }
   i = 0;
   n = atoi(argv[2]);
   str = ( char * ) malloc ( n * sizeof(char) );
   while ( ( !feof(fp1) ) && ( i < n ) ) {
      ch = fgetc(fp1);
      str[i] = ch;
      i++;
   }
   rewind(fp1); /* reposition the file pointer to the beginning */
   i = n-1;
   while ( i >= 0 ) {
      fputc( str[i], fp1);
      i--;
   }
   fclose(fp1);
}
```

Test Run

```
Original Contents of file test.dat
1234567890abcdefghijklmnopqrstuvwxyz

>kopy2 test.dat 5
>

New Contents of file test.dat
5432167890abcdefghijklmnopqrstuvwxyz
```

You can verify that the contents of the file after program execution by using type command on the command prompt.

In the above program, first the given file is opened in read/write mode. Next, first *n* bytes of the file are copied in dynamically allocated character array. Next we rewind the given file, *i.e.*, reposition the file pointer at the beginning of the file. Finally, we write the contents of the character array in reverse order onto the file. Thus, we are able to accomplish the desired task.

13.11 QUICK RECAP

In this chapter, we have learnt that

- If volume of the input data is very large, it can be best handled using data files.
- If the data generated by some instrument is in machine-readable form (binary form), then you have to use data file to pass on this data to your program.
- If the volume of output is large and can't be viewed on the screen properly, it is better to write the output to a data file that you can refer any time without re-executing your program.
- If the output generated by one program is to be used as input for another program, again the use of data files will be advantageous.
- A data file can be a text file or a binary file.

13.12 MULTIPLE CHOICE QUESTIONS

1. Which of the following is a default file pointer?

   (*a*) stdin (*b*) stdout (*c*) stderr (*d*) All

2. The function *fopen ()* when fails to open file, then it returns value

   (*a*) NULL (*b*) –1 (*c*) Null (*d*) void

3. The function *flose()* is, usually, used to

   (*a*) delete a file (*b*) disconnect file from program
   (*c*) read data from a file (*d*) write data to a file

4. Which of the following values is not a value of *from* in function `fseek(fptr,offset,from)`?

   (*a*) 2 (*b*) 0 (*c*) 1 (*d*) EOF

5. The task performed by function `fseek(fptr,0,0)` is

   (*a*) fclose (fptr) (*b*) ftell (fptr)
   (*c*) search (fptr) (*d*) rewind (fptr)

6. Which of the following is not a valid file opening mode?

   (*a*) r+ (*b*) +r (*c*) r (*d*) rt

7. If letter *b* is suffixed with the file opening mode, what does it convey?

   (*a*) file is to be opened for reading only
   (*b*) file is to be opened for writing only
   (*c*) file is to be opened for both read-write
   (*d*) file is a binary file

8. Consider the following code segment

```
FILE *fp;
fp =  fopen("inventory.dat", "rb");
```

What is the role of letter *b* in "*rb*"?

(*a*) Open *inventory.dat* file in binary mode for reading.
(*b*) Open *inventory.dat* file reading and writing.
(*c*) Create a new file *inventory.dat* for writing.
(*d*) Open *inventory.dat* file in binary mode for writing and reading.

9. Consider the following code segment

```
FILE *fp;
fp =  fopen("notes.txt", "r+");
```

Which of the following operations can be performed on *notes.txt* file?

(*a*) Reading (*b*) Writing (*c*) Appending (*d*) All

13.13 REVIEW EXERCISES

1. Name the various systems for performing file I/O in C.
2. Name the mode for opening a file named *text.dat* in binary mode for reading.
3. Is it is advisable to close a file explicitly opened for writing?
4. Name the function to close a file.
5. What information system gets by opening a file?
6. What you mean by a *file pointer*?
7. How a file opened with *fopen()* function is referred to in a program?
8. What the text and binary modes have to do with files?
9. How data is stored when a file is opened in text mode?
10. How data is stored when a file is opened in binary mode?
11. Suppose a program wants to examine every byte of a file, which mode will be more appropriate?
12. Name the function to write a block of data to a file.
13. What do you mean by term *offset* in reference to a file?
14. What is the task performed by the *fseek()* function?
15. What is the task performed by the *ftell()* function?
16. Which value is returned by the *fopen()* if some error occurs in opening a file?
17. By which method(s), the contents of a file can be altered?
18. What is the difference between *w+* and *r+* modes?

19. What a *rewind()* function does?
20. Explain usefulness of the temporary file, and the way they are used in a C program.
21. Name the standard files and list their file pointers.

13.14 PROGRAMMING EXERCISES

1. Given a text file containing some text. Write a program that prompts the user to input name of a text file, reads this file and outputs the number of vowels and number of words in the text.
2. You are given a binary file named *student.dat* that contains information about some students. The information about each student consists of — his/her roll number (an integer), name (25 characters), father's (25 characters), and address (30 characters). Write a program that permits to modify a student's record, whose roll number is given.
3. You are given a binary file named *student.dat* that contains information about some students. The information about each student consists of his/her roll number (an integer), name (25 characters), father's (25 characters), and address (30 characters). Write a program that permits the user to delete a student's record, whose roll number is given.
4. Given a text file containing some text. Write a program that prompts the user to input name of a text file, reads this file and replaces each occurrence of character 'x' with uppercase 'X'.
5. A beginner to the C language has typed the entire program in uppercase letter. As you know that the normal convention in C language is to type the source code using lowercase letters only except for macros and defined constants. Write a program that converts the source code into lowercase letter. Comments should be left unchanged.
6. We have to maintain a database of members of a club. The information recorded about a member includes his/her membership number (int), name (20 characters), address (40 characters), and telephone number (long integer). Write a menu driven program that permits the user to add members, modify member's information except membership number, delete member from database, and generate a list of members.
7. Write a function that takes two file pointers as its arguments and appends the contents of a second binary file to the first binary files.

❑ ❑ ❑

14 Library Functions and Header Files

Learning Objectives

After reading this chapter, students will have the ability to:

- comprehend the working of variety of library functions provided with the C compilers
- use them efficiently in their programs

14.1 INTRODUCTION

The C language provides a rich collection of pre-written functions, called *standard library functions* or simple *library functions*, whose declarations have been written and are available in the respective header files (**.h*). The machine code of the definitions of these library functions are available in the respective library files (**.lib*). However, it is important to note that the source code of these library functions, in most of the C compilers, is not provided.

As discussed earlier, a function *prototype* (function declaration) specifies the return type and the data types of the arguments. The main purpose of the function prototype is to prevent errors caused by data type mismatches between the values passed to a function and the type of value function is expecting.

The C compiler comes with a number of standard header files. These files contain declarations, definitions, and macros that may be useful to a programmer in certain circumstances. The main reason of using function prototypes is to provide a means of avoiding type mismatches between actual arguments and formal arguments when a user-defined function is accessed. The header files can give the same protection for library functions. Each library function provided with C compiler is associated with a header file. Thus, to ensure that you have not inadvertently called a library function using arguments of wrong data type, you need to include the appropriate header file for the function at the beginning of the program file.

In this chapter, we will discuss some frequently used library functions, which are not discussed earlier and in later chapters. If you remember, we have already used function to handle the input/output of all types from the console (keyboard and monitor/display) in *Chapter 5*. The library function required to perform the input/output from/to files are described in *Chapter 13*. The library function required to manipulate the strings are described in *Chapter 10*.

For using the library functions to perform input/output, you need to include *stdio.h* header file, while using functions to manipulate strings, you need to include *string.h* header file.

14.2 MATHEMATICAL FUNCTIONS

Many library functions are available for important mathematical calculations. Most of the function declarations are found in *math.h* or *stdlib.h*.

Square Root Function - It is declared as

```
double sqrt(double x);
```

It returns positive square root of a number. An error occurs, if the number is negative. For example

`sqrt(49);` returns 7.0.

Power Functions - There are two power functions – *pow* and *pow10*.

Function *pow* is declared as

```
double pow(double x, double y);
```

It returns the value of *x* raised to the power *y*, *i.e.*, x^y. An error occurs, if *x* is negative and *y* is not an integer or *x* is zero and the *y* is not positive. For example

`pow(2,4);` returns 16.0.

Function *pow10* is declared as

```
double pow10(int p);
```

It returns the value of 10 raised to the power *p*, *i.e.*, 10^p. For example

`pow10(2);` returns 100.0.

Exponential Function - It is declared as

```
double exp(double x);
```

It returns the value of e^x. For example

`exp(2.0);` returns 7.39 (rounded to two decimal positions).

Absolute Value Functions - These functions are declared as

```
int abs(int x);
int labs(long x);
int fabs(float x);
```

They return the positive value regardless of the sign. For example

`abs(-7);` returns 7.
`abs(3);` returns 3.
`fabs(-7.35);` returns 7.35.
`fabs(3.20);` returns 3.20.

Ceiling Function - It is declared as

```
float ceil(float x);
```

It returns the smallest integral value greater than or equal to *x*.

For example

```
ceil(-5.3);
```
returns –5.0.
```
ceil(2.1);
```
returns 3.

Floor Function - It is declared as

```
float floor(float x);
```

It returns the largest integral value less than or equal to *x*. For example

```
floor(-5.3);
```
returns –6.0.
```
floor(2.1);
```
returns 2.

Logarithm Functions - There are two logarithm functions – *log* and *log10*.

Function *log* is declared as

```
double log(double x);
```

It returns the natural logarithm of *x*. An error occurs, if *x* is negative. For example

```
log(2.5);
```
returns 0.916 (rounded to three decimal places).

Function *log10* is declared as

```
double log10(double x);
```

It returns the base 10 logarithm of *x*. For example

```
log10(2.5);
```
returns 0.398 (rounded to three decimal places).

Trigonometric Functions - There are library functions for trigonometric ratios. One of them – the *sin* function is described here. Function *sin* is declared as

```
double sin(double x);
```

It returns the value sine of *x*, where the angle *x* is in radians. For example

```
sin(90);
```
returns 0.894 (rounded to three decimal places).

Polynomial Function - It is declared as

```
double poly(double x, int n, double coeffs[]);
```

It returns the value of polynomial in *x*, of degree *n*, with coefficients *coeffs*[0], *coeffs*[0], *coeffs*[0], …, *coeffs*[*n*]. For example, consider the polynomial as

$5x^2 + 4x + 10$, and we want to evaluate it for $x = 2$.

Here $x = 2$, $n = 2$, *coeffs*[0] = 10, *coeffs*[1] = 4, *coeffs*[2] = 5.

Listing 14.1

```
/* Program to demonstrate the use of some standard mathematical
*  library functions  */

#include<stdio.h>
#include <math.h>
void main()
{
   float x;
   printf("\n  x   ceil(x) floor(x) log(x) sqrt(x) sin(x)\n");
   for ( x = 0.5; x <= 6; x += 0.5 ) {
      printf("%5.2f\t%5.2f\t%5.2f\t%6.2f\t%5.2f\t%5.2f\n",
             x, ceil(x), floor(x), log(x), sqrt(x), sin(x));
   }
}
```

Test Run

```
 x     ceil(x) floor(x) log(x) sqrt(x)  sin(x)
0.50   1.00    0.00    -0.69    0.71    0.48
1.00   1.00    1.00     0.00    1.00    0.84
1.50   2.00    1.00     0.41    1.22    1.00
2.00   2.00    2.00     0.69    1.41    0.91
2.50   3.00    2.00     0.92    1.58    0.60
3.00   3.00    3.00     1.10    1.73    0.14
3.50   4.00    3.00     1.25    1.87   -0.35
4.00   4.00    4.00     1.39    2.00   -0.76
4.50   5.00    4.00     1.50    2.12   -0.98
5.00   5.00    5.00     1.61    2.24   -0.96
5.50   6.00    5.00     1.70    2.35   -0.71
6.00   6.00    6.00     1.79    2.45   -0.28
```

14.3 RANDOM NUMBER GENERATION FUNCTIONS

A random number is a number that is selected from a set of numbers where each number has the same probability of being selected. Random numbers are very useful in many applications such as testing of software to generate test cases and gaming.

Each time a random number function is called, it generates another number. Basically it uses a mathematical function designed in such a way to ensure that each number in the set has the same probability of being selected, in other words to ensure that each number is truly random. As a part of the formula, the function uses the previous number.

Now the point left is the starting number. The starting number is called the *seed.* If no seed is supplied, the default seed (1) supplied by the system is used. However, the user can supply the seed number.

Since the algorithm used is same, it generates the same series of number, called *pseudorandom number series*. Only by using different seeds, we can generate different random series.

Therefore, we can generate the same series of random numbers or different series of random numbers each time we run our program. Some program requires series to be the same in each program run while other requires that each time series should be different.

There are two functions to build random number series – seed random number function (*srand*) and random number function (*rand*). These functions are described below.

Seed Random Number Function - It is declared as

```
void srand(unsigned int seed);
```

To generate the same series of random numbers in each run, either we omit *srand* or we can provide a constant seed, preferably a prime number.

To generate different series of random numbers in each run, we can use the time of the day as the seed. Since time of day keep on changing, so seed will be different for each program run and hence the series generated will be different. The call for the time requires *time.h* header file, and will be used as follows:

```
srand(time(NULL));
```

Random Number Function - It is declared as

```
int rand(void);
```

It returns a pseudorandom integer number between 0 and RAND_MAX, which is defined in the header file *stdlib.h*.

Listing 14.2

```
/* Program to demonstrate the generation of random numbers
 *  without using any seed value   */
#include <stdio.h>
#include <stdlib.h>
void main()
{
    int i;
    printf("\nTen random numbers generated without seed value\n\n");
    for ( i = 0; i < 10; i++ ) {
        printf("%d  ", rand());
    }
    printf("\n");
}
```

Test Runs

First Run

```
Ten random numbers generated without the seed value
```

346 130 10982 1090 11656 7117 17595 6415 22948 31126

Second Run

```
Ten random numbers generated without the seed value
```

346 130 10982 1090 11656 7117 17595 6415 22948 31126

As you must have noticed that, in every program run, the program generated the same sequence of random numbers.

Listing 14.3

```
/*  Program to demonstrate the generation of random numbers
   with system generated seed value from system's time  */
#include <stdio.h>
#include <stdlib.h>
void main()
{
   int i;
   printf("\nTen random numbers generated with seed ");
   print("generated by the system\n\n");
   srand(time(NULL)); /* seed value generated from system's time */
   for ( i = 0; i < 10; i++ )
   {
      printf("%d  ", rand());
   }
   printf("\n");
}
```

Test Runs

First Run

```
Ten random numbers generated with seed value generated by the system
```

6480 4088 13943 26115 15681 28492 15694 20656 24977 6176

Second Run

```
Ten random numbers generated with seed value generated by the system
```

7519 3441 13730 292208 14611 14875 14359 19884 9042 30709

As you must have noticed that, in every program run, the program generated the different sequence of random numbers.

Listing 14.4

```
/* Program to generate a sequence of random numbers in
   the given range. The range is to supplied by the user  */
#include <stdio.h>
#include <stdlib.h>
void main()
{
    int range, num, a, b, i;
    printf("\nTen random numbers in the given range generated\n");
    printf("with seed generated by the system\n\n");
    printf("Enter initial value of the range : ");
    scanf("%d", &a);
    printf("Enter final value of the range   : ");
    scanf("%d", &a);
    printf("\n");
    range = ( b - a ) + 1;
    srand(time(NULL));
    for ( i = 0; i < 10; i++ ) {
        num = rand() % range + a;
        printf("%d  ", num);
    }
    printf("\n");
}
```

Test Run

```
Ten random numbers in the given range generated
with seed generated by the system

Enter initial value of the range : 10
Enter final value of the range   : 20

19  11  17  13  16  20  16  19  12  15
```

14.4 CHARACTER FUNCTIONS

The character functions are classified into two groups – *classifying functions* and *conversions functions*. The prototypes of these functions are in *ctype.h* header file. Before learning about these functions, let us understand the classifications of character that C language uses. This classification is shown below in the form of a tree. You should read the tree much like a structure chart starting at the top and following the branches to the bottom.

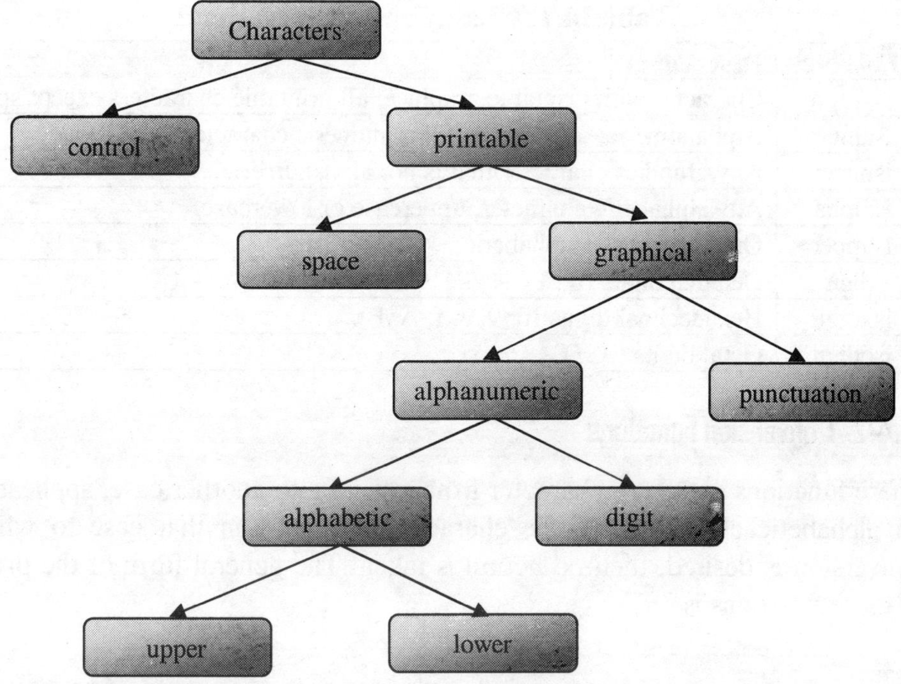

Figure 14.1: Classification of character type in C language

Note that control characters are not printable.

14.4.1 Classifying Functions

There is at least one function for each group. They all start with the prefix *is*. These functions examine a character to find out whether it belongs to the group or not. If it belongs to the group they return value 1 (*true*) else value 0 (*false*).

The general form of the prototype of these functions is

```
int isXXX(int ch);
```

where the function starts with *is* followed with the abbreviated name of the group.

Table14.1: Classifying Functions

Function	Description
iscntrl	Control characters.
isprint	Printable characters.
isspace	Whitespace characters – space character (ASCII code 32), horizontal tab (9), line feed (10), vertical tab (11), form feed (12), and carriage return (13).

Table14.1: Classifying Functions *contd.*

Function	Description
isgraph	Character with printable graphics; all printable characters except space.
isalnum	Alphanumeric: any alphabetic or numeric character.
ispunct	Any graphics character that is not alphanumeric.
isalpha	Any alphabetic character, uppercase or lowercase.
isupper	Only uppercase alphabetic.
isdigit	Decimal digits (0..9.
isxdigit	Hexadecimal digits (0..9, a..f, A..F).
isodigit	Octal digits (0..7).

14.4.2 Conversion Functions

There functions convert a character from one case to another case, applicable only on alphabetic characters. If the character is already in that case to which the conversion is desired, then no action is taken. The general form of the prototype of these functions is

```
int toXXX(int ch);
```

where the function starts with *is* followed with the abbreviated name of the group.

Table14.2: Conversion Functions

Function	Description
tolower	Coverts uppercase to lowercase. If not uppercase, returns it unchanged.
toupper	Coverts lowercase to uppercase. If not lowercase, returns it unchanged.

Listing 14.5

```
/* Program to demonstrate the use of classification and
   conversion functions  */
#include <stdio.h>
#include <ctype.h>
void main()
{
   char ch;
   printf("\nEnter a character to be examined : ");
   ch = getchar();
   if ( iscntrl(ch) )
       printf("\nYou entered a control character.\n");
   else
   {
       printf("\nYou entered a printable character, and \n");
       if ( isspace(ch) )
          printf("it is a space character.\n");
       else if ( isalpha(ch) ) {
```

```
            printf("it is a alphabetic character");
            if ( isupper(ch) )
               printf(", and in uppercase.\n");
            else
               printf(", and in lowercase.\n");
         }
         else if ( isdigit(ch) )
            printf("\nit is a decimal digit.\n");
         else
            printf("\nYou guess the group on your own...\n");
      }
   }
```

Test Runs

First Run

```
Enter a character to be examined : ^C
You entered a control character.
```

Second Run

```
Enter a character to be examined : A
You entered a printable character, and
it is a alphabetic character, and in uppercase.
```

Third Run

```
Enter a character to be examined : 7
You entered a printable character, and
it is a decimal digit.
```

14.5 MAJOR ERROR HANDLING FUNCTIONS

There may be situations when an error occurs but there is no way to recover from it. In that situation, we need to terminate the execution of the program. The C language provide two functions – *exit()* and *abort()*. Prototypes of these functions are in *stdlib.h* header file.

The *exit()* Function - Whereas the *return* statement terminates the function, the *exit()* function terminates the program irrespective of where it is executed in the program. While we use it to terminate the program because we detected an error, C language considers it normal termination. For this reason, termination is orderly as it closes all files, writes buffered output (waiting to be output), and then terminates the program. Prototype of the *exit()* function is as

```
void exit(int status);
```

This function passes the integer value to the operating system. While any integer value is acceptable, the normal practice is to use value 1 to indicate that program did not complete successfully.

The *abort()* Function - The *abort()* function is used to terminate the program abnormally. It is considered a non-orderly termination because the files are not closed and buffered output is not written. When *abort()* function executes, the control is immediately returned to the operating system. Prototype of the *exit()* function is as

```
void abort(void);
```

Turbo C/C++'s IDE provides very good features, and I personally feel every C/C++ programmer must be familiar with it. These features are in the form of on-line help. To know about any library function in detail, just type the name of the function, position the cursor on the name and press Ctrl+F1, you will the entire details. Even the Turbo C++ compiler goes one step further by providing examples that illustrate the use of the functions.

14.6 HEADER FILES

Though there are lots of header files, few of them that are frequently used are listed in Table14.3 along with the brief description about their contents.

Table 14.3: Important header files

Header File	Contents
stdio.h	Contains declarations for standard I/O functions.
math.h	Contains declarations for various mathematical functions.
stdlib.h	Contains declarations for various common types, variables, and functions.
conio.h	Contains declarations for various functions for console I/O operations.
string.h	Contains declarations for various functions for manipulating strings.
graphics.h	Contains declarations for various functions for manipulating graphical objects.
alloc.h	Contains declarations for various memory management functions.
bios.h	Contains declarations for various functions for accessing BIOS services.
dir.h	Contains declarations for various structures, macros, and functions for dealing with directories and pathnames.
dos.h	Contains declarations for various structures, unions, macros, and functions for dealing with MSDOS and the Intel iAPX86 microprocessor family.
time.h	Contains declarations for various structures and functions for dealing with time.
ctype.h	Contains definitions for macros for character type.

You may need to refer to the user reference manual provided with the compiler for information about appropriate header files, or you may consult your instructor for information and/or help.

Just to have a feel about the contents of the header files, the partial contents of *math.h* header file, provided with *Turbo C++ Compiler v3.0* as an example, are listed:

Contents of *math.h* header file supplied with Turbo C++ Compiler V3.0

```
/*  math.h

   Definitions for the math floating point package.

   Copyright (c) 1987, 1991 by Borland International
   All Rights Reserved.
*/

#ifndef  __MATH_H
#define  __MATH_H

#if !defined( __DEFS_H )
#include <_defs.h>
#endif

         :

#ifdef __cplusplus
extern "C" {
#endif

double  _Cdecl acos  (double __x);
double  _Cdecl asin  (double __x);
double  _Cdecl atan  (double __x);
double  _Cdecl ceil  (double __x);
double  _Cdecl cos   (double __x);
double  _Cdecl cosh  (double __x);
double  _Cdecl exp   (double __x);
double  _Cdecl fabs  (double __x);
         :
typedef enum
{
   DOMAIN = 1,     /* argument domain error -- log (-1)        */
   SING,           /* argument singularity  -- pow (0,-2))     */
   OVERFLOW,       /* overflow range error  -- exp (1000)      */
   UNDERFLOW,      /* underflow range error -- exp (-1000)     */
   TLOSS,          /* total loss of significance -- sin(10e70) */
   PLOSS,          /* partial loss of signif. -- not used      */
   STACKFAULT      /* floating point unit stack overflow       */
}  _mexcep;

#ifdef __cplusplus
extern "C" {
#endif
int     _Cdecl abs   (int __x);
double  _Cdecl atof  (const char *__s);
         :

long double _Cdecl pow10l (int __p);

#ifdef __cplusplus
   /* use class complex instead of cabs in C++ */
#else
```

```
struct complex        /* as used by "cabs" function */
{
   double  x, y;
};

#define cabs(z)       (hypot  ((z).x,  (z).y))
#define cabsl(z)      (hypotl ((z).x,  (z).y))
#endif

#ifdef __cplusplus
}
#endif

/* Constants rounded for 21 decimals. */
#define M_E           2.71828182845904523536
#define M_PI          3.14159265358979323846
          :
#endif  /* !__STDC__ */

#endif
```

14.7 QUICK RECAP

In this chapter, we have learnt that

- The C language contains a rich collection of library function.
- To use these library functions you need to include appropriate header file in your program.
- The mathematical library contains functions for almost all the mathematical and trigonometric function required for all sort of mathematical computations.
- A random number is a number that is selected from a set of numbers where each number has the same probability of being selected.
- Using the seed value generated from the system's time, we can generate different sequence of random numbers in each program run.
- Character functions can be used to classify the characters and to convert the case of the alphabets.
- In case an error is detected, the program can be terminated using either *exit()* function or *abort()* function.
- The *exit()* function terminates the program in an orderly manner that is with proper clean up.
- The *abort()* function terminates the program in an non-orderly manner that is no clean up task is performed, the control is immediately passed to the operating system.
- Every C compiler is contains a set of header files that contains prototypes of the library functions and other related declarations and definitions.

14.8 MULTIPLE CHOICE QUESTIONS

1. Consider the following segment of code

```
int i;
srand(1);
for ( i = 0; i < 10; i++ ) {
   printf("%d  ", rand());
}
```

   Which of the following statement is true?

   (*a*) In each program run, it produces same sequence of ten random numbers.
   (*b*) In each program run, it produces different sequence of ten random numbers.
   (*c*) All random numbers generated are equally spaced, *i.e.*, interval between successive random numbers is same.
   (*d*) None of above.

2. Which of the following function is used to provide the initial seed value for random number generation?

   (*a*) seed() (*b*) randomize() (*c*) rand() (*d*) srand()

3. Which of the following function can be used whether the given character is a decimal digit or not?

   (*a*) isdecdigit() (*b*) isdecimal() (*c*) IsDigit() (*d*) None

4. Consider the following segment of code

```
int x = -1.75, y;
y = ceil(x);
```

   The value of *y* will be

   (*a*) -1 (*b*) -2 (*c*) -1.5 (*d*) 1

5. Consider the following segment of code

```
int x = -1.25, y;
y = floor(x);
```

   The value of *y* will be

   (*a*) -1 (*b*) -2 (*c*) -1.25 (*d*) 1

6. Which of the following header file you need to include if you are using character functions in your program?

   (*a*) type.h (*b*) string.h (*c*) ctype.h (*d*) stdio.h

7. Which of the following function terminates the program abnormally?

   (*a*) exit() (*b*) break() (*c*) stop() (*d*) abort()

8. Prototypes of trigonometric function are in ______ header file.
   (*a*) maths.h (*b*) stdlib.h (*c*) ctype.h (*d*) None
9. Prototypes of *exit()* and *abort()* functions arc in ______ header file.
   (*a*) math.h (*b*) stdlib.h (*c*) stdio.h (*d*) ctype.h
10. Which of the following is a group in character classification?
   (*a*) Control (*b*) Alphanumeric (*c*) punctuation (*d*) All

14.9 REVIEW EXERCISES

1. What is the rationale behind the library function?
2. What is the difference between the library functions and user-defined functions?
3. What are the contents of a header file?
4. What is the rationale behind the large number of header files instead of one such file that contain prototypes of all the library functions and related declarations and definitions?
5. Differentiated between the working of *exit()* and *abort()* functions?
6. What is the difference between the working of *return* statement and the *exit()* function?

14.10 PROGRAMMING EXERCISES

1. Write a program to plot the sine curve.
2. Write a program that accepts a string from the user and converts the lowercase alphabets to uppercase.
3. Write a program that take following inputs from the user:
   - Value for integer variable *n*
   - Initial value of the range *a*
   - Final value of the range *b*

   The program should generate different sequence of *n* random numbers in the given range in each program run.

❑ ❑ ❑

15 Preprocessor Directives

Learning Objectives

After reading this chapter, students will have the ability to:

- comprehend the actual compilation process, and the preprocessing of the source code prior to compilation
- comprehend the usage of preprocessing directives
- use them for efficient program handling and making then generalized programs

15.1 INTRODUCTION

The C source code may include instructions for the compiler. These instructions are known as *preprocessor commands or directives.* Each directive begins with character '#' (hash character). Although, these directives are not part of the C language, they expand the scope of the C programming environment.

The C compiler is made up of two functional parts – *a preprocessor* and *a translator.* The preprocessor processes all the directives and as a result produces an intermediate code known as *translation unit*, which is then translated by the translator to machine code and places it in object file.

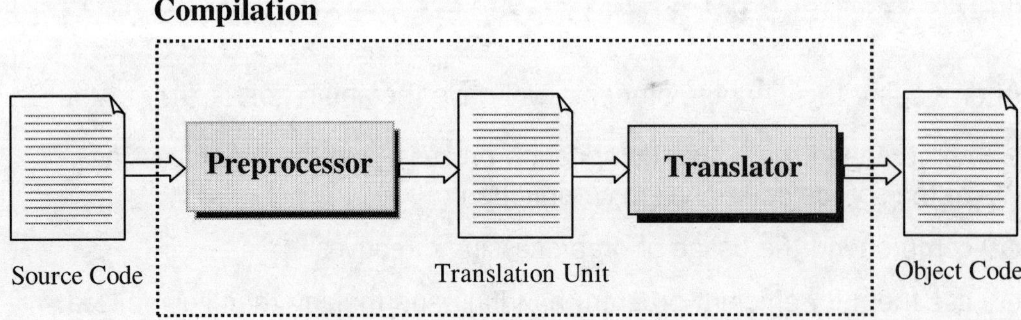

Figure 15.1: Compilation process

In this chapter, we will learn about various preprocessor directives and built-in macros.

15.2 THE #include DIRECTIVE

The *#include* directive, also known as *file inclusion,* instructs the preprocessor to copy the contents of specified file into the program. The files to be included are generally header files, though any file with valid C statements can also be included.

This directive has following forms:

```
#include <filename.h>
#include "filename.h"
```

The first form directs the preprocessor to include the header file from the standard directory while the second form directs the preprocessor to look for the specified header file in the user directory.

15.3 THE #define DIRECTIVE

The *#define* directive, is used to define an identifier and a character string that is substituted for the identifier each time it is encountered in the source file. The identifier is called a *macro name*, and the replacement process is called *macro-substitution*. The general form of the directive is

```
#define identifier string
```

Please note that the semicolon is not used after the *#define* directive. There can be any number of spaces between the identifier and the string, but once the string begins, it is terminated only by a new line.

For example, if we want to use *true* for a value 1 and *false* for a value 0, then we can do this as shown below:

```
#define true  1
#define false 0
```

Once an *identifier* has been defined, it can be used as part of the definition of other macro-names.

For example, the following segment defines ONE, TWO, and THREE to their respective values:

```
#define ONE      1
#define TWO      ONE+ONE
#define THREE    TWO+ONE
```

It is important to understand that macro-substitution simply replaces an identifier with its associated string. However, no text substitutions occur within a string.

For example

```
#define XYZ  "This is test string"
   :
printf( "XYZ" );
```

does not print *This is a test string* rather prints *XYZ.*

If a string is longer than one line, it can be continued on the next line by placing a backslash character \ at the end of the line, as shown in the following example:

```
#define LONG_STRING "This is a long string, \
       and is used to illustrate this feature"
```

It is a common practice to use capital letters for the defined identifiers. With this convention, anyone reading the program can understand at a glance that a macro-substitution will take place. It is always better to put all *#define* directives at the beginning of the program file or perhaps in a separate include file, rather than sprinkling them throughout the program.

The maximum use of macro-substitution is to define names for *magic numbers* that occur in a program. For example, you may have a program that defines an array and have several routines that access that array. Instead of *hard coding* the array's size with a constant, it is better to define a size and use that name whenever the size of the array is needed. If the size of the array changes, you only have to change it at one place in the file and recompile. For example,

```
#define MAX_SIZE 100
float a[MAX_SIZE];
```

The *#define* directive has another powerful feature — a macro-name can have arguments. Each time macro-name is encountered, the arguments associated with it are replaced by the actual arguments found in the program. This is illustrated in the following program.

```
#include<stdio.h>
#define MIN(x, y)   ( x < y ) ? x : y
void main()
{
    int a = 5, b = 20;
    printf( "\nMinimum of %d and %d is %d\n", a, b, MIN(a,b) );
}
```

When this program is compiled, the expression defined by *MIN(x,y)* is substituted except that *a* and *b* are used as the operands. That is, the *printf()* statement will look like

```
printf("\nMinimum of %d and %d is %d\n",a,b,(a<b)?a:b);
```

If you are not very careful in defining macros that take arguments, there can be some surprising results. For example

```
#include<stdio.h>
#define EVEN(x)   x % 2 ? 0 : 1
void main()
{
   int a = 5;
   if ( EVEN(a + 1) )
      printf( "\n%d is even\n", a+1 );
   else
      printf( "\n%d is odd\n", a+1 );
}
```

does not work correctly because of the way the macro-substitution is made.

When this program is compiled, the *EVEN*(*a*+1) is expanded to

```
a + 1 % 2 ?  0 : 1
```

Because the % (modulus) operator has higher precedence over the + (plus) operator, the modulus operation is performed on 1 first and then the result is added to *a*, which of course does not equal 0. To fix the trouble, there must be parentheses around *a* in the macro definition of EVEN as shown in this corrected version of the program:

```
#include<stdio.h>
#define  EVEN(x)   (x) % 2 ? 0 : 1
void main()
{
   int a = 5;
   if ( EVEN(a + 1) )
      printf( "\n%d is even\n", a+1 );
   else
      printf( "\n%d is odd\n", a+1 );
}
```

Now the expression *a*+1 is evaluated before the modulus operation. In general, it is good idea to surround macro parameters with parentheses to avoid troubles like the one just described.

The use of macro-substitution in place of real function is one major benefit*: it increases the speed of the code because no overhead for a function call is incurred.* However, this increased speed is paid for with an increase in the size of the program because of duplicated code.

15.4 THE #error DIRECTIVE

The *#error* directive forces the C compiler to stop compiling when it is encountered. It is used primarily for debugging. The general form of the directive is

```
#error error-message
```

The error-message is not between double quotes. When the compiler encounters this directive, it displays the following information and terminates compilation

```
fatal: filename linenum Error directive: error-message
```

15.5 THE #if DIRECTIVE

If the *constant expression* following *#if* is true, the code between it and *#endif* is compiled; otherwise the code is ignored by the compiler. The *#endif* is used to mark the end of a *#if* block.

The general form of *#if* directive is

```
#if constant-expression
   statement(s)
#endif
```

Consider the program given on next page.

```
#include<stdio.h>
#define MAX 100
void main()
{
   #if MAX > 99
      printf( "Compiled for small array" );
   #endif
}
```

This program displays the message on the screen because, as defined in the program, MAX is greater than 99.

This example illustrates an important point -- the expression that follows the *#if* is evaluated at compile time. Therefore, it must contain only identifiers that have been previously defined and constants; the use of variables is not permitted.

15.6 THE #else DIRECTIVE

The *#else* directive works the same way as the *else* statement that forms a part of the C language. It provides an alternative to the *#if* directive. The previous example can be expanded as shown here:

```
#include<stdio.h>
#define MAX 10
void main()
{
   #if MAX > 99
      printf( "Compiled for array greater than 99");
   #else
      printf( "Compiled for small array" );
   #endif
}
```

In this case, MAX is defined to be less than 99, so the part of the code between *#if* directive and *#else* directive is not compiled, but the part of the code between *#else* directive and *#endif* directive is compiled.

15.7 THE #elif DIRECTIVE

The *#elif* directive means *else if* and is used to establish an *if–else–if* ladder for compilation options. The *#elif* is followed by a *constant expression.* If the expression is true, that block of code is compiled and no other *#elif* expressions are tested. Otherwise, the next in the series is checked. The general form is

```
#if expression-1
   statement sequence-1
#elif expression-2
   statement sequence-2
#elif expression-3
   statement sequence-3
       :
#elif expression-N
   statement sequence-N
#endif
```

As an example, consider the following segment

```
#define US 0
#define UK 1
#define INDIA 2
#if COUNTRY == US
   char curreny[] = "Dollar";
#elif COUNTRY == UK
   char curreny[] = "Pound";
#elif COUNTRY == INDIA
   char curreny[] = "Rupee";
#endif
```

This segment uses the value of COUNTRY to define the currency sign.

15.8 THE #ifdef AND #ifndef DIRECTIVE

The directive *#ifdef* means *if defined*, and its general form is

```
#ifdef macro-name
   statement sequence
#endif
```

If the macro-name has been previously defined in a *#define* statement, the statement sequence between the *#ifdef* and *#endif* is compiled.

The directive *#ifndef* means *if not defined*, and its general form is

```
#ifndef macro-name
   statement sequence
#endif
```

If the macro-name is currently not defined by a *#define* statement, the statement sequence between the *#ifndef* and *#endif* is compiled.

Both the *#ifdef* and *#ifndef* directives can use *#else* directive but not the *#elif* directive.

15.9 THE #undef DIRECTIVE

The *#undef* directive is used to remove a previous definition of the macro-name that follows it. Its general form is

```
#undef macro-name
```

As an example, consider the following segment

```
#define  LEN 100
#define WIDTH 100
char a[LEN][WIDTH];
#undef LEN
#undef WIDTH
```

Both LEN and WIDTH are defined until the *#undef* statements are encountered. The principal use of *#undef* is to allow macro-names to be localized only to those sections of code that needed them.

15.10 THE #line DIRECTIVE

The *#line* directive is used to change the contents of __LINE__ and __FILE__, which are predefined macro-names. The __LINE__ macro contains the line number of the line currently being compiled and __FILE__ contains the name of the file being compiled. The general form of the *#line* directive is

```
#line number "filename"
```

where *number* is any positive integer, and the *filename* is any valid file identifier, which is optional. The line number is the number of the current source line and the file name is the name of the source file. The *#line* directive is used primarily for debugging purposes and special applications. As an example, consider the following program

```
#include<stdio.h>
#line 100
void main(void)
{
   printf( "\n%d\n", __LINE__);
}
```

This program specifies that line count will begin from 100. The *printf()* statement displays the number 102 because it is the third line in the program after #line 100 statement.

15.11 THE #pragma DIRECTIVE

The *#pragma* directive is defined by ANSI standard to be an implementation-defined directive that allows various instructions, defined by the compiler's creator to be given to the compiler. We will not be discussing it as it is used in advanced applications.

15.12 QUICK RECAP

In this chapter, we have learnt that

- The preprocessor directives are not part of the C language, but they expand the scope of programming environment.
- The C compiler has two components. The first component is the preprocessor and the second one is translator.
- The preprocessor process the directives and produces an intermediate file known as translation unit.
- The translator translates the translation unit to machine code and saves it in the object file.
- The most used preprocessors directives are *include* and *define*.
- The *include* directives is used in every program. It directs the preprocessor to copy the contents of the specified file.
- The *define* directives is used to define macro. Macros can have arguments as well and they simulate functions.
- The preprocessor substitutes each macro with the associated text if the macro is not taking any argument.
- If a macro is taking arguments, then the macro is expanded at the place of its call by replacing its arguments with the actual parameters.
- The other preprocessor directives include that facilitate conditional compilation, etc.

15.13 REVIEW EXERCISES

1. What is a translation unit?
2. What are the components of a C compiler? Explain the function of each component.

3. What is the difference in use when the name of the file is enclosed in angle brackets and double quotes with the file inclusion directives?
4. Explain the use of *define* directive with suitable examples.
5. What will be the output of the following program?

```
#include <stdio.h>
#define A 1
#define C 3
void main()
{
   #ifdef A
      printf("10");
   #endif
   #ifdef C
      printf("20")
    #endif
    #ifndef B
       printf("30");
    #endif
}
```

6. What will be the output of the following program?

```
#include <stdio.h>
#define  EVEN(x)    x % 2 ? 1 : 0
void main()
{
   int a = 5;
   if ( EVEN(a + 1) )
      printf( "\n%d is even\n", a + 1 );
   else
      printf( "\n%d is odd\n", a + 1 );
}
```

7. What will be the output of the following code segment?

```
#define XYZ   "This is test string"
printf( "XYZ" );
```

8. What will be the output of the following program?

```
#include <stdio.h>
#define MAX(a, b)    a > b ? b : a
void main()
{
   int max;
   max = MAX(2+3, 3+6);
   printf("%d", max);
}
```

9. Given a choice, would you prefer to use *const* over *#define* preprocessor in order to use a constant?

❑ ❑ ❑

Appendix **A**

Frequently Asked Questions (FAQs)

Question #1

Whether C language is *low-level*, *high-level*, or *middle-level* language?

Answer

The C language is a *middle-level* language. It is called a *middle- level* language because it has features of *high-level* language as well as *low-level* language.

Question #2

List the key characteristics of C language.

Answer

The C language was and will remain as one of the popular programming languages. Some of the key characteristics that add to its popularity are:

- It is a general purpose programming language, and therefore, can be used to solve vide variety of problems.
- It is supports structuring programming, and therefore, programs developed in it can easily be understood.

- It is free form, *i.e.*, no rigid format for writing programs. Any instruction can start from anywhere and end anywhere. In addition, a single instruction can span (can be written in) many lines.
- It is case sensitive. It distinguishes between lowercase (small) and uppercase (capital) alphabets.
- It was the first language to provide rich set of operators.
- It allows you, through pointers, to access any storage location and the devices connected to your computer through your program.
- It allows you to manipulate internal processor registers, and thus it is very useful for low-level programming.
- It is portable, that means any program written in it can be used on any computer without or with little modification(s).
- It allows you to develop your own library of functions that can be linked to your any program like standard library functions.

Question #3

What are various forms that *main()* function can take?

Answer

The *main()* function is a part of every C program. The C language permits following forms of *main()* function:

- `main()`
- `main(void)`
- `void main()`
- `int main()`
- `void main(void)`
- `int main(void)`

- The empty pair of parenthesis indicates that the *main()* function takes no arguments. This may be explicitly indicated by using the keyword *void* inside the parenthesis.
- We may also specify the keyword *void* or *int* before the word main.
- When the keyword *void* is used, it indicates that the function *main()* does not return any value to the operating system.
- When the keyword *int* is used, it indicates that the function *main()* will return an integer value to the operating system. Value 0 is returned to the operating system to indicate that the program terminated on completion of its intended task whereas the value 1 is used to indicate that the program terminated prematurely (could not complete its intended task).

Question #4

The output produced by a C compiler is an object code, *i.e.*, machine code, but not in a form that can be executed. Why?

Answer

Recall that a program can contain calls to library function as well as user-defined functions that are in other disk files and are not included using *file inclusion* pre-processor directive (*#include*).

The compiler doesn't have access to the definitions of these functions, and hence can't bind the function calls to function definitions. Hence, function calls are left unresolved. In addition, some more information is required by the operating system to run the program.

Question #5

Basically, what does the header files contain?

Answer

The header files contain declarations of library functions (prototypes of library functions) and useful enumerations and macros for the convenience of the programmers.

Question #6

What is the need of having large number of header files? Why not just one?

Answer

Note that header files are read by the compiler, which helps it in the process of compilation of the program. If all header files are combined into a single header file, this file will become very large and lot of compiler's time will be wasted. Further, note that in a program, we are not going to use diverse library functions in a single program, hence relevant declarations are put in different header files and relevant and meaningful names are given to these header files that show its intent.

Question #7

What is the difference between #include <...> and # include "..."?

Answer

There are two ways to include a header file:

```
#include <stdio.h>        and        #include "stdio.h"
```

The first form directs the preprocessor to include the header file from the standard directory while the second form directs the preprocessor to look for the specified header file in the user directory.

Question #8

What happens during linking?

Answer

The next step after compilation is linking, *i.e.*, to resolve the unresolved references to functions. This task is accomplished by another program known as *linker*. The linker takes object code(s) as its inputs and searches for unresolved references. For every unresolved reference, it searches libraries for their definitions and adds them to the end of final code being generated and fills its address at point of call. If search of any function is unsuccessful, the linker will generate a message like unresolved references and the also gives the name of the function called. Output of a linker is a machine language program that is in executable form better known as executable code or run file.

Question #9

What is the difference between declaration and definition of a variable?

Answer

Declaration only identifies the data type of a variable whereas definition causes the space to be reserved for the variable.

Thus, declaration is a place where the nature of the variable is stated but no storage is allocated whereas definition is the place where the variable is created or assigned storage.

Question #10

What is the difference between the following statements?

```
extern int k;    and    int k;
```

Answer

The first is a declaration indicated that *k* is a variable of type *int* and is defined externally, *i.e.*, in some another source file. The second is a definition and causes 2-bytes to be reserved for it.

Question #11

What is the restriction on the declarations and/or definitions of variables?

Answer

The restriction on the declarations and/or definitions is that they must come before the executable statements in a block, and hence they appear in the beginning of a block.

Question #12

Suppose a global variable and a local variable have the same name. Is it possible to access a global variable from a block where local variable is defined?

Answer

No. It is not possible in C. It is always the most local variable that gets preference.

Question #13

Differentiate between local and global variables.

Answer

Local	Global
❑ These variables only exist inside the specific function that creates them. ❑ They are unknown to other functions and to the main program. ❑ Local variables are allocated memory on the stack and they cease to exist once the function that created them has completed execution. ❑ They are recreated each time a function is executed or called. Local variables are not initialized automatically. ❑ Their scope and life is limited to the function in which they are declared.	❑ These variables can be accessed by any function contained in the program. ❑ These variables are visible throughout the program from the point of their declaration. ❑ They do not get recreated if the function is called. ❑ To declare a global variable, declare it outside all the functions. ❑ If the local variable is declared with same name as a global variable, then the function will use the local variable that was declared within it and ignore the global variable. ❑ Global variables are declared to 0 by default. ❑ Global variables are allocated memory on the data segment.

Question #14

Write a "hello world" program in C without using a semicolon.

Answer

```
#include<stdio.h>
void main()
{
   if ( printf("hello world\n") ) { }
}
```

Explanation: The *printf*() is a function that returns the number of characters it is able to print. This return value can be used in the *if* conditional expression. With this combination, we can print the required string without using a semicolon.

Question #15

What is the difference between *static* and *global* variables?

Answer

While the life of an object determines whether the object is still in the memory (of the process), scope of the object decides whether the variable can be accessed at that point in the program. Static variables are local in scope to the block or file in which they are defined, but their lifespan is throughout the program. For instance, a static variable inside a function cannot be called from outside the function (because it's not in the scope) but is alive and exists in the memory. It retains its old value between function calls.

Global variables persist throughout the program; scope is also throughout the program. It means that global variables can be accessed from any function, any file (unless declared static) in the program.

Question #16

What is the use of *register* keyword in the context of variables?

Answer

The register keyword specifies that the variable is to be stored in the CPU register, if possible. Variables are usually stored in stack and passed to and from the computer processor, as and when required, the speed the data is sent at is pretty but can be improved on. Almost all computer processors contain CPU registers, these are memory slots on the actual processors, and storing data there gets rid of the overhead of the retrieving data from the stack. This memory (in registers) is quite small compared to normal memory, therefore, only a few variables can be stored there. Having a register keyword for variables and parameters also reduces code size, which is important in embedded systems. The number of available CPU registers is strictly dependent on the architectural design of the CPU itself. The number of CPU registers is 32 in most cases.

Question #17

How do we make a global variable accessible across files? Explain the *extern* keyword.

Answer

If a variable is declared (with global scope) in one file but referenced in other, the extern keyword is used to inform the compiler of variable's existence. Note that the keyword extern is for declarations, not definitions. An extern declaration does not create any storage. Variable initializations should not be done with extern.

Question #18

What is a function prototype?

Answer

A function prototype is a declaration similar to variable declarations. Function declarations are generally placed in header files. Specifically, it tells the compiler

- ❑ The name of the function
- ❑ The type of the output returned by the function.
- ❑ The number of types of inputs (called arguments), if any, the function expects to receive and the order in which it expects to receive them.

Question #19

What is the difference between declaration and definition of a function?

Answer

Like variables, declaration of a function only identifies the return type of the function and the type of format arguments. The declaration of a function is usually referred as a *function prototype*. On the other hand, definition of a function contains the statements to accomplish the intended task. Like variables, functions also have an address associated with its name.

Question #20

Is the name of the formal arguments in a function prototype mandatory?

Answer

No. Only data type is mandatory. However, the name of formal arguments can be useful to know the kind of arguments that a function will be taking. This is explained with the help of the following example:

The *displayAt()*function accepts three arguments: row number, column number, and a string. It display the string starting from the given row and column.

The prototype of this function can be

```
void displayAt(int, int, char *);
```

But from this prototype, it is not clear whether row is to passed as first argument or column is to be passed as first argument. However, if its prototype is taken as

```
void displayAt(int row, int col, char *charPtr);
```

then it is clear that first argument will be row while the second will be column.

Question #21

What is the significance of storage class?

Answer

The storage class, in general, determines the scope and lifetime of a variable, which in turn helps to economize the memory usage.

Question #22

What is the difference between the following declarations?

```
const int *intptr;

int *const intptr;
```

Answer

First one is pointer to a constant *int*, while the second one is constant pointer to *int*.

Question #23

What is the difference between the following declarations?

```
int *ptr(int arg);

int (*ptr)(int arg);
```

Answer

First is the prototype of a function that takes an integer argument, and returns a pointer to an integer. Second one is declaration of a pointer to a function that takes an integer argument and returns an integer.

Question #24

What is the difference between the following declarations?

```
int (*a)[];

int *a[];
```

Answer

First one indicates a pointer to an array of integers, whereas the second one indicates an array of pointers to integers.

Question #25

How will you interpret the following declaration?

```
int *(*ptr)(int (*a)[]);
```

Answer

Since *(*ptr)(. . .)* indicates a pointer to a function, therefore, *int *(*ptr)(. . .)* indicates a pointer to a function that returns a pointer to an integer. Now within the last pair of parenthesis, *int (*a)[]* indicates a pointer to an array of integers. Therefore, putting pieces together, *int *(*ptr)(int (*a)[])* indicates a pointer to a function that takes a pointer to an array of integers as an argument and returns a pointer to an array.

Question #26

What is a dangling pointer?

Answer

It is a pointer that is not initialized with a valid address. Such a pointer can end up pointing anywhere in memory that may include the program code itself or to the code of the operating system. The use of such pointer can lead to undesirable results. Therefore, care must be taken to initialize pointers with valid address before use.

Question #27

What is a memory leak?

Answer

It is a situation where the programmer fails to release the memory allocated at run time in a module. Remember that when memory is allocated, a pointer variable is used to hold the address of the allocated block, however, when the module completes its execution, the pointer variable goes out of scope and there will be no way to reach that memory block. Therefore, care must be taken to release the allocated memory block in a module where memory was allocated.

Question #28

What is a NULL pointer assignment?

Answer

It is a situation that happens when a pointer points to address 0, which is called NULL. For example, it may happen that if the pointer variable is declared as global, since global variables are initialized to 0. Likewise, this can also happen for a local un-initialized pointer variable, particularly for local static variables, they are also initialized to 0. When it happens, and the pointer is used on the left-hand side of an assignment operator, the system generates a message "*Null pointer assignment*".

Question #29

What do you mean by *Lvalue* and *Rvalue*?

Answer

There are two values associated with a variable:

1. Its data value that is stored at some memory address. This sometimes referred to as variable's *Rvalue* (pronounced as "are-value"). We may think *Rvalue* as meaning *read value*. Both a literal constant and a variable can serve as *rvalue*.
2. Its address value that is its address in memory within which its data value is stored. This sometimes referred to as variable's *Lvalue* (pronounced as "ell-value"). We may think *Lvalue* as meaning *location value*. Only a variable can serve as *Lvalue*.

Question #30

Is any thing wrong with the following declaration?

```
int k = 1+2+3;
```

Answer

No. Remember that all constant expressions are evaluated by the compiler. Hence, above declaration statement will be treated as "`int k = 6;`" before compilation.

Question #31

Cite some cases where *switch* statement cannot be used?

Answer

The *switch* statement cannot be used when the variable or expression is not of integral type (*int*, *long* or *char*). The other situation is where conditions are of type that does not require exact match, such *amount* <= 1200.

Question #32

Is there any difference between expressions "*ptr++" and "++*ptr"?

Answer

Yes. The first expression accesses the contents of the current location and then increments the pointer whereas the second expression increments the contents of the current location.

Question #33

Can you write an expression equivalent to "++*ptr"?

Answer

Yes. It is "(*ptr)++".

Question #34

Among *gets()* and *fgets()* functions, which function is safe to use?

Answer

fgets() is safe to use. This is illustrated below. The prototype of *gets()* functions is

```
char *gets(char *s);
```

It reads a string of characters terminated by newline characters from *stdin* and stores in *s*. As there is no way to tell the size of the string there is always a possibility of overflow.

The prototype of *fgets()* functions is

```
char *gets(char *s, int n, FILE *stream);
```

It reads a string of characters from *stream* and stores in *s*. It stops when either it reads (*n*-1) characters or a newline character, whichever comes first. So overflow condition never occurs.

Question #35

Does reading a string using *scanf()* cause overflow?

Answer

Yes. Like *gets()* function, there is no way to tell *scanf()* function about the maximum size of the array for input string.

Question #36

What would be the consequence if the function prototypes are local to *main()* function?

Answer

If any other function calls these functions, the compiler will flag an error message, as these prototypes are not available in that function, hence the compiler may not be able to compile the program properly.

Question #37

When should the function prototypes be made global?

Answer

When the functions can be called from more than one function.

Question #38

Is the following nested comments are acceptable?

```
/* Outer comment /* Nested comments */ allowed/not allowed */
```

Answer

No. Note that anything that lies between /* and */ is treated as comment. Therefore, in the above case, from word *Outer* to word *comments* everything is treated as comment including /*. Hence the string "allowed/not allowed */" does not lie in the comment.

Thus, it is being improper statement the compiler will flag an error.

Question #39

When should we pass arguments by reference (address)?

Answer

Argument passing by reference (address) is useful in following situations:

- When we intend to change the values of actual arguments.
- When we want to save the memory by preventing the creation of large array and/or structure variables being passed to the function.

Question #40

Given a choice, would you prefer to use *const* over *#define* preprocessor in order to use a constant?

Answer

Using *const* is always a better choice because we can control its scope, which is not possible with *#define*.

Question #41

Passing arguments by reference (address), we can prevent the creation of large array and/or structure variables in the called function. Here the called function can change the values of array and/or structure variables. Is there any way to prevent the called function from doing so?

Answer

Yes, by prefixing the formal argument by keyword *const* as shown in the following example

```
void fName(const int *a)
{
    /*   some statements   */
}
```

Question #42

In how many ways can we pass arguments to a function?

Answer

There are two ways in which we can pass arguments to a function:

- By value

```
void f(int, int)  /* declaration  */
f(a, b);          /*  call    */
```

- By reference (address)

```
void f(int *, int *)  /* declaration  */
f(&a, &b);            /*  call    */
```

Question #43

Differentiate between call by value and call by reference (address).

Answer

Call by Value	Call by Reference (Address)
1. The actual arguments can be constants, variables, or expressions.	1. The actual arguments can only be variables.
2. The values of actual arguments are substituted in formal arguments which are ordinary variables.	2. The addresses of the actual arguments are substituted in formal arguments which are pointer variable.
3. Any change made to the formal arguments will have no effect on actual arguments, since the function will only be using the local copy of the arguments.	3. Any change made to the formal arguments will have immediate effect on actual arguments, since the function will be working on actual arguments through pointers.

Question #44

What is the purpose of *fseek()* and *ftell()* functions?

Answer

The *fseek()* function positions the file pointer at the specific location in the file. This position of the file pointer allows accessing the record in a random fashion.

The *ftell()* function returns the current position of the file pointer in the file. If *ftell()* functions is used when the file pointer is at the end of the file, the number returned by *ftell()* gives the size of the file.

Question #45

What is the difference between text mode and binary mode?

Answer

Differences between a Text File & a Binary File

Text File	Binary File
1. Data is stored using human readable characters.	1. Data is stored in the same format as it is stored in memory.
2. Each line of data ends with a *newline* character.	2. There are no lines or *newline* character.
3. There is a special character called end-of-file (EOF) marker at the end of the file.	3. There is an end-of-file marker at the end of the file, which is usually implementation dependent.

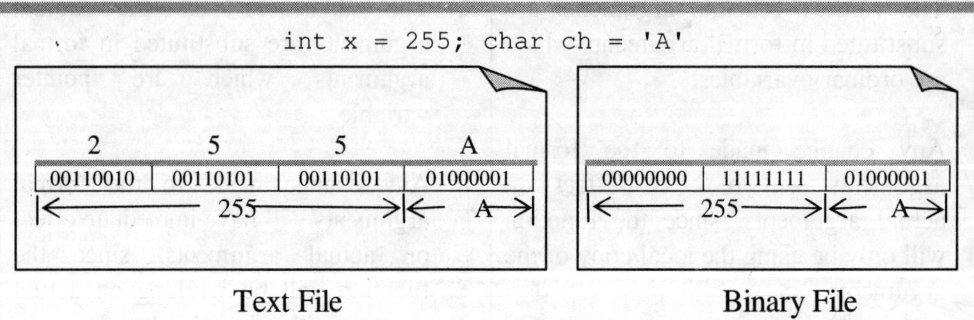

Question #46

Is it necessary to close the file and then open again if the file needs to be re-read in the same program?

Answer

No. The file pointer can be positioned at the beginning of the file either using *fseek()* function or the *rewind()* function.

Question #47

Write function call to *fseek()* function to position file pointer at the beginning of the file.

Answer

```
fseek(fptr, 0L, 0);
```

Question #48

Write the function call to *fseek()* function to position the file pointer at the end of the file.

Answer

```
fseek(fptr, 0L, 2);
```

Question #49

What is the main difference between *malloc()* and *calloc()*?

Answer

The main difference between *malloc()* and *calloc()* is that *malloc()* function just allocates the memory whereas the *malloc()* function also initializes the memory to zeros.

Question #50

What is free store/heap?

Answer

Free store/heap is area of memory from where memory is allocated at runtime using *malloc()* or *calloc()* functions.

Question #51

Recall that when we use *free()* function to deallocate the block, we only pass pointer to the block, then how *free()* function know how many bytes it should deallocate?

Answer

When operating system allocates memory, on call to *malloc()*, *calloc()* or *realloc()* function, to a program from its free pool of memory (also called free store), it keeps track of the address of the block and the size of the block. Therefore, when the memory needs to be deallocated, program need only to tell the address of block to the operating system.

Question #52

What are the advantages of using *typedefs* in a program?

Answer

The advantages of using *typedefs* in a program are

- It makes writing of complicated declaration a lot easier, which in turn helps in eliminating lot of typographical errors.
- It also helps in achieving portability in programs. Suppose, there are some data types that are machine dependent and we use *typedefs* for those data types, then we only need to change *typedefs* as we move to new machine platform.

Question #53

What is a void/generic pointer?

Answer

When a variable is declared as being a pointer to a variable of type void it is known as a generic pointer. Since we cannot have a variable of type void, the pointer will not point to any data and therefore cannot be de-referenced. It is still a pointer though; to use it we have to cast it to another kind of pointer first. Hence, the term generic pointer. It is very useful when you want a pointer to point to data of different types at different times.

Question #54

Why arithmetic operation can't be performed on a void/generic pointer?

Answer

The C language doesn't allow pointer arithmetic on void pointers. The argument being that we don't know the size of what's being pointed to with a void *and therefore can't know how far to seek the pointer to get to the next valid address.

Question #55

What is a NULL pointer?

Answer

A NULL pointer is conceptually different from an un-initialized pointer. A NULL pointer is known not to point to any object or function; an un-initialized pointer might point to anywhere. In *stdio.h* header file, NULL is defined as 0. Whenever a program tries to access 0th location, the operating system terminates the program with runtime assignment error because the 0th location is in the operating system's address space and operating system doesn't allow access to its address space by user programs.

Question #56

How do you access command line arguments?

Answer

A program is started by the operating system by calling a program's *main*() function. The *main*() function is the only function in C that can be defined in multiple ways. It can take no arguments, two arguments, or three arguments. The two and three argument forms allow it to receive arguments from the shell. The two arguments takes an int and an array of strings. When defining *main*() function any name can be given but it is convention to call them *argc* and *argv*[]. The first argument (*argc*) holds a count of how many elements there are in the array of strings passed as the second argument (*argv*). The array is always null terminated so *argv* [*argc*] = null.

Here's short program demonstrating the use:

```
int main (int argc, char *argv[])
{
    int i;
    for( i = 0; i < argc; i++ ) {
        printf("argv[%d] == %s\n", i, argv[i]);
    }
    return 0;
}
```

The integer *argc* is the argument count (hence *argc*). It is the number of arguments passed into the program from the command line, including the name of the program.

The array of character pointers is the listing of all the arguments. The *argv*[0] is the name of the program. After that every element number less than *argc* is command line arguments. You can use each *argv* element just like a string, or *argv* as a two dimensional array.

❑ ❑ ❑

Appendix B

Answers of Multiple Choice Questions (MCQs)

Chapter 2: Overview of C Language

1.	(*c*)	2.	(*b*)	3.	(*c*)	4.	(*d*)	5.	(*d*)
6.	(*c*)	7.	(*c*)	8.	(*c*)	9.	(*d*)	10.	(*d*)
11.	(*b*)	12.	(*d*)	13.	(*b*)	14.	(*c*)	15.	(*d*)

Chapter 3: Fundamental Data Types

1.	(*a*)	2.	(*a*)	3.	(*d*)	4.	(*b*)	5.	(*c*)
6.	(*c*)	7.	(*a*)	8.	(*c*)	9.	(*d*)	10.	(*a*)
11.	(*c*)	12.	(*a*)	13.	(*d*)	14.	(*d*)	15.	(*b*)
16.	(*a*)	17.	(*c*)						

Chapter 4: Operators and Expressions

1.	(*b*)	2.	(*a*)	3.	(*c*)	4.	(*b*)	5.	(*a*)
6.	(*b*)	7.	(*b*)	8.	(*a*)	9.	(*b*)	10.	(*b*)
11.	(*c*)	12.	(*b*)	13.	(*a*)	14.	(*c*)	15.	(*a*)
16.	(*d*)	17.	(*c*)	18.	(*c*)	19.	(*b*)		

Chapter 5: Standard Input/Output

1.	(*a*)	2.	(*b*)	3.	(*a*)	4.	(*b*)	5.	(*c*)
6.	(*a*)	7.	(*a*)	8.	(*b*)	9.	(*d*)	10.	(*d*)
11.	(*b*)	12.	(*a*)						

Chapter 6: Decision Making Statements

1.	(*c*)	2.	(*a*)	3.	(*d*)	4.	(*a*)	5.	(*c*)
6.	(*c*)	7.	(*c*)						

Chapter 7: Looping Statements

1.	(*c*)	2.	(*d*)	3.	(*c*)	4.	(*d*)	5.	(*b*)
6.	(*a*)	7.	(*d*)	8.	(*c*)	9.	(*b*)	10.	(*d*)
11.	(*c*)	12.	(*c*)	13.	(*a*)				

Chapter 8: Functions

1.	(*d*)	2.	(*c*)	3.	(*a*)	4.	(*a*)	5.	(*c*)
6.	(*b*)	7.	(*c*)	8.	(*d*)	9.	(*c*)	10.	(*d*)
11.	(*d*)	12.	(*a*)	13.	(*b*)	14.	(*c*)	15.	(*b*)

Chapter 9: Arrays

1.	(*b*)	2.	(*a*)	3.	(*c*)	4.	(*d*)	5.	(*c*)
6.	(*b*)	7.	(*d*)	8.	(*d*)	9.	(*a*)	10.	(*c*)
11.	(*d*)	12.	(*a*)	13.	(*b*)	14.	(*d*)	15.	(*a*)
16.	(*c*)	17.	(*b*)	18.	(*c*)	19.	(*b*)	20.	(*c*)

Chapter 10: Strings

1.	(*b*)	2.	(*a*)	3.	(*d*)	4.	(*c*)	5.	(*b*)
6.	(*a*)	7.	(*b*)	8.	(*d*)	9.	(*c*)	10.	(*a*)
11.	(*c*)	12.	(*a*)	13.	(*a*)				

Chapter 11: Structures and Unions

1.	(*b*)	2.	(*c*)	3.	(*b*)	4.	(*b*)	5.	(*c*)
6.	(*c*)	7.	(*b*)	8.	(*a*)	9.	(*d*)	10.	(*a*)
11.	(*b*)	12.	(*c*)	13.	(*b*)	14.	(*c*)	15.	(*a*)
16.	(*d*)								

Chapter 12: Pointers

1.	(*b*)	2.	(*d*)	3.	(*a*)	4.	(*d*)	5.	(*b*)
6.	(*b*)	7.	(*a*)	8.	(*a*)	9.	(*d*)	10.	(*c*)
11.	(*c*)	12.	(*b*)	13.	(*c*)	14.	(*c*)	15.	(*a*)
16.	(*b*)	17.	(*b*)	18.	(*a*)	19.	(*a*)	20.	(*a*)
21.	(*b*)	22.	(*c*)	23.	(*b*)	24.	(*b*)	25.	(*d*)
26.	(*b*)								

Chapter 13: File Handling

1.	(*d*)	2.	(*a*)	3.	(*b*)	4.	(*d*)	5.	(*d*)
6.	(*b*)	7.	(*d*)	8.	(*d*)	9.	(*d*)		

Chapter 14: Standard C Language Library

1.	(*a*)	2.	(*d*)	3.	(*d*)	4.	(*a*)	5.	(*b*)
6.	(*c*)	7.	(*d*)	8.	(*d*)	9.	(*b*)	10.	(*d*)

❑ ❑ ❑

Appendix **C**

Precedence & Associativity of Operators

Table C.1 summarizes the rules for precedence and associativity of all operators. Operators in the same row have the same precedence and rows are in order of decreasing precedence.

Table C.1: Precedence and Associativity of Operators

Operator	Description	Precedence Level (Rank)	Associativity
() [] –> .	Function call Array element reference Structure operator used with pointer to a structure Structure operator used with structure variable	1	Left-to-right
! ~ ++ — + – * & (type) sizeof	Logical NOT operator 1's complement Increment Decrement Unary plus Unary minus Pointer reference (indirection) Address of Type cast Size of an operand	2	Right-to-left
* / %	Multiplication Division Modulus (remainder)	3	Left-to-right

Table C.1: Precedence and Associativity of Operators *Contd.*

<table>
<tr><th>Operator</th><th>Description</th><th>Precedence Level (Rank)</th><th>Associativity</th></tr>
<tr><td>+
–</td><td>Addition
Subtraction</td><td>4</td><td>Left-to-right</td></tr>
<tr><td><<
>></td><td>Left shift
Right shift</td><td>5</td><td>Left-to-right</td></tr>
<tr><td><
<=
>
>=</td><td>Less than
Less than or equal to
Greater than
Greater than or equal to</td><td>6</td><td>Left-to-right</td></tr>
<tr><td>==
!=</td><td>Equal to
Not equal to</td><td>7</td><td>Left-to-right</td></tr>
<tr><td>&</td><td>Bitwise AND</td><td>8</td><td>Left-to-right</td></tr>
<tr><td>^</td><td>Bitwise exclusive OR</td><td>9</td><td>Left-to-right</td></tr>
<tr><td>|</td><td>Bitwise inclusive OR</td><td>10</td><td>Left-to-right</td></tr>
<tr><td>&&</td><td>Logical AND</td><td>11</td><td>Left-to-right</td></tr>
<tr><td>||</td><td>Logical OR</td><td>12</td><td>Left-to-right</td></tr>
<tr><td>?:</td><td>Condition (ternary)</td><td>13</td><td>Right-to-left</td></tr>
<tr><td>= +=
–= *=
/= %=
&= ^=
!= <<=
>>=</td><td>Assignment operators</td><td>14</td><td>Right-to-left</td></tr>
<tr><td>,</td><td>Comma</td><td>15</td><td>Left-to-right</td></tr>
</table>

❑ ❑ ❑

Index

A

B

C

D

E

F

Q

R

S

T

U

V

W

❑ ❑ ❑

PROBLEM SOLVING AND PROGRAMMING IN C

PROF. R. S. SALARIA

FEEDBACK FORM

1. Which topics from your examination point of view are inadequately or not covered in this book?

____

____

2. Is there any misprints/ mistakes/ factual inaccuracy in this book? If so, please specify.

____

____

3. What is your assessment of this book as regards the presentation of the subject-matter, expression, precision and price in relation to the other recommended books available on this subject?

____

____

4. Which competing books you regard as better than this? Please mention their author and publishers.

____

____

5. Any further suggestions/comments you would like to make for the improvement of the book?

____

____

PS: If needed, please attach a separate sheet.

Name : ____________________

College : ____________________

Address : ____________________

Email : ____________________

Mobile : ____________________

Please mail the feedback form at:

KHANNA BOOK PUBLISHING CO. (P) LTD.

4C/4344, Ansari Road, Daryaganj, New Delhi-110002

You can also email this feedback form at contact@khannabooks.com or Whatsapp at +91 – 99109 09320

BEST FEEDBACK WILL BE REWARDED SUITABLY